Leisure and the
Family Life Cycle

Leisure and the Family Life Cycle

Rhona Rapoport and Robert N. Rapoport
with the collaboration of Ziona Strelitz
Institute of Family and Environmental Research

Routledge & Kegan Paul
London, Henley and Boston

First published in 1975
by Routledge & Kegan Paul Ltd
39 Store Street
London. WC1E 7DD,
Broadway House, Newtown Road
Henley-on-Thames
Oxon. RG9 1EN and
9 Park Street,
Boston, Mass. 02108, USA
Reprinted and first published
as a paperback in 1978
Set in Monotype Imprint
and printed in Great Britain by
Lowe & Brydone Printers Ltd
Thetford, Norfolk

ISBN 0 7100 8134 0 (c)
ISBN 0 7100 8825 6 (p)

Contents

Figures and Tables

Figures

Tables

Acknowledgments

First and foremost we want to acknowledge the foresight and generosity of the Leverhulme Trust in making a grant for the study on which this book is based. Initially, the grant was via the Tavistock Institute of Human Relations and then through the Institute of Family and Environmental Research. Without the Trustees' recognition of the need to take a new view of the leisure field and the importance of relating it to the family life cycle, the study would not have been made.

Our next debt is to the people who allowed us to spend many hours with them in interviews. It is only with this kind of collaboration that meaningful family studies can be made. For obvious reasons, these people must remain anonymous but we want it recorded that our research is always dependent on their co-operation; we hope that they will feel that it has served some useful purpose. The names used in the case studies are fictitious, and details have been altered so as to retain anonymity.

Many colleagues and organisations have helped us at different stages of the study. Linden Hilgendorf and Barrie Irving reanalysed some of the Tavistock Stress Study data on hobbies and symptoms. Some of the interviews with young people and their families were conducted by Linda Thompson and Denise Newton. Diana Barker was very helpful in preparing materials for the chapter on young adults. Much of the case material on small town conformists comes from a study she conducted in Swansea. Michael and Phyllis Fogarty helped with the collection of materials for the late establishment phase. Denis Molyneux and Spencer Hudson gave generously of their time and knowledge in the leisure provision area. We are very grateful for their help, and while they are not responsible for what we have finally come out with, we do really think of them as collaborators. Michael Dower and Peter Downing of the Dartington Amenity Research Trust were extremely helpful in clarifying with us the potential connections between our social-psychological approach and the concerns of leisure providers. We thank them for their invaluable encouragement.

Victor Thiessen and Martha Moeller worked with us to develop the concept of enjoyment careers, and their help is much appreciated. Many other people helped in various ways. William Loving and Lorna Hubbard of the Pre-Retirement Association discussed with us the issues confronting people in the retirement phase. Hugh Mellor of the National Corporation of Old People and Barbara Spiers of the Camden Council of Social Services also helped our understanding of the late phases of the life cycle. A number of local authority officers attended a meeting to discuss the provider field with us. We also had particularly helpful discussions with some others in related fields. We wish to thank Colin Bonsey, James Kegie, Alan Reavill, Norman Perry, G. F. Hoar, Sylvia Law, Ray Maw, J. A. Jeffrey, Stanley Parker, Kenneth Sillitoe, Joan Davidson, Michael Smith and Martin Rein for helpful discussions of leisure provision in relation to social research.

We thank our project advisers—Asa Briggs, Liam Hudson, Adrian Phillips, Baroness Serota, Cyril Smith and Beric Wright—for the encouragement and comments they gave at critical points. While they are not responsible for the product any more than are the others we have mentioned, we hope that they will feel their efforts were worth while.

Parts of earlier drafts of the book were read by our advisers and by Michael Young and Peter Willmott. We thank them for their helpful comments.

Finally, we thank our colleagues at the Institute of Family and Environmental Research and the secretarial staff, particularly Marion Harrison, for their patient work on many drafts; and also our friends, and our children—Lorna and Alin—for their long-suffering toleration of our phase of involvement with the meaningful interest of leisure.

Beyond palpable mass demand

People usually have some 'freedom' to organise their lives. But a distinctive feature of modern society is the emphasis placed on freedom of choice as a social value. Economic and political advances are, accordingly, evaluated in terms of their power to make these choices available.

Changes in key variables: work and home

There has been an overall increase in time available to spend as one chooses and in the economic, technological and organisational wherewithal to make use of it. The working week has dropped from an estimated 70-hour, six-day week in 1850 to the present norm of a 40-hour, five-day week with strong movements in the direction of a 35-hour, four-day and other variants of a shorter working week.

Riva Poor, the 'apostle of the four-day week', has found strong support for the idea among managers in the USA who find it economically viable as well as humanistic (Poor, 1972). In Britain the idea has been resisted both by managers and unions. The recent 'natural experiment' of the energy crisis showed that for many industries 80 per cent of productivity could be sustained with the three-day week. It is too soon to say whether the experience will have produced any lasting adherents to the idea that a four-fifths week might be both feasible and desirable.

Not only has the 'normal' working day now been formally reduced but many preparatory and peripheral activities associated with work and previously considered part of the workers' 'own time' are now reckoned into wage agreements. The journey to work, washing-up time, lunch time, rest time, and so on, are legitimate parts of the paid work day for many salaried workers. This means that 'own time' is less taken up with occupation-related activities except where undertaken by choice.

The reality as well as the idea of a paid holiday as a right rather than a privilege has been established. Nearly everyone in the peak earning years takes at least one holiday a year unless they are very poor or disabled. The few who are neither poor nor disabled and yet do not take a holiday seem to do so as a matter of personal choice. A saturation point seems to have been reached by the early 1960s; since that time there has been a growth in 'second holidays'. In 1971 nearly 15 per cent of the population took two holidays or more; the proportion rose to 19 per cent in 1972 and 20 per cent in 1973. These holidays mainly involve the use of the motor car but when many off-season air-package holidays became less expensive than domestic holidays, they attracted an increasing part of the holiday market. By 1972 15 per cent took a holiday abroad as compared with 10 per cent in 1970. The proportion has since fallen slightly because of 'uncertain economics and foreign exchange situations' (BTA, 1973). The short holiday—i.e. less than four nights away—has increased even more markedly, though increased fuel prices and general economic problems may also slow down this trend in the short term.

There is a growth in second home ownership (Downing and Dower, 1973). The recent catapulting of prices for properties in rural and coastal areas indicates the trend. These areas are now much more accessible to metropolis-dwellers because of motorway networks. There are also signs that more and more of the metropolitan population who can afford to do so will spend increasing parts of their weeks, months and years in their secondary residences. Like hobbies, these residences serve many people as bases to which they may shift their centres of life interest as they grow older. Second homes are advertised and bought as pre-retirement homes. To those in the top percentiles of the population, economically, the second home away represents a happy combination of financial investment and social-psychological preparation for the retirement eventually to come. Where the second homes are abroad, the intercultural experience provides a range of stimulating interests—language and literature, art, food and the informal study of national character.

The age of retirement has receded from the traditional three score years and ten in the early part of the century to 65, and now there is a tendency towards 60 or even earlier. Male life expectancy has increased from 59 years for those born in 1931 to 68 years for those born in 1955 (Sillitoe, 1971). Because these changes are consequences of improved technology, they have been accompanied by increased rather than decreased levels of disposable income.

The top countries with per capita GNP of over 5,000 dollars per annum are the USA, Japan, the Scandinavian countries, France, Germany and Canada. The second level with per capita GNP of 2,000–5,000 dollars includes Great Britain, Switzerland, Benelux, Finland, Italy and the USSR. Although their per capita GNP is less than the first group, these all have a high level of economic development and consumer goods (Kahn, 1972). Even in Great Britain, however, there was an increase of 113 per cent in personal weekly earnings between 1956 and 1969. During the same period, prices increased 57 per cent, making for over 50 per cent in real income. By 1971 the estimated 'leisure £'—amount available to spend beyond the basic costs of living— was estimated to total £7,000 million in Britain. Morrell, in a market projection to 1980, estimated that by the end of this decade the amount would be £16,000 million (Sandles, 1973). (The trend may have been arrested by recent economic vicissitudes, but we cannot assess their ultimate effect.) This increase in cash available for spending on inessentials was not achieved by lengthening hours of work, though there is a sizeable minority who still work long hours because of overtime, 'moonlighting' and the like. It is also a feature of contemporary society that the 'leisure class'—in the sense of time at their disposal—is no longer the élite. The latter, now comprising the professional/managerial superstructures of the occupational system, work longer hours with more like mid-Victorian norms than like their contemporaries in lower-status jobs. But this has largely been a matter of choice. The greater flexibility with work hours and greater perquisites of their jobs as well as intrinsic interest partly compensate for the more arduous pace they accept. Differences in income levels have decreased rather than increased during this period; bricklayers can make as much as, or more than, university lecturers. Both pay and time differentials between the majority of white-collar and manual workers have decreased with increasing professionalisation of work. The more meaningful distinction now seems to be between salaried and unsalaried workers: the former seek to maximise their options by achieving organisational supports, and the latter by maintaining their autonomy, even though with less financial or other advantages than previously.

The same technology that has made for greater productivity and income despite shorter working periods has also affected qualitative aspects of life. The explosion of consumer goods is an obvious aspect of this. Many inventions which were developed for utilitarian or even military purposes have become instruments of enjoyment—for example, the radio, the motorcar, the aeroplane. The miniaturisation of machines developed in the industrial context has been applied on a massive scale to the domestic scene. As machinery facilitates housework, people have more time for other purposes. This change is illustrated in Quentin Bell's description of Virginia Woolf's life in her country home (1972, 55–6):

> To get there at all she had to walk or to bicycle for several miles or to go to the expense of a taxi or a fly. To make a light she had candles which dropped grease on the carpet, or lamps which smoked and had to be refilled with oil and trimmed every morning; heat was supplied

by wood or coal . . . the coal had to be carried about in scuttles, grates had to be cleaned, fires laid, and if they were not competently managed they would fill the room with smoke or die miserably. In the country you got hot water by boiling it over a stove. Cold water had to be pumped up into a tank every day and Asham was furnished only with an earth closet. There were no refrigerators or frozen foods, a tin-opener was a kind of heavy dagger with which you attacked the tin hoping to win a jagged victory. All the processes of cooking and cleaning were incredibly laborious, messy and slow. [Now in contrast] . . . in the evening you can make a light with which to read . . . by pressing a switch. The room is warmed by central heating, you turn a tap and hot water pours into your bath or into your sink, you pull a plug and cold water gushes into your lavatory. You may do your own cooking and your own housework, but you are probably assisted by dozens of mechanical devices, tins, and tin-openers, frozen foods, refrigerators and plastic containers. Heaven knows how many thousand horses give their power every day at the touch of your fingers. No very serious effort is demanded of you when ovens have to be heated, foods ground and mixed, floors swept, rooms lighted and fires made.

Apart from less time having to be spent on the basics of living, the hours 'set free from work', as Phelps Brown and Browne (1969) put it, are often applied to domestic 'do-it-yourself' tasks which may 'add something to the unmeasured amenities of households and to the goodness of life'. This movement, so prominent in British and American cultures, is now also gaining momentum in Europe.

The 'leisure explosion'

The increased basic wealth and heightened freedom of choice arising from the social changes described are also reflected in an increasing number of activities not directly related to work or home life (hence having an aura of the 'optional'). It is this area of activity people have in mind when they speak of the 'leisure explosion', though what this encompasses is neither entirely coherent nor consistent. The issue is more than definitional. Conceptually it is important not to reify the 'leisure explosion', but to see it simply as an array of linked variables in a more embracing societal change.

In 1950 there were $2\frac{1}{4}$ million private cars on the road in Britain; in 1960 the figure rose to $5\frac{1}{2}$ million and in 1970 to 12 million. It is estimated that despite a levelling off, the total by 2000 will be 28 million. Car use, when expanding so explosively within the fabric of associated cultural and institutional contexts, interferes with as well as facilitates freedom of options. Recently attention has been called to the low levels of personal mobility enjoyed by some—particularly the young, the poor and the old (Hillman *et al.*, 1973). The latest figures available underline this: 19·5 million people in England and Wales did not have the use of a car in 1971 (Hillman, 1974). Decentralisation of workplaces, greater flexibility of working hours, increased controls on vehicle circulation, new inventions of more 'socialised' vehicle systems, etc., will doubtless take form under the impact of this contemporary concern (Hillman *et al.*, 1973; Patmore, 1970).

But the immediate effect on the increase in 'freedom of choice' is one of shock. Demand overwhelms supply; over-use creates at best the danger of a self-defeating glut—in roads, parks, beauty spots, trails, sports facilities, etc. The alarm has been sounded by visionary observers, like Michael Dower, who wrote in 1965 (5):

> Three great waves have broken across the face of Britain since 1800. First, the sudden growth of dark industrial towns. Second, the thrusting movement along far-flung railways. Third, the sprawl of car-based suburbs. Now, we see, under the guise of a modest word, the surge of a fourth wave which could be more powerful than all the others. The modest word is *leisure*.

A town planner, Dower sees leisure in almost physical terms—compounded of increased population with higher income, greater mobility, more education, retirement and 'free time' generally. This amalgam of forces is seen to drive people by every conceivable means of locomotion in a quest for amenities—in and around the towns, in the country, in the mountain-tops and by the seashore and abroad. Dower estimates that the amalgam of leisure forces is such at present and into the immediate future that its thrust will exceed that of population growth by a factor of at least two to one in Britain. His image of congestion and devastation of the precious natural resources that unplanned absorption of this thrust will create is powerful and persuasive. On the cover of his report to the Civic Trust is a holiday beach crowd jammed together like the proverbial sardines (though less neatly) and inside is the observation that: 'If everyone in England and Wales went to the seaside at the same time, each would get a strip of coast three-and-a-half inches across.'

This dramatisation of the situation is highly effective but Dower is no 'doomwatcher'. He suggested various solutions for the different scales at which problems confront the country—urban, rural, regional, national. His suggestions draw on world experience, and proceed by practical steps. The formula is to search for and make an inventory of the resources available to the nation, region or local area (land, water, general topography, technology and finance) and to create plans using scientifically based guidelines and standards for capacity and usage, and then to implement them. Dower sees the job as one that must be tackled on a large scale, but at the same time requires deep local involvement. The co-operation of public, voluntary and commercial bodies is also called for to an extent not previously envisioned. 'This thing leisure', he states, 'requires powerful authorities with big resources and clear-cut channels of responsibility . . . the highest standard of co-ordination and expertise' (Dower, 1965, 188).

We shall return to responses to the 'leisure explosion' of public and private, national and local 'providers', in a later chapter. It is relevant here to note that the 'leisure explosion' confronts people generally with a number of issues—the main contours of which constitute the focus of the present work. The explosion of free time, of disposable income, and of available consumer goods has been accompanied by an escalation of 'wants'. Increased levels of education for ever-broadening sectors of the population have led to increased interest in all sorts of pursuits that can be followed with the resources increasingly available. Travel, literature, music, art, gastronomic delights and so on are in demand by ever-broadening waves of the population. Time and money, the two powerful elements which have in the past separated élites from masses most sharply, have now been made more broadly available, increasing access to valued resources of the world. The joys (and dangers) of jet travel are now available not only to film stars, tycoons and the wealthy leisured classes, but to school-teachers, bricklayers, shopkeepers and farmers. Festivals of the arts, treasures of exotic lands and ancient times, riding, golf and sailing—the sporting life—are now available to more people— and wanted by still more—than ever before. Of course, not everyone has shared in this relative ease of access. It is to be hoped that the new focus of concern with 'the cycle of deprivation' will generate some redress to seemingly intractable imbalances.

And yet, there are two nagging foci of concern: one that plagues the providers (or should plague them, as servants of the people) and the other that plagues everyman, more rather than less as his level of consciousness and his wants and desires escalate. The first is whether the meeting of *palpable mass demand* in the most direct and obvious way (i.e. adding more of the same to what has been delivered and found to be popular) is the best that can be done; and second, the concern of everyman, of how to use the available time, money and resources to create a *meaningful whole life*.

Palpable mass demand: the providers' vista

Every society and culture has an inventory of artefacts and social institutions that satisfies something in popular demand. Monuments, arenas, stadia, parks and open spaces, entertainment places—songs, dances, pageants, rituals, sport—all can be seen to exist as foci of popular interest and activity. Much of any period's 'leisure' resources is subject to readaptation as society changes. Boulevards and avenues laid out for military purposes, or to glorify the name of an autocrat, become people's promenades. Private mansions, abbeys and castles become museums, and games formerly enjoyed only by the aristocracy become folk sport. As with symbols and meanings, so with leisure facilities and activities: one may alter while the other holds constant, or both may change. Hence, we have physical artefacts which persist, while the activities they generate change; activities which persist while new or improved facilities are called for; and both activities and facilities evolving together.

A distinctive characteristic of the present is the explosive increase both in what is wanted and in the means to get it. Looking down on earth from a detached height might reveal a population agitated by a strange driving force to move about, to proceed by air, rail, road, cycle or foot to many points of interest away from routine places of work and residence. Making use of available places, things or events gives rise to secondary demands: for access routes, parking places, toilets, catering facilities, information and safety devices. If not properly attended to, these secondary requirements may not only create a residue of frustrated demand, but of disastrous consequences. An example is the disaster of Altamont, California, where masses of people came together for a pop festival without adequate controls on the mob psychology (fuelled by drugs and the juxtaposition of such incendiary elements as Hell's Angels and hippies).

This dramatic illustration is an extreme case of a wider problem, the self-defeating character of the explosion of palpable mass demand. Cars flooding out of metropolitan concentrations on weekends and at holidays make the search for calm and non-polluted environments elusive. People swarming through exhibits, trampling over fragile nature trails, stampeding over spectator barriers, etc., not only disrupt the proceedings but may destroy resources. The traffic, queuing, straining and anxiety involved in reaching many 'leisure' destinations, is qualitatively different from the suspense of sport or adventure, and often serves to kill rather than foster enjoyment.

The 'natural' response to these problems of over-running and congestion is to add more resources in the tried and true pattern of demonstrated demand. If the roads are inadequate for the cars, build more roads; if the parks are overcrowded, build more parks; if the pools are overcrowded, build more and larger pools; if the demand for books, concerts, exhibitions, etc., goes up from year to year (in attendance figures), make more of the same. Prototypical are the Sports Council's proposals for its 'Sport in the Seventies' programme. On the basis that existing sports halls, swimming pools and golf courses are used to capacity, and a simple extrapolation of this pattern, a multi-million pound programme for the provision of these three facilities nationwide was formulated (Sports Council, 1972; White, 1972). Up to a point, this is reasonable but it is necessary to question assumptions more, to experiment more with new forms and new uses of old forms, and to innovate more actively.

Except for a few resources such as television which reach almost everyone, most palpable demand may not reflect actual levels of demand. There are latent and potential demands as well as expressed ones. Palpable demand is influenced by the existing array of facilities. Again, though the class structure is vaguely pyramidal in its numerical composition, the demand for many of the desirable goods of life are disproportionately represented by those at the upper end of the pyramid. This is true both for costly elements—gourmet restaurants, theatre tickets, trips abroad—and for some of the 'best things in life [that] are free', such as nature trails, beach walks and public libraries. Not everyone demands as palpably or is as motivated and consumptive as the 'leisure explosion' image implies. Not all providers recognise the complexities of latent demand. There is a natural tendency to think of populations to be provided for, in 'block' terms. Thus providers and others may refer to women (as if they were all the same) as participating at low levels, or to the 'fours and fives' (the lower socio-economic status categories) as participating little in the facilities provided. To provide more effectively for individuals, closer attention has to be given to variations in the constraints that impinge on them. Age, sex and social class are not sufficiently comprehensive to guide social policy.

The danger of inequitous use in a society that strains towards equality of opportunity is seen not only in availability of money, education and taste, but of locality. A numbers-oriented public authority may provide a sports centre or a battery of tennis courts or football pitches which, in terms of quantities of facilities and expenditure, may seem like making a sizeable contribution, but in terms of use patterns may be used and enjoyed only by those near enough to reach the facility conveniently. The converse may also be true. Facilities like swimming pools, whose catchments are 'known' to be fairly local, may be monopolised by users outside the area who come a considerable distance with their clubs who make fixed bookings. Conventional wisdom about catchment areas may be based on inadequate assumptions. Empirical research like that of Maw and Terence Lee is gradually providing a more adequate appreciation of the variety of interacting factors that influence use patterns (Maw and Cosgrove, 1972; Lee, 1970).

Two factors seem to determine the overriding pattern of leisure providers. One is the rather mechanistic use of criteria such as seating, acreage, demand numbers and so on, to fulfil an organisational requirement and provide a clear-cut basis for evaluation. The second is the tendency to adopt patterns that are successful in particular situations as models or blueprints for large-scale situations, amplifying their size but not complexity. All those indoor sports centres must be good! More visionary providers direct their energies towards the continuous search for more equitable and flexible as well as more bureaucratically acceptable patterns of provision. Michael Dower and Peter Downing (1973) write that:

> It may be that little harm has resulted from our own, and others' outlook. One could argue that the demands are so palpable, and the supply of facilities so limited, that no harm can come from pressing ahead with the provision of a range of leisure facilities of types which are already familiar, and in which we are 'behind' some countries in Europe and elsewhere. But, awareness is growing that these facilities are posited on assumptions which may or may not be right, may or may not be the really significant assumptions. . . .
>
> We do not deny the need for action . . . [but] the . . . concern with supply and demand, with efficient use of resources, and with maintaining political support and the flow of funds . . . understandably leads to heavy emphasis on numbers as a criterion of success. 'Overseas tourists 12% up', 'historic house tops $\frac{1}{4}$ million visitors', 'sports hall used 7 days a week, 14 hours a day'—are accepted as quick but sure guides to the rightness of policy and the success of its execution. But let us remember that every digit is a *person*, to whom that holiday, that visit, that game of squash is an event important to his senses and emotions, either enhancing or diminishing or neutral to the pattern of his life. The other million people also on that trip are not irrelevant to his satisfaction but they can as readily diminish as enhance it—and certainly an entrepreneur preoccupied with the number of visitors is not necessarily so concerned with the quality of the experience offered.

We shall return in chapter 2 to some of the issues confronting providers as they pursue their various goals. The important point here is that there is a range of people who seek, in their roles in social organisations, to provide facilities. These people have one sort of perspective on the 'leisure explosion' which has, to some extent, a life of its own. They are concerned with performance, with resources, costs, political supports, standards and design, training and liaison, recruitment of staff, procurement of supplies, obtaining of sanctions and control and maintenance of the facilities themselves. While all of these considerations are ultimately relevant to users generally, the distance between providers and users is often great. There is also the tendency to become bogged down in organisational imperatives.

Added to this is the fact that the involvement in 'leisure' activities at the societal (macroscopic) level stems from multiple agenda. The field of leisure provision is a coalition: of people interested in improving health and preventing illness, delinquency or premature death; of people interested in cleaning up the environment and preserving the natural heritage; of people concerned with maintaining morals, building character or satisfying needs.

More recently, the pleasure content of leisure has been validated in its own right. The Lords' Select Committee on Sport and Leisure has recast the humanistic values of the American Constitution's Bill of Rights in the framework of a modern Welfare State. It holds that everyone in contemporary Britain is entitled to enjoyment (Lords' Select Committee, 1973):

> The state should not opt out of caring for people's leisure when it accepts the responsibility of caring for most of their other needs. The provision of opportunities for the enjoyment of leisure is part of the general fabric of the social services.

> Every County Council and metropolitan District Council and Regional Authority should have a Recreation Committee and a Department of Recreation under its own chief officer.

> Each Department of Recreation should be concerned with all forms of sport, physical recreation, the arts, museums and libraries and informal leisure activities.

And leisure/recreation was chosen as the topic for the Prince of Wales's maiden speech in Parliament—a topic which, like virtue, no one was expected to be 'against'. Yet, as has been indicated, the attitude taken toward specific provision depends on a number of factors. The public responsibility facet, emphasised in the Lords' statement, is, on the whole, less salient for private sector entrepreneurs who are more concerned with economic indicators of demand. Then there are the others in the coalition: medical people concerned with health; social workers concerned with the prevention of delinquency or vandalism or misery in housing, or boredom in retirement; educators concerned with recurrent education and government agencies with job readjustment.

Our concern in this book is more with the public than the private perspective on this—though each has a contribution to make not only to the satisfaction of people's life interests directly, but to one another's perspectives and methods of work. And each is a major element in the working environment of the other so long as our society retains its present form of mixed public and private initiative. Public sector pro-

viders have a good deal to learn from those in the 'leisure industries'—
about market-orientated procedures, about being alert to people's more
light-hearted needs—for 'fun' and enjoyment. Conversely the public
sector will not only be an indispensable ally for private enterprise in
many of its own ventures, but may temper the tendency in some enterprises in this field to show the 'unacceptable face of capitalism',
exploiting human weaknesses and insecurities with insufficient humane
safeguards.

Existing theoretical perspectives

Providers, both public and private, and indeed voluntary and informal
bodies, may be informed in their efforts by social theory and social
research. There are many relevant theories; the very profusion of them
creates problems of selection. The observations of de Tocqueville and
Veblen, supported in contemporary research like that of Young and
Willmott, suggests that there is a diffusion of valued resources relevant
to leisure provision from the élites to the masses. Many sports, elements
of technology, access to artforms, desirable experiences of travel and
recreation, have 'trickled down' from the rich to the poor. For de
Tocqueville this argued for the maintenance of the élites; for Veblen,
in the American setting, for keeping open channels for social mobility.
The 'American dream' of every man's possible ascent to the top keeps
the masses from the discontent that many may feel for their lot (de
Tocqueville, 1945; Veblen, 1957; Young and Willmott, 1973).

Indeed those in the Marxist tradition of theory and research argue
that the danger of supporting policies of leisure provision in a capitalist
society may detract from revolutionary potential. A recent illustration
of this is in the critique of the Mary Quant exhibit at the London
Museum by the Russian newspaper, *Pravda*. The enjoyment that has
been brought to young people by Mary Quant's efforts to disseminate
high-fashion flair to the masses (a kind of 'trickle down' effect in the
design world) has been seen as a capitalist device to placate youth—
whose critical assessments of the contemporary order might otherwise
have been more effectively directed against the system. Most contemporary social researchers simply observe the tendency for working-
class youth to *want* to emulate the middle-class life styles, albeit ambivalently because of the hated elements that this may entail. Emmett,
for example, indicates that while many young people use their own
relatively déclassé age groups as reference groups for norms, particularly in the leisure area, it is older people by and large who control the
social institutions which must be used to express these norms. She
says (1971a): '[there is] a tendency for working class people, as they
become better off financially, to emulate middle class people in leisure

pursuits as in other things.' Even where the creativity is firmly rooted in youthful working-class impulses—as with many of the pop groups from the Beatles onwards—the dependence on the mass media, entertainments industry, impressarios, managers, lawyers and accountants—all middle class—presents a dilemma to individuals who wish to carry this beyond their own enjoyment and that of their local friends: '[the creative working-class youth] must join the middle class which by and large provides the model for working class behaviour' (Emmett, 1971a). Emmett notes that there are, however, exchanges going on in both directions. The 'squares', often middle class, may use some of the ideas and expressive forms of the more 'way-out' creative groups (often, in leisure fields, working class) just as working-class performers or designers may use the institutions of the middle class. Diffusion goes on in both directions.

The social class interchange, apparent in relation to youth culture, may also be at work in the conventional world of middle-aged, established society. Heckscher and De Grazia noted the tendency in modern industry for managers and higher executives to be psychologically hard-driven—to work longer hours and more single-mindedly (in what is almost a caricature of puritanical devotion) than the workers. The latter, though less intrinsically fulfilled by their work and less gratified by amenities and perquisites of their jobs, are nevertheless 'freed' with energy and spare cash for the cultivation of other interests. The restoration of the ideal of multi-dimensional man may, under circumstances like these, call for upward diffusion of leisure influences (Heckscher and De Grazia, 1959).

If boats, golf courses, tennis courts, high-fidelity sound reproduction and the like are spreading from the domains of the privileged to those of everyman, is there a sense of fun, enjoyment and pleasure spreading in the opposite direction? This appealing argument does not seem as yet to find much empirical support. While workers have more time off and are less downtrodden in their work than previously, there is little to support the idea that they are increasing their overall life satisfaction by cultivating other interests. *Social Trends* analyses show a fairly stable level of satisfaction apparently independent of the leisure trends noted (*Social Trends*, 1973; Abrams, 1974). Many take their 'spare time' to 'work' more—either for pay or on home improvements, in which they follow middle-class tastes and patterns. There is little evidence to support the idea that they are generating new forms of *joie de vivre* which will make themselves felt by those in higher social-class positions.

There seem to be two implications of these findings. First, that there are a number of possible directions and channels for the diffusion of different elements of the leisure configuration. Time, ideas, activities, artefacts and personal orientations may all diffuse separately and in different channels. Way-out groups, workers who are leisure heroes, minorities experimenting with variation in cultural patterns may all influence the 'middle mass' of society in different ways. There seems to be an increase in the scope and number of variant subcultural groups who choose not to accommodate themselves to conventional cultural norms. Paradoxically the reciprocity between these variant groups and the mainstream of society may increase. This is enhanced by the encouragement of the creative experimentation in fringe groups by those who control the leisure industries and communication channels, so that they can take advantage of 'the possibilities of incorporating within the mainstream of mass culture successful discoveries and styles within the fringe groups' (Briggs, 1969).

Second, in addition to all its other complexities of definition, the idea of leisure has a peculiarly elastic character. One can fill one's time with work and other obligations without necessarily crowding our 'leisure activities' because they can be combined in so many ways. While managers and professionals work longer hours than their workers —not shorter as the nineteenth-century revolutionaries would have predicted—their work has a porosity and multi-dimensional character that makes it possible for leisure elements to be absorbed or combined with it. For others, however, work may be so alienating that there is little energy left for enjoyment following the work day (as writers from Marx to C. Wright Mills and Wilensky have noted); and there are inequities in the distribution of task which do not allow this plasticity of enjoyment to be easily combined with work. Women present a special problem, at least at our present stage of 'gender liberation'. The burdens of household work fall inequitably on married women, even when they work equally to their husbands. Weekends therefore become more a matter of overtime work for married women and more a matter of recreation for men. The movement towards more equitable definitions of domestic as well as occupational work may alleviate this situation eventually—but there are significant time lags in this, in socialist as well as capitalist countries.

From the point of view of the providers—and their tendency to concentrate their efforts on satisfying palpable mass demand—the question of how individuals and families use the resources made available to them is a private issue, an issue that will be worked out in terms of the *life style* that particular families evolve within the privacy of their homes (Laslett, 1974). The tendency among theorists in the socialist countries is to regard the 'privatisation' of home-centred trends in leisure consumption as anarchic and deleterious to the fabric of society. Part of their emphasis on the need to create a 'culture of leisure' supports the socially integrative functions of provision (Hollander, 1966).

Most Western analysis of leisure behaviour has stressed the central value of choice, and there has been a stream of research on actual patterns chosen (Kaplan, 1960; Larrabee and Meyersohn, 1958; Riesman, 1954). Wilensky has concluded that in the USA there are three broad leisure (life) styles which have emerged. These are: *class-determined patterns*—mainly operative on the lower end, where alienation at work, limitations of economic wherewithal and of educational level create the kind of situation described by Marx and Engels in the nineteenth-century European setting. About one-fifth to one-sixth of American workers seem to be bound by class patterns. *Individuated patterns*—which are responsive to the person's individual wishes for solo, deviant, fluid, 'freaky' patterns or eccentric creative patterns with little social significance or impact; and *family home localism*—probably the predominant American pattern, less alienated, less solo, less deviant than the other patterns, drawn more *towards* comforts of the home and family circle than *against* society as such.

Wilensky's work has been supplemented and enlarged on in Britain by Stanley Parker (who has refined the class variables by analysing specific occupational characteristics in relation to leisure), and by Young and Willmott (who have added a social change dimension) (Wilensky, 1960; Parker, 1971; Young and Willmott, 1973).

This work is relevant in the context of the present discussion. Providers, in making decisions about 'demand' for leisure facilities, base their plans and actions partly on the 'feasible' extension of what already exists and is known to be workable, and partly on a reading of people's 'needs' and social trends. Social research that looks beneath and beyond palpable mass demand may contribute to providers making optimal decisions. *The contribution that we seek to make to this effort is to suggest a perspective that supplements rather than replaces the perspective of social class and social change already mentioned. This is the perspective of the human life cycle.* Based on relatively constant preoccupations arising from psycho-biological maturational processes, this perspective cuts across and underlies class and sub-cultural patterns. Most commonly the life cycle plays itself out in the framework of family living, and it is this framework that we propose to use. It is important to enlarge perspectives in this way at this time, because of the *institutionalisation* going on in the field of provision; after the patterns are set and crystallised, they will be more difficult to alter than at present when they are in a state of some fluidity.

The people's side of the equation

As a great many studies have shown, and as providers are increasingly aware, there is a problem of relating what is done at the macroscopic level of social institutions to phenomena at the 'grass-roots', people's level. This issue is found not only in leisure provision, but in politics and government, in large bureaucratic organisations and in social life generally. It involves the relationship between individual and society, which in turn involves the need to understand the workings of each as a separate system and the ways in which they link. Concern with the quality of this interface is growing among researchers and policy-makers.

From the perspective of those in institutional roles—providers, administrators, etc.—the most widely used concept to assess the pheno-mena at the 'people's' level with which they seek to link their activities is *need*. Social policies, industrial products, services and facilities are provided in response to what are taken to be people's needs. Enlightened providers sometimes formulate these needs as 'rights' (Hudson, 1971):

> leisure rights—for variety, tranquillity and privacy, free association, space to play in, space to explore, access to materials that will deepen and widen experience, opportunities for exercise, experiencing sensa-tions, being surprised, being stretched and opportunities to succeed.

Or, as prescriptions by those interested in preventive medicine (Wright, 1971):

> People need to relax, they need to build up outside interests. And outside interests are not professional meetings, trade associations, committee meetings, dinners and God knows what. Outside interests are abiding interests in something outside work.

Or, by scientists, seeking to shape future societies to meet human as well as technical goals (Gabor, 1972, 136):

> in a technologically highly advanced mature society, young people at 20 may be in a similar position to that confronting those of 60 today. Nobody ought to leave the new (mass) university without having found at least one lifelong interest.

Gabor's use of the term *interest* is casual. He does not suggest it as a concept to improve or replace the imprecise concept of need to which so many policies and suggestions for policies are addressed. We use the term interest as a key concept in what follows. It is, for us, a pivotal concept—between the psycho-biologically based, often unconscious notion of 'preoccupation', and the manifest behavioural variable, 'activity'.

The concept of interest has been developed in sociology by Dubin and inch psyology by Strong. Foreshadowing some of the more recent work on life styles, Dubin noted that individuals, even within the same class and occupational groups, place different emphases on the components of their experience. While it may be that, by and large, professionals find their greatest satisfaction in work, and assembly-line workers find their greatest satisfaction outside, there are variations. Individuals can be classified according to where they find these satisfactions, or expect to find them—and this classification defines their 'central life interest' (Dubin, 1956). Dubin's original aim was to study what produced the more 'job-oriented' workers as distinct from those who were less job-oriented or indifferent. In the early studies, work and non-work were the contrasts; later this became differentiated into work, family and leisure, and various adumbrations were added in comparing different kinds of groups, some only with expectations and aspirations, others with memories. Strong, and those who used the interest scale developed by him, were primarily concerned with vocational and work choice (Strong, 1955).

Looking generally at the studies that have used the notion of life sectors and life interests, a number of points are now clear. They can be summarised as follows. (a) Work as a source of satisfaction increases as the status of the job rises. So job satisfaction is likely to be greater for the more highly skilled, more highly trained, more educated, and in more technologically advanced occupations. (b) Paradoxically, as skill, status, education, remuneration (and other linked variables) rise, there is a tendency for the *main* source of personal satisfaction to come from (or to be expected from) outside the workplace. Thus Dumazedier found that skilled workers indicated in higher proportions than unskilled workers that they derived their principal satisfactions from family life (Dumazedier, 1967, 97).

There are also sex differences. We found among British graduates that though career as the principal source of personal satisfaction is greater for women who want to work continuously than for those who wish to drop out of work for a period of domesticity, for women generally the family is expected to provide the principal satisfactions. Perhaps less conventionally expectable, however, was the finding that the majority of men also expect their greatest satisfaction to come from family life. Their expectations though are not as universal as among women. There are other factors beside the intention to have a continuous career that affect men's value orientations (Fogarty et al., 1971).

Odaka, in a study of five Japanese companies, found that like the French and British, family life was the principal source of personal satisfaction and that an 'integrated' conception of life style—work and non-work having complementary roles to play in their lives—was the most popular one (Odaka, 1966).

It must be stressed, however, that contrary to the indication of survey material, the priorities are not clear-cut for all individuals. The ways in which people manage their lives, and the energies they invest in various life sectors, are not necessarily conflict-free in any of these societies or occupations. It is one thing to favour a given pattern, another actually to enjoy it.

Bradburn, in an American study, found that marital happiness is a variable relatively independent of occupational status for men (with similar proportions of men reporting very happy marriages at each SES level); but for women, the likelihood of reporting a very happy marriage drops sharply in the lower SES level (Bradburn, 1969, 156). The crucial element is how much attention the man is willing or able to give to his family life. This interpretation is supported by Bailyn's finding in British graduate couples, that it was in the families of 'careerist' men that the lowest proportion of marital happiness was reported (i.e. men whose devotion to career did not include an expectation of major personal satisfaction from family life), and they were men who were predominantly high on the SES scale (Bailyn, 1970). Where women are unable to find fulfilment in such a situation, they become what Gavron called 'captive' housewives. Jessie Bernard argues, on the basis of American data (which may differ from data in other countries because of the differences in consciousness about sex role issues), that the single state is statistically more vulnerable for males, while for females, it is the married state. We have some indications of this, which will be reported in chapter 4 on the 'establishment phase', in Britain as well. We argue that the proximate cause for this vulnerability is the concentration of women's interests on domesticity and maternity to the exclusion of other interests, and to their own later detriment (Gavron, 1966; Bernard, 1972).

The concept of need is too gross to deal usefully with the kinds of findings reported. The pattern according to which satisfied high-status workers also seek to maximise their satisfactions from home life by cultivating a 'do-it-yourself' set of hobbies is only very loosely connected with a theory of needs. Is it because they 'need' to do something with their hands, or 'need' to have a home that reflects their status but lack funds to pay for it; or is it because they 'need' to have a haven from the jungle of competitive work life? If the last is true, why don't all their wives feel that their needs are being satisfied in this way? Is it sex differences in needs? If so, why do members of both sexes withdraw from external involvements when they marry and have their first child? Do they 'need' sociability or sport less at that point?

This reflects another problem with the concept of need. Sometimes need seems to be indicated by a demand activity; sometimes by its absence. Adolescents 'need' activity channels, as their restless behaviour shows. 'Captive' housewives 'need' interests external to the home even though they do not necessarily 'demand' them. Similar points can be made for old people, poor people, unaggressive people, children, sick people and so on.

Whatever needs may be taken to mean, and however they may be subject to change or variation, they do not correspond to palpable mass demand. Nor is there a theoretically formulated link between need and the kind of behaviour for which leisure providers cater—except in the most loose and *post hoc* sense.

In contrast, there is a growing appreciation of the importance of evolving people-oriented approaches to complement the traditional concerns with facilities. A study group of the Sports Council on research priorities has stated (1971):

> the social and psychological influences affecting the aspirations and motivations underlying leisure behaviour need to be understood more clearly if effective leisure provision and administration is to be achieved. So far, little progress has been made on these topics and the group can only repeat and underline the need expressed in its first report for these areas of work to be opened up and developed.

The counterpoint between 'what is good for the public' and 'what is good for specific individuals' is part of the issue, and Kenneth Harrop's response (1973) to Peter Hall's attempt to emphasise the need for improved devices for communications between planners and their publics is to conclude: 'Perhaps what is really required is research about people, not devices.' Harrop is concerned with countering public apathy—as distinct from learning more about it. This seems to us to entail problems of understanding how people's motivational systems articulate with institutions, and how they interact in the change process.

Veal, in a study sponsored by the Countryside Commission, the Forestry Commission and the Sports Council, supports this view, stating as follows (1973, 1):

> As recreation planning and research moves beyond the 'fact-gathering' stage into areas of policy formation and forecasting, it is increasingly apparent that knowledge and understanding of factors relating to motivation and preference are becoming necessary.

What does this mean? How is it to be done? We suggest that a return to first principles is required in the first instance.

First principles

We are concerned with the key problem of the link between individual and society, microsocial intimate small groups and macrosocial bureaucratic large-scale organisations. The large organisations—in this case, directors and staff members of leisure centres, pools, parks, libraries and local government departments of leisure and recreation—are not concerned with the same issues as the people who use them.

Sociologists who have concerned themselves with the relationship between macroscopic and microscopic dimensions of society have emphasised different aspects according to their theoretical stance. Crozier (1972, 241) has emphasised power elements in the relationship:

> no system of organisation can be constructed without power relationships, and all organisation is built around power relationships which afford the necessary link between the desired objectives and the human means that are indispensable to their realisation.

Crozier uses a games metaphor to analyse the relationships between those who hold the power and those over whom the power is supposedly exercised. He sees a major change going on in society from a model in which one set of 'rules of play' is displacing another. The older one is a more rigid and restrictive model, the newer one is more co-operative. This is, in the political arena, the counterpart of MacGregor's 'theory X' and 'theory Y' in industrial management. Emery and Trist (1973) detail this shift as a key one in the movement from the organisational models governing industrial society to those of post-industrial society.

Emery and Trist, Slater and others try to show how the relationship between people and their institutions must be analysed in a dual framework allowing for motivational and social structural analysis. This is particularly true when analysing change phenomena—as we are necessarily doing in the leisure field at the present time (Slater, 1971).

Our argument is that there is a gap between the institutions of leisure-facility providers and the wishes, 'needs' and requirements of people seeking to develop meaningful whole-life experiences. It is necessary for society to attend to both levels (organisations and people). How do we proceed to think about them systematically in relation to one another? We suggest the life-cycle framework as a useful (not the only useful) one, and one that has been insufficiently understood or applied. We are particularly concerned with the influences of the family in the individual's 'life line' of development, and in the way different spheres of influence interact at different times in the cycle. Individuals develop their lives along three lines—work, family and leisure. Individuals integrate influences and experiences in all of these life spheres as they create and live out a life career. This is, as Robert White put it, the 'enterprise of living' (White, 1952). While the three separate planes are conceptually distinct (as suggested in Figure 1), individuals combine them in characteristic ways to form whole life-style patterns.

Each life-line strand is thought of as a helix because at each critical status transition (such as getting married) people go back psychologically over ground covered earlier. The life revision that occurs, consciously or unconsciously, as each new stage is entered into and a new integration brought about, gives the process a spiralling or helical character. Because each of the points at which there is a necessary turning involves fairly fundamental revision, we think of each as a 'life crisis'. Together, the three strands form a 'triple helix' rather than three

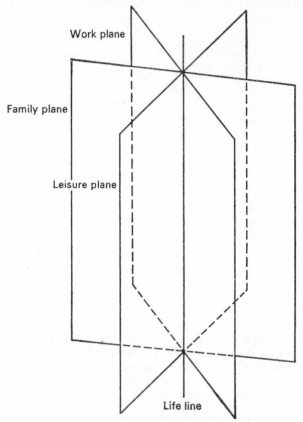

Figure 1 *Three planes representing sectors based on the individual life line*

distinct spirals because of the way each of the strands interacts with the others, an effect particularly notable at critical transitions. At the time of these critical transitions there is an 'unfreezing', a disorganisation during which established patterns are loosened. Then reorganisation follows. In the period of disorganisation a revision occurs which provides a potential challenge to develop new patterns for all strands, not only the one in which the transition occurs. For example, when an individual marries, his patterns of heterosexual and family relationships, his orientation to work and career, his pattern of involvement in peer group activities and his other life interests are all likely to be affected. Changes in jobs, changes in life interests (such as in sailing or a second home) may have similar ramifying effects not only within the specific life-line strand, but in the other strands as well.

Each life-line strand, then, can be seen as undergoing a 'career'. 'Career' has been used in the occupational plane primarily, often most usefully as a retrospective concept in which a pattern usually becomes visible only after it has occurred. But it can be applied, to some extent, to other interests. A child develops a play activity at home such as kicking a ball around with his father; this may later become an interest at school and he may become a member of the school football team. If he keeps football in his leisure line, the career of enjoying football remains a non-occupational one. If he becomes a professional foot-baller, his enjoyment of the activity may or may not continue, but the activity itself is differently classified. Only a tiny proportion of 'football-mad' youngsters become professionals. However, though careers in family, work or leisure can only be plotted for given individuals retro-spectively, characteristic patterns may be seen, and used, as a basis for social policy and social theory.

Influences from diffuse macroscopic sources such as the mass media, the larger institutional structures like the church (shown in Figure 2) to the more specific influences assignable to actual people known and interacting with one are at play throughout the life cycle. 'Normative agents' express attitudes of approval or disapproval, and provide both substantive content for what can be done and sanction as to what ought to be done by the individual in specific situations.

Most people try, less or more consciously, to locate or create congenial experience and environments. There are many difficulties in achieving this; there are barrriers and frustrations; sacrifices and trade-offs, con-flicts and struggles that occur in the process of evolving satisfying life styles. The construction of life styles involves dealing with resistances and constraints as well as taking advantage of opportunities and poten-tials. Figure 2 centres on the development of the life line. At critical transition points, influences from different spheres impinge on the individual and he interacts with them to give a structure to his involve-ment in those spheres. Experiences in each of the strands affect decisions and subsequent developments in the other strands. Interests can arise in any of the strands and either be contained within it, or diffuse to others.

Our thesis is that underlying observable life-style patterns there are socio-psychological dimensions of motivations that are important to appreciate if one is to understand people's life requirements. At the

most fundamental level, rooted in psycho-biological development, are
people's *preoccupations*, changing with growth in the course of the life
cycle. Preoccupations may be manifested in *interests*, which may change
or remain constant (perhaps with changing meaning for the individual)
and a given interest may be channelled into various *activities*.

Any particular *activity*—say walking in the park—has different

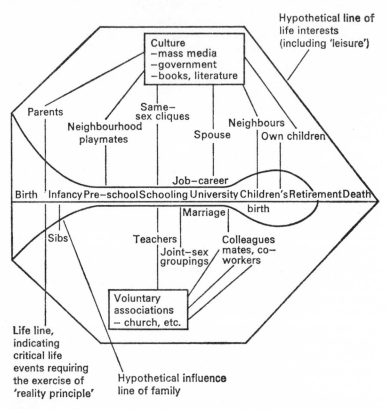

Figure 2   *Influences on the development of the life line*

meanings for different kinds of people in relation to the *interests* they are
pursuing. It may be a way of being alone for a young courting couple;
a way of exercising a pet for an old lady living alone; a way for a middle-
aged man to fend off the coronary to which he is at risk, and so on.
Similarly a given *preoccupation* (for example with a sense of excitement
and stimulation) may be expressed differently by different individuals:
through sports cars, drugs, sexual adventures, or in mountain-climbing.
Some may experience similar stimulation by visiting art galleries. For

many tycoons 'making a deal' provides excitement and the addiction to work of some businessmen and professionals can be better understood in these terms than in terms of economic drives. For a poet it may come by finding the right words to match his feelings, and for a scientist the right experiment to demonstrate a scientific principle. Is there any pattern in this, or is it all a matter of individual variation?

Variations observable in the life styles of individuals and groups while ultimately individual in detail have underlying patterns. These are determined by influences which can be systematically described. The variables which have been productive in social research for detecting and analysing patterns have included age, sex, social class, type of residence and education. Each of these, and clusters of them, are capable of explaining observable behaviour. It seems to us, however, that they are losing power as predictors to the extent that age, sex, social class, standards of housing and education become less socially divisive.

To the extent that static categories are indeed losing relevance for understanding people's behaviour and values, one requires a framework that is amenable to the analysis of change and variation. We want to explore the utility of the family life-cycle framework for this purpose. Individuals have life cycles, according to which they change their preoccupations, interests and activities as they develop—maturing and ageing in the course of the life cycle. But individuals vary systematically not only according to their biological drives, but to their social roles in relation to the family life cycle and family structure. The events of marriage, child-birth and all the subsequent critical transitions as children develop and eventually leave home are in and of themselves important as foci of interest and activity. In addition they signal re-organisation of life style, determined by social class and the other influential factors indicated in the overarching framework presented above.

The family life cycle is geared both to age and sex variables but it encompasses something more. It implies a changing organisation of roles and value orientations (for example in child-rearing) which partly reflect the large social environment, and partly the particular people. The key concepts reflecting the developmental nature of the changes that occur in the course of the cycle are the following:

1 *Preoccupations* are mental absorptions, less or more conscious, which arise from psycho-biological development, maturation and ageing processes as they interact with social-environmental conditions.
2 *Interests* arise in people's awareness as ideas and feelings about what they want or would like to have or do, about which they are curious, to which they are drawn, through which they feel they might derive satisfaction.

3   *Activities* are spheres of action—such as driving, dancing, participating in or watching sports, attending clubs, etc.

As we have indicated, there is no one-to-one relationship between
preoccupations and interests, and a given interest may be fulfilled
through different activities with a similarly non-specific link. The way
in which activities and interests are matched affects the level of satisfaction that different individuals derive.

Preoccupations arise at a relatively 'deep' motivational level in
'human nature' as the individual develops through psycho-social stages
of maturation. Given preoccupations may be present all through the
life cycle but they tend to become particularly salient at a given phase,
and to effloresce at critical stages. Interests take form out of the interaction between an individual with his felt preoccupations and his
social environment. Aside from providing (or failing to provide) the
content and structure for the cultivation of interests, society through
its various providers of facilities offers channels through which interests
may flourish and provide satisfactions.

'Quo Vadis?'

Published three years before Watergate, Slater's analysis of the corrup-
tibility of a national character produced by the overvaluation of technological products was startlingly prescient. His distress and anger at the
primacy given the expedient and manipulative mentality so produced
is relieved by a degree of optimism at attempts with creative revision.
He suggests that there is already present, particularly among the young,
the kernel of a 'new culture', emphasising humane, co-operative, con-
summatory values—as well as the hard-core set of institutions and
motivational patterns representing the 'old' culture of technological
primacy. In assisting the new culture to survive and become stronger,
persistent efforts need to be made at both the motivational and the
institutional levels. Unencumbered by so many institutional constraints,
many of the young express the wish to revise their motivational priorities: love and peace, pleasure and expressiveness. When they leave
school, enter work, marry and have children, the constraints increase,
and the difficulties in sustaining changes mount (Slater, 1971, 160):

> The new parents may not be as absorbed in material possession and
> occupational self-aggrandisement as their own parents were. They
> may channel their parental vanity into different spheres, pushing their
> children to be brilliant artists, thinkers and performers. But the hard
> narcissistic core on which the older culture was based will not be
> dissolved until the parent-child relationship itself is de-intensified,

and this is precisely where the younger generation is likely to be most inadequate. . . .

It is not that being child-oriented itself produces a narcissistic personality—quite the contrary. It is when the parent turns to the child as a vicarious substitute for satisfactions the parent fails to find in his or her own life that the child becomes vain, ambitious, hungry for glory.

Slater is talking about the difficulties that stand in the way of achieving change because of the interlocking between the parental and child generations in the life cycle. Emery and Trist indicate another facet of the problem. They note that forging new modes of experiencing life must be hammered out against the twin obstacles of one's early socialisation and one's inhospitable environments (Emery and Trist, 1973, 178–81):

> The prospect that the traditional distinction between work and play, made extreme in industrial society, will be replaced by a new modality in which the reality and pleasure principles 'co-operate' is both incredible and terrifying. The infrastructure of distress, which has a numbing effect on the rest of the affective life, has functioned as a defence against the degree of self-encounter required to meet this challenge. What capacity does one have for joy when the world created by 'the dismal science' (the queen discipline of the industrial society) has issued an injunction against finding out?
>
> . . . (recent psychoanalytic theory has illuminated the personal and interpersonal dynamics as established in the paradigm of the mother-child relationship) . . . the source of feelings of one's own goodness is in the experience of good feelings towards the other. This in turn involves recognition that the source of one's need satisfaction is in the other who has good feelings towards oneself. The experience of positive affects is founded on the recognition and experience of inter-dependence. . . .
>
> . . . becoming more mature in the psycho-social sense as well as the bio-physical sense . . . is required but it can only come about by a working through of the deep ordeals which have always belonged to the human condition to a far greater extent and by far more people than in previous societies. . . .
>
> Such working through is unlikely to attain a new general level unless a new social context emerges; for the present level is a function of the present context. The regulation of positive affects requires the identification of new values and the formation of new norms.

Emery and Trist detail how the early hippy attempts to emphasise only the positive—to create an alternative sub-world of joy—with badness and hate banished and displaced on the 'brutal society' is as superficial and unrealistic, they say, as are the more materialist or rationalist approaches of futurologists of the Kahn stamp (Kahn and Wiener, 1967).

We suggest that a useful concept, linking the organisational level with human development so as to foster change in the desired direction, is *resourcefulness*. Resourcefulness has two characteristics, as we see it. First, it requires the capacity to develop interests which have meaning in themselves as well as expressing underlying preoccupations; second, it entails the ability to carry through the interests to realisation in activities. This may be in an occupation, in the home, in personal relationships, or elsewhere. Resourcefulness means knowing and being able to make a meaningful life for oneself with the *realities* of one's existence as well as how to change these realities. So it requires being in touch with one's feelings on the one side, and one's environment on the other, and being able to manage the two in relation to each other.

A resourceful person need not be rich, though money may help. A resourceful person may be male or female, young or old. There are many people who waste away at retirement though they were highly effective in their occupations, because they are not resourceful at dealing with changes in their life circumstances. There are others who may not have been 'successful' but who are resourceful enough to develop interesting lives at later phases—and are thereby the richer for it in terms of quality of living.

Resourcefulness then is not the same as competence; nor is it the same as intelligence or virtue, though it may relate to all of these. Resourcefulness is not directly tied to social class. A resourceful person can take the intelligence he has, the competence he is able to develop, and within the framework of his material means and social values apply them to weave a life that is satisfying.

What then are the qualities that make for resourcefulness and how can they be cultivated? Resourcefulness differs in different people; it refers to qualities of mental orientation, of motivation and attitude, and of a willingness to meet and relate to new situations so as to make them into meaningful experiences; it requires a general orientation to making use of available experiences: in oneself as a person, in the family, the school and the larger environment. Resourceful individuals are those who have the capacity to discover interests in themselves, to develop them and to use their own and others' capacities to help.

Above all, resourcefulness involves considerable social-psychological work, in the sense of effort applied for specific purposes. We believe that doing this meaningful psychological work is a pan-human need —irrespective of social class, IQ or other bases for social inequality. It is part of the human make-up to need to be personally 'successful'.

This has been one of the key elements in human adaptation—and in the selective processes leading to human survival. While it may be expressed in occupation, this concept of 'work' is a broader one than that. For an infant it is seen in the pleasure experienced in such triumphs as learning to walk across the room; for a mental defective it may mean becoming able to weave a simple basket.

A consideration of leisure provision stimulates idealistic visions, because leisure is for the realisation of the *positively* valued aspects of living. In an ideal world, everyone would be sufficiently resourceful to develop interests to express their preoccupations, and to find activities to fulfil their interests without any outside assistance. All would have fulfilled lives and there would be no need for public facilitation. In the real world, however, this is impracticable for several reasons.

First, some people are less resourceful than others; some have fewer material resources, fewer psychological resources and some have less mental and social capacity for the cultivation of appropriate and satisfying interests. In a society that believes that 'everyone is entitled to share in what is available' some mechanism for countering inequality is needed.

Second, in a world that is increasingly complex, it is necessary to have organisation if there is to be the massive scale of provision required to facilitate people's wants. Transportation systems, sports facilities, media of communication and so on are required to create the facilities for people of varying degrees of resourcefulness to use. The very magnitude of this requirement creates a whole range of new problems.

While it is true, in one sense, to say as Schumacher does that 'small is beautiful', when it comes to matching human environments to a human scale of participation, it is also true that the current macroscopic pooling of efforts is making 'big' more prevalent than ever (Schumacher, 1973). Both bigness and smallness are and should be going on at the same time. Negative by-products of bigness—impersonality, bureaucracy, rigidity and so on—are hazards that must be kept in awareness and combated as a kind of social pathology. One way to combat them is to counter them by cellular organisations *within* (not instead of) the large ones, cellular organisations that are personal, flexible and humanistic. Only by working with paradoxes of this kind can the fulfilment of human preoccupations and interests be achieved—in work, family and other areas of human involvement.

In working out the interfaces between leisure facilities (which are organised on ever larger and more complex bases) and people's preoccupations (which are sensitive to the more personal and intimate kinds of influence), it is important both to have an appreciation of the nature of the 'institution–person' paradoxes in this field and a continuously exerted effort to work with them.

Resourcefulness in developing meaningful life interests varies not only with the personality of the individual, but with life-cycle stage. Even among the advantaged it needs channelling, and among the disadvantaged it needs positive facilitation. For some it means the harnessing of exuberant tendencies, for others the awakening of dormant ones; for some it means the compensating for earlier lost opportunities to develop interests, for others it means the modification of interests to suit changed circumstances and capacities.

One of the most important lessons that emerges from a wide range of studies on different groups is that there must not only be *facilitation for the development of interests appropriate to a given phase and situation, but also for the more generalised development of resourcefulness—resourcefulness to be able to readapt continuously and cultivate new interests.* Learning to learn, as well as learning how to cope with specific situations, is the new imperative in our society.

The importance we attach to these aspects of resourcefulness is a theme which runs throughout this book. It is requisite at all stages of the life cycle, and provides a linkage between the four life phases we distinguish: adolescence, young adulthood, the establishment phase and retirement. Although we treat these phases separately, each with a chapter of its own, the boundaries between them are fairly fluid, and our material shows that they are linked in other significant ways.

The phases we distinguish are based on the family life cycle, and that imposes a modality on the material we use, but we have tried to inform the book with a broad range of life styles within the family life-cycle framework. Our material is based on what we find useful in the work of others that is available, and on our own limited research. Much of our own work is based on biographical case studies. We present several cases throughout the book as centrepieces for discussing the ways in which people fit their preoccupations and meaningful interests with available facilities to form patterns of activity. In the cases presented we attempt to show something of the range of individual resourcefulness in our society; and, more importantly for the topic at hand, the ways in which realisation of a meaningful life is blocked or facilitated by environmental factors, including leisure provision.

The *biographical method* is meant to show how a systematic qualitative study of selected individuals in specific family and community contexts may be instructive. The case studies are not presented as substitutes for cross-sectional surveys. Ideally case studies should be used in conjunction with cross-sectional surveys which provide another kind of information and a contextual sampling frame. The case studies are like geological specimens taken from 'bore holes' in selected social environments. As this book is based on an exploratory study, we could not select them in the framework of a cross-sectional sample but only as individuals who provide examples of observable life styles delineated by key informants like teachers, youth club wardens and local young people themselves. Our orientation to the presentations is that suggested by such users of the biographical method as Erikson, Keniston and Briggs, who study and report on selected individuals as expressions of social forces. Erikson, who has concentrated on young people's development in much of his work, takes the view that the developing individual, in his search for a personal identity, finds it only in the context of the major themes of culture and history in his society (1953):

> I am convinced that only through meaningful development of his individual childhood in line with one of the major trends of history can an individual find his ego identity, be he a sedentary peasant or a migrant, a worker or a businessman, a scientist or a man of faith.

His study of the individual is in relation to these themes. In times of upheaval and change, as with the Industrial Revolution, he notes that there are inevitable disturbances of maturation. Studies of individuals' personal dilemmas, in this context, are made to illuminate the social process. His study of the young Luther was directed in part to this end. This is also the approach of Keniston in his *Youth and Dissent* (1971). Briggs, in his *Victorian People* (1965), states: 'The studies of individual people in this book are not designed as miniature biographies so much as explorations of value judgements and preferences of mid-Victorian society.'

There is plenty of evidence that there have been personal disturbances in times of upheaval but our point of view is that the cultural-history themes are only part of the influence pattern. They may be compensated for in various ways by individuals and institutions. Whole societies may dampen or avert some of the turbulence through provisions for the management of potentially disorganising forces. It is therefore important to try to understand how individuals interact with social and cultural elements in their environments. Different individuals, embodying different historical themes, may compete for influence on other individuals. A school-teacher who urges an able working-class boy to continue his education may be in competition with the local delinquent gang leader who is pressing him to try the quick pay-offs of street life. Both sets of influences reflect themes in contemporary society each with an historical as well as a contemporary grounding. Both are mediated by individuals with different institutional strengths in the situation and different kinds of interpersonal influences.

Most of the case material presented in the book focuses primarily on a description of individuals and the dynamics of their interest formation at different stages of the life cycle. While illuminating this process is the main contribution of the book, the focus must extend to the processes involved in the articulation of individuals' interests with provisions in their environment. Essentially this is a shift in emphasis, the starting-point being 'opportunities' (equated with facilities—physical and social) and the assumptions underlying their provision, the object being how actual individuals do in fact relate to them. To this end an exploratory area-based study was carried out on a fairly new housing estate in a residential district of an industrial town in South-east England. The town has a unitary leisure directorate, and as the study area is relatively discrete, physically, the provisions locally available, and their providers, are fairly easily specifiable. Of course no such area is an entirely closed system, but providers do assume that 'local' facilities will be used in particular ways, as well as facilities elsewhere. Discussions with four families there, and a group of young estate-dwellers, suggest how actual individuals perceive, interact with, and ignore 'opportunities' in their surroundings. This data is used in the chapters on young people and the establishment phase in particular.

We hope that providers, and those in leisure provision especially, will find our contribution helpful to improved service delivery. Each 'people chapter' contains a section on leisure provision as it relates to the life phase with which particular chapters are concerned. These suggest mainly *where* in people's lives providers can most profitably direct their efforts. In the penultimate chapter on provisions we make suggestions as to *how* they can do this, though our suggestions are neither systematic nor comprehensive, and often identify particular research programmes or experiments as starting-points. In our final chapter we suggest what a more concerted and informed effort *could* mean in large-scale social terms, over and above the obvious benefits accruing for improved provision and heightened provider–user interface at local level. While we believe that leisure providers have a special leverage in this, we hope that the 'people chapters' suggest that for a meaningful whole life to become more widely realisable, the challenge rests squarely with us all.

2

Young people and leisure

*Identity crystallisation**

This chapter focuses on the phase of the life cycle usually referred to as adolescence. We concentrate on the age group centring on school-leaving (between 15 and 19). During this period, young people are involved in critical life decisions—whether to continue with further education or to enter work, what kind of education or work, what patterns of relationships to sustain with family, friends and others following the transition from school. While the developmental processes in adolescence are biologically rooted, their manifestations vary by sex, class, locality, educational experience and sub-cultural style of life.

Adolescence is often a time of considerable turbulence both for the young person and for those in close association with them. The period may also be one of considerable creativity, experimentation and excitement. Young people explore their environments, look for new ones, sample new experiences—all in an attempt to crystallise their personal identities which will underpin a transition to greater independence. The paradox in considering young people and their leisure patterns is that while their experience is in one sense universal and phase-specific, in another sense they are incomparably variable; their attention shifts frequently, they like moving from one interest to another, they are highly labile in their behaviour from day to day, if not from hour to hour. Typically, when young people describe their 'patterns' of activity, they may include activities they have pursued only once, and intend to pursue again, or activities they are interested in pursuing in future. In this sense they are difficult to categorise, to pin down, and they tend to react *against* pressures to organise or plan *for* them though their malleability is not easy to grasp and is generally lost in reports based on

* This book does not deal directly with younger children. Much research needs to be done on children's leisure in relation to their families. There seems to be a particular dearth of facilities for the 7–13-year age group and less understanding of their underlying concerns than other sub-groups in the life cycle. It was not possible to include children in the scope of the present work but that in no way reflects on their importance.

survey data. On the other hand, providers of leisure, or any other facilities, like to be able to classify and predict the behaviour of the populations they are providing for and find it difficult to subsume such a high level of variation in their provision. If they can accept that the 'membership' of groups for which they cater may be highly unstable, their tasks may be eased; there are likely to be sufficient numbers of young people at any given time eager to pursue specific activities—both to sample the activities and the people there. This may suggest a reorientation to the goals of many providers.

Examining the process of transition to greater independence, in the framework we have suggested, young people are seen as moving along

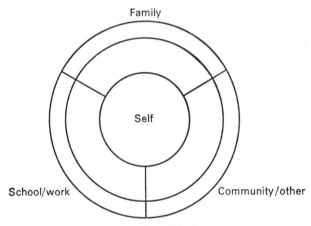

Figure 3   *Cross-section of the life line*

a developmental life line, with groupings of significant social influences impinging on them; family, school/work and community (see Figure 3). This is a cross-section of the life line presented in chapter 1. Within each sector of this model there are some figures who are close and who entertain personal relationships with the individual (parent, teacher, corner shopkeeper) and others who are more remote, known only through their social roles in organisations (the principal, the club warden) or even through the mass media (a pop idol, a famous footballer or a figure from a novel). Remoteness does not necessarily mean lack of influence; many young people go through periods in which major influences are derived from novels or plays; characters in Tolkien, O'Neill or Dostoyevsky may become very real and influential for them, as many figures in science, sport, religion or the entertainment world. The circles suggest degrees of closeness and each is divided into different spheres of life.

The shape and sizes of the different sectors of the life space vary by individual, as does the way in which they are populated and the influence that a given person or group will have on an individual. People vary in the extent to which they differentiate life sectors.

Most individuals develop categories which cut across those defined in formal terms; for example, people you can trust. Early patterns of relationship tend to carry over and generalise so that individuals who develop basic trust towards early family members are more likely to be trusting in other relationships as they proceed through school and into the broader spectrum of social relationships. Conversely those who have learned that distrust, suspicion and anxiety are prominent among the rules of life are likely to generalise these dispositions. Neither blanket trust nor blanket distrust is appropriate in a complex world. But adolescence is a period in which people and interests are intensively tested out and young people learn to discriminate those who can be trusted from those who cannot; between situations in which effort is worth while and those in which it is not.

Similarly for adults it is necessary to differentiate between different kinds of young people. Knowledge of their developmental experiences allows specific young people to be related to constructively as they are, rather than in terms of stereotypes.

For young people this may be the happiest time of their lives, but many are sad; they often seem frantically busy and impatient with their elders, but as often they impress their elders as idle (in the best sense described by Bertrand Russell) and view their elders' hyperactivity with scarcely concealed scorn; young people are idealistic and they are egocentric; they are sensuous and they are cold; they are engaging and emotionally removed; they are aggressive and they are shy; they are arrogant and humble; they are bright and they are stupid. They are people—and as such intrinsically variable—but it often seems that their variations are caricatures of other people's variations. They often seem, in the needs they express, to be a mass of contradictions. Sometimes they seem to need constant stimulation; at other times they seem to need to be bored; they seem to need to huddle together and they seem to need to be alone.

While a systematic description of young people's preoccupations, needs, attitudes, relationships and behaviours must be drawn in terms of tendencies, it ought not be taken to apply to all young people in the same way or to any particular young person consistently. The modal pattern should be thought of as a thread around which an appreciation of variation can be developed. The key concept we employ for this is the identity crisis.

The *focal preoccupations* of young people during the period which we are examining surrounds the struggle between *identity* and *identity*

diffusion, as described in the work of Erik Erikson (1950, 1959). The
adolescent, in breaking out of childhood roles, becomes preoccupied
with establishing for himself a satisfactory answer to the question 'Who
am I?' In his search for the answer to this question he tries out all kinds
of possible identities, seeks to experience different roles, experiments
with different kinds of relationships, explores his own mental and
physical properties and limits in a more active way than previously. The
outcome may be satisfactory to himself and others involved, if it fits the
requirements of the roles which he subsequently encounters at work, in
heterosexual relationships and in community life generally. Alternatively, if the young person fails to clarify and give structure to his
personal identity, he is likely to experience depression and despair, a
sense of meaninglessness, self-deprecation and dissociation; symptoms
of identity diffusion.

Zinberg indicates how experimentation with drugs does not itself
produce disaster, but is more likely to do so in young people who lack
the psychological foundations to experiment and draw limits to their
involvement, with the experience and particularly the hazards it could
lead to. Definition of these limits is one of the critical tasks in the
identity-formation process (Zinberg and Robertson, 1972).

A positive outcome of the identity crisis does not imply that the
young individual will persist with the same idea of 'Who am I?' for
the rest of his life. A satisfactory resolution does not lay the issue to
rest for ever more. Erikson suggests only that the identity-formation
issues are most acute and salient in the crisis of adolescence. The quest
may never be completely resolved, and the questions of self-definition
effloresce again in crises later in life.

While in the throes of the identity crisis, adolescents are prone to
great mood swings—from elation to despair, from supreme self-con-
fidence to extreme anxiety and self-doubts. Lidz describes adolescence
as 'a time of carefree wandering of the spirit through realms of fantasy
and in purusit of idealistic visions, but also of disillusionment and dis-
gust with the world and the self' (Lidz, 1968, 298). Anna Freud has
noted that the depressive signs in this period relate to a 'saddening
farewell to childhood, a renunciation of its pleasures and ties', while the
elation relates to the 'awakening and opening up of the joys and potentials of adulthood' (Freud, 1958). There is a new sense of physical
power and of sexual and libidinal feelings; at the same time there is
uncertainty about how to use and control them. Helena Deutsch refers
to the dynamics of this phase as representing a continuous 'clash'
between 'progressive' and 'regressive' forces in the formation of
character (Deutsch, 1968).

Adolescents are peculiarly aloof and often lonely even though they
may be active with all kinds of people; they are sociable, sensitive to

values and ideals, and highly involved in exploring themselves—their own personalities and life interests and to distinguish them from those received from parents and others. While they differ in how they make their explorations and in their resourcefulness in developing life interests, their focal preoccupation is the quest for their own personal identity. The preoccupation manifests itself in a number of *sub-preoccupations* which are experienced through characteristic *interests* (see Figure 4). The expression of these interests may be more or less facilitated through specific activities that are available. Providers of leisure facilities and activities may find it useful to be aware of these complexities. A given provision may be used differently by different young people and by the same person at different times. This is important for both the tactics and management of facilities as well as the strategic planning of systems of facilities.

Autonomy and independence are preoccupations in this phase, so young people like to 'do their own thing' out of the sight and control of authorities and to do things that may be prohibited. Provisions which make it possible for youngsters to take increasing responsibilities as they wish, self-programming and self-governed execution of activities, are ways of meeting this preoccupation. As with others that will be mentioned, this desire for autonomy will alternate with the wish for not taking responsibility and not being treated as an independent adult.

Stimulation and boredom are preoccupations which often alternate. Stimulation may be experienced through an interest in bright lights, loud music, fast movement, noisy roaring cycles, vivid colours, intense conversation. Complaints about being bored are so pervasive that it seems to be a preoccupation that may be met through providing opportunities to be bored, to be alone, to have quiet places for solitude. This is not as easy and obvious as it seems, as once a place is named as a quiet place, it may cease to be able to fulfil this function.

Provision for stimulation is also difficult. There are the issues of how permissive to be in relation to sexual, narcotic and other stimulants. Advertising and consumer-oriented stimulation provides excitement and arouses interest but may not always be felt to be in the best interests of the young users. On the other hand, in the public sector, given the public accountability of such enterprises, there may be a tendency towards staidness, dullness and lack of stimulation in provisions that are designed in such a way as to pursue a safe line.

There is a need to work on provision that is both responsible and stimulating. This leads to the issue of how to gain and hold the interest of youngsters. Entry points which stress stimulation may be effective elements of design (social as well as architectural). Then it is a matter of providing sufficient variety and novelty to maintain interest. This

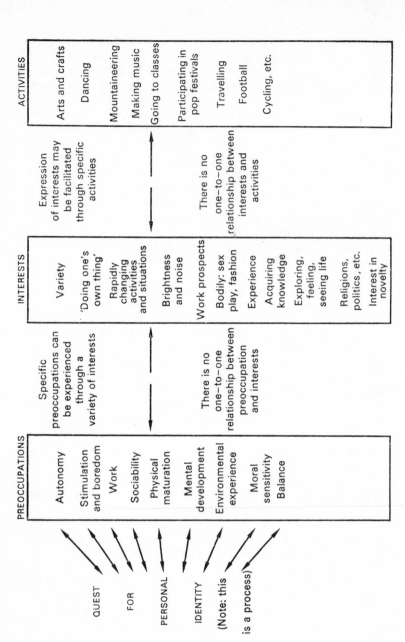

Figure 4 *Preoccupations, interests and activities*

may involve an acceptance that young people will come and go and not necessarily use the facility steadily.

Work is a preoccupation of young people and there are many kinds of interest taken in prospects, conditions, rewards and constraints of different jobs. Experiences are sought that will sharpen awareness of the meaning of work, and activities—both in and out of employment— are pursued in crystallising an occupational identity that will help to set a certain level of aspiration and salience of work in the evolving life style of the individual. Not everyone goes through these experiences in ways acceptable to those around them and some may face a lack of empathy with their difficulties in coping with the transition.

The provision of work experiences—on a community-industry, voluntary-work or other basis—may, in this context, be thought of as part of leisure provision, in so far as this is a preoccupation that goes on outside the youngsters' regular employment as well as in it. Many provisions, such as scouting, are explicitly geared to developing orientations that will be applicable to work careers as well as to life generally.

Sociability is a preoccupation of young people that is expressed in various interests—from pairing to mass events. Peer groups, representing different strands of youth culture, influence the way in which sociability is expressed. Existing provision often comes across to young people in terms of *exclusion* emphases rather than as channels for making contact with groups and sub-cultures that might interest them. Provisions making use of the concept of sub-cultural strands, enlisting the participation of youth groups, allowing for the creation of new groups, may satisfy this preoccupation. The interest of young people in making contact with and exploring the 'scenes' of others in different sub-cultural strands is powerful, though sometimes the exploration is accomplished through hostile encounters rather than friendly interchanges. Competitive as well as co-operative provisions may take these contrasts into account. The provision of variety so that there can be 'sampling', shopping around, movement from one option to another, would give scope for this preoccupation.

Physical maturation provides another preoccupation which is characteristic of this phase. The development of their more manifest sexual characteristics—breasts, body hair, muscles and so on—has been going on for some time, and the urge to experience their bodies, to experiment sexually and to learn about either enjoying or controlling the feelings involved may be overpowering at this stage. Usually these urges are expressed in the fascination with clothes, hairstyles, fads and fashions of adornment, etc. It is an awkward issue about how far public bodies might provide young people with places for sexual and other physical experimentation, but commercial bodies are heavily involved in this. It is a topic which should not be swept under the carpet as though it did not exist. The challenge for providers is what to provide and how to deal with this issue; the preoccupation will not go away by being ignored, though the Victorians tried. It then comes out indirectly and perhaps in less desirable ways.

Mental development is another preoccupation, even for those who are not academic-minded, that is not always met in contemporary provision. Improved television, improved books and comics, information games, etc., may begin to meet this need. The training of mental capacities and associated skills is the work of schools, but for many youngsters the schools simply do not 'switch them on', and they search for other ways to experience mental development, 'mind-stretching' and 'mind-bending' experiences. Alternative approaches might centre on the mastery of information, league scores, distances, heights, weights, machine tolerances and all sorts of things that allow expression of this interest without being organised into conventional disciplines of knowledge. For youngsters who are 'divergers', whose minds want to follow their own pathways of interest development, the school experience may only inhibit the lively potentials of their mental interests. This becomes a challenge for leisure providers to supplement the cultivation of mental interests together with school authorities, and to facilitate their development in ways that could lead either to future enjoyments or to future occupations.

Environmental experience is something that young people have tremendous but often latent preoccupations with, which are often not met. For all sorts of reasons, young people's environmental interests tend to get closed off or inhibited as they grow up. Urban young people learn from earliest childhood that it is dangerous to wander the city streets; it is difficult for them to make their way in the country. Young people in all sorts of settings need to explore new territories close to home, and to familiarise themselves with the potentialities of their larger environments. People from one area may have negative stereotypes of people from other areas, not only native-foreign, or rural-urban, but from one district to another or one type of family in relation to another. They distrust or disparage the food, the conditions of life and so on of others. There are many ways that could be envisioned for providing for the interest that many young people have with learning about other environments as part of their own identity formation. Interchanges within the same social settings as the individuals customarily live (seen with different eyes) or with other kinds of setting (city youth to the countryside, country youth to the city), travel with survival kits, exchanges, group host schemes are possibilities. They may be arranged in parallel with schemes already existing in sports or other contexts. If visiting sportsmen and others could get acquainted with one another as people, they might also be able to learn about and therefore be able to enjoy one another's environments. Exposure to new environments may lead to a greater degree of tolerance for ambiguity. But these exchanges and explorations tend not to occur spontaneously. Given all of the inhibiting factors, there is the need for 'animation', i.e. arousal of interest and leadership, to open up environment-consciousness in the young and to facilitate the acquisition of environmental experience.

Moral sensitivity is a preoccupation often noted among the young, and finds expression through interests in religion, political ideology and acute sensitivity to what is 'right' and 'wrong', 'just' and 'unjust'. This seems to relate to young people's feelings about themselves in relation to adults, their ambiguous situation in relation to whether they are included or excluded. They are, accordingly, particularly sensitive to discrepancies between what members of the older generation say and what they do. They may dramatise this sensitivity in demonstrations *against* one or another inequity in established institutions.

Provision that bears in mind this preoccupation and encourages expression of morally coloured feelings, gives opportunities for role-playing, institution-building, self-programming and so on, might effectively engage and give satisfaction to many young people. Voluntary social service activities—*for* the older, *against* pollution, *against* discrimination and so on may also deal with these interests. There is a need to devise new ways of making young people feel welcome and wanted *as people* rather than as children. Ways are needed to facilitate their expression of criticism of the way things are run by adults.

Balance. Young people are concerned with how to put together into some kind of balance their own disparate and sometimes contradictory preoccupations, and the often contradictory elements of life style they see as available to them from adult society. By experiencing dilemmas of individuals in various roles, the reaction against what is wrong with what they see in established practices may be corrected through experimenting with alternatives and arriving at an integration which may constitute a better balance for them.

Another aspect of this preoccupation is seen in young people's interest in developing the *capacity for living*. The particular juncture of history in which we live is one which has to be seen against the background of a generalised inhibition of the capacity to enjoy life. In our culture enjoyment is often felt to be dangerously close to sin and, perhaps worse, to sap moral fibre and the wish to *produce*. Youngsters feel that the lives of their elders have been stunted by this puritanical ethic, and many feel the need to restore a balance by an active effort at learning how to enjoy life. This is not nearly as automatic as it might sound, and provision for helping to free individuals to enjoy their lives is sorely needed if anything like a balanced life is to emerge. This may, for some youngsters, entail a phase of over-reaction—a hedonistic or Omar Khayyam phase—which is eventually put into perspective when a more stable balance is worked out.

To see how these preoccupations and interests are played out in people's lives, we turn now to an examination in high magnification of the process of interest development in some young people up to the point of leaving school. We use the biographical method for this. Twelve young people were interviewed intensively. There were five girls and seven boys of diverse social class background, schooling, academic ability and aspirations; they came from diverse family structures—single-parent family to dual-career families. Despite the heterogeneity of the individuals, there are many common elements. This reinforces the impression that there are focal preoccupations which are *phase-specific* and cut across social groupings; it is the way focal preoccupations are dealt with that influences particular outcomes. The person's individual make-up, family resources, the availability of specific provisions, the competence of mediators and so on, all *affect* the particular outcome, but they act on a *similar* set of developmental forces common to young people.

Three young people's lives are presented: Jenny, a middle-class girl; Katherine, a working-class girl; and Derek, a working-class boy. All three were in their last year or two in large urban comprehensive schools.

JENNY is a *middle-class* girl who thinks a lot about her life and her relationships; she is fairly articulate and while not completely accepting 'the system', she was prepared to co-operate with the researchers, particularly if her schoolfriend Clara could participate too. They were thus interviewed together most of the time. Wanting to do things together or in pairs was found characteristic of many in this age group.

Jenny and Clara were 17 at the time we saw them; both were attractive, natural in dress, without make-up, spontaneous and open in their remarks. Honesty was a strongly held value. They were seen together five times over three months, each interview lasting 2–3 hours. Jenny's parents and school housemaster were also interviewed. Both girls kept diaries for a full week and were interviewed about the contents and place of this specimen within their overall annual pattern.

Jenny is the second in a *family of three girls*. Her elder sister, Karen, is two years older and left school early after falling in with a 'good-time' group in the large comprehensive school they all attended. At the time of the study she was in the USA, trying to 'find herself'. Her sister Sally is two years younger than Jenny and is in a co-educational boarding school where she went after experiencing difficulties at the comprehensive school.

Jenny's *father* was once a successful industrial manager who developed a hobby of botanical studies. In his late thirties, he decided to throw up his business career which he detested as a 'rat race' and to take his chances as a free-lance scientific researcher and writer. He used a crisis in his firm as an occasion to opt out and began a new career based on his previous hobby, working from his home. Jenny's mother had been an art student and helped her husband in his work by illustrating specimens for his reports and publications.

In their younger days Jenny's father and mother had been interested in left-wing politics and their relationship developed on this basis and on their shared interest in music. They are temperamentally quite different—he is more removed emotionally and all-absorbed in his hobby-turned-profession while she is more expressive. In her youth Jenny's mother had led a rather bohemian life and had left a suburban background to live in digs in the city at a time when this was a daring thing to do.

When Jenny's father left business, he had a small cash reserve and a great deal of enthusiasm for pursuing his interest. However, the family's life became more insecure financially and there was a drift towards a lower standard as his fees were less able to keep pace with inflation. This meant that he had to take commissions that kept him busy day and night, often travelling to far-flung places to collect speci-mens and make studies. Jenny recalls that though her father was a dedicated naturalist and loved the countryside this enthusiasm did not rub off on the children: 'We'd go out to the country in the car and he'd sort of bomb around collecting specimens while we would get more and more bored.'

Her two sisters are temperamentally very different from Jenny, who is rather serious-minded, idealistic and even-tempered. They are both rather more volatile but in different ways. Karen was one of the first of a group of middle-class girls to enter a large comprehensive school which was located in a predominantly working-class area. She was caught up with the 'skinheads' and was enthralled by the excitement of going around with them. Jenny has this to say about her sister's experiences:

'When she was at the school she got in with a very tough lot of skinheads. . . . They used to break open meters and things; that's why they [parents] eventually had to take her out and send her to a boarding school. She's in a very bad state now because possibly we waited too long. She got very few O-levels, and got into a complete rut. She didn't want to do anything in particular.'

The family let her stay as long as possible in the comprehensive school as a matter of principle but took her out when it was clear that the gang she was travelling with was destroying her interest in education.

Jenny says that her father had generally been very absorbed in his

work and tolerant of what the children were doing, but when it came
to Karen's friends, or some of the people whom she later brought home
after picking them up in the park, he would 'blow his top'. These
friends were not prepared to be civil to the parents; indeed when there
were expressions of disapproval (for example about noise or their just
being around all the time and not doing anything) there were 'great
scenes with him banning them from the house and them telling him to
fuck-off and do various things'. Jenny's father notes that:

> 'We used to have pretty good battle from when she was around 12 or
> 13 and she was going out with boys, and parties and using drugs . . .
> and not getting on with her academic work at all . . . just talking,
> smoking, enjoying their own company and not wanting to do anything
> constructive at all.'

The problem eventually came to a climax at a birthday party when the
parents had turned their house over to their children's friends but things
got out of control. The father says: 'About eighty kids came in, when
she was 13, and they were drinking a lot and things got out of control,
and there was a mess generally . . . gate-crashers.' Jenny's mother says:

> 'Finally we had to haul Karen out [of the comprehensive school]
> and send her to a boarding school . . . out of London . . . this is the
> middle-class way of getting out of your problems and it went against
> the grain like anything. I am all for State education but there wasn't
> enough supervision in the school. They didn't know what she was
> up to . . . yet, I often feel I failed with her. Perhaps if I'd only had
> the courage of my convictions, I would have kept her in the school
> and seen her through it. On the other hand, she might have gone
> down the drain, or ended up in a borstal or something.'

The parents feel they were too permissive with Karen. Because of the
lessons learned and because the other children have different personalities, they have followed different patterns. None of the girls, however,
has shown any interest in their father's work. Karen has a 'natural
authority with children' and her father thinks she may still end up as a
good teacher if she learns to discipline herself. But he worries about
where the base for the discipline will come from. He feels that young
people nowadays have neither religion nor political commitment
'through which we thought we could change the world'. Where, then,
will they find the idealistic goals towards which the effort of discipline
can be organised?

The younger daughter, Sally, is quite different. Jenny says:

> 'She is spoiled a bit, like most youngest children. . . . She is such a
> strong character. She wants to be like us. When she is home she
> goes out to pubs [though only 14, looking much older] and my

mother gives her the same amount of money as me, which I don't like. . . . But she wants the same rights as us, and is so forceful that she gets her way.'

When they were younger they played together and Sally used to tag along after Jenny, who always had a group of friends. All three girls went to the same primary school and Sally followed Karen and Jenny to the comprehensive school. She had a better example before her in Jenny than Jenny had in Karen, but she still ran into trouble with the rougher lot from whom Jenny has been able to steer clear. Jenny's mother describes the experience as follows:

'Sally is a terrifically social person. She has friends all over the place, and if she is depressed she'll rush off to see them. Her friends are so important to her. . . . When she came into contact with that rough crowd at the comprehensive school, they gave her a very rough time. She was very interested in art and she dressed like a hippie. She had long wavy hair and looks like a Pre-Raphaelite, great long neck. And, she used to wear way-out clothes. Well, all the skinhead lads and lassies didn't like her because of this, and they used to form gangs and beat her up . . . and she being a tremendous pacifist and wanting to be friends with everyone. She tried to reason with them. She'd sit on the school steps, so her housemaster told me, and say "Now what is it you don't like about us, you just tell me and say what it is, I'm really interested and want to know". Of course they didn't want to talk about it, and so the girls sort of ripped her clothes to pieces and caught her hair, and it got so bad that she had to have protection going home. This was one of the reasons that we had to haul her out because she's the sort of girl if you said to her "Look, what you've got to do is sort of conform so they won't notice you", it's no good saying that to her, she wouldn't.'

Whereas Karen tried to 'join' the skinheads, Sally tried to change them. Both aroused sufficient anxiety in their parents that they were 'hauled out' and 'packed off' to boarding school. The family used their cash reserves for this, despite their economically precarious footing; this also violated their educational ideals, so tension in the family over these issues must have been great.

The mother's general aspiration for all her children, however, is that they 'be able to stand on their own two feet and be happy, good people, and not cause too much misery, try to help a little bit'. Sending Karen to the USA for a year to find herself seems very satisfactory to her father:

'It's the best thing that has happened to her. . . . I think she'll be a much better person when she comes back . . . she's got her independence which is one of the most important things that children have got to learn. . . . I think that university students would benefit by an interruption of this kind . . . one has to have two sides of one developed; one sees lots of people who are intelligent but who don't achieve anything with their lives. You have to develop your natural ability but you have to learn how to apply it in life . . . and this requires experience and experimentation.'

This is an example of the family issue mentioned earlier: of how much permissiveness and how much control, how much guidance in the youngster's preoccupation with experimentation is advisable. This issue has been a recurrent theme in this family. As in many middle-class families where the father is dedicated to a professional calling, the brunt of the day-to-day setting of limits tends to fall on the mother until a crisis arises, at which point a decisive intervention is made by the father.

Jenny recalls that her *early schooling* was pleasurable. She went to a nursery school so that, unlike her elder sister Karen, her entry to primary school was smooth. She had a teacher who was a communist and who treated all the children equally—poor kids and rich kids, white kids and black kids—and was 'nice to kids, a lovely woman'. From early on she had an artistic interest and liked dancing and music. Jenny's mother recounts her early school career as follows:

'She was a lively little girl—interested in everything. She did very well in school and the teachers liked her. She was co-operative and reasonable and worked hard and was interested in everything. She was a lovely little girl, super, you know. She did all the usual things, music lessons and dancing lessons, and when she was little we used to take her to all sorts of things—Covent Garden, operas, children's theatres—and then suddenly, when they get to secondary school they don't want to do it anymore. This isn't just Jenny, it's her sisters as well, and other children. Suddenly you're just dumped. They can't explain it themselves, it's just that going out with Mum isn't the thing anymore, though there are some who still do.'

Jenny's father describes her as different from her sisters: she is a worker, has got her five O-levels, is artistic and sensitive. In spite of this, he wonders if she will achieve as much as the others, partly because she is so sensible:

'She is good at many things, excellent domestically, cooks and sews and organises her time, very sensible in many ways . . . but she could never do what the elder one did in going off to America, and is much more shy with people than the third one— won't meet visitors we have in the house.'

And her mother says:

> 'She is a very reserved person . . . terribly different from my other
> two daughters, different as chalk from cheese. They are more extro-
> vert, she is very introverted. This is one of her problems. I think she
> knows it. She will have to get over it . . . she's like one part of my
> family while the other two are like the other part—it's fascinating to
> watch them grow up.'

Moving from the happy atmosphere of the local primary school to the
large and somewhat terrifying atmosphere of the comprehensive school,
where she had seen her sister getting into such trouble, was not easy for
Jenny; the entire style of work and way of life was different. When she
first came to the school, she found that she could join her sister and her
friends without any difficulty. However, as things developed she became
more reserved about this. Karen too was not prepared to have her
around. Jenny did not like the fact that her sister had developed a bad
reputation in the school, and she didn't 'look up to' her sister's friends.
About her school work she says:

> 'The first year I worked so hard, I came top in three subjects! and
> oh I was a good little girl! I loved science and maths and music—
> I've always liked music, I've always enjoyed it, you know; the only
> thing—I didn't dislike anything except games . . . all through school
> it's always been I'm pleased that I've got a period [and can therefore
> be excused games]. . . . I've always worked much harder than her,
> I've always been able to concentrate more. . . . I quite enjoyed the
> first year because it wasn't so strict—maybe in the third and fourth
> year they were sort of slowly bringing you to the idea that in a couple
> of years you'd have to take O-levels and you'd better start working.'

At this point Jenny ceased to enjoy school; she did not like having
to work for examinations and was not used to it, since she did not have
to sit the 11+. She had worked because she was interested in the
subjects, but she wanted to have a social life as well and felt that people
who worked all the time have a very narrow experience of life:

> 'That's what's wrong with our education in secondary schools today
> —I don't know anyone who didn't enjoy their primary school. As
> soon as they go to secondary school, it all just goes away, all the
> enjoyment, because it's something you have to do, and there's the
> gloomy sort of thing in the future of exams. . . . For some people,
> they go to school, go home, do their work, then they go and read their
> school books, you know; they just sort of work all the time, it's just
> a routine of work. They have no social life, or if they do, it's like
> going out with their cousin.'

Jenny and her friend Clara felt ashamed of their O-level results, but when they surveyed their classmates who had done well, they felt they did not admire them:

> 'You can tell them straight away. . . . [How?] Just the way they sort of act, their whole life pattern, everything—to me they're just cabbages . . . also I find that one girl in particular who works most of the time, when I talk to her about anything like psychology or the mind itself and things like that, she hasn't got any ideas about it, she hasn't really thought about it much, whereas I'd sort of thought about it quite a bit. It's very good to be well-read but if you've not experienced anything, you can't discuss it. You might be able to say, in such a book he said that—but that's just one psychiatrist—whereas if you've had experience, if you've known lots of people, you're much more able to talk about it . . . and another thing, O-levels come in such a bad sort of time of life, because you're so emotionally unsure of yourself.'

She felt that the menstrual pattern and how one was 'settling into it' made for emotional turbulence at this point; also the issue of what one wanted to do with one's life beyond taking examinations, the issue of school-leaving, life at home, relationships with friends and particularly with members of the opposite sex, and how to deal with the teachers who are pushing one for decisions on plans:

> 'There's a whole run-down of things that sort of all pile up together. Things like, you know, what you're going to do; can you see yourself staying at home for another three years or whatever, if you go on then to college; if you leave school, what can you see yourself doing; are you happy at school; you know—what happens if you don't get your exams, what happens if you do get your exams; all this contributes to one mass-turmoil of things, which you can't straighten out.'

In the course of her *social maturation* Jenny went through another series of intense experiences, based on her interest and involvement in groups of young people with different life styles. She felt that she had been a 'horrible bookworm' until she was about 12 and that her social development had lagged behind her intellectual development. Earlier she had gone to a youth club in a local church building but disliked the idea of organised clubs:

> 'I don't really like organisations like youth clubs. I started going to one when I was in primary school; it was very organised but later on it became less and less organised—there was a room where everyone used to smoke dope and stuff. . . . It was run by a vicar actually, a very nice guy—he didn't know it was going on. Completely innocent.

But he felt he had to make some rules because it was just going a bit too far, and he sort of said "There will be certain games, like you can play badminton and table tennis" and I thought, I don't want that. . . . I don't want to be organised and pushed about and have facilities provided for me that I can use, because I want to amuse myself.'

She began to smoke 'pot' while at this youth club and has since experimented with different drugs:

'There are some nice drugs and there are some horrible drugs—hash is nice, it doesn't do anything horrible to you; then there are things like sleepers and speed that may be nice when you're on them but they do you no good. . . . I once went through a stage of speed, you know, and I enjoyed it at the time. I took quite a bit, I got really irritable. I couldn't sleep or anything. But it's all worn off, I don't think there are any [permanent] bad effects. But I don't take any drugs now, even when I'm down; I think that's a bad thing to do because you get dependent on them.'

Jenny's mother recounts the drug episode as follows:

'Jenny got in with a rather questionable druggy group and this was a very worrying time. They weren't particularly nice people she was seeing . . . and Sally also got involved with them. I suppose this sort of thing happens everywhere now and it seems to be the thing for parents to jump on it like anything and forbid their children to go out and practically lock them up in their rooms. I didn't take this attitude and I allowed them a certain amount of freedom. If I thought things were going too far, I'd read the riot act. This was a few years back and parents were more frightened of drugs than they are now because they didn't know as much about them then; there has been a *Which?* report about it and so on, which wasn't very good but it helped to clear things up a bit. Also, when you live with a thing for a while, you get used to it. It's like living with the bomb, I suppose. I was pretty scared then but I didn't clamp down entirely and I've found that—touch wood—they are now very sensible, all of them, about drugs. Some other children that I know who were locked up in their rooms and sat on, went on being very difficult about drug abuse but now my girls are pretty sensible on that score.'

Jenny, echoing her father's philosophy that young people have to find out for themselves, says about the whole drug episode:

'I think a drug is worth trying whether it is good for you or not, so you can recognise it and know what it really is; recently there has been this thing on microdot, this acid, LSD, saying people went wild on it and things. Well, it's just a stronger dosage. A lot of my friends have taken it. It's just much stronger. You read the medical things about it, what it does to you physically and mentally but then you make up your own mind about it, I think.'

Jenny's mother fed her medical evidence and tried to sweat it out with her and is pleased now that she 'found her way through it'. Jenny's mother recalls:

'My husband was very upset about it . . . I was very frightened because I didn't know what it would do to them physically, and there were very few facts around at that point, even about hash. I tried to get all the information I could and give it to them . . . any article there was in the paper, I'd cut it out and say read this, which they did. I think it wasn't so much the drugs themselves that attracted Jenny but that she was doing something secret, and the family didn't know about it or she thought they didn't know. She was doing something on her own, independent. This is what was important to her at that point. Although I went through an awful time, it was probably a very valuable experience for her but it could have been dangerous.'

The other aspect of Jenny's social life that evolved outside school has to do with *sexual relationships*. Karen had been precocious sexually; she 'joined' the skinheads at 14 and adopted an active sex life as part of her life style. After having been through all this with Karen, her mother was not going to let Jenny get into things unprepared, and told her when she was 13 that if she needed any advice about contraception, she should discuss it with her; this rather shocked the more conventional-minded Jenny but also pleased her and helped the mother–daughter relationship to remain an open one. Her mother did not come to this position through any inclination of her own but through a recognition of how much things had changed since she was young: 'I didn't have a date until I was 18 and it took the boy three months to kiss me good-night. Nowadays young people seem to hop into bed very early.' She notes that the kind of hippie crowd towards which Jenny gravitated were in favour of natural things—no make-up, vegetarian foods and so on, although in relation to sex they favoured the pill. She thinks that this is a matter of survival in the competitive game of boy and girl:

'Jenny and her friends are great health faddists. They won't take any chemicals or drugs. They'll hardly take an aspirin, even if they have a terrible headache. And yet they take these pills which they know are doing all kinds of things to their insides that might not be desirable. The reason they say they do it is that the boys blackmail them. The boys say, or they think that the boys say, that unless they go on to the pill they won't sleep with them and if they won't do that then they won't go with them. They will find someone else who will. So they feel that they have to take the pill to keep their men.'

Jenny's present intense relationship with a particular boy went through a series of stages which she describes as follows:

'I've gone through so many stages. When I first started going out, I went with a very academic crowd. I was about 13 then. That's when I first started smoking cannabis and things like that. Then I moved on to another set of people—with them it was just drugs really. Only two of that crowd were academic, the rest had left school at 15. Then I moved on to another crowd—complete drop-outs. I just met them on the street one day when I was with a group of my former friends. There were a few guys sitting on a bench, they looked a bit hungry, so we said "Come home and have something to eat". We brought them home and I sort of got into their scene. Usually I bring friends home and there's no problem but with this crowd my father disapproved. He'd ask "What do you do?"— "Nothing." "I don't like them." And then I moved on again to a more intellectual crowd. I've met so many people—I've met junkies in a very bad state. I've met the complete opposite. I've met a really wide range of people.'

Jenny's friend Clara joins in at this point:

'That helps you to understand your own problems, your own position. If you think "Oh God, what am I carrying on living for?", you've just got to think "Well, I remember him—and really am I so badly off as I think?" You've experienced people in tremendously worse states.'

Jenny, though shy and somewhat withdrawn at home, has been very outgoing in making relationships outside. She describes how she 'gets into their scenes' and experiences life as it is lived in all its variety:

'I just go up to them and say, "Hello, I'm Jenny". Through meeting people and talking to them one thing leads to another and you meet others. I find it much easier to talk to males. I can't get on with females at all. Before I was going out with my boyfriend, I was going around with a crowd of nine or ten boys, not one girl, and I was quite happy. I had no personal attachment to any of them.'

Though Jenny disclaims friendship with girls, she not only showed a close attachment to Clara all through the course of the interviews, but her mother mentioned that she had been very close to another girl earlier in her school career:

'She had one very close friend at the school who has now left but I know that girl will always be Jenny's friend, always and always. But she has few close friends. When she was a baby the midwife I had for my youngest one got to know her and said about her that she will never have many friends but the friends she has will be real. And it's absolutely true. The friend from school who left dropped out. She was a problem child. Her family had no money and she had no father, and her mother got drunk or something. Because of this she had to get help from the local authorities, and they've got her a tutor and arranged for her to get into a dancing school and she's studying dancing in another part of London.'

Jenny feels that young people generally have to go through various phases of development, though of course there are variations in emphasis and in how much experience the individual actually has:

'First you go through a sort of giggly boyfriend stage; then settling down with a group of friends or going with various groups; then you have one steady boyfriend. There are different outlooks on how you see boys according to which stage you're in. A couple of years ago I saw having a boyfriend as a sort of status symbol . . . but now with Simon, he's someone I really enjoy being with and an attachment has just sort of grown up with us over the ten months we've been going out. A deep attachment has formed. I can't sort of describe the stages . . . we are just going around, just the two of us at the moment, no other friends, which I think is quite bad because though we meet other people and we're friendly with other people, there's just only one person we can call a true friend out of school.'

This 'pairing off' has been satisfying for Jenny and it has removed her from the hazards of the drug crowds as she spends all her time with her boyfriend, who is seriously committed to photography, first as a hobby and possibly as a career. Her mother, relieved that Jenny has come through the minefield of early adolescent perils, is not completely happy about some of the perils of premature settling down:

'He's a nice boy and a very bright boy. He dropped out of grammar school and kicked his heels around town for a couple of years—just did nothing living off his family. Actually Jenny has made him pull himself together and he's now got this job with a very fashionable photographer in town, and it's also his hobby. He's terribly interested in it. She's with him all the time. At weekends she goes over to his house and they develop films together and they work in the darkroom. She is very interested in art and she draws and listens to music but they seem to have reacted against all adult forms of entertainment; they never go to the theatre. She is very domesticated. She washes his socks and cooks him Sunday lunch and is playing at being a wife. . . . She talks of having lots of children and she's very upset that perhaps families are going to be limited . . . she's very puritanical and idealistic about motherhood, thinks that mothers going out to work is bad, and popping their babies into crèches and things like that are bad. She is almost sort of reactionary about it. Whereas our generation were fighting for day nurseries, there she is thinking they are bad and mothers should stay with their children.'

At the same time Jenny says that she wants to have a job and not be dependent on her husband; her mother encourages her to think this way. She wishes that Jenny would think a bit more about her own career and that the boy ought to help her with this rather than everything revolving around getting his career established. She tells Jenny that she ought to get out more, meet more people, have a life of her own, but at the moment it is not clear whether this is a phase that she must find her way through, as with the drugs, or an early commitment.

Jenny's *philosophy of life and the meaning of leisure* in the particular *life style* she has evolved may be understood in the context of her whole enjoyment career. In her primary school days she participated in a range of 'middle-class' activities—helped both by the school and by her mother—dancing, art, visits to theatres and museums. During secondary school, the distinction between work and social life became more prominent and her sister Karen's trouble with her social life became a negative influence for her. By whatever combination of this negative example and her own different temperament, Jenny steered clear of the skinhead crowd at school and developed a social life outside. She always had at least one close schoolfriend but for the most part her real friends have been outside school. She still continued to work hard at school and to use her work habits for the development of her other interests which became, however, primary for her:

'The teachers think I'm basically a good girl . . . at school I work steadily but the teachers know nothing of my outside life whatsoever. I'm in everyone's good books but if they knew of my outside life they'd have a completely different outlook of me and my work.'

Jenny feels that the split in her life between work and her social life came about because of the shock of transition from primary to secondary school. In primary school everyone enjoys themselves, but in secondary school it becomes 'gloomy'. So she feels that one has to develop interests separate from the school—'you need a change, you need new people, new atmosphere, everything.' School is 'just sort of routine, I've got sick of it.'

Within school she differentiates between the two subjects she likes best and plans to take A-levels in—art and geography—and all the rest. Art is more interesting and in her diary she classifies her time in the art programme as leisure. She feels that she could pursue some kind of a career like her mother's, illustrating books, and this would not be 'work' for her at all: 'It would be leisure because I like drawing so much, whether I had to do it in a set time for somebody or not, I don't mind.' On the whole, however, leisure means *not* being in school and *not* being organised or in activities formally provided *for* her. She experiences a shortage of places to go in the evenings. One of the few places, a coffee bar, to which she used to go with her friends is no longer available:

> 'It's all posh now—they wouldn't let us near it! . . . But I think if places were arranged where you could go, no one would use them, because they're arranged for you to use! . . . For myself, I would never go to anything that is provided for "young people" in inverted commas, you know.'

Shortage of money also restricts her but she does not want to take a Saturday or holiday job to earn money; she has tried it and found that she did not like the routine and feeling tired:

> 'I've had about six [jobs], but I found when I was working on Saturday mornings, I couldn't go out on Saturday night, because I'd feel so rough. . . . I was cleaning a lady's flat and I knew her, so it was a nice kind of job, it was friendly. But you know, I just couldn't make it on Saturday morning, getting up at nine o'clock and working for three hours.'

As has been described, Jenny's 'social life' has consisted of a passage through numerous groups in which she has tried out different identities and experiences, got 'into the scene' of different kinds of people, and formed an impression through this of the kind of person she is. Now, with her intense involvement in a pair relationship, her routine has changed. She still goes out, for example to pubs on Friday evenings, but there is less searching for new experiences:

> 'On Friday nights I usually sort of get a bit pissed, you know, it's just a sort of regular thing to break the monotony of life . . . not because I'm fed up with life, but because it's the end of the school week, I have to celebrate a bit. . . . I go out over the whole weekend, but Friday night is a particular pub night where we meet our friends. . . . I don't go to the pub as much as I used to, but they still know me there, and it's still my local pub.'

Apart from the regular Friday-night visit to the pub, Jenny feels that

leisure activities should not have a routine character and that spontaneity is the essence of the enjoyment of leisure time:

> 'We'd just decide to meet somewhere and we had a bit of money
> between us and we thought, enough to go to the country for the
> day—so we'd get on the train and go to the country, just out of the
> blue, not planned. We'd find that if we planned something, it doesn't
> turn out as well as if we just do it straight off; like one day we said
> "Let's go to Kew Gardens" and it was really nice in the hot-houses
> and everything.'

Jenny's diary indicates that she spends nearly every evening with her
boyfriend at his home. Weekends are spent with him at her home; the
part played in her life of the spontaneous excursions with friends has
dropped off considerably. Jenny's mother is concerned that she has got
into a domestic routine too early, and Jenny has begun to feel this too;
she now thinks of expanding her horizons *with* him. They were planning
to make a trip to Finland at the time the interviews were conducted.
They intended to go by motorcycle and the boy was learning to drive
one so that he could qualify in time for his licence. This aroused a new
set of anxieties in Jenny's mother.

Jenny went through a phase of differentiating work from leisure—
i.e. school work from 'social life'—of finding out about herself through
getting into relationships and 'scenes' with various kinds of young
people and through experimentation with drugs; but she is now trying
to reintegrate the different parts of her life. She hopes, for example, to
study art after leaving school. She wants her activities in work to be
activities which she enjoys; the 'feeling' part of it is the key to the
meaning of life and leisure to her. She is getting her boyfriend to do the
same, and organises her own life around his. In summary, when discussing the meaning of leisure and indicating how it means so many things
to different people, Jenny presented her own view as follows:

> 'It's just enjoying yourself. I can curl up with a good book and
> enjoy myself; I can talk to my mother and enjoy myself; I can go
> out for a walk in the park and enjoy myself; everything . . . it's
> to be happy in yourself and the people you're with and the whole
> situation.'

She describes how her more mature relationship with her boyfriend
differs from the relationships with the boys at school whom she regards
as immature:

> 'Lots of boys at school, if they met my parents or somebody's
> parents, they wouldn't really want to converse with them because

they're older; but Simon will willingly talk to my parents and he'll spend hours talking to my mother . . . and they can't accept females as having female emotions and things. They'll say "old bitch, she's off again, ugh, ugh, can't stick her, we'll have to chuck her in". They're not really willing to get into it and share it. That's the best part of a relationship, getting in and sharing all these moods and quarrels, and all the ups and downs—if you come out of a relationship having experienced it, it's well worth it. Simon moans about my being moody but he sort of accepts that all females are fairly moody and he just has to put up with them, you know.'

Jenny and Clara feel that the boys at school still want to go out with girls as status symbols, and to try out sexual relationships with them without any deeper involvement, 'not actually enjoying having it but just getting in there, managing it'. At the heart of what Jenny considers a mature relationship on which a good life style is based, is the need to develop independence and self-assurance, which she feels she has done; she feels her life should avoid too much routine, too much structure, and that she should be interdependent rather than too dependent on a close relationship.

Jenny's *family background* is obviously important in a number of ways in shaping her interests. Her father had thrown up a job that was materially rewarding, but which he did not like and could not approve of morally, for something he really liked though it entailed financial sacrifices. Her mother had put her own training and effort into support work for this, and their work as a home-based team had an impact on the children both as a model and as a set of conditions. The model has been taken up most actively by Jenny in the arrangement she has developed with Simon, whose hobby is becoming his work. He is totally dedicated to it, giving up everything to spend time on it while Jenny does the support work and cultivates her own hobby-cum-occupation.

Beyond this there are other elements in the family background and outlook that are apparently important in moulding the pattern that has evolved for Jenny and her sisters:

1   Both of Jenny's parents were very idealistic and belonged to a radical political action group when they were young. They did this as a way of trying to improve society. None of their children is interested in political action, but the idea that their parents were idealistic and that what they did was a bit 'way out' in their time seems to have influenced the children.

2   Jenny's mother was unconventional in her youth. Jenny recounts the family image of it thus:

'I think my mother is a very nice person because she's nonconformist.

I can talk to her easily and she's sort of travelled with the times. I think my father is still in the sort of age when he was a child—his beliefs about what people should do—but my mother has sort of grown up with it. [Would you say she's influenced you?] I would say she's been the main influence, I think. [How?] Partly to understand and partly to go along with the things I've done; she's sort of taken my things, like I come home and discuss the way of life at the moment or something, and she accepts it because she's thought about it. . . . She likes the freedom of ideas and she's always been a sort of arty type herself. When she was a student she was going around with loads of long hair and beards and cloaks, and she even had a friend who had a bicycle and a raven used to sit on the handlebars! Like the freaks of today, she would be like them in her day.'

3   A number of negative examples: both Jenny's elder sister and her mother's elder sister provided examples of the trouble one could get into if one followed the quest for excitement too single-mindedly, without a sense of responsibility. Karen's experiences have already been described; her aunt had several children and then split up with her husband, partly because she had a tendency to get wild ideas and then to act spontaneously on them, often getting them into trouble. Jenny's disapproval of this developed only after it was clear that sometimes it meant not fulfilling responsibilities to children—as when she had gone off after her divorce leaving one of her children in an institution. Another negative example is a cousin who errs on the other side, who is too much of a 'swot' and does all the 'good' things—goes to organised clubs and camping groups but is not the sort of person Jenny admires. She regards this sort of person, whom she sees in school as well, as a 'cabbage'. They have suppressed many of the preoccupations that she and her friends think important; as a consequence she feels that they have not developed as whole persons.

Jenny thinks her father is too withdrawn into his work—that he works too much of the time, too hard, and was too little involved with his children. He has explained this partly in terms of the characteristics of his career (with the switch to a less secure but more personally fulfilling kind of work), and partly in terms of the fact that he only had daughters and none of them showed any interest in the scientific part of his work, favouring more the artistic side, as expressed by his wife.

So Jenny's negative reference points are the 'swots' on one side (father, cousin, some of her schoolmates), and irresponsible, impulsive people on the other (her aunt and elder sister). However, her father feels that the schools should teach young people more about current affairs and try to get them thinking on positive lines about them. He recognises that the schools cannot do everything. They are, however, perhaps too concentrated on the cultivation of the mind and the academic approach to problems:

> 'I think it would be quite helpful to try to integrate their young lives into improving society but it's all in very broad terms; they just see this intensive academic work and the world in a mess outside and they're going to be tipped into it and many of them say, well to hell with it, we're not going to work, we're going off to India.'

Jenny's mother had seen Jenny and the other girls go through some hazardous pitfalls in the adolescent obstacle course—with sex, drugs and violence having been handled in various ways. The danger now with Jenny involves the precocious settling down into a conventional pattern; she fears that Jenny will not go on to get a higher qualification which may be essential for later life in a time when one knows one should not become totally dependent on a particular man; and also that the very close interdependence that she has formed so early may get her into new dangers, as with trips on the motorcycle:

> 'Jenny and her boyfriend are very close and I feel she's just not meeting enough people and in fact I feel she's really being a little unimaginative. Dropping back into the system again in a way does worry me a bit; I wish she'd be a bit more adventurous. Playing safe all the time. I would like to see her do more to fulfil her potential, I suppose. Also in our society as it is at the moment, you need a bit of paper with a signature at the bottom to be able to get a job very often. And if she is going to marry and have children and perhaps be left by her husband, a little piece of paper with a signature at the bottom may be very useful. It has happened to so many of my contemporaries . . . they've been let down and to be able to teach is an absolute life line . . . [also] further education gives them a few years to be able to think and sort themselves and meet other people, talk to other people and just broaden themselves.'

Jenny's mother has ideas on what she thinks would be helpful to young people at this stage, with their search for a balance of challenge, excitement, security and organisation in their lives. Characteristically she discusses these ideas with her daughter:

> "When I knew you were coming I said to Jenny, don't you think that more places where kids could go in the evening would be a good idea, because this has always been a thing of mine, in fact I was thinking of setting up a soup kitchen where people could come and just sit. You know, so that they would have somewhere to go. And Jenny said "Oh no, it wouldn't be a good idea at all, nobody would

want to go there because it would be specially for them and therefore they wouldn't want to go there".'

The young people tend to classify such places within their own rather shifting set of categories and the clientele as well as the classifications change. A place will be branded as for 'freaky' types or 'hairy types', or 'squares' or 'older drop-outs'.

In general Jenny's mother feels that the ways in which people fill their time and plan their activities is a very individual matter. She knows that some people conform more to a pattern and seem happy with it, but this has not been the way for their family. She thinks that young people do need a sense of adventure and excitement, and to be with people like themselves at least part of the time. One way in which this happens that she feels could be developed more is through pop festivals:

'this pop festival is a very good leisure thing for young people nowadays and I am rather cross with the way people are stamping on it. Now this they really enjoy and get a lot out of, and I've noticed that this last pop festival, apart from the fact that it's lost so much money, hasn't hit the headlines at all. I know why it hasn't hit the headlines, because there haven't been any nasty incidents . . . though I've never actually been to one myself, my children have and they've always come back very exhilarated, happy and positive; they like them very much. I think these group activities where you get lots of people together and there's a lot of good feeling, positive feeling. [They feel in touch with their generation?] Yes, quite. . . . I think they are tremendously good, provided they are well handled. My children went to one which was a sea of mud as far as I can gather and they got very cold and there wasn't enough to eat and there weren't enough loos, but if they are well handled, as people obviously see now they should be well organised, I think they are a very good thing. I would like to see a lot more good pop festivals. Though my girls come back very dirty and sometimes cold and hungry, you get cold and hungry if you go mountain-climbing, organised mountain-climbing, and these aren't organised . . . well, they are but the kids don't feel they're organised.'

KATHERINE is a sixth-former in a large comprehensive school in a working-class district in London. She is an attractive, personable girl and at the time of the interviews was 17 years old. She and Jenny have different social environments and experiences, different influences as they work out a congenial life style. Katherine has a working-class background, and her mother and father do not live together; she moved between mother and father while the issue of her care was resolved; she lives with her father and paternal grandmother. Neither her residential environment nor her school encourages her to raise her level of aspirations; this is in contrast to many aspects of Jenny's environment. The two girls are different in personality, social class, neighbourhood and family background; they are similar in sex, stage of life career and in some of their interests.

Katherine was contacted at the youth club which uses the premises of her school in the evenings. She was one of a clique of three girls; all were interviewed four times over a period of several months at the school or the youth centre; each interview lasted up to two hours. Briefer contacts were made, but not sustained, with her father, mother, grandmother and school-teacher. None of the family members wanted to be interviewed, saying they were too busy. Perhaps they were, though other explanations are possible. Their reluctance may have been an expression of their general disengagement from Katherine's life: she complains that none of them really cares about what happens to her, though granny is sporadically 'very strict', and both father and mother sporadically give her treats. Another reason seems to relate to an earlier bad experience the family had, in which the information obtained by an interviewer was used to their detriment.

After getting to know the interviewer together with her friends, Katherine was willing to talk freely about her opinions and experiences. As the relationship between the interviewer and the friends developed, she not only became more co-operative but took a leading role in arranging contacts so that the interviews could continue.

Two themes dominate Katherine's conceptions of life and leisure. First is the importance of 'free' choice: she feels that there must be an area of her life where she chooses freely and it is only then possible to see any activity as leisure. The content is secondary. The second is the sense of 'fair play': once an activity is chosen or a relationship entered into, she must follow it through, otherwise it is not fair to the others involved. This principle governs all spheres of her life. The first theme is pervasive among today's youth. The second, while a British cultural value, is particularly emphasised by Katherine because of her specific life history.

As for her more general orientation to life, Katherine functions with a sense of mood counterpoint, wanting periods of quiet and solitude alternating with more boisterous activity, social life and fun. The latter is the predominantly preferred mode, but she is clear that she needs and seeks out both kinds of situations and experiences.

Katherine is the elder of the two girls in her family. Her father was first a railwayman and later worked for a transport company. When she was 4 years old, about a year after her sister was born, her mother left her father, taking the two girls with her. The following three years were very unsettled. Katherine attended three different primary schools in eighteen months while her mother moved around. When she was 7, Katherine was taken back to live with her father and grandmother in her grandmother's house, where she and her sister have lived ever since:

'Well, first of all I lived with my mum and dad until I was about 4. My sister must have been about 1 year old when my mother went and I was left with my father and my sister; then my mother came and took my sister, and I lived with my dad for a long time—maybe three or four months. A lady who lived downstairs—we lived in a big house—used to come in and look after me and my dad used to take me to school and she used to give me money for dinner. It was rather nice because I had these nice cousins and my aunt—they weren't really relatives, they might have been half-and-half—used to look after me; I had four big boy cousins and they used to look after me and that was fun, cos' they used to have dogs and cats and everything else in that house. Then my mum came and took me.'

Before they split up, she recalls that her mother taught her to read early. This is an interest that has remained important to her ever since.

'I learned to read very, very early; she used to teach me simple maths—two-times—and she taught me how to read. . . . She was very particular about that; she also taught me to tell the time at a very early age. I can remember one occasion—we had a very small front room cum kitchen and it had a kind of divider; she used to sit on a chair by the fire and I was kneeling down; she had a clock, and that was before they split up, so I must have been about $2\frac{1}{2}$ to 3 years old, and she started teaching me to read, so I could read very early.'

Reading was a strong interest up to the time she began going to the youth centre; drawing has also been a central interest since the age of 3. She was taught by a man who lived in the flat below her parents before they split up:

'One of my dad's friends taught me to draw and he taught me to draw paving stones—you know, a lot of children draw them so that all the lines sort of coincide—well, he taught me draw them with a jagged line to make them look like paving stones—put one set there and kind of overlapping—and he taught me to draw things like that. I saw him a couple of weeks ago and I just about recognised him—I haven't seen him for years and he said "Do you still draw?" and I says "Yes".'

In the period following the split both parents tried to make it up to Katherine and her sister by giving them extra gifts or treats whenever possible. Father's treats were 'super':

'The thing that really used to make the day or week was when my dad took me to the yard—sometimes, when he wasn't busy, he'd come and collect me from the lady and used to take me down to the yard; he taught me how to drive one of those big steam ones, and he taught me how to drive the big diesel ones [trains] and, he taught me how to drive an electric train! Only 3 years old, and I started learning to drive a diesel! That was great that was.'

Katherine's mother came to take her away rather suddenly and in a tense emotional atmosphere. Katherine locked herself in her room and did not want to go, but finally she was taken off without her toys:

'I'd just that day gone to the library to get a book out and it was this big, lovely book and it was a brand new one and it cost about £3 I think. When I'd gone, he [father] just threw it out. My mum took me and she left all my toys because I had a lot of toys—lots of expensive toys and dolls' clothes. I never saw them again.'

She excuses her mother for this however, saying: 'It was because she couldn't carry them. My doll's prams and bike—I had two bikes.' While Katherine was with her mother, she found other compensations and interests. Her mother went out to work and she was looked after by some family friends who were addressed with kin terms and who had animals.

The picture that emerges is of Katherine using the opportunities given her for learning in spite of the disrupted family life; she found a good deal to enjoy so that even now at 17 she likes to 'go back to childhood' in the school holidays and play as she used to:

'I play with Lego sets; build puzzles; I go over to the swings; I read *Winnie the Pooh* all over again; I read Beatrix Potter again—I can't stand Enid Blyton, I don't read her; and I read lots and lots of history books which I used to do when I was about 9. . . . I used to have over 100 books. Altogether in the whole house there must be bordering on 200, because my sister's got a lot of books, my father has, my grandad's got a few and my nanny's got some; you know, we've got a lot of books; but my own, I used to have about 100.'

Reading was Katherine's main interest up to the age of about 12. Because she moved schools so much, she had some difficulty in maintaining friendships; reading was a solitary activity in which she could become completely absorbed as she still can now:

'I wasn't a very friendly person at the best of times; I always preferred being on my own and I used to make friends loosely but I never used to invite them up or play with them or anything; just to have someone to talk to so that you wouldn't feel left out when you were at school . . . [and now] I think I go through stages of preferring to be out with my friends; for a couple of weeks the thought of sitting at home really bores me and for a couple of weeks the thought that I've got to go to the youth centre tonight [doesn't appeal]. I'd rather read this. I sometimes walk along the road reading a book—I nearly got run over one day! I remember I went to the youth centre one night and I was reading this book; I came to a very busy crossing, at the road there it's always very busy, and I never take any notice because I've got this attitude that if you're halfway across the road the car isn't going to go straight over you, they're going to use their sense or else they'll get locked up for it! I was in that part of the road first—and I just walked across and I didn't realise—the car missed me by about three inches.'

Katherine's *relationship with her younger sister* has always been a rather protective one. She recalls the delivery of the baby which was at home and part of which she witnessed, and how she took a particular interest in 'the horrible little red thing in the cradle'. She was a bit jealous of her at first and of the big cot with bars; but then she used to get in and play with her sister. The protective relationship has persisted into the present with strong elements of ambivalence. She feels that her little sister, Tilly, has been indulged too much and has a moody and demanding nature. Two big issues that seem to cut across social-class lines—bedtime and pocket money—were recurrent themes between them:

'Up until I was 12, we used to have to be in bed by half-past eight, but now I'm older, I'll go in sometimes at ten o'clock at night—she'll still be up and my whole family doesn't accept the fact that she should be in bed before I go; when I say "Oh dear, you shouldn't be up now, you know, I didn't used to be when I was this age", everybody gets really stroppy about it . . . a couple of years ago I never used to get pocket money; if ever I wanted something, I used to have it bought for me or I couldn't have it; since last year we've started having pocket money and she doesn't get as much as me, but she doesn't respect the fact [that I'm older] and she gets a bit stroppy about it. . . . She goes through more phases than I ever did. She always needs more money, she always sort of moans when she's sent to bed and I never bother because it's a waste of time, but she gets in a bad mood then. She always wants her own way; in general she sees something she wants and when she's got it she won't want it anymore, whereas I always got plenty of use out of it when I got it; like we used to get Lego sets and she never used them. . . . She went through these phases and my gran, she always used to excuse it as a phase; it used to annoy me because if I'd done anything like that when I was her age, I'd've got told off and people wouldn't have accepted it.'

Nevertheless, Katherine is fond of her sister:

'You know, I feel great protection towards her. She's not a weak or ill person but she's had operations on her stomach. Any time it can occur again. At times I feel like banging her head against a wall and at other times I look at her and—she's a character, my sister. She can be sort of very sweet, she can come out with the nicest things and the next minute she can say "You're a nasty old so-and-so, you won't let me go out!"—you know that sort of person.'

This protectiveness is shown in Katherine's assumption that she should go along with her sister to look after her if her activities take her into danger. Tilly had an early enthusiasm for horse-riding and Katherine felt that she should accompany her. She felt some relief when Tilly developed a craze for ice-skating which she shared with a friend, so that Katherine did not need to accompany her: 'I'm pretty lucky this summer, it's ice-skating at the moment [for Tilly], so I don't have to go with her when she goes—she takes a friend along. She's good at that too.' Although Katherine has always found her sister's moods trying and has resented what she sees as 'unfair' indulgence, she basically accepts her sister and is generous in describing Tilly's talents and good looks. She also enjoys the meetings which both she and Tilly have with their mother: 'The three of us, we have great fun together.'

Katherine and her sister stayed with their mother for about three years before going back to live with their father and grandparents. Katherine says that her mother was having a hard time working and trying to look after them; also she was moody and not a very maternal sort of person. Since returning to their grandmother's house, they do not see much of their father who is often away and works odd hours; their 'nan' is the central figure in the daily domestic scene and they have regular visits with their mother:

'My father leaves, not so much discipline but hours to my nan, and she's very old-fashioned, but if I let her know a week beforehand and I'm very nice about it and I say I promise I won't be in late, she'll generally let me go out. But I never am really late; even from parties, I leave about 11. It all depends where I'm going—if I'm going out with a group of friends, it doesn't matter much, you know, 'cos she likes my friends. She's always saying, "Oh that Mary's nice", or "That Ellen is a nice girl"; if she knows who I'm with, I'll be able to say, "Nan, I'm going out with Mary, Ellen and Sue, I will be back fairly late". And she'll say, "If you're going to be back very late, ring me". But if I am going out with one specific person different, she doesn't believe in it. You have to work up to it. . . . Whenever we've got a show on at school or anything I take her ticket to her but I don't actually do anything with her. I might sit down and have a chat with her. We have great fun together; she's very nice like that. I like her a lot. And she's great fun to talk to— she's very helpful.'

At other times she resents her nan's lack of real interest or involvement in her affairs and dislikes the fact that her nan 'doesn't want to know'. But Katherine stresses that she is not the sort of person who confides in older people or looks up to them for help or advice, so when she is 'sitting down and having a chat' with her grandmother it is social rather than personal: 'I'm not a very confiding person. I like people to confide in me their problems, but myself, I prefer to work out my own problems.' She feels that neither her father nor her mother could understand her problems, 'and I never tell my nan because of her age, and that, she might not understand.'

Turning to Katherine's *school history*, we know she had several changes between the ages of 5 and 7. However, since she moved back to her father, she has attended the same comprehensive school. The first school experience that she recalls gives some insight into the source of her current emphasis on 'fair play':

'When I started school, when I was about 5-ish, my dad used to give me some money every day. I don't know why but I got told off by my teacher because it seems that she thought it was a crime to take money to school. Seven-and-six was a lot of money for a 5 year old, and I met my cousin coming up the road and he was three or four years older than me and he gave me about three bob; so I had over ten bob, I was quite well off. I went into the school and I put some of the money into the box they had there—a kind of charity box—I put in two shillings and the teacher saw it. She said, "What are you doing with all that money?" And I said, "My dad gave it to me." And she said, "He's not allowed to give you all this", so I got upset about it and I sulked for the rest of the day.'

Katherine felt that this was unfair and the fact that she was taken away that very night by her mother may have contributed to a sense of ultimate justice in the world. However, the next three years, with the changes of school that were involved, were worse than a waste of time. She felt that the schools did not appreciate her potential and did not bring out the best in her. They were in poor areas and the burdens on the teachers were severe. She recalls them as autocratic:

'I always used to hate these schools, I don't know why. Even when I was very little, I used to like to have a free attitude with the teachers; not so much as now, but I'd like to be able to do something wrong and not get told off for it, and they used to. But we used to have fantastic playgrounds in one of the schools and it had a load of apparatus in the grounds; we had a fantastic time in that. I enjoyed that because we used to go climbing—oh, it was fantastic. That was the only time I really enjoyed myself at that school. School meals were abominable; there were these two old ladies who used to march us from the infants' building across to the secondary building, where the dinners were and you weren't allowed to talk—I mean, that's ridiculous! We marched quite a long way and it used to be very hot weather; I've always suffered from hay fever and asthma; it used to be a bit much for me at times because if we'd just had a meal, they didn't let it go down—we just marched straight back across and sometimes when it was a very warm day it didn't really appeal to me and I got very stroppy about it. Silly old bags. Their attitudes were very old-fashioned and I never liked apple sauce and they always made me eat it and the fat with the meat. It used to turn my stomach up—it still does—I was made to eat it one day and I came home and I was violently sick, so my mum went rushing up the school and I didn't have to eat it any more.'

When she returned to her father's home, she went back to her first school and was pleased to find that many of the children she knew were still there. She considers that the teachers there were much better in bringing her out and she recalls doing well early on in maths because of the teacher's skill:

'You see, my teacher at my primary school was really intelligent— I'm sure he should have been a secondary school teacher because he used to teach us with secondary school methods. When I went to the secondary school part I'd already done algebra and geometry that all the rest hadn't because this teacher was very particular about it. Every morning when we used to come in for registration, before we went into assembly, there used to be a five minutes' gap; he used to have all these slides and it used to have a table on—you know, 7×7—and he used to hold it up and point to somebody, and if you didn't get it within five seconds, you were in trouble! So there it was $7 \times 7 = 49$; it was really so that by the time we left that school— we had him for two years—if anybody said "6×6?", we could roll it straight off; I can't do it now because we're not supposed to work like that. Also we used to be taught geometry: like shadows of things and measuring the heights of buildings; we were taught how to use protractors, set square and so on, and he used to be really strict about it. . . . We all thought he was a fantastic teacher; he was very, very strict. Once he got down on his knees in front of the class and said, "God, give me strength." Very embarrassing! We also used to learn French, history, and geography and science with him—oh, we used to do most of the subjects that no other primary school did. And we also did country dancing. I remember once, to get out of doing lessons, we spent three weeks measuring the school, to find out how much it would weigh! We measured it six times, all the way round, every pillar and post—oh, it was really good fun. We took ages on that and in the end the teacher got suspicious. We never did find out the weight!'

Katherine enjoyed school from the time she went back to the local primary school and went on happily with her classmates to the local secondary comprehensive school. The transition from primary to secondary school was smooth. She already knew the school, the building, the teachers and most of the students. She'd watched the construction of the new building as it had gone up while she was in primary school, and felt part of it all. Katherine recalls that the headmaster of the secondary school used to come down to give sweets to the juniors on their birthday, so when they went up to the secondary school he was not a frightening figure.

For the first three years at secondary school, Katherine's life consisted of going to school and reading at home. She did well academically and, although she liked history and art best, she was able to cope with maths without too much effort because of the good grounding she had received earlier:

'When we used to do maths, I used to get a load of paper out and I used to spend all the lesson, drawing. I used to sit next to a girl called Sue, and he'd say "OK, I'll give you ten to do before you go." So I used to put all my drawings away and I'd say to Sue, "How do you do this?" And she goes, "I'm not telling you!" So I said "Be like that!", and I used to ask Eve who was sitting in front, or then I'd ask Mary and nobody would tell me—Eve couldn't do it, Mary couldn't do it—so I used to work it out from the board and I didn't used to do too bad, although I never paid any attention to him.'

The main developments that were taking place at this time were social rather than academic. Katherine made friends with Ellen and Mary and began to feel the need for a social life in the evenings. Looking back, those first years of secondary school seemed empty by comparison:

'Last year my life—I used to go to school, come home and that was it . . . my life was very empty. At the time I could be sitting down one evening and I'd realise, I'm not doing anything. And looking back as well; but at the time I think it was only occasionally I felt it was empty because I'd spend a lot of time reading.'

Non-academic school activities that she enjoyed were drama and dancing, the only physical activity that she liked: 'I enjoy dancing—it's very tiring but because I'm not frightened of making a fool of myself —which you do—I enjoy it.'

Katherine and her clique of friends—particularly her closest friends, Mary and Ellen—see themselves as 'good' but rather fun-loving and inclined to act up under certain circumstances. Some of the teachers are strict and do not allow any joking about, but in other cases there is considerable playing up:

> 'What we are is girls that look very nice, helpful, co-operative, goody-goody; and we can be. But basically we are argumentative, non-co-operative and bad behaving. The teachers would never believe it. We had a French teacher and for the life of me I couldn't do the homework and I thought, "Right, if I can't do it, nobody else is going to." There were about nine others in the class. I made all the racket I could and I was a right nuisance. If a different teacher had walked in who I liked, whose lessons I really do concentrate on, they'd never believe it, I was being so awkward. Actually, we're very easy to teach if I do say so myself. We can be very quiet when we want to and if we're reading or something you wouldn't know we were there.'

This feeling that there is something underneath that is 'awkward' is a pattern that is often found among the 'good' students who have a bit of spark. Whether the spark comes out as troublesome 'fire' or not, depends on the situations and how it is handled.

Katherine's other school *interests* are more closely linked to what she would call leisure, but as has been indicated the element of free choice is so crucial in her concept of leisure that it is less that these activities—art and drama—are conventionally called leisure activities, than that she likes them and does them voluntarily:

> 'You can't really get away from school work, because there's home-work and things involved with school. Leisure means enjoying your-self—whether at school or at home. If someone says you've got to do something, whether it's at school or out of school, you don't want to do it so much.'

In thinking of her *life interests* generally, Katherine is mindful of her father's indulgence with her early play experiences. She had 'lots of prams and dolls and bicycles and all the other things that little kids have'. Her early reading experiences with her mother have stuck with her and reading still absorbs much of her 'free time'; her father's friend who taught her to draw is recalled as another important early influence:

> 'I was only about 3. Fancy being taught to draw when you're 3 years old. But he used to sit with me and draw me houses and pavements and things like that; he was very nice and very big and cuddly. He was the type that you always think of when you think of fathers, the same kind of jolly person, [but] they never had any children. . . . I always used to enjoy scribbling and my parents had a lot of rows when I was about 3 or 4 and I used to go down and sit with them.'

Her early experience of riding ponies at the zoo has had its impact too; she still enjoys animals. When her mother went to work at the time Katherine was living with her, she liked the family with whom she was left, partly because they had animals. These experiences of reading, drawing and playing with her toys represent islands of happiness and escape from the tensions of her early environment; she still returns to them.

At the moment Katherine seems to be in a transitional phase between her earlier pattern of more solitary activities and the more sociable ones connected with the youth centre. Dancing and drama activities begun in school are pursued in the youth centre. From this wide range of interests—beginning with the early ones of reading, drawing and riding, and continuing with the later ones of singing, dancing and acting—Katherine began to focus around the drama group in the youth centre. This was a social activity as well as one that gave expression to some of her earlier interests. Within it, technical drama engaged her most. In the youth centre and the drama group she and her friends developed the habit of seeing one another outside school over shared and non-compulsory interests:

> 'I think as I grew older my friends started getting more interests outside school and perhaps seeing each other during school wasn't enough—you might say "Come to my house for tea" or "We'll go to youth centre together", and I think it works up from there really. The main thing was—here it all comes, Mary!—Mary liked a boy [in the technical drama class at youth centre] and that's the reason we went to technical drama—and from there it just kind of snow-balled.'

This change is seen as a major one; looking back over her development of life interests so far, it is the main landmark:

> 'Yes, this [school] year, since September, it's rare that I'm actually home during the week, whereas last year my life—I used to go

to school, come home and that was it. And then September, you know, I was 14 and I was interested in drama—it just sort of seemed different. I used to—when I came home from school, I didn't look forward to doing homework and watching TV or something; all of a sudden I would be able to say, "I am going out tonight". The thing I miss now is—going out all these evenings—I can only read say two books a week, whereas before I'd read one a night—a big difference.'

The social side of Katherine's life centres on having fun—playing up, larking about, 'having a good laugh'—and having friends. The two are connected: when she formed the relationship with Mary, who is her best friend within their small clique, it was over a good laugh that they had together. Mary had just come out of hospital recovering from an injury and had to walk with the help of an appliance. The teacher asked for volunteers among the other students to look after her:

'You know, to make sure no one run her over. . . . Well I knew her fairly well; I didn't know her so much as a friend but as a person in the same classroom. So I volunteered and little fat Suzy volunteered. Mary came in and the three of us he chose to look after her; we're all kind of very exuberant, outward-going people and when Mary walked in in this brace, we didn't stop [larking about]; it didn't seem wrong to us, you know, we're all rather lunatic . . . we were all rather natural.'

One incident was particularly remembered where Mary fell off the bed in the school's medical room, which everyone found hilarious: 'We were all rolling round! It was hysterical, that was. From there, you know—I mean seeing Mary falling off the end of the bed—I mean you can't really not be friends!'

Three or four of a loose-knit group of girls started 'going round together' after this with others joining them or 'drifting away' after break-points like summer holidays. The core group are Katherine, Mary, Ellen and Peggy—the first three of whom participated in this study and were often interviewed together. The fourth girl, Peggy, initially did not like Katherine but was 'bullied' into liking her by Mary. Mary notes that Peggy is moody and generally difficult to get on with. Katherine speculates on why difficulties may have developed between her and Peggy; in so doing she gives some insight into her own situation and the meaning of friendships to her:

'Normally if a person doesn't like me I don't notice it because I'm oblivious to the fact that a person likes me or dislikes me. At first the meeting was very hostile, I don't know why; I think of myself as well, not a nice person but somebody easy to get along with. I don't sort of walk around saying "Oh, I don't like her because she's got a big nose" or anything, so I never take people for what they look like and I didn't really get why she didn't like me. I think perhaps it was because I've got this habit of talking about things I've got, things I do; I can't help it because at home I can't go in and say to my nan "Oh, I've been down town" or "I've been somewhere today" because she's just not interested and I've got nobody to talk to. But my mum takes me to lots of places where other people can't afford to go—she's only got herself to look after. And when I come to school, I chat about where I've been, perhaps to a foreign country or something; and I think perhaps that might have something to do with it. But I have to have somebody to talk to about things, like.'

The small group of girls, then, emphasise friendliness, having fun together and communication. They feel that they are all alike and yet different and that they complement one another. This keeps them from getting bored in one another's company as one thing leads to another. The group also acts as a 'huddle' to protect its members against male incursions. They are at an age where one or two of them are playing around with the idea of pairing off; the group seems to resist the idea and provides protection for the member if she wants it. One of the girls, Ellen, is being hotly pursued by Derek (who is described next). Katherine has been getting somewhat interested in Bill. While the girls refer to their 'boyfriends', they say that the boyfriends are not the exclusive property of the particular girl but that they are friends of the group. Ideally the two ties are compatible, but in fact they sometimes produce strain. Ellen, speaking of her relationship with Derek, said:

'The thing is, it's a bit awkward with us because if we do get involved with anyone, our little group gets quite embarrassing afterwards; that's what I was worried about with Derek. It just didn't work, trying to be "just good friends".'

The group developed a joking attitude towards boyfriends, minimising the sense of emotional involvement. The girls developed an explicitly exploitative attitude toward the boys, as though to reassure the group that the individual member is not interested in him for himself but just because 'he buys me presents' or it is 'a bit of a status symbol and one feels badly not to have one'. The boys and girls go in crowds—wanting neither to pair off exclusively as couples nor to form separate, single-sex groups. Katherine describes how the two sets of friends overlap and articulate as follows:

'There's always a crowd of us, so it's never six or seven girls on one side of the playground and eight or nine boys on the other. We're always very mixed. We don't talk to each other all the time—one day

I might talk to Judy or next day I might stand there and talk to Paul; but, you know, we just sort of talk to each other and in our set it's just as easy to talk to a boy as it is to talk to a girl; you don't go "Coo! She's talking to a boy!", sort of thing. It's good fun. You get two sorts of views on a subject, you get a girl's view and you get a boy's view. And he doesn't mind—he doesn't get stroppy if I go and talk to his friends and I don't get stroppy if he comes and talks to my friends. I couldn't care less. Sometimes his friend Julian puts his arm round me and we have a laugh and he doesn't mind, but some boys tend to get a bit stroppy about it.'

Possessiveness is strongly disapproved of by the group. Derek tends to be very possessive about Ellen. Ellen said of a recent party: 'I had the most boring evening—had to spend the whole evening with Derek and that's one thing I hate at parties. I like to get around a bit.' Katherine adds: 'That's why I won't go to a party with Bill.'

Boyfriends are 'for taking you out', 'for having fun with' and as a 'status symbol' but not yet for intimacy or confiding in. The tendency for the boy clique and the girl clique to be semi-closed communication networks has its positive aspects. Ellen says: 'The thing with boys is, you can tell them that you don't like one of your best friends or some- thing like this, whereas you can't tell one of your other best friends, because they'll tell your other best friend that you said it!' The girls recognise that later stages will produce conflicts and note that already some of them use as an excuse for not going out with their friends the fact that they are seeing their boyfriends that night. Katherine says that her own relationship with Bill has not yet reached this stage:

'A lot of girls, when they've got boyfriends, use it as an excuse not to go out with their [girl] friends—"I'm going out with so-and-so tonight, I can't come around with you lot tonight". If I ever felt that I was tired of this lot, I could use the same excuse but I don't. I try and make sure that I never go out with Bill more than I see my friends. Normally we all tend to go around in a big gang anyway; all the boys we go with at school usually come to the youth centre as well.'

The way Katherine and Bill began their semi-pairing off was symbolic of the way in which the ties with the same-sex group have to be broken. They were on a school trip to Scotland and events developed as follows:

'He'd been up to Scotland with us and it all started because my torch wouldn't work when I decided I was going out for a midnight walk. I wanted to go over to have a chat with one of my friends about something, only my torch ran out. Bill was there and he said, "Where are you going?" And I said, "Just for a walk", you know, "nothing to do with you", sort of thing. So he says "Can I come?" So I said, "Well, let me see the colour of your torch first." So we started walking and it was very dark. And we felt that someone was following us, maybe Suzy, and it was dark and you couldn't see the path you were walking along. Me and Bill, we've both got long legs but Suzy hasn't, so he switches off the torch and he goes "Right! We're going to run", and get away from whoever it was that was following us. So we started running and poor old Suzy couldn't keep up with us, so she said, "Oh, I'm going back!" Anyway, we got to the bottom and we climbed over a gate and we walked nearly to the village, about three miles away; we were just talking and we walked back and then we saw one of the sixth-formers behind us with Gerald. She had a right go at Bill and was treating him as if he was a kid—"You've got no right to go off on your own"; it's not as if she was his mother or his sister or anything and I got very annoyed, and that was the first boy I went out with.'

Back in London, she and Bill go out on their own to the cinema, to restaurants, dancing or visiting with his family:

'We go to dinner; we went to one or two dances and we didn't really like it. Normally, I either go and I spend all night having a chat to his mother or else he takes me to the pictures or to dinner. Once we walked from the Tower of London to my house. It was quite fun actually because he said he was going to throw me in the Thames! . . . I don't believe in it [equality of paying]. Bill does only when he's broke; he doesn't believe in it otherwise. Last night we went to see *Fantasia*—his mother paid for that. Whenever he takes me out to dinner he doesn't pay—he says to his mum, "I want to take Katherine out to dinner, can I have some money?" So she gives him about £4. We go to Berni's because, you know, they go there a lot, and he takes me there usually and we have steak or scampi or duck; I like the coffee they give you at the end with a mint. . . . Sometimes we just go out and have a Wimpy or something, or we'll go and see a film. But I never normally go to one—he wants to take me out to dinner and he gets really annoyed about it—he'll say "Do you want to have something to eat?" and I'll say "Oh, no, I'm not hungry but if you are, we'll go somewhere and I'll just sit there with a cup of coffee", and he says "NO!" and he gets really stroppy about it.'

The groups of boys and girls cohere as a mixed-sex but non-paired group at the technical drama activity in the youth centre. This is an activity group involved in drama productions and they are all very enthusiastic about it. The activity is available all year and gives them a place to go outside school and home.

In turning to Katherine's *occupational aspirations*, we find her main interest is in design. This builds on her prime interests of drawing and artwork. While she aspires to be a 'second Mary Quant' she is unsure whether she will be able to qualify for the London College of Design (where she wants to train) because she is having difficulty with her O-level requirements. Katherine's conceptions of work and leisure are fused, despite her class, neighbourhood and family backgrounds, where work is usually separated from the enjoyment of leisure. She says:

'I've always liked drawing—I'm not very good but I like it. Some of my designs I've turned out, people like. Not so much the drawing but the design itself; it just kind of appealed to me. It seemed easy work because when I draw, it never is work to me. And I thought, Wow, if I can do that kind of thing for a living. I got some notes on it —I'm not at all business-minded—and there's all this having to see principals and getting O-levels and making sure you see him a year before you want to go—and you know, it just didn't seem right that you should have to go through all the trouble. And then there's this matter of fee: I always expected that the government pays for it but I found out differently. I mean my father, he gets a fair wage but not enough to keep me. . . . I suppose I could get a grant, but I'm not sure. I couldn't understand it, it seems to be so garbled—they talk about everything at once. So, I still want to do it but I doubt if I will do it.

[So what do you think will happen now?]

'Well, I don't know. I don't like offices. I've got a thing against offices. I don't want to work in a shop, because—I'm not saying that I'm a genius, but I think I'm too intelligent to work in shops; it would kill me. If I'd been slimmer and prettier, I would have liked to have done dancing and things like that, but the thing is if you're going to be good at dancing, and if you're fat, like me, it just doesn't look right. Every dance teacher I've ever seen seems to be slim. So that was out. . . . I probably will end up as a teacher. I shall have to overcome all my fears and all that, standing in front of the class; but you know it is frightening just to stand in front of a lot of people.

[Where did you get the idea of being a teacher?]

'From a Forestry Commission man [in Scotland]. He was driving us up to the Forestry Commission and he was telling the teacher that the children have to go twenty to forty miles a day because the teachers won't teach up there in the very small schools. Schools of five or six kids are shutting down and 6-year-olds and 7-year-olds are having to travel thirty-five or forty miles and I just didn't think this was right and I got very militant about it; I decided there and then that I was going to be a teacher. Then I realised that I had to teach 5-year-olds and upwards and I don't like children, so that nearly put the idea out of my mind. But I think I'd suffer just to be some help to society. . . . When I was younger I never used to think about being a help to society—being a dress-designer was something I wanted very much. . . . But I suppose really it's silly to think I want to be famous and that, because I suppose everybody does inside, just sort of everybody knowing what you're doing and people seeing that something; other times I feel, oh, you know, I don't care if I'm going to be a teacher in the back streets of Scotland, if you're going to be of help.'

It seems that Katherine has not been supported in exploring the possibilities of her most deeply felt wish—namely to be a designer. Whether or not her talents are sufficient to become a 'second Mary Quant', she appears to be sufficiently competent and motivated to be able to have some kind of a career in design work, but she is unable in her present environment to find her way through the thicket of requirements, interviews and so on to be able to bring this off. She does not know where to turn to facilitate her wishes. So she starts to think of being a teacher, something she neither likes nor feels she is good at but it would be preferable to being an office worker. The kind of life she wants is one in which enjoyment can be found in all spheres, work and non-work. Being a teacher is more likely to lead to a split between work and non-work and the feeling that work can't be enjoyable. However, the idea of being a teacher has the support in her peer group:

'We're all going to support society. Police lady [Mary], nurse [Ellen], teacher for maladjusted children [Peggy]—I think that's rather good. . . . I shall never have children—they bore me too much. . . . I like looking at them—if I see a little child in a pram or walking along the street, it doesn't matter if it's a pretty child or not, I like looking at other people's children. I buy them sweets and things like this; an hour before my little cousin goes home I get really fond of him, and I buy him things, but when we've got him all week, like we have at the moment, I think that's what turns me off kids, I detest looking after them. Children demand too much of your time. I'd rather just sit there and read or play records or something; but if you're looking after a child, you can't sit there and read because they demand your attention all the time.'

Katherine's idea of working at something she could enjoy, so that her life would be all of a piece, thus seems to be in abeyance for lack of adequate encouragement and guidance. How this guidance could have been provided is a difficult issue. School staff members may be too

harassed to offer a counselling service geared to the problems of developing the interests of ordinary students. Katherine's social class is also
relevant, because supportive as her parents are they simply lack knowledge of how to 'work the academic system' for the necessary information, coaching and access to situations that would facilitate the development of their daughter's current primary life interest.

The implications for the development of Katherine's life interests are
clear. With one set of influences, she may have been able to develop
what she wanted: a life style in which occupation and other meaningful
life interests are fused. Without facilitation, the life style she is likely
to evolve will be compartmentalised. If there are mediating influences,
they are not reaching her effectively at present. The youth centre provides activities which she enjoys and which allow the social aspects of
her development to flourish. It does not come to grips with the issue
of resourcefulness and whole life development.

DEREK was first interviewed when he was an 18-year-old sixth-former
who regularly attended a youth centre. In the six following months, he
was interviewed four times at the youth centre, as was his girlfriend
Ellen. Before the interview series had ended, Derek had left school. He
highlights the transition between adolescence and young adulthood—
the next phase we describe—not only because he leaves school (which
we take as the event formally distinguishing the two phases), but
because his focal preoccupations are increasingly with his identification
with social institutions.

Derek was not very articulate in the interviews except when he was
talking about football, his favourite activity. Three themes were prominent throughout. One was a concern with potential violence in life—
both within himself and in the environment. He described himself as
having a violent temper of which he often lost control, but he felt he
was learning to calm down and think before hitting out blindly. His
concept of leisure relates to this in its emphasis on releasing tension.
Leisure is to 'let off steam', to 'find some action', which means an
opportunity to work off surplus energy.

The second theme, occupational achievement, was striking because
of the incongruity between his ambitions, his behaviour and achievements. There was a conspicuous gap between his fantasies which
emphasised high professional achievement and his poor record, both in
O- and A-level examinations. In sports he has done well, but he
aspires to a line of work where attainment depends on scholastic
accomplishments.

A third theme, also striking for its contradictions, is Derek's familistic
orientation. At first he overstated an anti-family attitude, saying family
life was not that important to him. He spent little time at home and was

vehement about not 'settling down' until he was at least 35, and even then football would come first! By the third interview, six months later, he was using much of his time to design a house for Ellen and himself, envisioning a happy family life in the suburbs—this in spite of Ellen insisting that they were 'just friends' and saw little of each other. It became clear that family life was important to Derek but that he had not yet worked out how to handle his conflicting feelings about it.

In the early interviews Derek projected an image of tough masculinity —keen on football, unafraid to fight, speaking of girls as 'a nice bit of stuff' who would never take precedence over football in his life. He saw himself as a potential architect and in spite of failing his A-levels this did not change, although his self-image in the later interviews softened. But he had problems within himself with which he was struggling—his temper and moods, and his failure to perform academically in a way that could translate his long-term goals into reality:

'Every now and then I get very depressed and sick in the head and I like to go by myself. It comes in periods. Sometimes I like to mix, and sometimes I like to be on my own. At the moment I'm in between.'

Derek presents a picture of a rather confused working-class boy who has developed aspirations for social mobility without the wherewithal to realise them; his enjoyment interests, family relationships and school/work relationships are highly interconnected as he struggles to work through the various conflicts he experiences.

While Derek still lives at home with his parents, his sister (now 22) has married and retains little contact with the family. Derek's father is a self-employed builder subcontractor. His mother works at Derek's old primary school, helping with the children's dinners. His father's hobby is building boats, and although he sells them, he does the work for enjoyment rather than financial gain:

'Wednesday night is his usual night. Building his last one now—it's getting more and more expensive and he isn't getting younger. He's building a 21-foot sailing boat. I think it should last him out. He says he's going to pack it in; I don't know if he's going to keep this boat—we'll see.'

Derek was inarticulate about his relationships with his parents, about which he seemed to have thought little. He recalls that he spent more time at home than he does now but he cannot recollect doing anything specific with his family or going out anywhere with them. He does remember that he was not allowed to play out on the street until he was 9 or 10: 'My parents didn't let me out on the street. I wasn't

allowed to cross the road until I was six.' He did not play with his
sister at all: 'She was the goody-goody and I was the little devil, sort of
thing. Usual thing. We both liked to belt each other [Did she try to
boss you at all?] Tried to—I never let it bother me.' Over the issue of
parents and homework, he reiterated:

'Oh, she was the little goody-goody, she always done her homework
—as far as I was told anyway—don't believe it! Mind you, she's got
a couple of 'O's and an 'A'—one's in geography—ugh!—a subject I
didn't like. Maths, English, British Constitution—good luck to her!
She went to a very good secondary school. She sort of adapted herself
to it, and that's it—I think that most girls do.'

But she left home three or four years ago:

'Mainly because of arguments with the old man—every time she
comes home he sort of puts on the act a bit, that he's pleased to see her;
after she's gone, he couldn't care tuppence . . . when she brought
home her boyfriend, he [dad] was very nice and we told him [boy-
friend] "You were lucky he was in a good mood; if he was in a bad
mood, you wouldn't stand a chance", but he wouldn't believe us.
It was lucky for him that he was in a pretty good mood. You just
can't force him to do anything; we went out to see her at Little-
hampton [where she now lives]—mother's idea!—she wasn't at her
house, she was at Robin's house, her boyfriend—'course he didn't
like that—his mother was there, his brother was there—not that they
could get up to much anyway—but we went over, we were invited in
—"Where's he, the old man?" [she asked] "He's out in the car"—
"Go and offer him a cup of tea." I went out and asked him in, but
he wouldn't come. She went out there—he still wouldn't come. You
could say she got down on her knees and begged him; eventually he
came in, didn't say much, just sort of stood there, grunted; then went
home again.'

Derek perceived his father as strong-minded, awkward and not very
accommodating. He rarely mentioned his mother, saying that he found
it easier to talk to his father although Derek also had more rows with
him: 'When I was younger, I used to be frightened of him—he seemed
to dominate the place, he was a he-man sort of thing.' His father seems
to be his model for the stereotyped masculinity he now shows, and
the racy humour which goes with the toughness:

'When I met my girlfriend, she wondered where I got some of the
ways I acted from. When she met my father she found out—all
these quick jokes, turning one thing into another, it all comes pat—I
never get the chance to do it at home 'cos he's the master.'

Derek recalls that his father took an interest in his education, and checked up on his homework:

'The children rush through it as fast as possible in order to go out—"Finished! I'm going out to play!" "Let's have a look—punctuation, spelling—all wrong, do it again!" So you finally get the idea, do it correctly once, take your time—that's it. Mind you, I never used to do much homework.'

Neither Derek nor his father wanted him to go to a grammar school:

'It was being rebuilt at the time and it seemed a good place to come. My teacher wanted me to go to a grammar school and I told him where to go. I told him I didn't want to go to a grammar school. [Why was that?] You're joking! I saw a television programme once about it—I can understand a simple question—two and two—somebody puts his hand up—"Four". "Why is it four?" It's a good question, but you've just got to say, well, those two numbers when they're added up become four whether you like it or not. But when he couldn't answer, the teacher really had a go at him, called him out in front of the rest, told him: "You're here to learn—learn! Go and stand in the corner." That put me off grammar school for life. And my old man, he says, "You're not going to a grammar school." I said "Thank you".'

While Derek and his father were in accord about secondary school, Derek felt that his father was often inconsistent:

'My old man, when I started work, he says, "Well, it's your life"—five minutes later: "And another thing, you'd better pack up going to the youth centre!" I spend more time up there than ever—well, I used to; I never stay at home at all. Sometimes I'd come to school in the morning, play football after school, couldn't be bothered to go home because I'd go straight out again, and I wouldn't get home till about ten. "Where you been?"—"Out"—that kind of thing.'

However, Derek seems to have had less conflict with his father than his sister had; he thinks that parents worry more about girls and are stricter with them. Still, when he was 15 or 16 he began to resent his father exercising authority over him; for instance he used to 'get on to him' about having his hair cut, but Derek ignored this until it began to get in his eyes at football and he missed some goals.

The family moved house when Derek was 16; he willingly helped his father redecorate and during school holidays he worked for his father for pay. He does not have any regular allowance, but found his father reasonable about giving him money: 'I'd ask for a couple of bob and he'd give me ten bob, no trouble at all.' Derek feels his relationship with his father has improved as his father has given him more freedom. They have established a rough, man-to-man relationship; for instance if his 'old man' were to 'thump' him, he would 'thump' him back:

> 'He brought me up hard, because it's a kill-or-be-killed world; when I was younger, I got into more trouble than enough. I didn't tell him about it, and he just told me one day, he didn't think I had it in me, but he's found that I have. I didn't go running to him saying "I got into trouble, have a go at him!" sort of thing; I just go and sort it out for myself.'

Derek's father's attitude persists. A short time before the interviews Derek had occasion to 'sort out' a boy who had been giving Ellen unwanted attention:

> 'One night when Ellen was walking home from school some kid tried to be fresh with her; one of my mates with his girlfriend came across the road and sort of told him to shove off but he wouldn't go; I was told about it by one of the others. I was trying to get it out of her who it was, but she wouldn't tell me 'cos she knew I'd kick his head in, or I'd get my head kicked in. Anyway, when we put a show on up here, he happened to turn up. *She* didn't tell me it was him, but one of the others did; he tried it again—I kept myself scarce, 'cos I was hoping he'd try it again, and he did, and she was almost in tears, so I just took him outside and gave him a hiding. I went home—bloody nose, split lip and a cut eye; and my old man says "What's happened to you?" and I said "Would you believe a lamp-post or a door?" "No." "Er—tripping over chairs?" "No!" I says, "All right, I've had a fight, OK?" He says, "You got any other injuries?" I says "No." He says, "Good, get cleaned up." '

They have disagreed about Derek's future; although his father wanted him to do his homework and get some O- and A-levels, he wanted Derek to get a job when he left school at 18 and not go to college to become an architect: 'He is trying to get me a job, encourage me, but at the moment I'm not interested.' His father's ambivalence is clear. He wants his son to better himself but he has the small working-builder's scorn for architects:

> 'He hasn't got a good word for architects—the ones he's met don't know anything. They draw up the drawing and expect the workman to get on with it. Some of the drawings I've had to do, I'd like to change them, but I can't, you know—it's just that I can visualise how it's got to go, it's going to be bloody hard on the poor workman who's got to do it. . . .
>
> [Did your father fancy the idea of you following in his job then?]

'He told me that if I ever came into the building trade I'd have to be an electrician. Make myself useful. He calls the building trade a disease—there's no guarantee of work, you see. . . . He left it up to me.'

[Did your mother have any ideas what you might be?]

'Not really, well it's my life—they keep saying that to me. Mind you, if I was to pack in the job now and go on the dole, he'd give me a right rollocking, the old man! But he'd still say it's my life.'

When Derek failed to qualify as a full-time architectural student and began work as a trainee, it seemed to satisfy both his father and himself. It put him to work at something more mundane and postponed for a long time the professionalisation that would separate father and son socially.

Derek's grandparents are now dead, but he recalls his maternal grandfather whom the family visited annually:

'I used to get on very well with him. He just used to take an interest in me. If he saw I was sulking around the house, he'd come and ask "What's wrong?"—tried to cheer me up—go out for a walk on the sea-front.'

But sometimes he preferred to be left alone when he was in a bad mood and then, as he got older, his grandparents 'seemed to try to mother you more, sort of look after you more, and after a while you get fed up with it'.

At the time of the interviews Derek was between the stage of dependence on his family and the independence that entry into work signifies. His father would still 'have a go at him' about getting his hair cut, his parents and uncle would still quizz him, half jocularly, about his interest in girls. Financially he has yet to 'cut the cord'. 'At the moment I'd like to be independent but I don't want to open a bank account, I put in through my mother's. It's pay-day soon!' He feels that he still earns too little to live away from home. He also finds it difficult to make his pay last out the month. He gives his mother a couple of pounds a week for his keep, and is paying back some of the money he borrowed from his father when he was at school. He says that he doesn't really mind living at home because he cuts himself off mentally: 'I can sit anywhere, I can ignore everything and everybody, so it doesn't affect me. Someone says something—you just don't hear it—they come over and give you a shake. That's it—cut yourself off.' When at home he draws, listens to records, reads books and just sits around. But evenings he is mostly 'out'.

When talking of his *school history*, Derek recalls that he went to nursery school, but remembers few details of the experience: 'it was OK, but there was nothing to it, just lark around; I suppose it's just to take you off your mother's hands so she's got more time.' Derek was asked if he found it easy to mix with people at primary school: 'Not at first, I did make friends with two or three.' In general, he feels that he has always been 'a bit of a loner' and didn't make any really close friends. Derek's feelings about primary school are mixed. He feels that it was 'educational'; at first it was half play and half learning, later more learning, but not in a way that he could really get interested in. He said that he had often been bored and thought a lot about 'how I could get off school'. He didn't like the teachers:

'They didn't have no control; stand there ranting and raving and shouting their heads off, getting no response—at the time it was all good fun. [But you wanted to get away?] Yes, I used to play hookey quite a bit. [Bored?] Yes, the things they done were so sort of straightforward and drab, boring, the lot, you were pushed into the same thing over and over again. I was always getting told off for [not eating] school dinners—I couldn't stand them.'

One thing he did enjoy at primary school was football; he first took this up when he was about 9:

'They had a primary school team, and as soon as I was old enough I went to the team practice; I don't know if I was any good but apparently they thought I was and so I got into the team. I dunno why—I never did any playing. We'd watch any junior school, lower school—they just push the ball about—when I look back at that, it seemed marvellous!'

Derek becomes noticeably more animated when discussing football. He also likes swimming. On balance, his views about secondary school are very mixed. Derek felt that the first and second years were mainly spent in 'mucking about' but were interesting because there were many things to do. The third and fourth years were 'boring' because there was a lot of repetition, and the fifth and sixth years became more interesting because they did new things again. He complained that not enough work was set in his A-level metalwork class, so that it was difficult when it came to the examination. But he praises the teacher who was also the warden of the youth centre for his tolerance when they wanted to let off steam after a day in school and became rowdy in the evenings: 'He sometimes really gets at us, you know, but he takes it all in good fun, I'll say that for him.' On the other hand, he criticised a games teacher for pushing him into doing a long-distance run which he could not do well. Achievement in sport is central to Derek's self-respect and he resented being persuaded into something he could not do well:

'Last year they pushed me into the mile [race] and I didn't have a chance of winning 'cos the champion was running and he won. I came in fourth and there were only about six running. They were more or less making up the numbers; they got me into the cross-country run—that was the biggest mistake of my life. I'll never forgive him for that, the games teacher; he said it's only a 2½-miles course—it was 7½ miles, I found out in the end. He admitted that it was a mistake. I said, it's the longest 2½ miles I've ever run! I could've kicked him!'

Derek's relationship with teachers is best described in the context of his changing attitude towards working at school. Initially he enjoyed 'messing about'—and testing the limits. For example:

'See how far you could push the teacher before they crack or send you out to the head teacher for a bit of stick. The best of it is, you wait outside the head of the school's room for about half an hour so you miss the lesson anyway.'

After 'mucking about' initially he decided to work for his future and this made him make a *distinction between his work and leisure*:

'When I was younger—in my spare time—I used to muck around all the time—couldn't be bothered. Soon as I got into the third year at school, I just changed completely. I realised what I had to do with my spare time, I didn't sort of mingle it with my school time, so it all gets balanced out.'

He was 14 when this happened; it was after a parent–teacher's discussion:

'I was listening to the parents talking to the teachers, listening to both. It went through one ear and out the other, but that night I got down to thinking about it, my future. I've got to work for it, no one can help me . . . that's when it started to sink in! When I realised what it was all about, I tried to drum some education into me—it was going to be important for the rest of your life. One of my teachers pointed out that people with O- and A-levels get further than those without; and there's more people without than there is with; stand a better chance if you've got a better education. I just got to thinking about this: "Sod this, I'm going to climb up the ladder a bit—I ain't going to be a road sweeper or something like this." Once I become an architect, you know, get my RIBA, I can sweep roads for all I care; I've got my qualifications, I can always find a job.'

Derek indicated that home life affects attitudes to education too. He said that his parents:

'. . . couldn't understand me maths for a start! So it wasn't worth asking them. But you know, if you notice, quite a few of the parents let their kids run wild, yet some of them have got the potential to work. Now if their parents got them down to work, they'd stand a good chance, but half of them don't. They become troublemakers and hooligans at football. Yet one bloke, his father's a jeweller, during the week he's the nicest person in the road but on a Saturday afternoon I wouldn't go near him—he'd kill you!'

Looking back, he said that although there was homework in his school the teachers did not push one to do it, 'it was really up to you'. They would push for a couple of weeks and then give up, so it was up to you to make the effort if you wanted to get on.

Derek took four O-levels: maths, physics, technical drawing and engineering, and failed maths and physics. When interviewed he was working for maths and physics again, and in addition English, though he seemed uncertain whether to take language or literature. He was also working for two A-levels, art and metalwork. He enjoyed his A-level subjects, but he did not like maths: 'I like art, for instance. How you feel, you work; whereas in maths, you're just set a problem and you've got to work it out whether you like it or not.' When he was seen six months later, he was asked what had happened with his examinations:

'Not very good, I'm afraid! One I failed, and one I got an O-level pass for. The art I failed and I've got the O-level for the metalwork one. There's only one thing I haven't got yet—my maths paper's gone astray—they're holding an inquiry into it at the moment. They put me down as not sitting the exam. Yet according to the register—the teachers are swearing I was there, they saw me take the exam. Just gone missing. [That must be worrying?] No, as long as they find it— I know I've got to sit it again if they don't. They won't give me the O-level otherwise.'

Derek said that he could confide in the teacher who is also warden of the youth centre. He does not feel as free to discuss his problems with his parents:

'Well, to start with, I've never been able to talk to my parents about me failing A-level art until just recently. I was a bit worried about how they were going to take it and when I found out about my maths paper going astray, I said "I failed my A-level art anyway". "Oh? Well, never mind. Sit it again if you want to." Suppose I will in time. I still do a bit of art. [For pleasure, or to get the qualification?] More 'cos I enjoy it, but I still want the qualification.'

Derek gets depressed at his poor performance at examinations:

'When something gets me down I like to be on my own. Usually when I get a bad result in my exams, I feel really bad, but for some unknown reason this year it hasn't got me down—I just took it as it comes. The only one I was worried about was maths, and that hasn't really got me down.'

He hopes to continue his education towards an architectural qualification in his spare time by going to evening classes three nights a week.

Derek has had a series of *interests* which developed in overlapping fashion, though he remembers little about his earliest years. He did not like to read much, but sometimes used to paint—'mainly the back yard!' he joked. He had always liked art. He began to take an interest in football as a supporter of Arsenal when he was about 7, and liked to be taken to watch their matches with his uncle. When he was old enough to go alone, it was difficult to find the money when the price of admission went up to 50p and he was still at school. When he was 9 he played in a primary school team, and when he was at secondary school he played for a pub league, again in connection with his uncle. In the early years, before he went to comprehensive school, he liked to 'muck about'. His description of 'mucking about' is similar to that of the other working-class boys in our series, and the working-class girls in the area-based study:

'We used to go over the fields a lot, breaking the rules, just for the kick of it; these park-keepers chasing you, which is a good laugh really. We used to go round causing riots, shouting our heads off till people started complaining—we used to tell them where to go. We used to have three or four of them chasing us down the streets.'

In school holidays he used to hang about with friends on the streets or indoors, or go to the pictures. He recalls one person in the local neighbourhood he used to visit in the holidays:

'Where I used to live, there was a battery shop on the corner; used to go round there, have a chat with the old boy. Used to make batteries up, put all the terminals together. I was fascinated by the work—he pours the lead or whatever it is, and in three or four seconds it's set.'

'Mucking about' is partly curiosity about what is going on and how things work, and partly it is the search for excitement and what Derek called 'action':

'Just walk around and look for places—sort of go in and if they weren't no good we'd move off. Discos and places like that. An awful lot of people think they're the best thing going, but they're not. . . . Working off energy . . . physical. I'm more or less sitting down all day at the drawing board; I really get depressed and sick in the head, so to speak.'

Part of the 'action' is the sheer moving about in and out of places where there are young people, noise, music, excitement. He describes the sort of release that the discos give:

> 'Freedom to do what you want, within reason. Then again there's a tense atmosphere, as if something's going to happen; I've had this a few times. . . . You just can't concentrate on what you're doing. If you're dancing, you're always looking over your shoulder to see if someone's coming to have a go at you. If that happens, half the time I just walk away, go out and go for a walk.'

'Mucking about' also has a sense of potential violence. Although he does not go out looking for a fight, he is always aware of the possibility that someone might 'have a go' at him. Derek perceives violence in himself and the environment; he is always prepared for trouble. When he's walking around the West End on his own, for instance, he feels:

> 'as if someone's going to have a go at me. Sometimes they do. It's what you expect in that area; gang of about four or five; there's going to be some trouble. So you don't run or you've had it. You just keep on walking and hope for the best. Half the time, they're just as scared as you are and they just pass you by because they don't know what [weapon] you're carrying.'

He says that he does not enjoy fighting, yet it helps to satisfy his recurrent need to 'let off steam'. This form of tension release has persisted since leaving school: 'If I've really been got at during the day, anyone who comes up and says something, I immediately kick a hole in the roof, it's all the fun and noise of a slanging match; we all feel better for it afterwards.' Although he prefers not to fight unless pushed to it, when fighting he enjoys it:

> 'Because I get the feeling that I didn't start it, they pushed me into it. Sort of "God help them—they can take the worst of it". But I don't sort of walk into it. It's all their fault if there's any broken limbs or anything. Half the time, four or five of them don't know who they're hitting; if you crawl out from underneath, they carry on fighting each other—just stand there in the corner watching them. Get a good laugh from them.'

Aside from street-fighting Derek's main way of relaxing the physical tensions he feels so acutely is through *football*: 'you can always find excitement up at the lot . . . not only playing it, but watching it too. You can get into the game by watching it.' In contrast to the peripatetic search for excitement—which tended to concentrate on Saturday nights —football had weekend and weekday outlets in school and 'free time' groups. It has provided his most consistent enjoyment:

'It's hard work but you think of it as a great achievement if you win; if you set your heart to win, you know, you won't be disappointed. . . . I've known quite a few goalkeepers get out of my way rather than stop one of my balls—quite a few say "What you got, steel toe-caps?" It gives you reassurance that you're not losing your touch.'

Keeping physically fit is an important function of football. When an injury kept him off the field for a few weeks, he felt that he became physically unfit and 'fell apart'; he felt terrible till he had played a few hard games again and got back on form. He did not want to play for the school football team because they wanted him to stick in one position and he liked to change around. He began playing for a pub-league team that his uncle was in while he was still at school, but gave this up because the others did not take it as seriously as he did:

'I'm out of that now. They wanted me to sign up again but they used me too much last season. They sort of took advantage because I like playing football; just weren't getting nowhere, the team and all that; not that I'm exceptionally good but I like to play with a good team. These ones couldn't care two monkeys about it . . . all they thought about was "let's get the game over and have a drink!" '

Sometimes there was an outbreak of fighting, but characteristically, Derek emphasised that he fought only when he was pushed:

'Well, you just feel better for it; get it out of your system. It all boils up. Like when I used to play at school, football, you get kids saying "You can't play for nuffin!", and it just builds slowly up and up, and the first thing you do is change sides, if they're on the other side, and you slowly belt the ball at them, and work it across till you get someone in the face—"Oh, we'll get you for that!" and just pile in, that's it.'

Derek also enjoyed swimming and badminton. He learned to dive by accident when he was pushed off a board; he entered a couple of competitions but was disqualified for losing his temper—if someone says he is no good, he tends to turn round and 'thump' them. He used to enjoy badminton but gave it up after leaving school. At the end of his school career he used to come in early to practise darts for the match between the staff and the sixth form; in previous years each side had won once, and he was very keen that the sixth form should win this year. He enjoyed the 'constructive competition' with the authorities.

In his last three years at school, Derek attended the youth centre, taking an interest in technical drama, particularly lighting. Though he enjoyed productions, football remained his main interest. He liked the youth centre as somewhere he could sit around and chat with his friends, or go to the art room because he could do what he wanted there or to be alone.

An interest which is currently important started a year or two ago—motorbikes and the country. When we first met Derek, he had had a bike for just under a year, though it had only been on the road for about three months. He had taken it apart and rebuilt it, but 'the problem is the thieving arabs round where I live' will steal any part you turn your back on. He enjoyed working on the bike although he does not like getting his hands dirty; he does not regard maintenance and tinkering about with it as 'work'. He used to go to motor maintenance classes at a local adult education institute; he did not think much of the teacher but picked up a lot of useful tips from the other people in the class. He was looking forward to buying a better bike when he started work and had some money. Derek describes the enjoyment he gets from riding the motorcycle:

> 'Well, you have time to think again but you also have to concentrate. I have come off this bike quite a few times—once seriously, the others not too bad; you sort of get up, have a look at the bike, say "Sod it" and carry on. . . . I still don't like doing right-hand corners because I came off at one. I always slow down. Left-hand corners all right. [What else do you enjoy?] Fresh air. Out in the country; with a car you don't get much of it. The only thing against bikes is in the winter, it's very cold.'

Derek's friends share the joys of motorcycling with him: 'If there's something important going on, they'll always call round for me. We've all got bikes—they also used to come to this school and they live local.' They are not the leather-jacketed, Hell's Angels type of bike enthusiasts; nor do they use their bikes to play 'chicken' or in irresponsible ways. Derek says that he wears a helmet and does not go fast except where there are clear stretches of road. They meet at the local pub and it has been a fairly regular weekend activity to have an outing together: 'One Saturday, just for the hell of it, we went down to Southend. This was just something to do. We didn't get back till eight o'clock that evening.' They have informal races on the open stretches, seeing which bike can overtake the others and compare notes on size, speed, maintenance problems, strategies of purchase, payment and dealing with agents.

The pub did not play much part in Derek's life; he liked to go for a drink with his father on Wednesday evenings when the 'old man' regularly went after building his boat, which Derek sometimes helped him with, and at Sunday lunchtimes 'if I'm up in time'.

Since Derek has left school and started work his pattern of 'free time' enjoyment has changed. Saturday night is no longer the all-important night out that it used to be. His pursuit of enjoyment is more spread out over the week:

> 'To everyone at school it's Saturday, especially if they've got a Saturday job—get their money and it's a big spending spree, oh boy! You lose that. During the week it sort of evens out. Whereas before, you really let go on a Saturday. Once you've left work, it's up to you where you want to go; even during the lunch hours you can go out. And it's spread out evenly.'

Derek said that he feels the need for 'action' less now than when he was at school because he is busy with study and work he does at home voluntarily.

At the time of the study, the courtship of Derek and Ellen was an important part of the interaction of Ellen and her girlfriends, and an important part of Derek's development. They went around together on Saturdays, participating during the week at the technical drama classes together with others at the youth centre. Derek was 18 and Ellen 15. Ellen's parents began to get anxious about her getting 'involved', and her mother asked whether there was any sex in the relationship and whether Ellen knew what the dangers were. Derek's father and uncle would just make remarks such as 'Don't do anything I wouldn't do' or 'take care', with a sly wink.

While at the start Derek maintained his air of braggadocio—stating that he would not let a girl interfere with his football (they'd have to carry him off the field with both legs broken before he'd stop that)—he changed his attitude as time went on. He began to get involved and she sought to withdraw. With her friends the talk was all about 'packing him up', being fed up with his possessiveness—'Thank God he's left school, because at breaks he'd always be hanging around—so at least I get my breaks to myself now.' Yet Ellen did not want to break away completely. Something about his violence seemed to fascinate her. She thought of him as a typical skinhead and liked the idea of his fighting for her when unwanted advances were made by another boy at school.

When they were together, the main questions were where to go and what to do. Cinemas and cafés were the main places they could 'just be together', without it costing too much. Discos were expensive, and though they went to one pop festival together, these were infrequent and also expensive. Derek still felt the need to 'let off steam', apart from the times he could do this playing football or riding his motorbike. He was losing his enthusiasm for discotheques, which he had previously enjoyed, when he wanted to use up surplus energy. He said that he had smoked pot:

> '. . . quite a few times but I still got the same effect—nothing, complete blankness—so I couldn't be bothered. It's a waste of money

anyway. I've got self-control—like with smoking, I proved to myself that I could give up something, or stop myself taking something.'

The theme throughout his enjoyment career had been the evolution of ways of coping with physical energy and tension. At first it was more or less random 'mucking about' with near-conscious provocation of physical fights; then it became channelled into football, technical drama and motorcycling. The part played by courtship—real and fantasied—in his effort to control and channel the aggressive energies has been marked.

After failing his A-levels, Derek got a job as a trainee-architect through a local Youth Employment Service officer. At the time of the third interview he had been *at work* two or three weeks and he described his initial response: 'A bit nervous at first. But when I found out that quite a few of them were about the same age as me, I settled in very quick.' He says that he was not really keen to go to work and would have preferred staying at school. Having left school, he feels that he has 'lost contact with quite a few people'. It is a long haul to look forward to—seven years—before he can hope to complete his qualifications this way. The content of his day-time activities seems little changed to him: 'It still hasn't struck me, now, that I'm at work. Because I used to do a lot of drawing at school—it's virtually the same thing. The only difference is that I'm pulling in money at the same time.' He doesn't feel that he is treated differently or has changed as a person in his work role yet. He gets depressed if people at work belittle what he feels is his main strength as a potential architect, namely knowing a bit about building:

'They think I know nothing about the building side of architecture; but my old man's in the building trade and during the summer holidays I used to go and work there, so I know more than most of them. Except for one; he knows all about plumbing. I can't argue with him.'

Sometimes he gets very bored at work:

'If it's very slack, you just sit around doing nothing. Occasionally get a drawing that you have to alter. There's all these jobs—we get drawings back to check and revise, then we send them to the site engineer; they're on strike and they stop them. We can't do any more until they come back.'

Doing nothing was hardest for Derek, whether at school or at work. The football team at work helped him to become accepted:

'Well, I've a team at work, I'm glad to say! It took me a while to get into it, but I'm in it now. As usual they're always a bit dubious about newcomers. But luckily I had a good game first of all. So I'm in.'

Could Derek ever cut himself off and go into his own world, when work was slack, like he did at home?:

'I daren't! Because my month's trial is just up and I'm expecting a letter to say a month's notice or I'm staying on, so I've still got to play my cards right; you know, no time to go for walks, I've got to look busy—it's difficult sometimes. Rub out a line that's already there and draw it again; and rub it out and draw it in again!'

Nearly six weeks later, the routine of work and study had become more established; he started to attend college three evenings a week and he was busy at work as the builders' strike had ended. He was having no trouble with his temper at work or with people 'getting on to him' as he had felt at school.

After two months at work Derek's career ambitions were unchanged. Although he found it hard to study in the evenings, particularly for resitting his O-level mathematics—an essential qualification—he was undeterred. He does some work of his own at home, trying to design his own house, and thinks of 'settling down'.

Analysis of case studies: social influences impinging on young people and the proliferation of their preoccupations

In addition to the three young people described, we interviewed an additional nine and some of their family members and teachers. These were selected to provide a broad range of young people from the London area. While this limits our direct information to situations prevailing in a large metropolitan setting, for the purposes of our exploration this is not a crucial limitation. For understanding the processes associated with the channelling of focal preoccupations into meaningful life interests and then into activities, and how the interests articulate with facilities provided, we believe that the insights derived from these case studies may be applicable to a wider range of situations.

While we presented only three case studies in detail above—Jenny, Katherine and Derek—we draw on materials from all twelve and from the literature on young people in the discussion that follows.

Our data illustrates how the focal preoccupation of young people is the quest for a satisfying sense of personal identity. We see a proliferation of preoccupations associated with this quest as young people sample the world around them in a kaleidoscopic fashion. Each of those interviewed indicates that this preoccupation is both a conscious concern and that it operates at a deeper level. Awareness of the proliferation of young people's preoccupations conveys some understanding of the search for enjoyment or gratification in actual experiences.

Different *influences* surround each person. In analysing the cases we use the framework of focal preoccupations and show how the influences impinging on the different individuals channel their expression into the observed behaviour patterns of each. We first review the influences already discussed in the literature on young people.

To consider *family influences* first, it is notable that adolescence is usually a problematic period in family life; there are few general cultural norms about adolescents' relations with their families, and both parents and their young may find themselves in turmoil. While adolescents do not 'need' parental care in the same way as when they were younger, they are not entirely independent of their families; most live at home at the beginning of the phase, but by the end, many have left. Till now, most have experienced family members as central figures in their lives, and extensions outwards to teachers, friends and 'mates' in the other sectors relate in some way to the family paradigm in nature and quality. Most adolescents are busy working out the best balance between attachments to home and family, and attachments to others.

At some point during this period, young people tend to earn their own money—at first at part-time jobs, later, if they leave school early, at a full-time job. In many families contribution to the cost of food and lodging is expected from earnings and there may be family pressure for the young person to leave school at the earliest possible point.

Whether to live at home or not is an issue that occupies the minds and emotions of many adolescents and their parents. While the parental home is a shelter, saves money and may offer warm and supportive family relationships, it is the place where one was a child. Even if one is not closely supervised and controlled any longer, being reminded of the child role is difficult to avoid and is the last thing most adolescents want. On the family side, there is enormous variation in the capacity of parents to alter their relationships with a growing child to accommodate the latter's changing capacities and interests (including his/her overt sexuality).

Theodore Lidz (1968), Derek Miller (1966) and others who have written about adolescents in the family context have stressed the difficulties on both sides: the adolescents have to give up idealised conceptions of their parents and parental values (as well as of the gratifications of being looked after as an infant in the parental home); and the parents have to learn to relate to an independent-minded, often rebellious, sometimes seductive individual whose youth and situation may be envied. The authority and autonomy conflicts are one aspect of what is generally meant by the *generation gap*.

The 'generation gap' has been used to indicate various phenomena. Another aspect involves rebelliousness and a perception of breakdown in communication and sharing of values across generations. This phenomenon is very characteristic in family life at this stage of the life cycle. It relates in part to the separation aspects of the developmental process, whereby the younger party asserts that established values are dull, boring, stupid, reactionary or simply useless. Many observers have noted that if the parents can tolerate the negativistic phase, there often follows a period in which the young person adopts very similar values—but as his own. Eisenstadt has stressed the sociological importance of this process in the reassertion of values from generation to generation—a necessary link for socio-cultural continuity (Bengston, 1970; Eisenstadt, 1956; Rosenmayr, 1972).

The value conflict is also expressed outside the family context, as when pressures are exerted by a younger group, say students, to get an older group, say administrators, to do something they want. The particular expression of intergenerational conflict may be seen as a manifestation of young people's heightened moral sensitivity, or as an irrational rebelliousness against a society that has overstressed parental permissiveness.

In the family context the emotional problems aroused at this stage may remain fairly covert or become more overt. The ways in which the turbulence is dealt with may have critical and lasting effects on subsequent ability to be resourceful about developing meaningful life interests for both the young person and the parents. Parents vary in how explicit they make the problems and how able they are to deal with them constructively. The main issues that arise can be presented as shown in Table 1 (overleaf).

There is considerable support for the idea that adolescent development is related to family environment; apparently the development is best served by a balance between permissiveness and punitive control (Devereaux, 1970; Elder, 1971). The good family is one, according to Kovar, which is good to start out from (encouraging new ventures and interests, not clinging on) and which creates the feeling that it is good to go back to (Kovar, 1968). For the young person, the problem of achieving autonomy may present special problems in a particularly tight-knit, as well as in a particularly restrictive family. Breaking away against strong ties may have to be done explosively. Parents who are indifferent present fewer constrictions but they also present a less rewarding set of relationships, and fewer family bases for the development of a range of meaningful life interests. Nevertheless, remarkably little is known about how parents and adolescents either share interests, or mesh their diverse interests in the context of family life to sustain a 'good family' base. Douvan and Adelson feel that 'basic solidarity between generations will continue to develop' around points of sharing, like mealtimes together (Douvan and Adelson, 1966). The family

Table 1   *Issues in adolescent development*

Issues	From parents' viewpoint	From children's viewpoint
Limits	How permissive to be? In what way? Phasing? Hours? Friends? Use of stimulants? Sex? etc. Where to be adamant; where to be indirect; where to lay off?	How far to press the boundaries set? How daring to be about doing things *probably* dis-approved of? What to battle over and what to bend with?
Communications	How much to probe into the children's private lives? How much to discuss one's own personal problems?	How much to tell about what actually goes on (especially when it may be near or over the limits set)?
Participation	How much to allow children's participation in decision-making? How much to expect their participation in the family chores? What to do together?	How much to participate? How much to respond? With what spirit? What time and activities to spend with parents?
Programming	How much to organise the children's behaviour? How much guidance to offer without being asked? When? How?	How to handle parental organising (controlling; fussing; protecting; caring) efforts? What to accept, how, when and with what loopholes?
Distancing	When to keep 'hands off'? How to stay clear without implying you don't care?	How and when to opt out of family things? How to distinguish between 'their' (parental) concerns and 'my' concerns without too much guilt?
Sibling relations	What sort of sibling relationship to encourage? How much co-operation? Segregation? Constructive rivalry? Differences versus favouritism?	How close to be with siblings? Can they be friends? Their friends' friends? Can they keep a secret?

integrative potentials of leisure provisions, both in the home and in programmes offered by the public and private sectors, may facilitate this, if effectively exploited.

School influences provide important constraints and opportunities for young people. The educational system provides a potentially valuable structure within which interests may be aroused and cultivated. Even more important, people's resourcefulness to develop their own interests may be developed. If schools are too orientated to academic or vocational goals, to examinations and grades, they may stifle or divert the awakening of more personally meaningful interests except in those who attune their personal values to those of the regimen. The sense of wonder, curiosity and delight that comes from the enjoyment of activities, is often lost when performance pressures are imposed on them. Some 'progressive' educational establishments try to combine rigour with enjoyment.

Other factors are critical for the school experience. Most research has been concentrated on the social class variable, charting the constraints on students from working-class homes (where the speech codes are discrepant from those valued in schools, where the cultural objects and channels are constricted and the pushes toward high aspiration are feeble or even negative). There is much to support the idea that children from middle-class backgrounds are more likely to be attuned to the school's value system. Aside from being more likely to develop personally meaningful interests within the school, middle-class children are less likely to leave school early. They are less likely, therefore, to fall prey to the paralysis in interest development that frequently attends early school-leaving (cf., for example, Bernstein, 1967; Bone, 1972; Maizels, 1970; Morton-Williams *et al.*, 1968).

Nevertheless, generalisations from statistical tendencies tend to blur the presence of significant minority patterns. Sugarman, in a study of secondary school students, found that the relationship between IQ, achievement motivation and middle-class values has to be heavily qualified. With IQ held constant, class background seemed to have negligible impact on performance (Sugarman, 1966; 1968). The values critical for achievement, individualism, activism and future orientation are not exclusive to middle-class families. There are many middle-class school children who are passive, hedonistic and present-orientated. Similarly there are many working-class students who are ambitious, activist, future-orientated and who perform well.

The present academic system emphasises achievement performance and tends to polarise reactions to students. Those who cultivate interests appropriate to career advancement are 'good', those who do not tend to be devalued in school. This is one of the basic arguments in the 'de-schooling' position which emphasises rather the importance of each

individual's development (Illich, 1971). Where the student leaves a disliked school to enter an unattractive situation, he may have the advantage of continuity (as Carter and others have emphasised), but these
can hardly be seen as opportunities for developing positive life orientations (Carter, 1966; Wolfenden, 1960).

The question is how to revise school experiences. De-schooling is a
provocative idea. Gabor advocates more attention to what he calls the
'ethical quotient' by which he seems to mean the type of 'character
building' long emphasised by many old-fashioned voluntary bodies, but
in a secular context (Gabor, 1972; Smith, 1968). We argue that, while
the development of a moral or ethical sense is vital, perhaps even more
relevant—and more attractive to young people who resent 'moralising'
—is the need for the cultivation of a *resourcefulness quotient*. This would
emphasise the capacity to develop interests that are meaningful and
the capacity to carry them through to realisation in activities. Understanding the preoccupations that are pressing on the individual may aid
him to channel them into interests. While much of the stimulus to
develop a high 'resourcefulness quotient' comes from family background, it would seem that the school's mission is not only to inculcate
skills that can later be transferred to occupational tasks, but which can
also be transferred for the enjoyment of life. This is what the French
mean in their distinction between *savoir faire* and *savoir vivre*.

School-leaving, particularly for those who leave early, is a very mixed
experience in terms of young people's preoccupations. On the one
hand, early school-leavers quickly become financially independent. On
the other hand, they tend to obtain jobs at the low end of the occupational totem pole and are liable to be treated like 'dogsbodies', with
relatively chronic low esteem, low pay and infantilisation on the job.
They may feel resentful and relatively powerless in their low positions
at work. In their time away from work they may not be as accepted in
the various community activity groups as they would like—the sudden
absence of school facilities being experienced often as an abrupt withdrawal.

One local authority recreation officer described a characteristic problem for such a school-leaver in relation to recreational facilities as
follows:

'He may have come from a family that is perfectly good from the
point of view of love and care but which may not have had much
experience in relation to the contemporary range of clubs, and may
not have taught him very much about how to relate to adults who
have other kinds of interests. His neighbourhood may not have provided many facilities like clubs. He has to find out about what there
is, and try to guess what it would be like in them so as to match his

own interests—usually based on no experience—with what they offer. He has to make an approach, explain his interest to people who are ordinarily much older than himself and not necessarily keen to have youngsters in, particularly if they do not seem to be dressed right, or to talk right, or show that they are really keen. Their experience with exploring such situations rather than awakening their latent interests and aspirations may close them off for ever.'

If the resentment at work spills over into 'free' time without finding outlets, this may feed the tendency to be against 'the system', to become delinquent and the like. These are alternative interest channels for the preoccupations of young people.

People's involvements outside the family and the school/work situations bring them in touch with what we call *'community influences'*. These influences may be exerted self-consciously by community agencies, or they may exist simply as a property of being *there*. People experience them through the networks in which they operate, and the level at which 'the community' impact is most effective for awakening interests varies with people and their groups. Some young people with the will, the knowledge and the means may explore far and wide— travel the Orient, America, the Mediterranean and across the Sahara, 'just to see' what is there and to meet others on the same circuit. Others will be most susceptible to community influences at a very local level, and yet others may be equally responsive to a world community, 'cosmic' issues, their national environment and their residential neighbourhood.

There are different ways of looking at young people's responses to their environments. The model from Matza's analysis—though now dated—is useful, as it emphasises the network element. He distinguishes between 'conformist' and 'non-conformist' styles. The conformists use available facilities—at school, in clubs and at work—in ways that are socially approved in the adult world that provides them. They 'play the game' in life as on the playing fields. The non-conformists, into which category many adolescents fall at least transiently as part of the normal developmental process, he describes as falling into three types—the bohemian, the delinquent and the radical (Matza, 1964). Explorations, particularly by the bohemian groups, often carry young people to the edges of, and beyond, what established society will accept. Some variant young groups make a point of exploring and 'going as far out' psychologically as possible, to 'edge city', the very boundaries of sanity and existence (Spate and Levin, 1972). For a while, Timothy Leary lent the patina of academic psychology to the quest for ecstasy through drugs; and the Maharishi and his backers have lent the patina of oriental religion to the quest for love and certainty through mystic experience.

For the delinquent-orientated young, the 'edges' have to do with the laws relating to larceny, assault and battery and disturbance of the peace. These are illustrated by gang sub-cultures like the Hell's Angels and a range of street gangs which emphasise daring, toughness and defiance in their flamboyant and aggressive flouting of authority. While Matza and Sykes refer to this group as 'the last leisure class', stressing the analogues in concept if not content of activities to leisure class groups described by Veblen, with their emphasis on daring, rejection of prosaic work, flair for conspicuous consumption and respect for 'manly' demonstrations of power, this resemblance should not be pressed too far.

The radicals, as Keniston has pointed out, have been drawn more from middle-class backgrounds and are intellectual and idealistic, but reject established modes of realising these ideals (Keniston, 1971). In Britain, the channels for the expression of radical life styles outside the universities and professions include the radical or alternative press (*Time Out, Kids, Oz, North Devon Snail*, etc.) and a number of radical action groups.

Young people's groups often seem to comprise a variegated, chameleon-like and kaleidoscopic array. The groups may change their memberships, and the groups and individuals may change their self-conceptions and their social programmes of activity at different points in their histories. The distinctions between individual young people who conform and those who dissent or renounce established social institutions are only partly applicable to whole groups. There are many anomalies and constant change.

The kaleidoscopic pattern of young people's motivations and participation patterns can be seen as determined by a range of factors, from their own developmental dynamics to the attitudes of society toward them. Many sociological writers have commented on the importance of society's attitudes towards the adolescent since Margaret Mead's famous work in the 1930s and 1940s, in which she demonstrated that many of the adolescent 'problems' which are experienced in our society are a product of the social structure in which they are kept in infantile roles past the time of their physical maturation, because of the way specialist education has evolved in industrial society. This contradiction was considered confusing. More recent writings stress the importance of ambivalent social attitudes in determining at least part of young people's behaviour (Leigh, 1971; Smith, 1968; E. M. and H. Eppel, 1966; Jephcott, 1967).

Adults who perceive the young as potentially out of control, posing threats of delinquency, licentiousness and anarchy, want to strengthen controls. The young may be seen as 'barbarians at the gate' and fault is found, perhaps, in their having been too permissively treated. Other adults, who may ambivalently envy the young as vital, creative, idealistic, uncorrupted by compromises and vested interests that take over the adoption of established adult roles, may react by encouraging young people's expressive and audacious experiments with life. As Cyril Smith has pointed out, these different perceptions find their way into professional analyses as well as popular stereotypes. Consequently, most of the writings on young people—whether on leisure, family life, politics or education—tend to have a bias; they either portray the young in a specially favourable light (perhaps as oppressed and misunderstood by their elders) or in an unfavourable light (perhaps as overindulged and irresponsible) (Smith, 1968; Leigh, 1971).

What in fact happens to young people when they leave the umbrella of the educational system for the more diffuse and less controlled congeries of environments of 'the community' is of interest to many kinds of providers of leisure facilities. Commercial providers recognise a ready market in the school-leaver, who is earning but has not yet incurred the heavy economic burdens of marriage and home-building. This is the market of entertainment, fashion, music, motorbikes and sports. As boys and girls move out of schools and leave the public-supported youth service clubs, they begin to pursue their interests according to what their purses will bear and where their values and inclinations take them. The city itself is a major magnet for youth, and many studies have noted that rural and small town settings are shunned not only because of job opportunities, but because of the poverty of entertainments (Bone, 1972; Leigh, 1971; Smith, 1966).

Within the conurbations there is entertainment, acceptance into youth groups and stimulation galore, anonymity and social space to experiment with building one's own identity. There is also callousness, malevolent and exploitative influences, loneliness, boredom and exclusion through social filters and barriers of new kinds. This is often irritating, confusing and depressing. There may be heightened intergroup tensions and this may entail a shock in self-image, unthreatened in earlier environments (Emmett, 1971b; Maizels, 1970; Jephcott, 1967).

How young people build their lives at this stage is affected both by their family influences and by the opportunities presented to them in their environments—some of which are made available by leisure providers. We have explored this in considering above a few cases from metropolitan London.

At the beginning of this chapter we indicated that the quest for personal identity is the focal preoccupation of young people; we describe how this proliferates into many sub-preoccupations. We identified some of these, though doubtless they could be differentiated in other ways. What is important is that it is only for this stage of the life cycle that there appears to be the need to conceptualise a proliferation of preoccupations. This fits with Erikson's description of the process of developing a sense of identity. The danger during this phase is that instead of ending up with a sense of personal identity, the diffusion of identity will remain uppermost. It is this diffusion which is expressed in the many preoccupations that young people show. Some are so overwhelmed by the different underlying passions and concerns, that they are unable to channel the preoccupations into meaningful life interests; others are better able to translate the preoccupations into selected interests which they then pursue. For most, it is probably true to say that they undergo both sets of feelings. The 'swamping' that may occur at this phase may also account for the feeling that many adolescents hold—for longer or shorter time—that the world is meaningless so that it is impossible to develop meaningful interests. It is crucial to come out of this period in such a way that one's inner resources are developed to the point where it is possible to turn underlying preoccupations that may be pursued in real life. Without this, the risk of increasing meaninglessness and lack of interests later in life is great.

Katherine, Jenny and Derek all showed their preoccupation with the need to separate and become autonomous people, and the struggle involved in doing so. They all alternated in their need to be stimulated and to be left alone and quiet. (This is an important point for providers to note—young people, contrary to stereotype, do not need continuous outlet channels.) They are all preoccupied with the issue of work in its broadest sense. For some work means school—which may be an unpleasant set of experiences in which one is told all day what to do rather than finding out what one wants to do. One response to this is to truant. Others, like Jenny, will do their 'dull' school work but will then look for enjoyment outside the school-work context. Thus she developed photography as a hobby, and this may later be transferred to a work interest that she can enjoy. Katherine shows how her preoccupation with work was not satisfactorily channelled. Young people develop their generalised work orientations within institutions—school, club or apprenticeships. These may then be applied to an occupational career or to non-occupational enjoyments, or some mixture or alternation of the two.

Sociability and relating to others was a marked preoccupation of the young people interviewed. Even those who characterised themselves as 'loners' had a friend or group with whom they developed many of their interests. Katherine and her group of friends are inseparable, in and out of school. They form a phalanx against the predatory incursions of boys, and a sounding-board for the development of views autonomous from family members and teachers. Their sexual morality is more conventional than that of Jenny's sub-group, and so they chose their exposures more gently and cautiously. The group reassures individuals, and also their parents, whose surveillance centres on the issue of how long they

are out and with whom. Peer groups also channel interests into behaviour and allow expression of preoccupations with the environment,
and with moral issues. It is in the social group that pubs are explored
or drugs or sexual relations, or pop festivals or motorbikes or travel.
Individuals feel pressures and influences from these sub-groups representing different streams of youth culture, but they also get support
from them and exposure to them facilitates exploration of their underlying preoccupations. But joining a social group may create tensions with
friends who are non-group members. Thus Derek's participation in a
semi-skinhead group created tension with his girlfriend.

Physical and mental maturation are of major concern to young people.
Stature, weight, secondary sexual characteristics are intensely interesting both to individuals and to their friends. As girls mature earlier than
boys they tend to look outside school for heterosexual relationships. The
odd girl who has an affair with a much older man while she is in her
early teens is an object of tremendous interest if not emulation by the
others. The boys in the same setting may disavow any interest in girls,
or may be irritated at the girls' feeling that they are immature compared
with the 'men' that they know. They may, under these circumstances,
confine their demonstrations of maturation to physical exploits such as
sport, motorcycle-riding, or various forms of braggadocio seen in skinhead groups. Contemporary young people are more sophisticated and
experienced with sex than their parents were at their age; and they hide
their sexual feelings and desires less. Interest in sex magazines, touching
and feeling, exploring their own and others' bodies is prominent and
overt. The capacity of the mind is of concern along with the capacity
of the body; in many ways the young people studied indicate an interest
in the layers and dimensions of mental processes. While most of them
know about drugs and many have experimented at least with cannabis,
few are involved in the active cultivation of mind-expanding or mind-
exploring experiences via the use of drugs. They seem to recognise that
they need time to think things through and assimilate them, that the
mind has levels and that they need opportunities to integrate mental
experience.

The urban young people whom we interviewed show various forms
of preoccupation with the physical environment. Their class and cultural milieux, particularly their families, play a critical role in this. The
children of less affluent families have a more restricted knowledge of the
environment beyond their local areas, and less appreciation of the
potentials of the environment for aesthetic pleasure. For many the
streets are places for games and play but also places of danger—from
people and traffic.

For children from middle-class families there is often exposure to a
wider range of environments—not always appreciated in infancy but

later part of an evolving identity. As a little girl, Jenny was bored when her father pursued his botanical hobby and she had to sit in the car while he 'bombed about the countryside collecting specimens'. Later, sharing the interests of her boyfriend, she finds endless pleasure in going into the country to photograph natural life.

A heightened concern with what is 'right' or 'fair' is seen in young people. Katherine is concerned with being fair with people and expecting the same from them. Her friends, Ellen and Mary, want to take up socially useful occupations. They want to be teachers or social workers, to help the less fortunate and to do something morally commendable. In their school they visit old people and help out as part of a voluntary action group. Katherine herself, however, recognises that she does not like doing this kind of work and that it therefore is not the kind of interest she wants to cultivate. Moral sensitivity is shown by Ted and his friends, who demonstrated against apartheid in South Africa. Jenny and her friends are active conservationists and health food enthusiasts. They have well developed positions on Women's Lib and other ideological issues.

Balancing one's preoccupations, interests and activities, is very evident among girls and boys irrespective of social backgrounds. Jenny's preoccupation with not being a one-sided 'swot' is an example. In addition to reading about people, she wanted to get to know them. Derek's preoccupation with his emotions and his body—and handling the build-up of tensions and feelings of violence—are being balanced by his interest in winning the approval of his girlfriend. This involves not only curbing some of his violent inclinations, but attempting to concentrate on some of his course work in order to be able to achieve a better occupational situation. Katherine too is concerned with the issue of working out an integrated life pattern. She wants to enter a line of work that will be more than just a source of income, but which reflects her interests in drawing and design. She does not accept that the interests of her friends should be the guides to how she should work out an integrated pattern for her own life.

The case studies, illustrating the preoccupations of young people, provide a basis for understanding the interaction between young people and those who provide leisure facilities for them. The linkage may be studied via the concept of interests into which the preoccupations are channelled.

Leisure provision for young people: understanding their interests

There has been an interesting evolution of attitudes about leisure provision for young people. Concern with them has come from various quarters: the social services; educational authorities; recreational councils; and a wide range of private interest groups like folk dance and song societies, ramblers and camping associations, hobby clubs, etc. Government departments concerned with health and social services are concerned with specific subgroups of the young: the ill, the disabled, the delinquent, etc. But the greatest part of public interest in the young comes from the Department of Education, through the Youth Service.

In the early days of the service, in the 1930s and 1940s, negative rationales tended to predominate, i.e. to 'keep the kids off the street', to prevent delinquency and vandalism, to make work for idle hands that might otherwise be used to do the 'devil's work'. But there was inadequate training for youth leaders, no career structure, and facilities were poor. By 1950 the morale of the service was recognised to be very low, because it had also become manifest that most of the young people it was intended to serve were not, in fact, responding.

The Albemarle Report (1960) made recommendations which became widely accepted. It de-emphasised negative and antiquated social service conceptions, highlighting positive concepts like the use of physical recreation, co-operation with the young to develop mutual respect, variety and flexibility of provision instead. It emphasised the three aims of *association*, *training* and *challenge* in the lives of young people. Specific suggestions included an improved system of training and better organised career structure for youth leaders, and the improvement and enlargement of facilities like national parks, waterways, camp sites, swimming pools and sports centres.

Prior to Albemarle, variant and anti-social adolescents were considered 'unclubbable'. Following Albemarle, they were considered 'unreached'. In 1972 Dennistoun Stevenson's report commissioned by the Department of the Environment, *Fifty Million Volunteers*, defined the problem as one of organisation in the community of various interest groups with contrasting youth cultures, around their own sub-cultural emphases (Stevenson, 1972).

The young have always been the focus of the great bulk of public investment in recreation facilities. Apart from the isolated Cambridgeshire Village Colleges experiment, it is only recently that this bias has been questioned (Cambridgeshire Education Committee, 1970). The main grounds on which it is challenged are economic—that the use of expensive facilities by young people during school hours and their non-use out of school hours is wasteful. This has prompted a considerable degree of 'dual use', strongly encouraged by central government, primarily through the Sports Council. What the form of 'dual use' that is becoming rapidly institutionalised usually involves, is the use of facilities by young people in school time, while the adult population has some access at other times. The notion that temporal segregation of the school and non-school populations is not always necessary, and may at times be undesirable, has met far greater resistance. The cases where this idea has been supported for its own sake, leading to a genuine 'community use' of facilities, are few (Strelitz, 1972). While policies of community use, so termed, are more widely adopted than previously, the concepts on which they are based are often very limited, and the 'community' element is more apparent than real. The housing estate which formed the context of a provider–user study for the work reported in this book contained a perfect example. There the use of the 'community centre' was rigidly age-segregated, with young people rarely able to participate in activities *together with* adults, and at times excluded altogether.

We now consider the nexus between provisions and young people on that housing estate, using it as a window on the world of the linkages individuals are able to make with leisure provisions in their expression of interests in a concrete situation. By delimiting the area, we are able to specify the range of provisions available.

Young people and leisure provisions on a housing estate

There is little in the study area that people can invest with personal meaning. The estate's environment is relatively simple: its physical components all have specified and committed uses. The main part, the residential fabric, is barely differentiated by other uses; the non-residential facilities which do exist are sited in two clusters—one at the centre, one at an edge of the estate. Perhaps a group of garages or a telephone booth are the only facilities with that interstitial quality that enables people to overlay them with definitions of their own.

The estate is situated at the edge of a town; public transport links to the town centre are fairly poor. Some 10,000 people live on the estate in what is generally agreed to be good quality housing. At issue is the quality of 'what goes with it', i.e. the estate's 'social provision'. This has always lagged behind the housing. In the estate's earliest days, some sixteen years ago, there was none. The bulk of non-residential provision, now contained in the community centre, followed thirteen years later. Other provisions now available comprise: some schools—one infant, three primary, one secondary; three churches—Anglican, Roman Catholic, Methodist—and a Pentecostal church without a building of its own; two parks, i.e. grass areas containing play sites with swings, etc.; a group of some ten shops and public toilets in a semi-covered square. There are also two pubs, a medical clinic, a petrol station, some squash courts—privately and expensively managed—a swimming pool and separate changing pavilion nearing completion.

The social facilities accommodated in the physical structure are more extensive. In part this stems from a degree of multi-use of most facilities—a youth club in the secondary school; a playgroup in the Anglican church; weekly bingo in the Roman Catholic church. The main locus of provisions is the community centre, jointly sponsored by the housing, social services, education and leisure sectors of the urban local authority. Management is vested in the leisure department, though in respect of policy for young people's activities, the education department have overriding authority. This stems from the insistent tradition that the youth service, based in the education sector, has exclusive responsibility for young people over 14 years old.

Physically, the community centre contains a variety of spaces, lending themselves to many uses. The range of provisions offered at the centre reflect the interests of its mixed sponsorship: daily pre-school playgroups; lunch club and afternoon activities for elderly people; a public library; and numerous clubs structured on a variety of activities from the 'serious' through the 'sportive' to the 'social'. Young people's activities, whether more social or more particularly oriented towards specific interests, are invariably provided via club structures and for specific age ranges (e.g. 8–10; 11–14). There is also a coffee bar, which, aside from the two pubs with their statutory age limitations on admissions, constitutes the only public venue for casual meeting and refreshment on the estate. Predictably, demand for its use has been great, and the management say it is for this reason that restrictive admission policies have been adopted for the coffee bar.

The personalities who are most influential in channelling the centre's impact are the local authority's leisure director and the local level management personnel, the centre manager especially. Their purposive views of recreation—'not amusement, but recreating, mentally and physically'—coupled with somewhat negative stereotypes of the estate's population (shared, incidentally, by estate-dwellers themselves) underlie their orientation. The centre manager conceptualises his aim as 'to promote standards—of conduct, behaviour, respect—the whole issue, at a higher level than people have in their own homes'.

The overriding implication of this is 'that there are certain minima to be adopted' in provisions at the centre. The delicate guidelines the centre manager employs in selecting what is offered are 'those activities which will attract the most people, i.e. cater for the majority that is the minority'. In essence this refers to the most popular activities 'above' the perceived minima, ones which therefore exclude activities like 'art'.

In addition to these general conceptions surrounding provisions on the estate, there are particular conceptions relating to young people. The centre manager feels that while in general 'the teenager is a bored animal', young people are roughly divisible into three groups: 'those interested in youth clubs, those interested in other things, and those interested in nothing.'

These conceptions of young people explicitly influence provisions and admissions on the estate. For 'the third interested in youth clubs', the centre manager considers that provisions are good, as there is some youth club activity offered each evening either at the centre or the secondary school. 'Other things' are defined as more specialist activities like judo or further education—and also homework—of interest to those young people 'with more purpose', for whom the centre manager feels provisions at the centre and elsewhere in the town are also good. Another of the centre's staff members agrees that young people in the area are well provided for. This she bases on the observation (extrapolated largely from her own children's experience) that the average young person is 'pretty fully stretched in an average day'. After school, sport, homework and reading, she sees that very little time is left open: 'It is the low-intellect young person who is bored.'

In terms of this classification it is the third sector of 'uninterested youth' that seems to be overlooked. Not only are all provisions at the centre for use via membership in structured clubs, but it is policy that young people in particular may not use the refreshment bar—intended for casual use—unless they join a club. Although this is rationalised in terms of limited capacity, it must hit hard at young people whose interests are not being stimulated or absorbed at the centre, and who— too young to attend pubs and limited in transport or fares for trips to the town centre—have little else in the way of available facilities to which they have access on the estate. The discussion with 'users' suggests that simple classifications of young people—a common expression of 'block-thinking'—not only disguise the complexity of young people's interests, but result in exclusion measures against some, and have other adverse effects. The town's leisure director is not so exclusively aligned to these achievement-oriented emphases in the activities he is prepared to sponsor. He has twice met delegations of disgruntled youth in the town, but found the meetings unproductive, as delegates were unable to specify their requirements beyond increased provision of discos, offering choice between various types of music, and for different age groups.

Discussions with families on the estate confirm the impression that some young people are being overlooked. One couple with small children of their own had helped to run a teenagers' disco at the centre; they saw clearly that 'the youth club isn't everyone's cup of tea', and that 'If they're going to oust young people who don't conform in manner, etc., they're pushing away those who maybe most need some-thing.' They support their observations by querying the policy of dis-allowing young people use of the coffee bar at the centre unless they join up for an activity, citing the example of a 'young boy who got really angry and upset because he wasn't allowed to have coffee in a *community* centre'. They feel: 'It is always the same kids, and the same types of kids, who are drawn in to the centre's activities. Those who are "otherwise" are in fact not allowed to partake.' Another couple, who had had teaching and social contact with young estate-dwellers, put it this way: 'There's not much of a scene for young people here. There's a sense of rigidity. They can only do what's offered on the conditions that they're offered.' This appears to be a function both of there being little choice of activity overall, and of what is available being geared to very specific tastes. This couple see the young people as frustrated: 'You can see them hanging about with nowhere to go.'

All the adults spoken to—both providers and estate-dwellers—themselves raised the issue of violence and vandalism in reference to young people. Although all made the association, some families felt that its reported incidence on the estate has been dramatised. Nevertheless all believe that in so far as these negative forces do exist on the estate, they mediate between young people's interests and deficient provisions, constituting an index of frustration.

The leisure providers at all levels, on the other hand, are preoccupied by the vandalism, destruction and other forms of 'anti-social behaviour' they attribute to young estate-dwellers. The leisure director explains the issue of control as 'basically, the preservation of the physical fabric of facilities'. While he feels that, *inter alia*, vandalism is positively correlated with the level of provisions, he does not believe that it is exclusively the expression of frustration. Similarly he rejects the view that some physical destruction to the property may be viewed as a cost of its use. In part he would doubtless be inhibited from supporting this view by the difficulty of conveying its meaning to those to whom he is accountable. Nevertheless it stems in large measure from a strength of feeling that 'we must insist on some basic civilised standards'. At the local level, the centre manager experiences his main difficulty in this area—implementation of controls over physical destruction which he too deprecates. He concretises his problem as 'the need to police the building without having to create hostilities'. He sees a solution in the recruitment of extra personnel who may undertake the 'policing' role, freeing him of associations of supervision.

The discussions which follow are centred on one family, the Smiths, who have five children, but are caught up with their teenage daughters above all.

Some parents' views

MR AND MRS SMITH are intensely concerned with the activities of their teenage daughters; they have keenly felt opinions about young people's provisions on the estate. They recognise inherent tensions in the young: 'Teenagers are an awkward group. They want money, yet they are too young to work.' Some, they point out, are not even old enough to be allowed a weekend job or paper round. The Smiths see it as quite normal that their children want money to spend on activities, clothes, etc., yet they have difficulty meeting their daughters' requests, and think that this problem is exacerbated by continual demands emanating from their children's schools:

> 'The girls have to take so much for cookery lessons. Only yesterday they had to make fresh fruit salad, and bring the ingredients. They also have to pay for professional players, and that. Our children are spread over three schools—and they all come home with financial demands.'

What the Smiths find especially hard to bear is that much of this money goes, they believe, on experiences their children do not really enjoy. They refer, for example, to recent and forthcoming visits to historic houses, and say there is a strong social pressure exerted both by the school and other pupils for parents to yield to each demand, 'even if all the children know they aren't going to enjoy it'. And then, the Smiths point out: 'The children won't accept that though they've had these things at school, they can't get pocket money. They say of the school activities: "That's education!"' They then feel obliged to sponsor activities which their daughters will actually enjoy.

The Smiths are uncertain what in particular characterises those activities their daughters do enjoy, but point out that whereas only a couple of years previously the girls much enjoyed participation in the Red Cross and in Guides, this no longer interests them. Mrs Smith had insisted that they remain in the Guides, although she realises that it 'doesn't offer them enough'. The parents point out, too, that their daughters are 'boy mad', and anxious to enjoy themselves away from the company of adults, including their parents. Recognising these interests in sociability and autonomy, and their own financial limitations, the Smiths stipulate the type of provision they believe their children require: 'What the kids need is cheap or free entertainment that appeals to them in a way that Guides doesn't.' They feel this is not provided on the estate. That which interests their daughters is either not provided locally or is expensive:

> 'The bus fare from here to town is 20p and then they would need money for the pictures. The disco up the road is 5p—and that is only held once a week at the centre, and our girls have to sneak in because they're over age. There's nothing else really. Even table tennis at the centre is 10p—and that only keeps them busy for half an

hour. And even swimming—that's difficult to get to. There's no direct bus to the nearest pool, and then the bus service is bad, and there's a long walk at either end. It needs about 50p—even for swimming.'

The Smiths say what their daughters currently do most is go to the park every night: 'We don't like the kids going to the park every night, but we let them.' The parents realise that the attraction at the park is the venue it provides for a crowd of young boys and girls to meet away from supervision. Another current attraction for the girls is a disco, held on Friday and Sunday evenings at a boys' club near the town centre. Mr Smith takes them there, and collects them. They are not permitted to attend on Sunday evenings. They feel that 'trouble, violence, fighting' which they see as characteristic of the teenage stage is in much greater evidence on Sundays. They suggest this is because 'whatever else is available in the town centre—not much—is closed on Sundays'.

The Smiths make two more observations. First, they say, there is nothing on at their girls' school after school hours, and the youngsters may not even be on the school ground in the afternoon. The Smiths feel the school should be opened for something in the evening, although they suggest this is probably impeded by the school's use for evening classes. Would their children like to go to school in the evenings? They are not sure, but feel it likely if the programme offered were sufficiently varied and attractive.

Their second point is that the youth activities they remember from their own younger days required only a small blanket cost for membership. Payment each time an activity was engaged in was not necessary. This, they feel, was a far more enabling type of provision.

In overview, Mr Smith volunteers:

'The violence at the shops can't be swept under the carpet. They can hide it, but that doesn't sweep away the cause. The kids need something to occupy them—maybe a speedway track. The town lacks in entertainment. It has closed down most of the major dance halls; it has closed down the milkbars where the kids congregated. Now the kids are put on the outskirts of the town, where they certainly can't afford the fares into town. They are left on the open estates to find their own entertainment, and theirs is throwing over old ladies, and throwing stones through windows.'

The Smiths say that some young people had hung a rope swing from a tree in the park, to swing over the river, but that the police came several times to remove the swing. They feel that any damage to the tree or even the children's swings is simply a cost which should be borne in the circumstances. Similarly, Mr Smith suggests, in relation to young people and the disco at the centre: 'The half that can't get

into the disco start throwing stones and that—because they get resentful.
Lots of kids get turned down so often that they won't bother any
more.' To the Smiths, these correlations they perceive are self-evident.

Three girls—aged 13, 14, 15

This record of some young estate-dwellers' activities is based on a discussion with the Smiths' two teenage daughters and one of their friends.
The girls' discussion was led by one of them, the others contributing
mainly when their own experiences or opinions differed from those
described. The discussion was structured in terms of an average
weekday, Saturday and Sunday. They spoke about holidays separately.
   Claire describes life on a weekday as follows, starting from the time
she arrives home from school. Immediately on arrival home, she changes
and then does homework till tea. After tea she joins in domestic tasks,
which the children in the family do on a rota system. Then she feeds
the dog and waits for Kate to come for her. What they do then depends
largely on the weather:

> 'When it's raining, we listen to the wireless in our room, or at our
> friend's over the road, or we stand in the passage. When it's not
> raining, we go to the park, or go for a walk. If it's really nice, we
> go to the field. It's quiet there and we can talk about what we want.'

Kate adds: 'Sometimes we just walk about the streets.'
   The passage, park and field require some explanation. The 'passage'
is the space of a few feet between the end of the terrace the Smiths live
in, and the tenant next door. The girls have clearly differentiated this
as a particular place. Standing there constitutes an activity. On the
evening Mr and Mrs Smith were first visited, it was raining, and Claire
and Kate were standing there. The 'park' is that part of the green space
at the edge of the estate where the children's swings and mown grass
are situated. The 'field' is simply the part beyond it where the grass
grows high.
   Kate says that sometimes she goes to the club at the centre on
Wednesdays (for 11–14-year-olds), where she plays badminton, table
tennis, records, etc. Sometimes she has a drink at the centre's coffee
bar afterwards.
   The girls say that the disco at the centre is for 9–12-year-olds. Only
Diana has therefore been strictly entitled to admission, but says she
once got turned away because it was too full. Claire says she got turned
away because she is too old. This made her angry but she went to the
coffee bar. She points out though that she was not allowed in without
buying something. The girls add that when the boys get turned out,
they start breaking bottles. Kate generalises this: 'There's nothing to

do, so they keep breaking stuff.' Diana points out that the discos at the centre are anyway not enjoyable because 'there's lots of little ones tiddling about your feet'. She knows something about a club 'for older ones', but says 'you must be fourteen to join'. She is too young for this. They say the minimum age for youth club membership at the secondary school is 15.

The girls say that there is dancing at the secondary school on Fridays. They do not attend this as it used to clash with their Red Cross activity, and now it clashes with their disco attendance at the boys' club nearer the town centre. The girls are very enthusiastic about this disco; they all 'go there on Friday evenings'. It emerges that so far Kate has attended several times, Claire has been once, and henceforth intends to go regularly, and Diana has not yet been, but will go this week for the first time, and thereafter plans to go regularly. What makes this disco distinctively attractive is clear: 'It lasts till ten, has the latest music, it's dark in there, and there's flashing lights.' It obviously caters for a variety of the girls' interests. The costs are considered manageable: '10p to get in, 5p for a drink, 13p for a hotdog outside.' The last item is considered expensive but unnecessary as the girls eat at home before they go. They are 'taken' by Claire's father in the van, and he takes other young people who wish to join in. The girls say they cannot go to the Sunday discos at the same club because then two other 'lots' come fromelsewhere in the town, and there are fights. They say that two boys were stabbed the previous week. Diana seems to know that there are varied activities at that club on non-disco evenings. None of the girls has attended these; they say that other evenings are more exclusively for boys.

On Saturdays the pattern of the girls' activities vary more. Kate, from a family with fewer children than the Smiths, has more money to spend and can therefore do more. Claire and Diana are more restricted by lack of funds. All the girls like to go swimming, but only Kate goes regularly on Saturdays. The minimum sum required for swimming is 15p, before refreshments. Sometimes the girls go to the town on Saturdays: 'We go in a whole party and muck about. We go in the shops and get kicked out.' Kate sometimes goes shopping with her mother on Saturdays. The girls say 'it's too dear to go to the pictures'. Kate has been once to an afternoon matinée with her mother, and recalls that it cost almost £1 for the two of them. The girls also speak of Saturday-morning shows in the cinema in town, with only 5p admission for a cartoon, serial and adventure film. Kate says she still goes sometimes. Claire and Diana used to go regularly but are no longer allowed to, as if they go, the other children in their family also want to, and fares and admission for all would be too expensive. They point out that if their father did not work overtime on Saturdays, he could take them

all in the van. The girls say that the park is the 'main place' for Saturdays. They 'muck about' there, and 'play on the kid swings'. They tell
about the rope swing which used to provide much fun, but which 'the
men from the council have taken down'.

Do the girls' activities vary in winter? Only Kate seems to have
experienced a winter 'out of childhood' so far: 'In winter we go to the
park till it is really dark, and then we walk up to the chip shop [in the
shopping square], or to the off-licence to buy coke and sweets, but the
walk's the main thing, just walking up and down to the shops.' Kate
says she also used to go to the Girls' Brigade last winter.

The girls say that on Sundays both of their families go out, but they
no longer like to join in always. The main reason is that they like to stop
and talk to boys, while their parents 'don't let us muck around'. Claire
and Diana illustrate this: they went with the family to a park at a
nearby town and afterwards their parents wanted to go to see the old
church in the vicinity, but they 'hate history' and lagged behind to talk
to some boys. Their father spoilt this by coming back to fetch them.

The 'hate of history' is generalised. Claire had been on a school visit
to an historic house that day. She describes the visit:

'The coach on the way there was OK. There was a wireless and we
were waving out the window to men. When we got there, they allowed
us half an hour to talk to boys, and that was nice. There were lots
of boys—loads of schools on the visit at the same time. But then we
had to go into the house. It was so boring. We were in there for
1 hour and 20 minutes. When we came out we went to the souvenir
shop. It was so expensive—5p for a postcard; a candle was 75p—it
was ever so dear. I bought a drink instead, and that was 10p.'

The girls point out that they 'have to go' on these school visits.

What would they like to do? They say that there is only one choice
really—the park. Or they can walk around the streets. They find provisions specially limited when it rains. Like most young people, they like
places where they can have 'peaceful talks'. They suggest that if the
disco at the secondary school were programmed for a different evening,
they would be able to go. The new pool, they fear, will be too small.
They also talk of a disco in the squash court, but say that they are not
allowed in, as they are under 16. Those attending it are older, some
having their own cars, and driving up from the next town.

The girls isolate mobility as a critical factor. They say they would
welcome more to do on the estate, but if they could get to the town
centre, would discover what was available there. They are impeded in
this by the price of fares. Kate says that her brother had nothing to do,
so her father bought him a motorbike. For Claire and Diana at least,
the obstacle of immobility is unlikely to be so easily overcome.

In general, the girls say they do not watch television. Claire says her mother buys her a record once a week—instead of pocket money. Claire chooses the records, and Diana may play them if she asks first. Kate receives 50p pocket money each week, and 10p each weekday. The girls read when the weather is wet, otherwise 'it's boring to read when there's a chance to go out'.

Kate and Diana both say that their special hobby is swimming. They swim once a week at school. Kate also goes each Saturday but Diana cannot afford it every week. Claire is mad about horses and has been taken horse-riding once by her father. She points out the prohibitive costs: 60p an hour for initial instruction, then 50p an hour. She suggests the better value is £2 for the whole day, but says that sum is far too great.

All the girls look forward to leaving school as soon as possible—mainly so that they may earn money.

Interests as a basis for leisure policy

Going back to first principles about young people's preoccupations is a starting-point in analysing how they articulate with the institutions and roles available in their environment. This we did in detail with Jenny, Katherine and Derek. The intervening step is to analyse the main kinds of life interest expressed by young people. It is at this level of *interests* that the discussion with the three girls on the housing estate was pitched, and that exploratory study firms up our opinion that the connection between interests and lines of activity is the most effective potential point of articulation between providers and users. Still, that case study skirts the processes involved in the expression of interests and activities only lightly, though it does show that the same interest may be satisfied by different activities and that the same activity may be an outlet for different interests. We now spell these out in more detail. This process is easily blocked or frustrated. The need for *facilitation* by those who provide leisure services, and other community services, can be clearly seen.

Interest in variety

Surveys of leisure and recreational activities indicate that young people are the most active sub-population. Our case materials show that individual adolescents often try out and experiment with a wide gamut of activities in expressing their interests. They feel they need to try for themselves and not to be prescribed for or to be tied down to any particular place, person, activity or relationship. Neither surveys reporting on activities nor 'head count' surveys indicate this fluidity, which is at the heart of the adolescent pattern.

A policy implication of this is that facilities should not be too strongly focused on a particular kind of activity or concentrated in one place for them (unless it allows for considerable circulation as in something like an Oriental *souk*). There should, ideally, be *many* places—in and outside the school. The places should be *different in content, different in milieu, different in personnel and in organisational structure*. Diversity and contrast should be provided. Stating the need for variety is necessary. However, how to provide variety at all may be a major problem particularly in new settings. In new housing developments the lack of variety is a characteristic problem though this may not be recognised outside new towns.

Interest in novelty

Young people are interested in what is new as well as what is on. There is a tendency toward fads and fashions in what is done, who goes where, what is worn and said, and what is 'in'. But just because an activity is 'in' does not mean that everything else is 'out'. Most young people like to have the reassurance of being able to return to familiar things, people, places and activities which function as bases from which their excursions into novelty can be undertaken without so much anxiety.

A policy implication of this is to work towards conceptions of provision that are flexible and which allow for storing what is 'out' and bringing them back when they are wanted again. Society as a whole does this, in a way, with its tolerance of a multiplicity of institutions and interest groups even when these are not in favour of those at the centre of power or fashion. Fundamentalist religions, for example, were nearly abandoned by young people until the recent revival of 'Jesus people' as a novel youth cult. They were kept alive in the interval by a relatively small proportion of devotees who were considered odd or old-fashioned by the majority.

Interest in awakening new experiences

Whereas many older people, particularly those with enervating jobs and little prior educational basis for the cultivation of interests, need to be pushed to try new experiences, young people are generally eager for them. This eagerness makes many adults anxious—with fears of drugs, 'way-out' experience or relationships capturing the youngsters.

On the other hand, young people have many kinds of fears and inhibitions about new situations, or misconceptions about them that can make their approach to them awkward for others involved. Often, in approaching new experiences about which they have anxieties or misconceptions, adolescents may put on an air of indifference or of defiance, which belies their real interest. Reactions to their surface attitudes may confirm their fears. It is easy for them to be put off, discouraged or disillusioned with experiences that they try, and if they are put off, this may result in enduring inhibitions.

Awakening experiences are often sought and experienced in the company of others. Chums, mates, friendship pairs and cliques, gangs and other peer groups serve an important function in this. Though there are some who are 'loners', most young people seem to use one or more friends as supports in testing out new experiences, talking about them and testing their reactions against those of others.

The objective of the search for new experiences is, in each individual case, the development of a personal identity. By having both positive and negative experiences, lasting orientations are formed at this stage. It is important that these experiences have enough that is positive to be able to form the base for subsequent enjoyment. Otherwise there may be guilt, anxiety, diminished self-esteem and distrust of authorities which can interfere with subsequent use of facilities and the enjoyment to be derived from it.

A *policy implication* of this is to train providers to deal with the delicate area of young people's awakening experiences in a way that will enable the development of enjoyment capacity rather than inhibit it. The technical aspects of providers' roles are too often those that are in focus in their training and in their role performance. While this aspect is essential, it is not sufficient. It is not enough to be a good parks-keeper, pools-keeper, house-warden or whatever in purely technical terms. The role should incorporate facilitation of interests. This requires an understanding of young people's developmental patterns: their defensiveness, their clique behaviour, their testing out behaviour. Handling these issues is not simple, as they often involve behaviour that is difficult to take or which presses the limits of toleration of those required to maintain responsibility for facilities. Nevertheless it is important that they be handled, either as part of the role of the leisure-facilities managers, or as an ancillary role. For the failure to handle them leads to failure of many young people to overcome the fears and anxieties which often underlie their off-putting behaviour, with consequent inhibitions or destructiveness of their orientation to equivalent facilities.

Interest in living

In contrast to the interest in awakening new experience, this is the wish to experience intensely the things that are already known. This sometimes involves pressing the limits—of speed, of aggressiveness, of closeness—that can be achieved. It usually involves an element of challenge or adventure, a degree of risk and a degree of revolt against authority. Sometimes it involves an 'after' phase of reliving an experience, savouring it, incorporating it into one's being, talking about it until it becomes part of one. Many physical experiences lend themselves to this two-phase pattern: for example, rambling and mountain-climbing, where one battles with the elements and arrives home or at a hostel wet, weary, but feeling perhaps a sense of achievement at having conquered natural obstacles and come out of it alive and well. The sitting around, drying out, having a drink, a sing-song, a romance or whatever, is part of the *après* phenomenon that is an important part of experience. Sometimes this reliving of an experience—embellishing it with retelling—helps the individual to make status with his peers and in his own self-esteem. This is seen in skiing, football (even for spectators) and other forms of physical or mental exertion. It may also apply to intellectual experiences, at the pub after a lecture or theatre performance. Clawson and Knetsch have described the cycle of enjoyment in terms of four stages: anticipation, travel, experience and reminiscence. The most important aspect of such experiences is by no means always the activity itself. For young people this seems to be particularly true. Telling and retelling of their exploits, the discussion of encounters between the sexes, etc., are high points for most of them, and this recounting helps identities to take form (Clawson and Knetsch, 1966).

One *policy implication* is to search for experiences that can allow intense climaxes, more than is usually possible in 'tame' provisions. This may involve provision of places and facilities for doing things harder, louder, longer than has conventionally been possible. Sometimes it may involve constructive conflict with the authorities. In association with such intense experiences possibilities should be available for enjoying the anticipation and reliving, which heighten the meaning for the individuals in social contexts.

Another *policy implication* in the educational sphere is to orientate curricula and teachers to the educational goal of living. Education for performance—academic, vocational, etc.—is not enough. It should be balanced with attention to the enjoyment of life in a socially responsible way. This implies a wider accountability than has been usual for specialists in protected institutional niches. Understanding and tapping informal as well as formal learning resources is a problem, but many young people prefer to learn about life in informal rather than formal ways.

Interest in solitude

There are a number of interests that relate to solitude. This shows in reading, having a think, going off by oneself. It may seem simple enough to accomplish, but for the urban child, often in sub-standard housing without a room of his own, in the midst of crowded places with people 'going at one' for one thing or another suspicious of loitering, distrustful of layabouts and disapproving of the lazy—it is not easy just to be alone doing apparently nothing but obtaining the relief of pressures and expectations on one that is necessary for achieving new levels of integration. Some young people's interest in oriental religions seems to be in response to this—the emphasis on psychic withdrawal, meditation and the like.

A *policy implication* would be to provide quiet places, quiet periods for reflection—places in schools or clubs or adventure playgrounds or programmes of learning or activity where one need not do anything; one need not interact; one need not perform; one could just be. It is important to see this as useful and necessary and part of valued provision. Sometimes this applies to mental phenomena as well—the need to have the right kind of place and people to talk things out, get things off one's chest, express what one feels, including outrageous views, without being censured. These all require spaces and opportunities for self-selected groupings of people for private purposes. Once again, such provisions may try the patience and tolerance of leisure managers, as young people may use them for activities which are difficult to tolerate within the framework of administrative responsibility. The fact of setting places aside and labelling them as 'quiet places' may present the kind of demand or expectation that contravenes the purpose.

Interest in making close relationships outside the family

Interest in finding others in whom one can confide (who are not family members), others to whom one can be nurturant and from whom one can get personal help (who are not one's own siblings or relatives), as well as others with whom one can share interests, appears to be common among young people. The dissolution of local communities, the atrophy of face-to-face, extended family relationships, the complications and conflicts of family living, widen the manifestation of many interests which may formerly have been relatively confined to family relationships. Interest in making a close relationship with a local shop-keeper or artisan would illustrate this; interest in joining a group that perhaps expresses closeness by using kin terms—brothers, cousins, mates; interest in helping older people. Young people's participation in such groups as Task Force and the Samaritans seems to channel this interest to some extent, sharing with others a meaningful kind of activity which puts the relationship onto another plane.

The *policy implication* is to provide channels for young people to express these interests through social service activities which are not rigidly organised. This might best be worked out in relation to volunteer interest groups within which young people could fit and influence.

Interest in the environment

For many adolescents this is a great potential area of awakening. Urban-dwellers become fairly mobile on their own early on. They can explore both the wider range of urban experiences that are possible in the city's endless mini-environments and the possibilities for enjoyment of the countryside. The challenge for leisure providers is how to awaken their potential interest in the larger environment in such a way that the people get the most out of the experience, and that they become welcome rather than unwelcome visitors in environments other than their familiar local ones. Neither goal is achieved if the probes into the environment are confined to motorbike races along the throughways. Comparable observations can be made about the young rural-dweller's excursions. Young people from both settings have potentials for developing interests both in their now larger environment and in the contrasting environment. They may have in common and share as an interest the concern with such issues as environmental pollution, different in manifestations and remedies in the two settings but comparable in noxious potential. While there are many possibilities for building social bridges here via the cultivation of shared interests, it is likely that this is one of those areas where considerable 'animation' is required, as the relevant interests are ones which have been systematically inhibited in the course of urban modern living.

Policy implications would include the provision of opportunities for young people to learn more about their environments in ways that are acceptable to them, ways that 'make the penny drop' both as learning experiences and as enjoyment experiences. Working on projects which aim to beautify the environment, make it more accessible for enjoyment or make it more understandable to them—make it their own—are desirable. Youth projects, environmental design projects—not only in play centres and sports centres, but in country parks and waterways—are all part of this thrust of provision. Once again, this is a particularly challenging area for providers and for the managers of provision because young people (pressing the experience as hard as possible) often use provisions in unorthodox ways. The challenge is how to channel these interests in 'getting into' things, by marking things up, changing them around, taking them apart, etc., while at the same time maintaining responsibility for the facilities provided, so that others can come and also enjoy them. In this area, as in many others, we have the impression that *extended and repeated exposure to, say, the countryside is necessary for the real development of interest in it.* An expedition, say, once a year may be pleasant, but it is not likely to set the basis of a developing interest. Therefore active leadership and stimulation—*animation*, to use the French term—is likely to be called for to fire the latent enthusiasms of young people in these fields.

Interest in putting family relationships onto a new basis

Adolescence is a period of breaking away to some extent from the ties that bind one to child roles. This is often accompanied by overt declarations of independence from the family. Nevertheless we are impressed that what is wanted by most youngsters is a *revision* of the relationship—putting it on a new footing or arranging its various parts to be played in a new key rather than dropping the relationship altogether. While there is often parental exasperation, fear about the trouble adolescents can get into if given too much independence too soon; and sometimes the opposite, fear of the child not being independent enough—the tendency is for parents too to want a new relationship. Sometimes it will mean that the father will be able to relate to his son as a 'mate' in a new way; sometimes it will mean greater freedom for the mother to re-enter work herself. Many parents feel relieved of the burden of having dependent children or glad to have the extra income that a child entering work may bring.

A *policy implication* is to arrange family events which allow for elements of togetherness and separateness. Families may be able to go and come together, as on a package tour, but while there do things separately—connecting periodically for a meal, a drink, a chat or a game. Safe boundaries allow parents to relax, while flexible internal arrangements allow children to do their own things by themselves or with their own peers.

The evolution of vital policies will be enhanced by relevant research. We elaborate on possibilities in chapter 6.

3

Young adults

Identification with social institutions

In chapter 2 we focused on young people until the time they left school. The age of leaving school and the level of personal development by that time is variable. However, we took the phase leading to that point to be one mainly concerned with the tasks of adolescence in which the search for identity crystallisation was foremost. This does not mean that by the time young people leave school, they have accomplished this identity crystallisation; in fact, the quest for a viable 'personal identity' probably continues in some form throughout life. In adolescence, however, it is at a peak. At the point of leaving school, young people are catapulted into more adult roles, whatever the level of their psycho-biological development. While the boundaries are flexible, we take the young adult phase to start with school-leaving and to continue through the first few months of marriage. Just where it ends is also variable. There are subtle clues for indicating that couples are no longer 'young adults', but have entered the early establishment phase. The latter often begins with pregnancy but may begin before. However, these are not absolute indicators, as many individuals will not marry, and of those who marry, many will not have children. Nevertheless, both in terms of the 'psychology' of the individuals, and of the ways in which they are treated in their social roles, these gradations seem to be widely applicable.

While these phases of the life cycle are not strictly age-bound, there is a loose correlation with age. If we take the young adult phase as starting somewhere around 16–19 years, it probably ends for most (but not all) people somewhere around ten years later. In 1971 the average age of men marrying in Britain was 24·6 years; for women it was 22·6 years. During the nine or ten years after leaving school, young adults tend to 'settle down' into positive identifications with adulthood, though they may alter these identifications later on.

Those who stay on at school after the minimum school-leaving age are likely to reach a different level of development by the time they enter the young adult phase; their resources for developing interests and expressing their preoccupations are likely to be richer than those who leave school as soon as it is legal to do so. On the other hand, they may lag behind in other ways; confronting the responsibilities of adulthood later, they may be more harshly shocked into recognition of these, than those young adults whose experience of youth had been less prolonged and insulated. Once out of school, young adults go directly into the work force, or expand their interests and resources by travel, study at institutions for higher education, or live in groups that are 'anti-institution' or somehow adopt a life style that people accepting the established way of life find difficult to tolerate. There are also those young adults who are faced with unemployment on leaving school and begin their adult status without the prime institutional identification in our society. Life styles are influenced by other people all through the life course, and the particular configuration of influence affecting young adults at this point is critical for the social alignments they make. We discuss four sub-groups of young adults, representing a limited range of life styles. They are: young conformists living in a provincial town; students; involuntarily unemployed; and young adults who have elected to live alternatively during this phase at least from the life styles they perceive in 'straight' society. These represent a compromise between what we see as the most important sub-groups and information we are able to obtain with available resources. 'Straight' young adults in the metropolitan setting are conspicuously absent from the presentation.

Young adulthood is a life phase which has been little studied. Shortly after leaving school, people pass out of the purview of the Youth Service, the Youth Employment Service, the education system (except for college and university students who have been provided for but not studied much from the point of view of their changing interests), and the juvenile courts. Having left these age-graded institutions, young adults have been a difficult category for social researchers to sample. Until very recently, those under 21 were not listed on electoral registers, making them difficult to identify or locate in the population. Even now, young voters are underrecorded; they are often out of their homes— at work or play—and they tend to be geographically mobile so that attempts to use medical registers as sources of addresses have also run into difficulties. Sponsorship for studies of young adults has usually come from agencies like the Youth Service, with very specific concerns about limited aspects of people's lives. After reading research on youth clubs, it is not difficult to come away with the impression that those who leave clubs at 16 because they are more interested in courting (youth clubs do not usually cater for courting interests) are perceived as 'deviants'. While several questionnaire studies and some qualitative work (for example Leigh, 1971) of young adults' 'leisure' have been undertaken, they tend to cover young people up to 18 or, at most, 20, so their usefulness for understanding the preoccupations of a range of young adults is limited.

We have constructed a picture based on the spotty and heterogeneous information available and our own case material to obtain a general overview of the preoccupations and interests of people in this phase. We regard the *identification with social institutions* as the most salient preoccupation of young adults. While the concern with establishing and maintaining a satisfactory 'personal identity'—focal for young people—continues at this phase, the new preoccupation with a 'social identity' is usually in ascendancy. Young adults gradually, often tentatively and experimentally, build up new commitments which may be longer-lasting and will affect their views of themselves in their new social roles. Along with the quest to find institutions with which to affiliate and in which to develop satisfying interests, there are the concomitant social-psychological concerns of *intimacy* and *commitment*. Developing a capacity for intimacy, in the sense of being able to live with something or someone in close association, for a long time, seems crucial in this period. This is based on an idea of who one is oneself and what kinds of persons and situations one wants to be deeply involved with. Prototypically, the development of a capacity for intimacy is played out in the selection of and cohabitation with a mate of the opposite sex. While this is usually within marriage, it increasingly occurs outside marriage—at least for a time, though there are those who do not want to marry at all. For some, intimate relationships with partners of the same sex, or within group settings, are preferred. These are no longer to be deprecated as immature or pathological, but as variant adult patterns particularly favoured at this phase. Finally some people seem to relate more intimately to an institution *per se*, rather than the people involved; thus there are people for whom it is important to *be* married without it being crucial to have a close intimate relationship with the particular spouse.

Just which institutions people focus on at this stage varies by sex, class, life style, early influences, personal history and so on. While women now work more than ever before, the social influences countering women's careers are still so strong that most women identify less with the work situation than most men. Some women and men are much more identified with their work tasks and organisations than others. But, for women generally, marriage still tends to be the cardinal institution for playing out the preoccupations with social identification, while for men it is work affiliations that have conventionally been paramount.

In discussing the psycho-social stages of development that people go through, Erikson (1950, 255) talks of the young adult who:

emerging from the search for and the insistence on identity is eager and willing to fuse his identity with that of others. He is ready for intimacy, that is, the capacity to commit himself to concrete affiliations and partnerships and to develop the ethical strength to abide by such commitments even though they may call for significant sacrifices and compromises.

There has been a significant change in social expectations in recent years; while it used to be that affiliations made at this stage had to be 'abided' by, sometimes until death, there is greater acceptance now that commitments may be altered. While it may be important to be committed to an occupation to which one affiliates as a young adult, it is not necessarily expected that it be until retirement. While 'uncareers' may still be marginal, multi-careers are much more acceptable than they were previously, as also are changes of job (Cooper, 1974). Similarly, with the increase in *de facto* divorce, marriage is less universally seen as a matter of 'until death us do part', and more as a relationship that should continue to be voluntary, or not at all. Experimentation, merging into full role rehearsals of the different kinds of institutional involvements, is now not only more acceptable but considered positively desirable by some. Flexibility, established as a resource at this phase, can be applied beneficially at later phases.

The focal preoccupations of young men and women in this phase tend to be channelled in *four different sets of interests*: occupational interests, interest in forming relationships with persons of the opposite sex (whether or not in marriage), parental-family interests (including relationships with siblings and other kin), and friendship interests. The way individual young men and women express these interests will affect and be affected by their life styles. Accordingly, some show one set of commitments while others show contrasting ones. Some accept conventional social roles, sex conceptions and so on, while others do not; some engage in a great deal of physical mobility, others still live at home; some live in a metropolitan setting, while others reside in a small town or suburban setting. There will be differences among them in the use of 'leisure provisions'. These will be considered in more detail after they are portrayed in the case material below.

Four sub-groups of young adults

Young adults' interests in large social institutions are not always played out with conformative acceptance; the individual will not necessarily accept what is given. There are those who find it relatively easy to accept established frameworks, while others reject them angrily. We consider four contrasting sub-groups for which we have collected data.

Small town conformists: the centrality of courtship interests

It is in small towns that the conventional patterns are most firmly established; the 'goldfish bowl' quality of life in such settings reinforces the sustaining quality of social sanctions. We have drawn on a series of studies at the University of Swansea to provide an account of how the preoccupations of this phase are played out in a small town context, particularly through the interest in forming heterosexual bonds in courtship (Barker, 1972).

Courtship is a dominant activity of many young adults in conformist sub-cultures. For females especially it may become so paramount that other interests become inarticulate and involvements with other activities are submerged in the process. A courtship career may begin before leaving school, but it is usually afterwards that a more sustained commitment is undertaken. Both boys and girls in Swansea begin to reflect heterosexual interests when they are 12–14 years old. The girls enter into more committed relationships during the last year or two at school, while the boys wait until they are 17 or 18. After one or two such 'steady' relationships, the serious business of courting begins; the average age of formal engagement in Swansea in 1968 was 19 for females and 21 for males. Marriage followed a year later and the first baby arrived within the next two or three years.

During the earlier phases of this heterosexual career, males and females tend to spend their 'free' time sampling scenes outside the home, in ways previously described in chapter 2 as characteristic of young people: 'hanging around' in youth clubs, coffee bars, recreation grounds, chip shops and on street corners, in age-graded groups. As individuals drift through, leaving and joining the groups formed in each locality, they have chances to 'pick up' a member of the opposite sex by 'chatting them up', listening to discs, or offering a smoke or a drink. Commencing these 'adult' pastimes—being accepted at a pub, getting drunk (and being seen to get drunk)—is a rite of passage.

The Swansea studies confirm the findings of Schofield that early pre-courtship heterosexual encounters begin with acceptable events like going to the cinema or to a dance; they then progress to dates with less well specified destinations and activities (Schofield, 1973). Holding hands and kissing goodnight proceeds through the more extensive explorations of petting and eventually, among some, to sexual intercourse.

While at school, those with academic aspirations have less of the time and money required for heterosexual involvements than those who are just waiting for the minimum leaving age. Early school-leavers are freer to take jobs after school, during holidays and at weekends as they have no homework to do (Crowther, 1959). As parents have to subsidise dating activities, particularly of males, the academic-minded tend to encourage participation in school societies for economic as well as cultural reasons (Wynn, 1970). Thus, while the more academic go out less than other young people, they engage in a wider range of activities ordinarily thought of as recreational—sports, voluntary organisations, travel abroad—and critical as sources of sustaining life interests (Crichton *et al.*, 1962).

After leaving school, males who earn are minimally controlled by their families, though there are complaints that they are 'out' too much and treat the home like a 'hotel'. Females are more closely watched and parental complaints centre around their being out too late, making themselves look too 'available to men', etc. By 17 nearly 90 per cent of boys will have gone out with a girl and though males continue activities with their mates (football, darts, motorcycling, pigeons, fishing, surfing, horse-riding, etc.) they will ask girls out as well. Females, in contrast, begin to discard their sports and school/youth club activities as 'childish' or 'unfeminine'. They think instead about where they can meet boys and how they can attract them; hence they give up youth clubs because the boys who go there are too young and 'not yet much interested in girls'. But as it is easier to go around accompanied, girls soon move into a phase of having a 'boyfriend' who will take them out. This confers prestige, a 'chaperon' when going out and a source of entertainment (usually the boy pays)—but it makes a girl dependent on the boy because she finds it difficult to be both 'one of the girls' and have a steady boyfriend. Gradually the girl's social affiliations change from a group to a network, in which she associates with others according to the nature of her relations with boyfriends at the time. If a girl dances and her boyfriend does not, she may continue dancing for a while, going with a girlfriend, but as the relationship with the boy deepens, he is likely to object, referring to the dance hall as the 'knocking shop'. The boy's nights out with the other boys at the pub may be imitated by the girl and her friends, but usually does not last. Rather than going around as a group, girls tend to establish individual relationships for specific activities, and at this point they may strengthen relationships with kin—chiefly mother, aunts and sisters. Girls do not go to pubs alone; if not escorted by their boyfriends, they go with other girls. While the boys go in for convivial drinking and darts—usually initiated by their mates when they take their first jobs—girls go in to be with the men, not drinking as much, and just sitting while the men drink, play and tell stories. The town pubs are sophisticated dating and courtship centres, using soft lights, carpeting and music.

As casual dates change to steady dates, and steady dates merge with formal engagement—heralded by meeting each other's parents—the couple spend more time at home (usually in the girl's home unless she does not get on well with her parents or the house is crowded with

younger children). Visiting with friends, listening to records, watching
TV and drinking tea or beer is the pattern from this point onwards;
often the front room is turned over to the couple to sit in—the room
ordinarily reserved for holidays and special events like funerals. By
this time the couple are likely to have been 'living in one another's
pockets' for two or three years. It is difficult to break off such a relationship, even though one or the other may become bored with it—
feeling like old married people too early. The young couple in courting
may come to associate with one or another set of parents on a couple
basis more like friends than in the preceding phase. This makes the tie
between the couple harder and harder to break.

Though the couple start saving at some point as their courting
becomes serious, when they do go out they like to go to pubs, clubs and
licensed dance halls, which exclude younger people and are liked for
their atmosphere and the possibility of drinking. In Welsh society the
twin institutions of chapel and pub are of key importance in the courting
lives of young people; they may be either pub-orientated or chapel-
orientated. The interchangeability of the two is suggested in the response
of a young man who, when asked what his religious denomination was,
replied 'I'm a Cape Horner', naming his local pub.

Pre-marital intercourse is disapproved in Swansea but the couple are
often left alone when the parents go to bed. On engagement, domestic
presents are given and 'serious saving' commences. The boy then works
long hours overtime and the girl stays at home or drops around to see
his mother. Interminable discussions on wedding preparations begin.
The man reduces his contacts with his friends at the local pub, and
most of the couple's activities are together. They may join up with
one or two other couples and go dancing, for a drink, a run in the car,
baby-sitting or to the pictures. The girl's money is saved and the young
man meets nearly all expenses. They open a joint savings account into
which both put what they can. Saturday afternoons are spent looking
at furniture together, and then looking for a place to live after they are
married. When a place is found, weekends are spent decorating it.
This is a period of intense togetherness and communication—perhaps
never to be repeated in subsequent years.

The additional time spent at home and the ratification of the relationship by engagement usually results in increased acceptance of the
fiancé(e) into the family group:

> 'She [his mother] no longer talks *to* me about "our Tommy"—she
> talks *about* me as "our Eileen", and she shows me photographs and
> talks about what he was like when he was little.
>
> 'Once we were engaged they trusted me to look after the shop!
> And they talked about family matters in front of me.'

Thus a young woman narrows her range of interests to those which are courtship-orientated, and as 'going out' declines in importance, her activities centre more and more on her relatives. Her pre-engagement activities are no longer suitable because they involve going with girls to places where there are unattached men. Her friends are usually one or two girls—typically engaged or just married also—on whom she drops in to chat, and the couples with whom she and her fiancé go out. This pattern continues after marriage. The woman depends on her husband to take her out and is in many ways physically constrained. The conventional dictum—'A woman's place is in the home'—refers not only to the centre of her interests being within the home, but also to her physically remaining in the house as far as is possible.

Since male groups' activities are much less exclusively courtship-orientated. The tendency for young men to continue their membership in male peer groups is not inconsistent with courtship and marriage. They can therefore sustain some involvement in activities like sport, unlike their females who do not.

For those couples who are church-orientated, church youth clubs continue to provide channels for social activity outside the home later than the secular youth clubs of the Youth Service. The latter are more geared to the cultivation of activities on an individual basis—providing hobbies and developing interests for youngsters who need to blow off steam, or feel that they have 'nothing to do'. Some youth clubs have a distaste for courtship as an activity. Church youth clubs, in contrast, may take a different view and, in a sense, it is part of their goal as most marriages are in church among this group. Encouraging young people to court within the confines of the church reduces intermarriage. Perhaps the enthusiasm that some young adults feel for the newer or nonconformist crusade types of religious group—from the Jesus People to the Perfect Master of Divine Light—comes from the possibility these groups provide for conducting courtship activities under a moral umbrella at a relatively low cost. In Wales, the Welsh Nationalist movement seems to have a similar function. The Welsh League of Youth (Urdd Gofaith Cymru) meets in a chapel near Swansea, and it is said that 'many marriages are made in the Urdd'.

A case study of a young Swansea couple illustrates the conformist, courtship-orientated pattern.

ANNE AND BRINLEY show many elements of the small-town pattern. Though they might, in the course of their family cycle, take on what we describe in chapter 4 as the *new-conventional* pattern rather than repeat the conventional pattern of their parents, their attitudes and experiences typify those of conventionally oriented couples in our society.

Anne is a talkative, attractive, purposeful young lady who, according to Brinley, 'has her head screwed on alright, knows what she is doing, and can handle money'. Brinley is more 'easy-going' and sociable. He has had several girlfriends—'a regular harem'—before settling down to a steady relationship with Anne. She likes him because he is 'soft' and 'kind' and 'lets me have my own way'.

During the time the interviews were conducted, the couple had reached the serious saving phase; most evenings were spent in Anne's home—mostly in the back sitting-room—with various members of the family wandering in and out, taking the interviews as part of the available entertainment. The rest of this repertoire included TV watching, drinking tea or milky coffee, companionable chat, visiting back and forth with relatives in the neighbourhood and occasional excursions to clubs, pubs and bingo halls.

Both of *Anne's parents* came from the same industrial-dockland area of the town; her mother had lived all her life in the same 'two-up and two-down' terrace house where they were at the time of the study. They had courted for several years before marrying and then moved in with Anne's mother's family because of her father's low earnings as a van-driver. The war and his departure for the Army prolonged living in the parental home. During the war, Anne's mother, who was the youngest in a family of four and had remained at home partly to care for an ailing mother, took a job on the railway; she continued working there until Anne's birth following the return of her husband.

When Anne's father returned, he took a job driving a bus; this he has retained ever since. As his wages were low, Anne's mother returned to work which also provided her with 'company'. She has worked continuously at the same job as a janitor in a factory from 7.30 a.m. to noon each day.

Relations between Anne and her mother are close and warm. The mother is characterised as 'soft', having spoiled her daughter partly because she was an only child (following a stillbirth and two miscarriages). The parents love children and would have adopted another child if they could have afforded it. The mother provides a continuous presence in the house from noon onwards, sitting and drinking tea in front of the fire, popping next door to visit a neighbour who is 'like a daughter to me' (and is referred to by Anne as a 'cousin'). She is the one who visits relatives and keeps family ties alive; her only other pursuits are 'knitting and bingo'.

Anne's father is the elder of two sons in a family of four; the other son moved away and died; the two sisters still live nearby but less in close contact than Anne's other relatives. Her father spends his spare time with friends and neighbours at the local pub or the Railwayman's Club in the centre of town. The pub and the 'telly' are his main non-working-time activities.

Brinley's mother was a local girl, but *his father* came from England with the Army when he was 19 and married his mother a year later, after meeting her at a dance. She was 19 when they married and he was promptly sent abroad, leaving his new bride to live with her mother for the next five years, during which time Brinley's older brother was born. Brinley was born five years later, after his father was demobbed. They got a council house on the fringes of Swansea, and it was there that they were living at the time of the study. Brinley spent most of his life in this house and knew all the neighbours. The woman next door was 'like a mother' to Brinley's mother, and Brinley's maiden aunt lived down the road, as did an unmarried uncle and Brinley's maternal grandmother who was still alive and living in the original house. An additional uncle and aunt were married and living in other parts of South Wales. Much less was seen of his father's family, with visits only 'every couple of years'. Brinley's father went into the same trade as his own father and brothers, namely bricklaying, sub-contracting jobs for builders and employing up to three assistants and a labourer. Brinley's father died six months previous to the study, and the bereavement process proceeded along with the courtship. Brinley's elder brother had only recently married, and with Brinley's leaving imminent, his mother was feeling the losses greatly. She would be left with only a young daughter of eleven at home; apart from the personal loss, this meant the loss of financial contributions from two working sons. She was working, and in her non-work time found solace in the church, with bingo being her only other diversion. Brinley was in the habit of taking his mother to bingo in the car every week. Brinley's mother communicated a feeling of bitterness. Some of the relatives who were interviewed commented that Brinley may have allowed himself to be 'organised into getting married' by Anne partly to escape from the unhappiness at home. Anne called Brinley's mother 'Mrs Thomas', in contrast to Brin's form of address to her parents as 'mum and dad'.

Anne lived all her life in the same house in Swansea. She went to local schools and so knew many of the young people living nearby. Although her mother wanted her to stay on, Anne did not particularly like school and left at 15½. She went to work in a local factory, in the clerical section. Starting as a messenger girl, she worked her way up through five different jobs to being a shorthand typist for a manager at about £15 a week. To do this, she had been to night school and on day release to the local technical college for a year to learn 'book-keeping and English and secretarial duties'. But she was not excited by or involved in her work:

'the job gets on my nerves sometimes—but I suppose any job would. It's alright. . . . I suppose I can't go much further in my little

department. The next job up is secretary. And there are only five
secretaries—all been there for years.'

Anne always assumed that she would get married and had thought
that she would like to get engaged when she was 21 and married at 23.
Yet she courted a boy when she was 15–17 and they thought of getting
married; in the event she married Brinley when she was 19. In large
measure this is because courting and getting married are of such paramount importance in girls' lives—there is little else in prospect or as
exciting even if, as with Anne, they feel vaguely dissatisfied.

When asked what she thought she would be doing in, say, twenty
years' time, she said:

'Don't know really. Can't say I've got anything special in mind. I
want to get a house in about two years . . . then kids straight away.
I'll stop work when I've got children—he'd play merry hell if I
didn't. Go back when they're old enough. [How old is that?] Five
[Brin interjected 'Twelve']. I'm not going to stick in the house with
the dishes. I may have to go back to shorthand-typing I suppose. . . .
But I don't want the same life day after day; don't want security. . . .
Average marriages are dull. I think my parents—like most people—
live from day to day. I'd like to do something different. [How will
your marriage be different?] He washes the dishes, father doesn't!'

Anne and Brin, like the majority of young people in Swansea, lived
at home until they got married. Anne suggested that she had lots of
arguments with her parents, especially with her father. These usually
centred around her going out and the time she got in:

'They used to complain about my staying out—till six to seven
months ago [when it was established that she and Brinley were going
to get married]. Never go out now—got no money. They used to
complain if I went out every night. I used to have to get in at 11 p.m.
or before. But it's anytime now.

I usually did tell them where I was going. If I wanted to go I'd
have gone, so may as well tell the truth. That's why we quarrelled so
much! One place they did try to stop me going to was the Embassy
[Ball Room]. I loved going there—it was a *dive*. We had rows every
time I went there. Mother let me. But father . . . oh no! But if I
cried! . . .'

Her parents kept a watchful eye on her and because they knew the
district so well they knew who her friends were. Her father replied:

[Did you ever guide her away from a particular friend?] 'Yes.
Remember that Jones boy? She listened too. She didn't resent it.

Went out with him twice—till I told her who he was. Nice boy but not the right type. Illiterate. Very backward.'

Anne's parents also exerted some control over what she did in her 'free' time until she left school. Although she was given a little pocket money each week, this was only for 'sweets and the like'; if Anne wanted money for the cinema or a dance, she asked her mother. Anne suggested she was always canny about money: that she used to 'bank' her pocket money and when she wanted some sweets, she would ask for a few pence to go 'down to Auntie Lil's' (who had a shop). Similarly with her clothes: 'she had what she wanted. Wasn't worth fighting— if she didn't like something, she wouldn't wear it. No point in buying clothes to hang in the cupboard. Spoilt she was.'

This idea of 'spoiling' is important. Because parents convince their children that they (the children) have been treated exceptionally well, the children are under an obligation to behave extra well towards their parents. But equally the children are able to boost themselves by retailing how they 'always got their own way'. That they don't want to leave home because they 'know when they're well off'.

Anne summed up her relationship with her parents thus:

'We get on OK really—apart from the few odd words [her cousin interjected 'You get on exceptionally well']. I get on with my mother better than my father. Don't know [if I understand them]. Never really thought. You never think of parents as people. Don't think they really understand me. Never have heart-to-heart talks with them. Theirs is an average marriage. I'd like to do something different. If I had a personal problem, I'd talk to Brin.

The only thing I do regularly with my parents is quarrel! No, to be serious, the only thing is shopping with my mother. Not every Saturday, but sometimes.' [This ignores the many hours she spends with her mother at home.]

Anne said that after she left school she 'went around with a girl, Susan. We went dancing and to the pictures. Don't see her now. Lost touch when I started courting'.

Her first serious boyfriend was Alan: 'One of the very first I went out with. I was 15 when we first went out—lasted 2½ years. . . . We thought of getting married but we just didn't get on. We used to quarrel.' She had told Brinley about this boy, but not about the 'few—not many' (six when she counted up in her head) other casual boyfriends she had had. 'Alan's the only one he needs to know about':

'After I broke up with Alan I went around with Mary. She lives nearby and we'd known each other from school, but only friends in the last two years. We used to go dancing, to the pictures, to the

Grand [Theatre], the beach and for walks. Now see her just once a week—we go to the Grand on a Monday.'

Another friend, Jean, she saw only at work. Her other current friends (four girls living over a radius of five miles) were 'halves' of couples with whom she and Brin went out. Most of these had been her friends for a fairly short time; all except Mary were engaged, getting engaged or married. Two were also her workmates—the other two were the girl-friends of Brin's friends. Some of Anne's most important companions were not friends but relatives. When asked which of her kin she saw 'regularly', she promptly rattled off ten of her kin and twelve of Brin's. Other relatives visit and are visited 'when they bring presents [at Christmas and birthdays] and when they want to borrow something', or they may be met at the club or at the shops in town.

Brinley was the middle child in his family with a brother three years older and a sister twelve years younger. He was much quieter than Anne but opened up and was well able to speak for himself in general conversation and against Anne's joking. Like her, he had left school at 15; he then took up an apprenticeship as a welder in a pipe-making firm. He was unenthusiastic about his job and thought that one 'should leave work at work', not carry it over into outside life. He finished his time (six and a half years) at the pipe works and then left for another job in the same trade. From this job he was made redundant, and he had since been to eight other firms which he had left because he did not like them. In the firm he was with at the time of the interviews he was reasonably content, because he was on maintenance work and was constantly moving around. Nevertheless, he was looking around for something somewhere else. He was even thinking of joining the police. No one else in the family seemed to take this suggestion seriously.

When asked what he saw himself doing in the next twenty years, he said: 'Being a welder. I'd like to set up on my own. Can't see it though. Could sub-contract but the equipment is so expensive and I've no capital.' He smiled sympathetically at Anne's insistence that she wanted her life to be 'unconventional'; but he agreed with her cousin who, when Anne said that she didn't want security, said, 'You wait till you've got children'.

He thought his parents had had a happy marriage and he expected that his would be pretty much the same as theirs. He said that he got on well with his parents, though they had 'numerous arguments': 'I used to discuss football with my father and he used to come and watch me play and then we rowed over it.' By his account his parents had never tried to restrict how much he went out, nor where he went, nor what time he got back. He never discussed his girlfriends with either of his parents; they did not discuss such matters. None the less, he felt he understood them and they understood him and the family got along pretty well.

After leaving school, Brinley went around for a bit with another boy: 'just two of us boys'. Then at about 16 he started courting and the boys' group became a 'gang, going to dances and drinking'. When he was 'about 18½' he started

> 'going with Wendy. Lasted off and on for about nine to ten months. We parted good friends. Just decided to call it a day. Little quarrels —like she'd want to go to a dance and I wouldn't. [Had you thought of marriage?] No, not really—we were too young.
>
> Then there were lots of others I saw about eight times—and about ten or twenty where it was only once, 'cos I found I didn't like them! [Have you told Anne about them?] Not all of them. (Anne: 'He gives their names away bit by bit. We tell each other everything— only he doesn't tell me their names.') Doesn't do to be too candid. Nothing came of it—so why tell? She [Anne] does throw it up in a quarrel later.'

It was the gang or 'all the boys in work' who came to his twenty-first birthday party—'in the Queen's in town' (a pub). His relations did not come, though they gave him presents. After these casual relationships and the gang, came Anne. He now had two close male friends, both of whom were engaged: 'My friends are her friends.' But when a couple was cited, Brinley gave the man as his friend, Anne gave the woman.

He sees a lot of his kin—his grandmother and aunt and uncle every day. The young couple met through their mothers because the two women once worked together (in the same factory as Anne, but in a different department). Anne said:

> 'His mother's watches kept going funny, so his mother asked my mother to take them to this man. Brin brought them round. He was going with this other girl [Wendy]. . . . I went for a walk with my mother to get her 32s [the watches having been mended and paid for] to the garage where his mother worked. He'd finished with his girl, hadn't you? After all that, we'd forgotten to take the watches! He came down on the Wednesday to pick the watches up. I was looking scruffy, so he said "How long would it take you to change?" I said, "Five minutes—why?" "Take you into town for a drink." The first week we saw each other twice—the Wednesday and Friday. And then about every evening since.
>
> It's funny, you know, to explain [how we decided to get married]. Just something we settled into. He wanted to get engaged early on. I said no. Don't know why. I just said "later on". He didn't actually ask outright if I'd marry him—just sort of hinted.'

Brinley: 'It was like this. A couple of nights previously, Anne's auntie was down. She tells fortunes. She was reading Anne's tea-leaves. Said something about a ring. We'd been quarrelling—she kept saying "I don't know where I am with you." I said "You know that ring? You can have it any time." She said she'd think about it.'

Anne: 'We just decided on the spot when to get married. He'd asked me ages before. I just said no. Suddenly I said: "It's about time we got married." He thought I was joking! It was in a pub in Swansea—the Three Lamps or the New York.'

Anne and Brinley were unusual in their local group in that they were courting for only a year altogether and they did not get engaged. In large measure this was because they did not have to save up to get a house and furniture; they planned to live with her parents and to save for two years after they were married. Anne said:

'Six months [between deciding that they would get married and the wedding] is just about the right length of time. Then it seemed a long time; now it seems just right. Enough time to back out! And [enough to] make arrangements and get everything ready. We're lucky I've no brothers and sisters and can live with my mother. If we'd had to get a house, it'd been different.'

The chief changes in their pattern of activities since they started courting have already been mentioned: the changeover from one girl-friend and a gang of boys to a shared group of engaged couples; and going out less—or going to places which cost less—in order to save. Anne represented them as still leading a hectic social life; she sketched out what they would do in a typical week:

'Sunday— nearly always go to the Naval Club at Aberavon.
Monday— [Anne goes to the theatre with her girlfriend, Monday being the cheap night at the local repertory theatre.] Brinley sometimes goes but he feels a bit awkward. If he doesn't come, he often picks us up in his car [or since losing his licence, meets them and comes back with them on the bus].
Tuesday— stay in.
Wednesday—either Dai and Diane come over or we go over there.
Thursday— go up the Ferryboat. The Ferryboat's good because they have a sing-song. Sometimes we go to a club—the Trostre Club . . . a friend's a member. Occasionally we go to the pictures.
Friday— we go to a club at Llanelly (a friend is in a group which plays in various clubs).
Saturday— go out with Bob and Jenny. Varies what we do.'

But at other times she contradicts this by saying: 'We generally go out at the weekends—stay in during the week. We're saving. We play records or cards, watch TV or have friends in.'

Both Brinley and Anne give 'a fair bit of help in the house', partly together—decorating, gardening and cooking. They decorate for her parents, his mother and other older relatives.

The young couple are highly integrated into their two kin groups. For example, in one of the interviews, Anne was at home but Brin was not there, so she fetched him. He had been to her house before she was back from work, and after chatting to her mother for five minutes he went down to the other end of the terrace to see one of Anne's uncles who was ill. He was there for 'the best part of an hour'. These relationships become a major interest. For small town conventional couples the platitude about gaining a son rather than losing a daughter has more reality than in most urban settings.

The two sets of parents see very little of each other. Among some of Anne's and Brinley's friends, they did not meet until the engagement party, and in a few cases not until the wedding itself. Anne's and Brinley's mothers knew each other from work, and the two fathers met at the club Brinley and his father belong to. Anne's parents 'came up one night'. But even had Brinley's father not died, it would have been unlikely that they would have made an effort to see each other again. The mothers occasionally bump into each other in town shopping; in future they will meet if both sides come to visit the young couple at the same time, for example at Christmas. Otherwise there is unlikely to be any contact.

Brinley and Anne felt marriage would make few changes in their pattern of interests and activities. Brinley said: 'Maybe on a Monday I'll go to the club while she goes to the theatre. But otherwise together, same as now.'

It seems that courtship and the early months of marriage are channels for excitement for these young people. Their jobs are experienced as boring. The courtships that they and their friends experience introduce a new element of drama. They evolve stories about the strangeness of their meeting, the bids and rebuffs, tactics and course of campaign in the process of getting engaged, and then the decision to get married. Anne's announcing (before an audience) that she did not want security had this element of drama—in what was taken to be a departure from conventionality. Similarly her overplaying of the number of times she and Brin go out each week, suggesting that they enjoy a 'mad social whirl' and her emphasis on how different (unconventional and companionate) her marriage is going to be, provide this kind of excitement. Brin is less given to such representations but he is much attracted to it in Anne.

For the people in this conventional working-class group there was a sharp division between time spent in 'money-earning work' (job) time, and out-of-job time. Within this out-of-job time there was some that was spent on particular *activities*: bingo, knitting, watching TV and going to the pub were mentioned by the older people; dancing, going to the pictures or theatre, walks, going to a pub or club, having a sing-song, football, playing records or cards and having friends in were mentioned by the young couple. These activities tend to be undertaken with friends while the companionate sitting and chatting tends to be with relatives.

Students: a moratorium in identification

Full-time students comprise a substantial minority among young adults (about 20 per cent of those aged 18–21 in Britain). They are, in a sense, the obverse of the unemployed, having no 'non-work' time. There is no standard work week for students, presumably all of their time being involved in developmental experiences. This assertion needs elaboration. There is a continuing discussion about the purposes and justification for higher education in this and other countries. While its assumptions are questioned by some, many subscribe to the view that one aim is 'education of the whole person'. Certainly this aim is central to what has been called 'the conservative ideal' of university experience, but is likely to be shared by many who subscribe to a more radical version also. Differences occur on issues like whether physical and social separation from the wider community in an encapsulating university environment is desirable or not in attaining this aim, and whether or not students more than others should be beneficiaries of 'education of the whole person'. A summary of the different ideologies involved, and their implications, is presented in a critique of traditional and new concepts of the university by the Joint Unit for Planning Research in their recently published *The University in an Urban Setting* (1974).

In focusing on students in the universities, the plurality of objectives suggested by the Robbins Report (1963) would seem fairly widely accepted:

> 'We begin with instruction in skills suitable to play a part in the general division of labour. . . . But, secondly, while emphasising that there is no betrayal of values when institutions of higher education teach what will be some practical use, we must postulate that what is taught should be taught in such a way as to promote the general powers of the mind. . . . Thirdly, we must name the advancement of learning. . . . Finally, there is a function that is more difficult to describe concisely, but that is none the less fundamental: the trans-mission of a common culture and common standards of citizenship.'

While these are neither integrated nor ranked in importance, it is clear that many people believe—though they do not conceptualise it in our terms—that students should cultivate the capacity to develop meaningful life interests. This holds for their time spent at lectures, classes, labs, in reading, writing essays, and for their other activities. The traditional ideal portrays also informal discussion with staff and peers drifting from academic subjects or religion to politics, sex, emotions, films or football. Developing skills in arguing, participating, experiencing, reading to find evidence to support particular standpoints, experimenting with new food and drink, sport or music, is not only relevant to training for work, but to training for life (Marris, 1964, 2–3):

> Most people who have faith in a university believe that [it] can give [a liberal] education, and that this is its particular justification. The ideal implies . . . the development of a generalized rational understanding both from the courses themselves and, equally, the social environment in which the student learns. For him university is not so much an institution, as three or four years of his life, when living away from home, making friends, falling in love or realizing his religious convictions may be as important as studying for a degree.

However, all universities are not identical sorts of institutions. In many, getting a degree or other vocational qualification is of overriding importance. Not all students live away from home, especially among those attending the large urban universities. The ideal of liberal education that Marris portrays is largely attainable only by the élite of the student élite, and is no longer as universally desired as it was formerly.

Students have been the most widely studied young adults. Butcher and Rudd (1972) state that in the last ten years 'higher education has been a growth industry and research into it has been growing even more rapidly'. Nevertheless, important gaps in the information persist. Little is known of specialist colleges (architecture, art, drama, physiotherapy, agriculture, etc.), of colleges of further education, or polytechnics. Our account thus deals largely with students in universities. Even here, little is known of actual differences students experience in the various types of university environment, for example in the new suburban universities as compared with the more established metropolitan ones. The JUPR's study (1974) of student (and staff) experience at Bedford College in London is a start in this direction.

Next is a problem of orientation. Much of the research is formulated in a framework of industrial bureaucracy. Accordingly attention is given to 'wastage' and inefficiency of performance (for example through protests, drugs and neuroses). There is comparatively little analysis of the developmental experiences of students. The focus tends to be on aptitude testing of entrants, teaching methods and objectives, the academic

profession, finances, therepy, etc., rather than on the process of facilitating the cultivation of students' personal resourcefulness.

Each institution of higher education has its own ethos and structure.
Its students have distinctive characteristics—especially in terms of
socio-economic background. Different institutions select for particular
skills and personality types. Some institutions are more favourably
placed in terms of staff–student ratios and other facilities (library
space, residential accommodation, playing fields, access to towns with
good theatres and cinemas, or the presence of an arts centre on the
campus). Some are reputed to be specially élitist; some are reputed to
be particularly strong in certain fields—perhaps in an unconventional
way. All these factors affect how institutions of higher education are
chosen by and how they choose their specific sub-populations—affected
by and affecting the life styles to be found in each. Many students in
the JUPR's sample, for example, chose Bedford College because of the
availability of London facilities (JUPR, 1974, 141).

One of the most useful British studies remains Peter Marris's *The
Experience of Higher Education* (1964); he covers a wide range of topics
related to life from the students' viewpoint at four institutions—
Cambridge, Southampton and Leeds Universities and Northampton
CAT (now City University, London).* CAT's no longer exist, and
though the material is dated in other respects as well, we use it as a
baseline for the discussion in this section, with more recent findings
supplementing it where they are helpful.

Marris describes the way in which students rarely stop to consider
what further education can provide but rather accept the bureaucratic
structure and go on purposefully up the academic ladder. They do an
honours degree if they have the ability; they go to a CAT or polytechnic
if they failed to obtain university entrance qualifications rather than
wanting what the polytechnic, etc., has to offer.

Because of the great pressure to get good A-level results and the
assumption that university is *the* goal, many students arrive at college
and 'seem at first to wait passively for some inarticulate but great
fulfilment'. Many become disenchanted—academically and socially—
when their romantic dreams (Marris, 1964, 35) of:

> gaiety, freedom, intellectual excitement and graceful surroundings
> crumble. [Also, they are] so long conditioned by the logic of com-
> petitive selection that they hardly [know] how to respond. By the time
> they [have] lived down their misconceptions, and [realised] how

---

* This research was undertaken as evidence for the Robbins Committee. The
Institute of Community Studies and the sponsors—Leverhulme and Rowntree—
felt that more discursive interviews were needed to supplement the statistical
information. Interviews were carried out from Autumn 1961 to Spring 1963.

much they must rely on their own initiative to realize their opportunities, the final year with its examination pressure was approaching and it began already to be too late.

Those who opted for a CAT are less disillusioned; but those who go to a CAT who wanted to go to a university are very critical of the 'cultural' aspects. The majority of students continue to study the subjects in which they have done best at school—only economics, law and social science are seen as new possibilities into which to move. A sizeable proportion of males from middle-class backgrounds changes to study of applied science. Marris contrasts the more instrumental, calculative approach of the middle-class with that of the working-class boy in two ideal types (1964, 31):

> There is the upper-middle-class student who goes from public school to his father's old university. He sees his university career primarily as a means of qualifying for an occupation similar in status to his father's, and he feels his parents to have been a more important influence on his application to university than his school. He chooses a course which provides a recognized preparation for a profession—medicine, engineering, law, or rather less specifically economics; or he may be equipping himself to take his place in the family business. By contrast, the working-class student is more influenced by his grammar-school, and sees the university more as the final prize in the competition for education, whose vocational usefulness he takes for granted. He is vaguer about the future to which it will lead, and sticks to the academic specialization with which he is most familiar, in which he has proved his ability and acquired an interest. Neither student has the social or intellectual opportunities of the university uppermost in his mind.

Marris does not give an ideal-typical picture for women students, but it is known that women, irrespective of class background, tend more to read arts or social science—which puts them with those who see coming to university as an end in itself and a general 'qualification' for later life. The social side—finding a husband of similar status—is also important, because of the strong, though lessening, tendency for a woman's life style to be dependent on that of her husband.

These findings seem compatible with Sandford's (1962) for the USA; for the middle class college is a social necessity, for the working class it is a means of social advancement. This applies not only in the vocational areas which Marris emphasises, but also to what Robbins refers to as 'the transmission of a common culture'—the area of life style and personal interests. But Marris's sample suggests that many students see their university courses helping little to develop their more general interests. The effect of specialisation may even be negative (Marris, 1964, 66):

> On the whole the students we interviewed were too preoccupied by the demands of their curriculum to take . . . initiative in their general education. Only a fifth of the students at each university had attended any lecture outside their course during the term. At Northampton, liberal studies—such as Psychology, Logic, History of Science, or English literature—are included in the course, though students are not examined in them. Over half our sample had attended them, if not regularly, and about a third had also been to some of the open lunch-time lectures which the college provides—but these were often related to their subject. It seems to be rare for students anywhere to attend lectures of another course; he finds time, if at all, only for the open lectures. Nor is there much leisure for general reading. Altogether, a quarter of the scientists had not opened a book at all during the term, apart from their studies, and another quarter had read only light fiction, or motor-racing manuals; while 15 per cent of arts students had read nothing and 8 per cent merely light entertainment. Outside Cambridge, only around a fifth had found time for more than a couple of serious books.

The main frustration reported was lack of time. Marris's indices of 'general education'—extra-curricular lectures and reading—are of course limited. If other indices are considered—socialising and attending theatres, cinemas, exhibitions, playing sport, or participating in civic activities, etc.—then the student sample at Bedford College at least was shown to be fairly active in pursuing 'general education'. How much students want to devote themselves to their subject, to get involved in 'university life', or to 'broaden' themselves culturally, varies with the individual and presumably also with the type of university, but there is a conflict between the requirements of a 'programme' of training and the desire for freedom to develop independence of mind and self-organisation.

According to Marris, science students feel the lack of time most acutely, partly because they have more lectures and laboratory work but also because, unlike arts students, intellectual interests other than those intrinsic to their subjects are excluded from their official curricula. Nevertheless, he suggests even if specialist teaching requirements were reduced, students would probably still spend most time on their special subject because of the importance for future occupational prospects of doing well in examinations. There is a 'general feeling, especially among technologists, that cultural interests [are] best postponed until their degrees [are] safely pocketed'.

An aspect of student life which has subsequently been well researched is residence (Brothers and Hatch, 1971). The studies show how difficult it is to untangle the influence of residence from that of all other factors. This reflects well in Marris's contrasting interview situations (1964, 3):

At Cambridge, the interviews took place in the students' rooms—with tea and biscuits, sherry, port or coffee; a hospitality at once informal and scrupulously polite. Evidence of a varied undergraduate society everywhere caught the eye—the posters in hallways and cafés; the rows of club programmes and creative invitations propped on a mantelpiece; an oar slung over a landlady's ormolu clock, a pile of OTC kit on a shabby sofa, an electric guitar and box of black Russian cigarettes on an austerely functional divan. Friends would call during an interview about a game of squash, the editorial meeting of a magazine, a textbook or a motor rally. No one seemed isolated except by choice, from the activity around him. Elsewhere most students preferred to meet us in the university buildings during the day before they scattered for the evening meal. We would sit in the corner of a crowded coffee lounge, a deserted music room or a nearby pub. Activity crowded around the refectory serving counter, the hallway of the students' union. The press of students hurried past tables offering Marxist tracts or poetry magazines in smudged mimeograph, a blackboard announcing the next CND demonstration, notices of holidays abroad or quiet walks for religious meditation; and piled heaps of duffle coats and university scarves along the radiators as they stood in line for their cottage pie and chips. . . . Even in the halls of residence, the students' rooms we did visit seemed impersonal. The rows of beer mats along the curtain rail, the maps on the walls, hardly redeemed the institutional neutrality.

Although fashions in clothes, political protest and wall decorations have changed, Marris, biased towards the cultural richness of the Oxbridge collegiate ideal, portrays the flavour of some student life. But it is known from subsequent studies that many people feel very lonely at Cambridge, and a landlady's digs can be even more depressing in their decor than the white walls of a 'box' in a tower block. Again, a flat shared with other students may be a stimulating, friendly supportive unit. The continuum—from compact social units all physically close in the university which dominates the town, through suburban campuses with high proportions of students ideally on campus or close by (though often several miles away), through urban centre universities with many students in hostels or digs, to scattered teaching buildings with few social amenities and no accommodation, to which many students commute (sometimes from over twenty miles away) and where social life is reputed to be divorced from the college which becomes 'a place you come to every day to learn engineering'—covers the range to be found in university education. As yet relatively little is known of the extent to which the key features of these stereotypes do in fact hold for the various situations.

Those who speak out for university colleges and halls of residence aim in part to facilitate 'cross-fertilisation'—to stimulate students to make friends with those doing other subjects. Marris reports that, despite a crowded curriculum, scientists he interviewed did manage to join in the social life of the university almost as fully as readers of humanities. He argues that in most students' experience the stimulating exchanges were not between those studying different academic disciplines, but between those with different social backgrounds, religious or political interests or ethnic groups. For in social groups they discuss not academic work, but faith, nuclear war, racism, class and education, sex and personal relationships, sports and careers, politics and current affairs.

Life interests rather than academic departments determine the social groups within the student community. Cliques form around sport, student politics and societies, popular meeting places and activity locales. It is in the provision of these opportunities rather than in academic content or standards ·that the contrast between the universities and the technological colleges is most significant. Marris suggests that the social life in the technical college is much more confined: there are no arts faculties or facilities to diversify the intellectual range, the social facilities are meagre, the students come and go at different times on sandwich courses, frustrating both personal relationships and the ability to form organisations; in addition he feels that the students, as technologists, feel themselves relegated to a subordinate role in intellectual culture. These students are under the disability that *they* have to initiate any activities they participate in (Marris, 1964, 115):

> Art students not only may have more time to give to plays, concerts, discussion groups, political and religious societies, literary magazines, but they can relate to these interests directly to their studies, and sometimes to the careers they hope to enter. A university can therefore foster a much wider range of social activities at a higher level of sophistication, than a community of engineers have the time or the confidence to tackle by themselves. And a university scientist may find time to take part in them, where he could not organize them himself.

While all the details of his portrait do not relate to all universities, for example London University or most of its colleges, the relatively interstitial quality of student life that Marris characterises remains fairly universal (1964, 126):

> A community of students is a relatively uncommon form of social grouping in our society. It draws together men and women of a

similar age, ability and interests, making them aware of each other as the academically privileged representatives of their generation. Their years at university are an initiation into the *élite* of their society, and the sequestration, the ceremonies of graduation, recall the rites through which the age grades of some African societies traditionally passed. Most young people in our society are never so withdrawn from everyday preoccupations, from contact with other age-groups, nor graduated into adult life so formally and with such evident marks of status, A university absorbs its members more wholly and more selectively than school, which remains for most pupils only a day-time community, enclosed within their life at home. And a university is also more detached, more autonomous in its values, repudiating too close a concern with the later careers of its members. Under-graduates are estranged from their past and their future, within a community more diverse in opinion and background than any they have known, or will know again, and yet extraordinarily homo-geneous. This is the outstanding attraction of university life, and also the source of a pervasive anxiety.

This anxiety arises from being in a state of limbo in relation to the kind of life style that one will practise—rather like being in national service for a brief period. Many students feel they are isolated in a closed, unreal, artificial community living an irresponsible life. Hatch and Moylan (1972) suggest that this dissatisfaction has grown and was an important factor in the student unrest of the late 1960s. Paradoxic-ally technical college students feel that their curricula are more clearly related to life. The drawbacks for them are poverty and pressure of work. The diploma students studied by Marris felt it useful to do part-time work in industry—they became more worldly-wise and saw how they would fit into work later, even if their particular experiences were not enjoyable or professionally useful (cf. also Jahoda, 1963).

The whole area of student unrest, radical political actions and extreme rebelliousness had not come to a head when Marris was writing. Though only a minority of students are extreme in their counter-cultural emphasis and activism, they have come to prominence, led rebellions, influenced attitudes and policy; universities, for better or worse, will never be the same. Taken by surprise, the faculties of many modern universities were split on how to deal with students who treated them, the faculty, like enemies. Were they simply to be treated as one's own children, tolerated with affection as they acted out their rebelliousness in the search for identity? Or were they dangerous enemies of the social order, whether as independent actors or as tools of others with sinister purposes? When they trespassed, destroyed property, banned dissent, interrupted teaching—were they to be suppressed like criminals or delinquents? Or were the deficiencies of the universities as bastions of privilege, expensive harbours of antiquated practices, purveyors of confusion and hypocrisy to be recognised and made the object of attention? Were the cultural revolutions of England, the USA and France as counter-productive as China's? Was the system at fault, or was it something endemic to the intergenerational tension in a situation of change and the liberation of new ideas and interests?

These are problems beyond the scope of our study, but we note that there is a problem of how young adults who defer participation in the 'real' world' of social action can find ways to relate their ideas and feelings to tangible activities. University students often use their vacations to re-establish contact with the 'real' world. Three-quarters take paid work in the summer—for the money and for the experience. Some deliberately choose non-vocational jobs which enable them to mix with other kinds of people. Relating to others in a meaningful way is the focus of the interests of many. Travelling far and wide is an activity whereby this is channelled.

The Hale Committee on *The Use of Vacations by Students* (1963) viewed the lack of study in the long vacation with dismay. But the contacts made by work and travel are important, as are students' feelings of personal and social integration through this extra-curricular form of development.

Sending students out—or having them oscillate between 'ordinary' life settings and those of the university—has been a fairly widespread pattern. The sandwich programmes (or 'co-operative education' programmes as they are termed in the USA) are turned out with various fillings and packagings. 'Junior year abroad' is an extension of the constructive use of the school holiday. However, bringing into the university elements not conventionally part of the structure—i.e. people who belong neither to the faculty, the administration nor to the narrow age band of students—tends to be seen as a far more radical change. Summer programmes for whole families as at Carnegie College; multiple use of cultural and sports facilities by the community; the off-season use of residential facilities for holidays or conference venues, are some ways of opening universities on limited and defined bases. There is still little interaction between the 'other users' and the regular users for whom the university is built and functions. In some cases there is little awareness that interaction is beneficial, or indeed possible. Alternatively, despite awareness of the potentials of interaction, it is resisted (Strelitz, 1972). Thompson's account of the city of Coventry's persistent failure to obtain a high degree of mutual participation with Warwick University provides one example (Thompson, 1970).

On a more mundane level, the removal of the life of the university from the realm of ordinary human interests and concerns may lead to low student morale, apathy, neurotic complaints, underperformance and high wastage. Dorothy Zinberg, in a recent study of a London science department (staff and students), found that what had produced excellence in the faculty produced apathy among the students. Faculty members who were selected because they were dedicated to science had little by way of training or even professional values on which to build communities of interest with new students fresh from school, lonely and uncertain of themselves and with unformed life interests and values. The 'sink or swim' mentality of the élites may serve to produce a small proportion of highly motivated professionals, tempered by the psychological ordeal of the competitive performance system. However, in a society with wider manpower concerns and humanistic concerns with the development of its citizens as people as well as specialists, the 'creaming off' of the few high-flyers is not enough. Zinberg notes (1972, 42-3):

> Knowledge is not transmitted in a vacuum. Even the most theoretical formulations of the fundamentals of a discipline are taught within a social milieu which has a force of its own. Although it is related to the curriculum, it operates separately from it. For example, to know whether or not a student likes a course, or believes he's learned something from it is not sufficient to understand why he decides to continue . . . or shift out. Neither are grades sufficient indices of what's happening to the student's attitudes over the course of the year . . . those students who scored the highest marks in their examinations were among the most vociferous critics of the year's experience.

'Creaming off' can easily slip into a less discriminating selection for conformity and mediocrity rather than excellence, the 'real cream' in a more creative sense passing centrifugally to other fields. This presents a paradox: excellence depends on specialisation but over-specialisation upsets balance. Balance depends on breadth and articulation with human interests. However, this may slip into blunting of keenness on which so many professions depend for their development and excellence.

There are some observers of the university scene—particularly in the USA—who emphasise the importance of reversing the priority of these values. People like Reich and Keniston emphasise the possibility in an affluent society for human values to be restored to ascendancy without disaster. They feel that if there is a path to disaster for society as a whole, it is in the unadulterated pursuit of competitive and materialistic values—in which the purpose for which such values evolved is forgotten in the single-minded lemming-like trek for 'more' and 'bigger' achievements (Reich, 1970; Keniston, 1971). Changing the situation of the student in university will surely take place in conjunction with the

changing relation of the universities to the community. As this change
is likely to mean a loosening of university boundaries and proliferation
of external linkages, students will probably come to share what is now
a special and fairly exclusive opportunity for the development of cultivated life interests with members of the wider society.

Involuntarily unemployed: time on their hands

Earlier we discussed the confusion which arises when 'leisure' is
defined as a particular type of unpaid, non-work time. Dennis Marsden
(1975) argues that it is only when people cannot get a job that the work/
non-work division of time assumes meaning for them. Drawing heavily
on Marsden's material, we give some account of the effects of unemployment on young people: of what it is like to have only imposed non-
work time.

In our society work is still perceived as morally good. Work also
provides money, sometimes allows self-expression, is absorbing and
organises one's time. People are placed socially by the work they do—
so work also gives status. Its stamp is pervasive, as Denis Pym suggests
(1972, 1–2):

> Your answer to my question 'What do you do?' leads to a wealth of
> additional categories, and becomes the basis for guesstimates about
> your origins, place of residence, income, family possessions, etc. etc.
> The question also invokes the tyranny of your public self. Although
> you may not wear the totem on your shirt, you carry its constraining
> tag on your head from where it exercises infinitely more power.

Yet many people have little emotional investment in their work and
for some it is negatively charged and stressful. So might not unemployment represent a release and an opportunity for such individuals? Certainly public or press reaction to the unemployed involves mixed feelings: envy, because it is felt that for the unemployed life is a long
holiday with pay; suspicion, because the workless are seen as perhaps
not looking for work, or that they are not suited for the particular work
which they insist on trying to get; hostility, in case they are work-shy;
and sympathy, because many of the unemployed are the victims of
circumstances beyond their control, and that it could well happen to
anyone.

The numbers of young people without work fluctuates with the
general level of unemployment, but they are substantial and occasion
widespread anxiety. In early 1972, 10,000 school-leavers remained unemployed compared with 5,500 the previous year. By autumn 1972, at
the height of the school-leaving bulge, and high national unemployment,
there were 55,000 boys under 18 and over 30,000 girls registered as

unemployed. This is an understatement; it is known that many young people do not register for work at the Employment Exchange. Yet if we look at studies of young people, with very few exceptions (Ferguson and Cunnison, 1956), the unemployed young (other than delinquents) have been socially invisible (Willmott, 1963; Morse, 1965). Marsden found them much more difficult to contact and to talk to than older unemployed men.

Unemployment therefore affects different age groups differently. It also differentially affects different skill groups and has variable affects by locality. Unemployment rates for unskilled men run at $2\frac{1}{2}$ times the national average; and the farther one moves geographically from the South-east region, the greater the unemployment. University graduates also face unemployment—a socially visible minority. In 1966 less than 3 per cent of graduates had not found a job by the end of the year (5 per cent unaccounted for), but in 1971 almost 8 per cent of new graduates were still looking for work (10 per cent unaccounted for).

For many unqualified young school-leavers, unemployment grows slowly out of a feeling of being on holiday. Initially it is fun but then they get bored and feel they have no place in life. They make energetic attacks on the job market till obvious lines are exhausted. Then they despair, perhaps solidifying attitudes which make it difficult for them ever to re-enter work. Others find themselves temporarily employed as youthful helpers but thrown out of work once they become old enough to earn men's wages. Or they are disillusioned when they realise that they are in so-called 'apprenticeships', leading nowhere. Others become redundant under the rule of last in, first out. They leave the work situation feeling exploited or personal failures.

A crucial problem faced by the unemployed is how to fill their time. Marsden found that in his sample in the North-east, they hung around their homes, becoming more and more bored and starved for company. The eternal accompaniment of transistor radios, records and comics becomes indiscriminate food for their boredom (Marsden, 1975):

The phrase being 'stuck in the house all day' expressed very clearly the sense of having no work or substitute work and no desire and no legitimate reason to be part of the home world of women and children. And this feeling was voiced most acutely by teenagers who, almost with one voice, described their days of unemployment as 'crap', 'boredom' or 'murder'.

'Oh crap! Like you're in the house on a Monday, on a Tuesday, Wednesday you gang down the dole. On a Thursday to the dole to sign. That leaves you with Friday, Saturday, Sunday and all the way like that again, the same week. Only one day you could get out and that's a Thursday. Well, I got up, like, went down the shops for summat to eat like. Went down to the dole, just signed, went back home, and that was it. I was in till the following Thursday.'

'Oh, its boring. I used to go and play football or something like that, sit about the house and play me guitar, and I just got fed up. Me mother was on at us. She was always saying 'Get out and try and get a job'. You can hardly wonder you were made depressed when you got turned down.'

The lack of a job as an organising activity is also important. Many of those who are unemployed find their biological rhythms disturbed. They are wakeful at night and tired during the day. Some spend much time in bed or they become generally apathetic, losing interest in previous hobbies. Marsden's teenagers mentioned growing laziness as a worry—they were afraid that they were losing the will to work, that they were becoming unemployable layabouts—a fear shared by their parents. This may lead to the ruin of previously meaningful family relationships.

Unemployed people suffer a change in morale, indeed in identity, with continued rebuffs from employers and jokes from family and neighbours. There is pressure from employers, the Labour Exchange and possibly also kin, to change one's ideas about what job one wants and what wage is appropriate (i.e. to change one's occupational identification, status and self-evaluation). Other people reinforce the negative aspects of the 'unemployed' identity: 'You're in a pub, and inevitably the question comes up "What do you do?", and if you say you're unemployed, they don't want to know, they just turn away.' This is partly a matter of the social vacuum that is created when one has no work experience to discuss but is also due to the inability of the unemployed to reciprocate in buying rounds of drinks, and to the stigma associated with unemployment.

Some respond to this situation by making work-like activity for themselves, which can be seen, felt and talked about if not paid for. But this does not provide a permanent solution. One of Marsden's informants who had been unemployed for several years, just after he was married and while living with his in-laws, did a lot of house decorating, which sufficed for a while. But then the comments from his father-in-law drove him out, and he spent all his days on an allotment, meeting his unemployed friends in a hut. In this little retreat unemployment was the norm. Others do handicrafts, which they sell cheaply or window-cleaning and painting and decorating in the neighbourhood as a 'fiddle', since they are on national insurance or supplementary benefit. Or they may 'acquire' a pseudo-occupational identity: for example, one young man always wore a British Road Services jacket to explain why he was walking around the housing estate in the middle of the day.

To be able to find meaningful interests accounts for the enthusiasm which many unemployed young people expressed for doing, for example, paid community service. Community Industries (a voluntary group, funded by the DEP for projects in areas of high unemployment) gives work to under 18-year-olds who have been unemployed for eight months to a year. Boys and girls are given jobs needed by local authorities, for example, decorating old people's homes, digging their gardens and the like. While the wages are low and this is explicitly seen only as a short-term expedient for the unemployed young, they express predominantly grateful attitudes. Work, for most, is simply better than idleness: 'This job, like, it's better than being on the dole, like, really. It gets a bit boring at times, like, but better than being on the dole.'

The limbo of unemployment can be experienced either as an opportunity for development of personal interests or as a stressful situation to which various retreatist solutions are sought. Some unemployed young persons pass their time and get emotional support from a gang or clique, supplementing their dole with a bit of thieving. Alternatively the time may be spent to develop new interests which might never have been born. *New Society* published a description of a youth who had made his way via a clique in a café to acquiring an identification with students (O'Brien, 1972):*

Young Nick spends his days in a coffee bar and his nights dossing in his mates' pads. He did not make the grade at the local tech. and, failing to get jobs which he was prepared to consider, he drifted—without any visits to the Employment Exchange, and thus without ever figuring in statistics of the unemployed—into the 'in' scene. He is 17 or 18 years old. He passes as a student. He left home after parental pressures to get a job. He cadges enough 'coffee, nosh and cigs' from students and girl friends to be entirely self-supporting. He supplements this with nicking a few bits of jewelry and selling 'pot' made from joss sticks to the gullible. He goes to parties and pop trips and pub sessions because his friends 'wouldn't think of leaving him out'. More recently, after meeting some real students, he has now a political reason for not dropping in. 'They' are always in charge so why should he contribute?

O'Brien ends his article thus:

Yes, you could say that Nick was a layabout, and in the clinking and the smoke and the laughing, the coffee bar holds many like him. Coffee bars, of course, exist even in the smallest towns of the land, and must collectively contain quite a few Nicks. There seem to be

* This is a summary of Terence O'Brien's profile of 'Young Nick'.

just two queries to utter: is the 'unemployed' really a bigger group than 'they' say it is; and is there any possibility that being 'unemployed' may be a good career?

The answer to the second query seems to be that it is for some—those who fill their time with interests which they find meaningful, and who are able to do so either in the context of a socially approved activity (like Community Industry or further education) or who insulate themselves from social sanctions by forming groups with alternative values—as will be described next.

Absence of a structured work role can be handled in different ways. Passivity, boredom and depression are the least resourceful. Restless activity of an indiscriminate kind, 'filling' time with TV, radio and comics is perhaps the most common but not much more of a developmental solution; acquiring a new identity with new interests is the more promising and constructive prospect but the most difficult to achieve without facilitation.

'Alternative' groups: no contrast between life spheres

One adaptation to unemployment which we have already mentioned is to 'drop out', though dropping out occurs also for other reasons. The drop-out does not look for a job but does whatever he finds meaningful; if his quest for meaning excludes paid employment, he does not mind living off the State. Conventional family and work life may be positively rejected in favour of other interests. These other interests may be study, art, writing, politics, group child-rearing, exploration of the mind (in psychological, religious, physiological modes), or simply in the attempt to find an alternative mode of existence within a society he finds unacceptable. The contrast between work, leisure and family life for such individuals is meaningless, and they attempt to merge the spheres in various ways. Work is not undertaken for remote goals or for gains other than the intrinsic enjoyment of the experience. Time is not divided into work time and other time. Relationships with others are sometimes in a quasi-family mode, with 'communal' living arrangements of various kinds expressing attempts at new groupings for intimacy. Paradoxically the fusion of various elements of living may (as with the unemployed) sometimes have the effect of creating a new appreciation of their distinctiveness.

It is easier to pursue an 'alternative' course if one has the company of like-minded people, together with whom one can construct and confirm **a** shared 'reality' (Berger and Kellner, 1964), employ boundary-maintaining actions to counteract the force of conventional mores, for example with food symbols—only eating 'health foods'. Living together may act as a reinforcement. Such groups vary in size, degree of integration and stability, and contain individuals who are there for various reasons. Some groups have an explicit ideology, purpose, philosophy or rationale for life together, while others are fortuitously sharing accommodation or facilities. There is a range of self-conscious living arrangements and rationales for alternative life styles. We contrast some characteristics of 'hip' communities and life style as portrayed in the literature with our own case material from an 'expedient' housing group in short-life housing in London.

'Hip' communes may be urban or rural, organised around a charismatic leader or not, may or may not experiment with family, may produce their own goods or not, and so on. The central common element is the attempt by young adults to form alternative ways of living independently of established patterns. Many do not sustain the alternative form; some communes fail and many individuals go through communes only to return home after a disheartening experience, an illness or hunger. On the other hand, the degree to which this is a stable though heterogeneous social movement, regardless of the foreclosure of particular groups (even whole districts like Haight-Ashbury in San Francisco), makes it an important element in the contemporary social change scene. It leaves traces that stimulate changes, even if unintended ones.

As Mills (1973, 5) demonstrates, the 'hip' ideology is focally, if not always explicitly, concerned with some of the central issues of this book:

> A story is told of a meeting between one of the more charismatic leaders of the London 'Underground' and an old friend who was insensitive enough to ask him what work he was doing. In magisterially contemptuous tones came the reply: 'I don't work, I play'. If a single attitude was required to express the essence of hippie values this is probably the one that would be chosen, both by hippies themselves and their commentators. 'We are secret agents of a future society free from the routine degradation of work', says the leader of the London Street Commune. 'Drop-outs are anticipating future economic policy', writes Richard Neville (1970, p. 270). 'Tomorrow you may be paid not to work—can you take it?'

Enriching the quality of working life, and of life generally, increasing resourcefulness and the capacity to develop personally meaningful life interests, are goals of the 'hippies', and increasingly those of 'straight' society as well. Hippies may be less equipped to realise their own goals than are the people whose life styles they castigate, but their function has been to arouse consciousness of the issues, to stir others from complacent embeddedness in deadening life patterns, and perhaps themselves to evolve through a life-cycle stage of 'hip' emphases to later integrations and adaptations to the larger realities of 'straight' society. The alternative society groups have not existed for sufficiently long to know what subsequent life careers their participants make for themselves; it would seem that those who use them as transitional experiences probably emerge with a range of resolutions from a reversion to a conventional pattern to new integrations of various kinds.

Davis points out that the USA counter-cultures are essentially a middle-class movement whose members have been 'nurtured at the board of consumer abundance' and are in revolt against the dominant elements of consumer society (Davis, 1973). Rizzo however suggests that many of those who went to Haight-Ashbury went not just in revolt against the materialistic life style of their parents. Some had deviant identities of their own (legal, political, sexual or religious); others wanted to get the positive experience of having been 'where the action was'; and still others wanted to get away from unsatisfactory home situations without reference to particular ideologies—for example where there was marital tension and discord (Rizzo, 1972).

The public image of 'hip' communes as emphasising free sexual expression and protest against war ('love and peace') gives only part of the picture. Their way of life forms a culture complex with different emphases in different groups but with a common thread of preoccupation, which makes it possible for young people to move around within the culture on a world-wide basis, visiting communes, exchanging gossip, telling stories, reading poems, teaching recipes, discussing philosophy or politics, passing on drugs and so on. Unlike the earlier colony-like bohemias—Paris' Latin Quarter, London's Bloomsbury and New York's Greenwich Village—the 'hip' culture or its variants have diffused widely in cellular units through Western society. The emphasis is everywhere on a rejection of the conventional values of consumerism, competitiveness, high valuation of material possessions, status and the individualistic ethos. Some concentrate on the construction of purely local and personal alternative societies, others see their experiments with alternative life styles as part of a militant spearhead aimed at the destruction of the dominant society and value system. 'Alternative' groups focus consciously on relationships—rather than activities—as a meaningful life interest.

Many adults secretly admire young people's stand for their ideals (for example, in protesting against racism and bloodshed and allowing freer scope for their sexual and other feelings) and have given them tacit support. Sometimes they have even tried to join in on a partial, part-time or transient basis. Some of the 'encounter' and other 'experience' groups can be seen as an attempt by adults to try to free themselves of the emotional fetters that they have felt trapped into by growing up in an earlier, more puritanical era. Some camping and 'straw-hut' holiday groups have an explicit *temporary* 'hip' society element in their ideology and practices. The hippies themselves do not necessarily accept as authentic the way their elders experiment with counter-cultural experience.

Roberts observes (1971, 104):

> The hip communalists berate sensitivity group members for copping out by not dropping out of their comfortable sanitary lives. Most sensitivity members look at the costs paid by hip communalists (including venereal disease, bronchial disease, and 'communal cramps' from dietary problems) and reply 'too much'.

Alternative life styles have various components—long hair, unisex and other exotic dress habits, free sexual attitudes and behaviour, interest in new experience—including drugs (in protest against the inhibitions and constraints of conventional 'uptight' society) and the emphasis on being déclassé (in protest against the inequities of the class system). Along with this there is frequently an emphasis on ecology, health foods, peace, love and philosophy of one kind or another. These may be used as symbols for saying 'we belong to a group that is concerned with relating to *people*'.

Davis has discussed the hippie cultural complex as an amalgam of contra-culture and pro-culture. Hippies are not only *against* the plastic culture of middle-class life but they are *for* the consumption of natural products; they are not only *against* the impersonality of modern urban technology and bureaucratic life but are *for* quasi-familial arrangement of the commune family or 'tribe'; they are not only *against* the perpetual deferral of gratification but *for* immediacy of experience; they are not only *against* the substitution of spectator experience for real participation but *for* everyman's 'doing his own thing' and the general appreciation of the effort. He says (1973, 11):

> modern man, has since the industrial revolution become increasingly a spectator and less a participant. Less and less does he, for example, create or play music, engage in sports, dance or sing. Instead he watches and listens to—sometimes first hand though more often remotely via sound recording or video tape—professionally-trained and infinitely more accomplished others perform their acts while he, possibly, indulges in Mitty-like fantasies of hidden graces and talents within himself.

Here too, as with the dilemma of compulsive consumption, in rejecting the gamut of middle-class values hippies are, willy-nilly, fashioning (rediscovering is, perhaps, a better word) possible solutions to underlying problems posed by a rapidly changing socio-technical order. They are doing so by turning away from the virtuoso standards of high culture; by substituting an extravagantly eclectic (some would say reckless and tasteless) admixture of materials, styles and motifs from a bewildering variety of past and present human cultures; by producing such household-based homespun and hand-made articles as candles, leather belts, simple woven goods and ham-mered jewellery—what is condescendingly referred to by the devotees of high culture as 'artsy-craftsy wares'; and most of all, by insisting that every man can achieve expressive fulfilment if only he would relax and let the socially-suppressed spirit within him ascend into vibrant consciousness. To all intents and purposes the manifesto is: all men are artists—and who cares that some are better at it than others; all can have fun.

The importance of spontaneity, of appreciating what each individual can do or give as 'beautiful' because it is '*you*', are central hippie values. In place of materialism, spiritual attitudes are adopted; in place of occupational and economic status symbols, a universalistic attitude with identities ascribed by the stars may be adopted; in place of competitive achievement-oriented society with its fear of failure and its deferral of rewards for an uncertain time in the future, immediate experience or 'happenings' are emphasised; in place of close and exclusive possessive-ness, accumulation and individual property, monogamous marriage and close and exclusive parent–child ties, sharing and communalism of varying degrees may be a focal concern; in place of a separation of work and leisure, life integration is emphasised. These elements are built up into an ideology which consciously focuses on relating to people as a central life interest. However, as with all ideologies, the practice at an interpersonal level may or may not show this concern.

Many communal groups attempt to restore the kind of work–home relationship that prevailed before the Industrial Revolution. Farms and craft factories of the cottage-industry type are common. Working from home, restoring contact with natural processes—the sea, the earth, etc.— are part of the general picture, though in urban communes that empha-sise withdrawal from earthly instrumental activities altogether, there may be less of this.

Negative reactions of society are as seen in the kind of phenomena portrayed in *Easy Rider*. Hippies are distrusted as irresponsible, feared as unhealthy (for example in spreading venereal disease, the use of drugs, and negative public health practices) and disliked as hypocritical (for example in begging for money from those whom they revile for making the money, or in cities, buying more expensive, organically grown food).

In Britain responses to 'alternative' groups and their activities— for example, some of the reactions to squatters—have been mixed. There has been a strong thread of benign reaction, in keeping with the

British tolerance for eccentricity so long as it is kept within the bounds of social responsibility. Mills (1973, 196) observes:

> In essence [society] tries to control [the hippies] and to save them, and so long as it measures only what it set out to do and not what else resulted, it may lay claim to some success. When methylamphetamine was being abused, stocks were destroyed by official intervention, with the result that abuse of heroin increased. When heroin abuse increased, the response was to limit supply, and one result was the increasing injection of barbiturates. When young people slept in the parks, the parks were closed, so they walked the streets; when they walked the streets, they were moved on; when they moved on, they had to steal to find money for accommodation. . . . By and large, society showed no particular vindictiveness in such attempts at control—they were seen to be both for the general good and for the particular good of the people involved.

Mills favours a 'benign neglect' of such groups, allowing them opportunities to use the self-regenerative processes of the groups they form to create alternative life styles in which individuals may find a basis for the personal development that they felt they could not achieve in the larger system. Not only are there differences among communal groups in how hostile they are to established society, but also in how competent individuals are to make their way back into established society after a transitional hippie experience (Mills, 1973, 165):

> Among the groups in which I moved, it was never wholly clear who were the ones who would be able to get by in conventional society and who were those, so bereft of the skills it requires, that they would be destitute outsiders all their days, but that there are many of the latter was quite clear.

Among people who themselves enter the general world of communal living, reactions are diverse. Though it is too early to know the full range of outcomes, there are some who report sufficient dissatisfaction with various elements of the experience to cause them to put it firmly in the past for them as far as their own efforts to develop a meaningful form of life experience. For some the unexpected degree of jealousy felt at actually sharing sexual intimacies is intolerable, however acceptable the idea may have been that monogamy is a manifestation of the capitalist property concept; for others communes as cells of effective dissent and radical revolution may have been experienced as inadequate, and the leaders as having feet of clay, however much their heads resembled Castro, Guevara or Lenin. For still others the physical and psychological discomforts of group living overrode the theoretical advantages. Perhaps the most pervasive lesson to be learned across the whole spectrum of response, is that the 'hip' communal variant is a form of developmental experience which is widely appealing for many young people, though as a permanent life-style pattern it suits few. It is a transitional learning experience.

Within the many 'expedient' housing communes, in which there are mixtures of various types of marginal individuals and sub-groups, one sees 'natural experiments' created in ways proposed by Mills. We examine an example of an expedient housing group with communal characteristics in their living patterns and with some other elements of communal living, contrasting different types of people in the group.

There is a wide range of living groups of a semi-communal kind made up of people who come together more or less expediently in the urban environment. Some simply share flats without any ideology of communalism; others live communally but lead 'straight' occupational lives. Some are militant political groups or anarchical collections of individuals; some are dependent or inadequate people looking for supports in an impersonal and friendless world, while others are simply trying to minimise housing costs and family obligations in order to get on with something else, their personal thing. Many groups use London's 'short-life' housing: 'street people', 'squatters', student housing groups and communards. They make up a sizeable semi-underground world within the life of the metropolis.

One such group in London consists of a network of sub-groups inhabiting short-life housing. The organisation has an agreement with the local authority. The agreement is that the former takes responsibility for allocating housing, collecting rents and policing conduct within limits. This suits both parties: the occupants are not squatters but tenants on low rents; the council avoids keeping properties empty while so many are homeless. The group's small headquarters' staff collects the rents, assigns the buildings and does minimal supervision of works undertaken to assure that a certain level of safety and hygiene is maintained. Within the network of houses are some tightly knit, purposeful, politically oriented groups and some purely expedient groups in which people are thrown together by chance. They vary in their degree of communality and their counter-cultural orientation. We worked over a three-month period with one group toward the expedient end of the continuum, though within it were individuals of a more purposeful contra-cultural bent.

The house contained five adults and two children; three were women, two of them mothers of the children; the third was pregnant at the time of the study. The two young adult males were friends who moved in together, having known one another previously for about eighteen months. Two of the women had been friends for several years since college days; they had met the third on the Continent and renewed their acquaintance in London where they all decided to live together in short-life housing. None of them had the idea of a 'commune' in their minds when they registered for the housing. The two males (in their early twenties) were looking for cheap accommodation where they could follow their desire to form a successful pop group. The three women (who were several years older) wanted cheap accommodation and a situation which would provide supports for them as mothers living alone with their children, and trying to study. Only one of the three had been married to the father of her child. The other two had had children in the hope that this might give their lives a purpose and meaning, after having drifted from relationship to relationship unsatisfactorily for a number of years.

The group had in common a loose-knit set of ideas and feelings that made for a sense of commonality, despite their differences in background, outlook and problems. The common elements were based on a degree of counter-cultural orientation—all shared the reaction *against* the kind of life their parents had led and that the larger society had pressed them towards. This was despite their very different backgrounds: from Tom, brought up as the child of a minor civil servant in an African colonial situation; to Joanne, brought up as the child of an Irish schoolmaster and an intellectual mother; to William, whose father was a fire-brigade chief, former naval officer and autocrat. They all felt that the established way of life was not for them.

Their 'anti-' orientation to middle-class norms and values was shared, but they were people who had been around and learned in their different ways that relationships based entirely on negative feelings were not viable for long. They shared a dislike for authorities, the police, anyone who tried to tell them what to do or how to organise their lives, and had a common emphasis on some values of 'alternative' groups, such as the emphasis on freedom for sex, for the use of drugs, for the expression of emotions and feelings, on living for the present, not deferring gratifications, not planning and organising and on generally being helpful and 'human'.

The members of this group (ranging in age from their early twenties to their early thirties) are older than many hippies. They had passed through the stage of aimless wandering, 'bumming around' and just reacting to situations. They did not want a stable pattern in the established way of life but they were at a stage in which they were making some kind of compromise. They wanted to do something, not just opt out: the men to form an entertainment group, the women to have their babies and to study—art, psychology and politics. However, they wanted to do it their own way, at their own pace. They can be understood as a sort of transitional community with a limited life, but which allows

members to develop their own attitudes towards social institutions—
work, family and participation in community interests and activities.

Below are two case studies of members of this housing group, showing more concretely how they see their lives in relation to the conventional divisions between sectors, what influences have operated on them
in the course of their development, how their interests are evolving in
relation to the styles of living that they currently enjoy and how, for
Joanne, at least, relationship is so dominant a life interest that it
squeezes out others.

JOANNE was 30 at the time of the interviews. She was separated from
her husband and living on social security while looking after a 5-year-
old daughter. She came from an intellectual Roman Catholic background. Her father's father was a university professor in Ireland and
ambitious for his son:

> 'I don't think my father was an easy child to bring up 'cos he was
> expelled from school at the age of 8; had a private tutor, and in the
> end went to study in France. He got five degrees but he went on 'til
> he was 33. When my mother picked him up, he was a drunk and
> was going around with philosophers and thinking of non-being and
> so on. I think my father was totally in a kind of fantasy world and
> trying to work out what he did believe in and what he wanted. I
> think he met my mother and made the decision to get married, it
> was a very definite decision, that if you are going to get married he was
> going to look on it as a kind of vocation. Either he was going to re-
> main single, but if he was going to get married he was going to have
> children, bring up a family and be responsible for them.'

Joanne's mother was ten years younger than her husband; her father
was a psychologist who experimented with hypnotism. Her mother
(who was her father's second wife) ran away with a writer, leaving her
children; her father then remarried three times. Joanne's mother went
to a progressive English school and there was always money. Before
marriage, she was well known as an original screen-printer: 'She did
dress lengths at her own studio in Paris and was doing very well before
she met my father.' Joanne's parents met and married in France. They
left France before the war and went to Ireland, where their first son
was born, followed three and a half years later by Joanne. The family
then left Ireland and lived in the UK, where her father taught in
various universities. Two more children were born.

When Joanne was 5, the family moved to the USA when her father
got a university post teaching philosophy. They lived: 'twenty miles
outside a city where my father was going every day and we were deep
in the country—couldn't see another house. And those seven years were

very wild years. More and more children being born. Mother was always pregnant.' Five other siblings were born—making eight children in all. Joanne saw her large family as the fulfilment of a parental ideal: 'I think with their psychological and religious backgrounds they decided that big families are good psychologically. A lot of the children's problems, whatever they were, would kind of work out among each other.' The family moved back to England after her father lost his job in the USA: 'They thought he was a communist and he was there in the McCarthy era. He couldn't get a job in a university over the whole of the States after they suspected that.' On arrival in England, the children were split up and farmed out to relatives for four months until Joanne's father bought his present home in London. The move back to England brought an occupational change for her father: 'He was too old to get a job in a university then, so he got jobs in public schools, which he's worked in ever since.' For Joanne the move was very disturbing. She had lived as an active country child and always looked down on city children. She had not looked to outsiders for friendship, since she and her sibs had formed a united group. She was not happy at her school in the USA:

> 'School seemed to be a very separate thing. . . . I hated school right from the start. I just couldn't understand what it was. . . . Somehow it didn't click with me. . . . All those lessons, being in class. I just wanted to be home doing my own thing. And when examinations came around I can remember sitting in front of the paper and just not understanding. Asking things about Florida, O they were all things which just meant nothing to me. They were just names. And my reality was very definitely like watching the crocuses and looking at the butterflies and climbing trees.'

This became even worse on her return to England. After re-entering the established way of life in Britain, she felt her parents put a new pressure on their children to excel academically. But: 'I just hated that [school]. I didn't like the nuns . . . after the freedom we'd had, it was just too much to take.' Her relationship with her parents also changed:

> 'We didn't see too much of our parents when we were in America because we were always out doing something. . . . I used to like [my father] but I didn't feel really close to him. I didn't feel he had much to do with my life . . . he was always at work, or we were always out playing. He kept on reading his books.
>
> In England we were much more in the house. We had much closer contact with my parents. It was the first time I got to know them as people. There were more fights, the house was just too small to contain us; it was a big house but it was the first time I can

remember being beaten by my father—things like that. . . . I started hearing my father talk, and I'd never listened to him before. I'd seen him doing practical things, like he built a lot of the house in America, but now I heard him talk and when he talked it was all philosophical or poetry—it was all very high stuff and I suppose that's where the separation—I realised there was—I thought he didn't understand me and I didn't understand him.'

Partly because of a pressure to achieve academically and in order to understand her father better:

'school became so much of my life . . . it seemed to be the only thing to do in the city and I'd been so useless at it in America, I just had to get control over it . . . so I really worked at it, at everything, but it was through fear rather than through interest, and I suppose that's where my fear started, because I picked up a lot of fear somewhere. And I did get control of it.'

In the end, she obtained her A-levels and a place at university but she chose instead to go to art school. This choice may relate to family dynamics as well as to her personal interests. Her father's pressures seemed paradoxical to Joanne. She points out that while he encourages people to become professionals, once they succeed he loses interest in them. Given that this is her perception of his attitude, her choice may reflect the fear of his losing interest in her again. In her behaviour during the last years of school, she tested to the limit how far he would go for her. She questioned her given religion, she questioned the value of educational achievement, she wanted the freedom of staying out all night at parties, and in choice of friends:

'My father really objected to my boyfriends. I think he realised a lot of it was sexual and they weren't the kind of man he could talk to. He had always been this figure for younger people . . . the wise old man for countless number of groups, but always of a certain calibre of intelligence, and always if you're doing something quite special and different. Otherwise he hasn't got much to do with them. . . . He only does things if he thinks he's getting somewhere, has got a reason for it. My boyfriends were the kind that wanted fast cars and coffee bars and clothes and dances and all-night parties, and it was right out of my father's life. And I intended to do it. . . . And I always got my way.'

When she started at art school, her relationship with her father improved for a time, as her friends were more to his liking. But when she was about 20, she left without completing her course and 'ran away' from home with Adam, a boyfriend from art school whom her

father 'really despised'. The couple lived in Colchester for a time:
'. . . . just to go somewhere . . . I just wanted to get out and live. Live
in my own way. I thought art school was just hanging on.' But while
she respected this boy's intelligence and abilities as a painter,

> 'he only satisfied one bit of me. I wanted somebody much more
> physical, much more instinctual, much less intelligent, much less
> clever, who was just kind of at a slower speed than Adam . . . I
> wanted more experience of other people and he was getting very
> possessive about me . . . so I broke it up.'

She left Adam for Brian, whom she had also met at art school—but
while he satisfied another bit of her, he didn't offer emotional security:
'He was very hard to me in those days. He wouldn't have much to do
with me. He was always having other relationships.' She then entered
a phase of having 'loads of other relationships' which lasted for the next
few years. While a desire to get away from her family was an element of
her rebellion, she continued to see her family and to get news of them
since her friends continued to be those she made at art school. She
heard that Adam had been on drugs after they had parted and had been
in hospital, that he was having a book published and he might be on
television. 'I met him accidentally at my father's', with whom he then
'had a very close relationship'. Some time later she:

> 'started publishing a book with my father. I was working at [a firm]
> as an artist there, using all the equipment I could to publish things,
> these litho things and that . . . then I met Adam again and he started
> taking an interest in this book that I was publishing and he started
> helping on it. While we were both working on this book, we started
> up a relationship again and I became pregnant in a couple of weeks.
> And that's what drew us together.'

Joanne asserts that it was wrong both for her to have had a child at
that time and to have married Adam. But:

> 'I was unhappy and he was one person who had a kind of key to
> how I could deal with myself, you know. He was on drugs; he was
> unhappy as well. I think our relationship was based on similar pain.
> . . . I was going through a very down phase at the time. He was some-
> body from the past who I knew and he wanted to marry me then.
> When I became pregnant, it clinched it. . . . I ran away from it for
> a time . . . my aunt, who I'm close to, said I should have an abortion.
> But it's one thing I couldn't face doing for religious reasons. . . .
> Physically and mentally at the time it was very wrong for me to
> have a child. It was very wrong for me to get married. Definitely
> done in an unstable state of mind.'

Her daughter, Linda, was born when Joanne was 25 years old. The new family lasted only two years:

> 'I needed other people. I needed people who weren't unhappy. I needed people who weren't on drugs. I needed people who had ordinary interests in life. Adam's interests were bizarre and almost totally on the other side—seemingly evil at times. . . . I wasn't going to make him change anyway, but I didn't see why I had to remain with him, or why I shouldn't satisfy what I wanted to do. He didn't like the people I wanted to see and physically it was really bad. And I wanted other sexual relationships. And that really screws up a marriage. I wanted to be separate from his writings and his books; I wanted to be myself. I didn't want to revolve my life around his. I wanted to find out about my own life.'

So the marriage broke up and Joanne went to the USA for six months with another man. When she came back to England, she had several attempts at reconciliation with her husband: 'But he couldn't accept that I'd keep leaving and starting up other relationships.' She was also in touch with Brian, and Susan—a girlfriend from art school, who shared a flat with Brian and two others. Joanne then moved 'home' to her parents' house, where she stayed for about eighteen months. Since Joanne's art school days Susan has been an important friend:

> 'I always find it very easy with Susan. I don't find any pressure from her. . . . Like if she didn't feel something for me, she wouldn't do it and the same for me for her. We've done quite a lot for each other. . . . I don't have to be anything but myself. I feel that she knows what I'm like and can put up with me, that there aren't any pressures for me to be anything other than myself. We like the same kinds of books and music and have the same kinds of attitudes about people. . . . I didn't get too close to her until I split up with my husband and moved in with Brian, 'cos she was living at Brian's; then when Brian and I broke up—*whenever* Brian and I broke up—Susan and I would come together. She would have lots of things against Brian in a way . . . I suppose sometimes the difficulties are that when I have a relationship with a man, it leaves Susan out. It separates us. But then I know if Susan had one she would be separate from me. We accept that in each other. There usually comes a point in my relationships where I start to feel that the relationship I have with Susan is far more real than the relationship I have with the man, and at that point I break up and it's me and Susan again.'

At some stage while Joanne was living with her parents, Susan moved in too.

Joanne reported that when her relationship with a young man was good, it was negative with her father; but when, for example, she and Adam split up, her father and Adam became very close.

With the advent of Linda, she felt that her parents' disapproval switched from her boyfriends to how her way of living would affect Linda; her arguments with her parents become focused on her child-rearing practices. Her parents expected her to make sacrifices for Linda, but she felt:

> 'it was my child to bring up my way. Eventually, through lots of fights, I got my way. Things like at the dinner table, sometimes; that's when I was eating with my parents, if she wanted to muck around with her jelly, I'd let her do it. But it would annoy my mother.'

This led to a gradual separation, and Joanne's eventual departure. Linda and Susan and another friend moved into the short-term housing already occupied by Tom and William (see case study of Tom, below). The grandparents now have the child to stay from time to time. Without the possibility of Joanne's mother 'taking over', because Joanne is no longer living with her parents, 'relationships are now very, very good'.

The grandparents seem to be very fond of this particular grandchild (though they have several others); Joanne says her father and mother play with and are stimulated by this child in a way which Joanne did not recall from her own childhood.

A relationship with Adam continued. He came to see Joanne and Linda each week:

> 'We take Linda out and talk and he gives me books that he thinks are good . . . and we talk about problems. You know, I can be pretty open with him . . . and we talk about our relationship. I enjoy being with him . . . he can face up to his problems . . . and he's going to solve them inside himself. He's not going to become part of a group to solve them.'

In addition, she sees Brian from time to time, and also a married man who comes at weekends. While the interviews were underway, she was beginning a relationship with William.

The leitmotif running through Joanne's accounts of her life is the tension she feels between freedom and involvement: between wanting sexual adventures and lasting emotional relationships; wanting the freedom of her own opinions and life style and wanting to be loved and accepted by her parents. In many respects she reached an interim resolution in the semi-communal setting. She can look to her co-residents for companionship and support, and also keep contacts with friends and family outside. Many of these friends and her parents have known each other for many years. Thus she can look to different people for different things—just as she described herself doing with her sibs in her child-hood.

Since she no longer has a job, she goes at her own speed, seeing friends when she wants to, doing essential household tasks when she wants to. Most remarkable is the amount of *time* she puts into her personal relationships and to the consideration and working out of her feelings, which she says tend to be so 'emotional—overemotional'. She is in fact extremely gregarious day and night. Over a period of two days for which diaries were kept, she was alone for only 2 per cent of her time.

But Linda does not really fit in with this arrangement. With regard to her child Joanne still experiences her familiar ambivalences:

> 'Linda sometimes gives my life total meaning and at other times she appears to destroy my life. . . . I often have to do things I know that she needs but I don't feel like doing them; I have to wash her clothes, I have to feed her, I have to listen to what she says and listen to the demands. At times I really enjoy it, and at other times I know that it has to be done. I believe there is a way to enjoy it but if I'm involved in myself somewhere else, I don't see any point in having a child—that doesn't fit into my life at all. It's very inconsistent, 'cos some-times it can be meaningful. The same things that sometimes can be leisure can also be work.
>
> Really in a way I see myself through Linda. Lots of things she does, she does so much better than me, and it gives me an idea of how people are meant to be—how open one ought to be, what are the right things to love. The right principles to have are no principles at all except what you yourself feel and have the nerve to demand what you want.'

A source of arguments between Joanne and her mother has been her mother's attempts to teach the child, to guide and encourage her to play:

> 'I wanted her to be much freer than they would allow her to be. They interfered a lot. My mother was always trying to get her into certain things and I wanted to watch her natural growth more. I didn't want her to be guided . . . I didn't think it was important to teach Linda reading or writing, not necessary to encourage her drawing or any-thing like that.'

When Linda came home from nursery school, she was never asked questions about what she had done or how well she had done—and the child was seldom if ever told that she was clever. The pressures were all to do with relating: Who did you play with? Do you like such and such a child? Who are your friends?

Joanne is emphatic that she does not push things on to people, that she does not try to change them, does not expect them to expect her to change or to be faithful. She tends to reject people whom she sees as accommodating themselves to a given system—such as Catholics or university students. She sees her ideal life as when she was a child in the country with her family group. As then, she tries to live a life guided by her feelings—and as these feelings change or become satiated or dulled, she looks elsewhere for satisfaction and stimulation.

To Joanne, leisure is:

'Things which I enjoy doing. Things which are new while I do it: while I'm doing it, it feels like I'm finding something out. . . . Whereas work to me is something which I know has just got to be done. . . . There's always another reason for doing [work] apart from my own enjoyment . . . it's when I'm not going at my own speed; if I'm doing something for money; I'm doing something because I know it's got to be done, because if it doesn't get done there's going to be much more to be done tomorrow because the thing just starts getting too big and it becomes very, very difficult to tackle. Or doing something because somebody else wants it done and not because I really want to do it and I don't want to lose them and so I do it [i.e. leisure involves some element of choice].

Work is . . . an inner attitude to something . . . it's just a mental attitude, because I'm sure you can have a mental attitude of leisure towards everything . . . I suppose work also comes into my fish and my plants, because they have to be kept up or they'll die. One moment they're not work and another moment they are.'

Similarly, speaking of her child, and her obligations towards her: 'The same things that sometimes can be leisure can also be work. It depends on my inner attitude.' She points this up by reference to her mother:

'My mother tends to sometimes . . . make her leisure into work. I can feel her attitude isn't right sometimes. Like she'll be sewing, but she won't necessarily be enjoying it but doing it for somebody else because she thinks it's a good thing to do and I call that work. . . . She's got this religious thing that can turn everything into work. I feel there tends to be a thing in [my elder brother] to make leisure into work rather than work into leisure and I'm always taking it round the other way.'

After the interviews with Joanne were finished, she experienced some changes that made her judge the case write-up to be obsolete— how she was a few months ago, but not now. First, she had moved from the house in which she was living to another house nearby that was a 'proper squat house', in part because the first house had become too much of a 'music house'; another group of musicians had moved in as well as Tom and William and their group, and music dominated the life of the house. Perhaps even more important, there were no children for Linda. Linda used to come along herself to the house in which they now live to play with some children of people squatting there. In this same house was Joanne's ex-husband, Adam (now with another girl), and the ex-husband of her friend, who lived there with a group of political radicals. Joanne was going through a psychologically very difficult time and felt that she needed some sorting out. Just as Linda had been drifting over to this squat house, she herself had been drifting over to a local house of the Philadelphia Community; when a vacancy occurred, she moved in, and Linda moved in with her father. She spent six months there, and:

> 'I met people who taught me how to live. I worked at it, learning how to create order in relation to these people; and one can continue to do it, even if one knows it is going to get all fucked up. One can continue to do it and enjoy the making of order.'

Joanne now lives in this large squat house with the others as a matter of convenience, but she no longer feels one of them. She has not been involved with a man for months, and has been trying to keep her own territory in the house somewhat clean and orderly. Occasionally she sets to and cleans up the 'shit' that the others leave behind them in the hope that they will follow the example, but despairs that they are really capable of it: 'Nobody likes to clean up. People like to be dirty.' She spends most of her time alone, except when cooking or eating. She sees them all doing their own things and listens to what they have to say, but now sees many of them as having wasted lives: 'Trying to get attention; out to do each other; trying to be cleverer. I've done it all and seen it, how lost people are.' She feels that she must organise her own life better—but that she is 'not strong enough' to take on other people's problems. She feels still that she should be able to find pleasure in each thing she does, and that the meaning of life comes in the concentration on each thing to find the pleasure in it. However, she also reckons that she must make some decisions about her life: does she want to live in London or somewhere else; does she want to try to get a room or a flat or not; what does she want to do herself?

In the house in which she now lives, the children are a unifying force—not music or politics. While there are advantages in the space available, in the sharing of food, etc., there are also disadvantages. Linda wonders why they can't have a house—as she proceeds into the primary school and compares her life with that of others, this will become a more pressing question.

In order to give her life meaning and direction, to have her actions 'take effect', Joanne feels she's got to take positive steps:

'If you treat something as precious, you'll feel that it is, and you'll teach your child that it is. You've got to get *order* in yourself; children pick it up. If you're full of hate or anxiety, they pick it up.'

So she tries to introduce order into their room: fixing windows, polishing furniture, cleaning clothing All this goes against the norms of the group in the house, and she has to resist their criticism, and their intrusion into her territory. She feels, however, that it is now in her own hands:

'You've got to *invent* yourself—discover yourself. So much of me is what my parents made me. I need to destroy that to find myself. Nobody but me can discover myself. I desperately wanted my parents because they weren't around. I felt that something must have been wrong with me. When you feel you're nobody, that little feeling can do you down. You need to feel in yourself that you're important. And you need to find it in yourself.'

TOM was another member of the group Joanne first lived with. He was nearly ten years younger than she—23 at the time. He is the youngest of three sons of an accountant who worked as a local government officer in East Anglia until Tom was 4. Then the family moved to a town in Africa where his father was Town Treasurer. In Africa the family moved several times and prospered—ending up with their own specially built house and swimming pool and several servants.

Tom went to two local schools until he was about 13, when his parents decided to send the two younger boys to school in England. The two boys lived with families in England, attending State day schools. They stayed with one family for two months and another for two years—until their parents returned to England. Tom's parents found the adjustment to life in England, with the fall in income and lowered prestige involved, unacceptable; they returned to 'white' Africa six months later. By this time Tom had taken his O-levels and decided to abandon his A-levels; he returned with his parents. He was then 16. However, once back in Africa, he discovered he disliked the job he got, the relative 'straightness' of the society, and the prospect of military service and 'having to go out and kill people'; so he returned to England.

In the five years since his return, he had eleven changes of abode and three trips into Europe (totalling eleven months). He has lived in the semi-communal house for less than a year.

Associated with this unsettled residential history, Tom has had a series of jobs. After leaving school in East Anglia, he took a 'fill-in' job for a few months in a bookshop until he went back to Africa. There he started a sandwich course, working as a cable salesman and attending technical college to study for a City and Guilds electronics diploma. Although he was less than enthusiastic about the job, he stuck at it, mainly because of pressure from his parents. However, he was made redundant and got a job with the Civil Service; this he saw as a way of getting the fare back to England. On arrival in England, he again got a clerical job but he found it so boring that he quit after a fortnight.

Tom, then aged $17\frac{1}{2}$–18, got accepted as a trainee in an electronics firm. He worked as a recording technician with a big recording company for eighteen months. He was moved from one department to another, to 'see how things worked'; after a time he looked at people who had been there longer than he and who still had not managed to become fully-fledged engineers. He decided that he was being used as a dogsbody and thereupon talked himself into a similar job in a small studio, leaving the large one.

He worked happily in the small studio until he was sacked—nominally for leaving a door unlocked late at night but, he suspected, really because the studio did not need him full-time. He has continued to work for the same boss on a part-time, freelance basis; this earns him enough money to get by, but allows him flexibility.

He is now forming and rehearsing a 'progressive' music group with hopes of 'making it' as a musician. This means more than just making a living. It means making a way of life as a famous pop musician; he dreams of becoming a 'superstar'.

Thus Tom has been intermittently employed with his present employer for several years. He likes the security and money that a job brings and has never left a job of his own volition without having organised his next job. To be acceptable to him now, a job must be enjoyable, flexible in hours and allow him to dress as he pleases. It must offer likeable colleagues and an opportunity for personally meaningful involvement in the work. He was unhappy in work until he found what he wanted to do and circumstances broke the parental pressures to simply have 'a career'. Until he left Africa, there was a clearly differentiated split between 'school and work' and times when he was 'not working'; the former having negative connotations, and the latter positive.

The initial stages in Tom's chosen occupation of recording engineer were not satisfying, but as long as he felt he was within reach of realising his ambition, he was happy. When he felt he was getting nowhere, he acted decisively. Nevertheless, at the time he was interviewed, he said that he was 'just drifting', though he was also making evident progress with his group, drifting in the direction he found pleasing.

Distinctions between work and non-work are not meaningful since

Tom's work and non-work activities are now identical. He and his friends are totally immersed in establishing their group and in attempting to find audiences. Their money may come from anywhere—social security, occasional recording stints, his friends' families; the meaning comes from the musical work which, in his fantasies, will make them rich as well as happy in the future:

> 'Leisure has very little meaning for me . . . whether [what I was doing as a recording engineer] was a work or leisure thing became meaningless because half the time when I was going to work I was having a better time than when I wasn't at work. . . . When I started working at [the small studio], splitting my life between work, leisure and that sort of thing got to mean less and less and now it means absolutely nothing. I have very little schedules or times that I have to keep. Sometimes sessions or something I have to do, I have to make, but that's very little, very little hassle that . . . but after I was fired, the whole time was leisure time. In fact, doing nothing really. I really had no purpose in life at that time. I had nothing really that I was interested in.'

Since then, playing in a group has become his main interest:

> 'What other things do I do besides working and playing music? Nothing, I don't think. . . . If I'm not working, then I usually get up and play if there's somebody to play with. And besides that I just sit around and do basically nothing. . . . I suppose I'd call that waiting for something to happen.'

In his plans for the future Tom hopes he will earn his living by playing, and he feels that the music group should live together so that they know what to expect from one another and can respond to one another on stage. He was prepared to turn down work from the studio if it clashed with rehearsals. But his job as a recording engineer has been important in his out-of-work life, because through it he has built up technical knowledge and skills, it has given him contacts for buying cheap, second-hand equipment for the group, provided him with contacts for recording services, and made him realise that 'superstars' are not superhuman and supertalented; this enabled him to overcome a 'put-down' received from his father: that he would never make the grade as a musician because he was 'tone deaf'!

Another consequence of Tom's unsettled residential history is that he has constantly had to make and remake his social life. In marked contrast to Joanne, friends do feature in Tom's descriptions of his earliest childhood activities, and he has far fewer old friends and close interlocking networks than she. Like her, however, he is gregarious and does few things on his own.

In his early years, before he was 4 years old, his activities with friends are described in such a way that it would appear that he and his two brothers not only shared their friends, but were friends themselves. After 4, though he still did things with his brothers, he developed his own friends in the neighbourhood. At about 8, 'girls' as a group appear in his recollections. By the time he was 13, his brothers had more or less been phased out as friends (he still sees his middle brother) and he had few friends from his neighbourhood. Rather his friends were part of particular sorts of groups with which he went round—for example, Teddyboys, later Rockers, then a group in pubs or gate-crashing parties and, on his return to Africa, long-haired drug-users.

The group of friends he developed since he returned to England was a more structured, small, intense network than he had had in the past—though this distinction may be more apparent than real. Each of the groups he 'hung round' has provided small, intense networks and each has passed and been forgotten by him. He has had six girlfriends—the first when he was 13+, the first 'steady' when he was 16. None of the relationships lasted very long. The last four girls had rooms or flats which he shared as long as the relationship lasted. When they broke up, he moved on.

His friends appear to have been important influences on him at several points in his life. The first girlfriend had the effect of making him lose interest in school: 'When I got back [after the holiday], I just wasn't interested in working at school anymore. I was just into going out and having a good time.' Another friend was important, in that when he returned to Africa with his parents and was unhappy with his job, '[a friend] showed me an article about being a recording engineer in a studio and I really decided that that was what I wanted to be.' When he was made redundant and came to England, he followed through on this aspiration.

An important influence which shaped his behaviour occurred when he was about 17 and was introduced to smoking marijuana:

'I first started smoking marijuana. I wouldn't take it at first because of the connotations of it in Africa. The way you read about it in newspapers, being supposedly something that makes you go crazy. But then this French guy . . . he was a descendant of some aristocratic family in France . . . had a flat and he was an insurance salesman, and he used to smoke a lot. He persuaded me to try and I really liked it after that.'

Six months later he had his first really 'mind blowing experience', when:

'I met quite a few people . . . the few long-haired people that were there all knew each other and they were all doing pretty much the same sort of thing. This group of guys, about four/five, used to be called "the Vacant Lot"; they were a psychedelic group and they were all taking speed and there was this guy called "Hippie Mike" who wandered up from J— and they had this little hut on a hill, on the outskirts of the city, which was called "The Funny Farm"; they used to have parties there, and the one party that I went to . . . had been going for about two days before I got there. All the long-haired people in the city were there; it was the first really psychedelic experience that had ever happened there I think. Inside it was just a round hut and they had a lot of food and fruit and dope; on the ceiling they had this big American flag and they had this record-player, and people sat around just getting spaced out of their heads. . . . That was really one of the few things that I enjoyed there, that weekend on that farm. Everybody was just spaced out of their heads. It was really nice. Lucky it wasn't busted.'

When he was about 18–19, taking acid led directly to another non-work activity: 'writing songs . . . was one of my fantasies from taking drugs.' A third important influence which was to shape his life style came from flatmates/friends. Here there was music: 'we used to get into things like spontaneous chanting and spontaneous music'; and someone who could teach Tom how to play his guitar: 'and that was the time when I started playing guitar. . . . There was this Greek guy in the flat . . . who showed me a few chords and I used to play along behind him.' The other flatmate/friend who was to play an important part in Tom's life was William, whom he met in this flat and with whom he started to play the guitar. Tom, William and the 'Greek guy' were involved together when Tom produced his first record: 'after about three months [in the local studio], I'd brought in this guy . . . who was living at our flat and played guitar, a Greek guy. I engineered and produced—that was the first record I produced.' William did his share of musical backing. Tom and William started to play together, and from this twosome the present music group evolved together with the plan to earn their livelihood this way in the future.

To Tom 'leisure' is 'doing just what you want to be doing—playing music, getting stoned, being with people you like to be with'. 'School' and 'work' were seen as alternatives to 'leisure' in the first eighteen years of his life. Once he enjoyed his work, he found it meaningless to use a concept to distinguish 'free time' from 'work'.

On the other hand, when he was fired, and doing nothing, while he could call this leisure time, he was reluctant to do so since leisure involves for him elements of enjoyment and choice, as well as being 'free' time. For him 'excitement' is a component of leisure, since the time he became involved with women and when he discovered drugs in Africa and guitar-playing in England.

At the time we met him he had no steady girlfriend, his guitar-playing and drugs were integral parts of his life and no longer novelties. He was free to choose his working hours—when he was awake and when he was asleep, when he worked in the studio for money, when he worked with his group, when he did his cooking and cleaning—and when he sat around talking and smoking. He did what he wanted to do, and most of what he did he enjoyed. He found his colleagues congenial—many were people he lived with, chatted with and smoked with.

Thus Tom does not differentiate between his work and leisure; he also does not (and would like increasingly not to) differentiate either from his 'family' life: 'It is all one and the same thing.' In part 'squatting' in the commune was a means to an end—a cheap way of living while he and William got the group going. But he also had a commitment to live with the people he played with: to de-differentiate his life as much as possible.

Review of the case material: narrowing of interests in young adulthood

The range of case material is striking for the mixture of stability and change it suggests. The four sub-groups we describe to portray young adulthood were taken at the same point in history in the same country, yet the realities of the various individuals appear to be so different. The worlds of Anne and Brinley are quite unlike Joanne's or even Tom's. An implication of this is one of the basic messages of the book: that while at each life cycle phase there are regularities in people's behaviour and concerns that are relevant to leisure provision (among other things), the individuals comprising 'people' are infinitely variable. They represent configurations of characteristics, varying around certain themes at their particular life-cycle phase.

Even where the regularities are sufficient to facilitate the definitions of 'types', the realities of individuals in those groups are more complex than implied. The life styles people adopt are not consistent and watertight packages. If Anne and Brinley are traditional in their orientation to courtship and marriage, do they necessarily fit the traditional mould in all respects? Anne, for one, differed from other 'traditional' girls in her orientation to work. Finding the prospect of prolonged domesticity unappealing, and expressing interest in occupational involvement after marriage, she was more 'modern' than many of her friends. This is untraditional in the Swansea setting, and Anne knows that Brin will 'play merry hell' if she does not stop work after having children. So young adults, in the way they identify with social institutions, cannot be too neatly classified into sub-types which align with complete packages of affiliations. Some do, others do not.

In part young adults' likelihood of creating their own blends of social affiliation will relate to their environmental settings. Geography is part of the picture, and in the small town 'goldfish bowl', the negative pressures on falling out of line with particular affiliations are stronger and more evident than in the city. Yet one can feel one is in a goldfish bowl in the city also; networks are another important element in the picture. Joanne in London began to experience pressures from her group not to break with the norms of its orientation. One crucial difference between Anne and Joanne is that Joanne, away from her parents' constant gaze and based in the city with its higher tolerance of heterogeneity, was freer to choose the network which critically influenced her. Yet while the social identifications they are making relate to influences in the environments with which they interact, the particular blends and resulting life styles will have to do, above all, with the individuals' own resourcefulness. Thus Joanne is thinking of leaving the communal house and finding a new direction, while Anne—for the time being at least—casts aside aspirations for a fuller occupational involvement. Similarly, while many involuntarily unemployed seem to collapse in apathy, Nick has 'made it' as a 'student', with new vistas opening to him.

So far we have emphasised the variability of young adults. If the variation it encompasses is so great, what makes young adulthood distinguishable as a coherent phase at all? We suggest it is marked by two specific characteristics.

All young adults, though in very different ways, seem to share focal preoccupations which they explicate through four major areas of interest: occupation; intimate heterosexual relationships; family; and friends. Much of the variation in the ways they express these interests is related to how much they differentiate separable life spheres. Second, for young adults of all the types presented, the expression of their focal interests impinged on their involvements in all other activities. This was as true for the university students meeting the requirements of their specialisms, as for Joanne with her overriding concern with 'relating'. It was as true for Anne and Brin whose lives were dominated by rigid adherence to a prescribed pattern of courtship and marriage, as for those young adults who began to be completely overtaken by the vacuum created by involuntary unemployment. This gradual squeezing out of meaningful interests, other than currently focal ones, seems characteristic of this phase, except perhaps for especially resourceful individuals.

The nature of involvement with one set of interests affects and is affected by the involvements with the remaining set. This holds particularly for occupational interests.

Occupational interests involve deciding on what kind of work one wants to do, what kind of job to have, what kind of personal commitment to the job, to the organisation and/or professional career that the occupation provides. Involvement in the experience of work, combined with the characteristics of the work itself, makes for different degrees of commitment to the occupation, with implications for interests outside the occupation. For most young men and women an important new affiliation is with having an occupation. While many who are against prevailing culture do not align with occupational institutions in conventional ways, they are concerned with the underlying involvements none the less. Alternative groups are, therefore, important to study, for they suggest new integrations which may emerge. Tom and William remind us that occupational interests may be pursued outside the formal job structure—living on social security while trying to develop their musical skills as aspirant pop musicians. So does Robert (who has not been described in detail), who freelances as a domestic cleaner and feels bad about accepting payment for the jobs he does, while trying to further his photographic involvement. Others may participate in the occupational structure in a regular way, but with little identification or interest in the work they do. Of special interest are the founders of Uncareers, who produce a *Directory of Alternative Work* that has met success—and now, with the rationale intrinsic to Uncareers, they have to resist professionalisation of their involvement in it (Cooper, 1974).

When people finish school, most face the issue of 'earning a living'. This may or may not coincide with the issue of where to commit oneself, to what and to whom. Almost everyone who leaves school and does not enter higher education goes to work. In this context, higher education is a time of 'occupational affiliation', i.e. the acceptance of the role of student. For some, there may be little question—because of a particular history or family situation, a person may know exactly what he is going to do, not have to think about it much and just slip into it, for example in a family business, or line of work one has always known one wanted to do. For others the decision may be agonising and involve a great deal of self-scrutiny. For still others the issue may revolve entirely around the availability of jobs one can do.

While the issue of where to put one's personal involvement runs through everyone's life, the issue becomes critical in the young adult phase. There may be many stalling tactics such as being a student or taking a 'fill-in' job, but somewhere along the line most people will decide what they want to 'do' occupationally. The decision is of course not entirely a personal option, but is based on an interaction between what the person might be inclined to do and what is made possible—by job availability, acceptance at university, trial experiences with varying degrees of satisfaction and success, etc. Pre-adolescent ideas about occupational identification tend to have a fantasy quality; then there is a stage of experimentation during adolescence, and by the young adult stage there tends to evolve a more real identification. Later, in the establishment phase, this may turn to heavier commitments and fewer degrees of freedom for making changes. Alternatively people may then decide to make a clean break with the identification they made as young adults.

People vary in how much of themselves they put into their occupational interests. For a long time now, work has been considered as the basis for men's lives—their social identities and self-images. While young adults do not necessarily think of the implications, the characteristics of different occupations, and the way occupational roles are played, affect life patterns outside work not only in terms of economics and social status, but also of how they see themselves and what they do in their family lives and 'leisure time'. The related conceptions young people have internalised about various occupations are likely to influence the alignments they make as young adults. Some may identify greatly with particular occupations and be attracted to 'total institutions', such as hospitals and monasteries, which require their members to do almost everything within their confines (Etzioni, 1961; Goffman, 1961). Others show a more neutral attitude, perhaps opting to be transient labourers at this stage of life, enjoying some of the characteristics associated with the work such as meeting new people, being physically active, mobile, etc., but they are unlikely to care much about the work itself or to have a powerful occupational identity. The geographically mobile *au pair* girl may have similar interests, using the occupation merely as a vehicle for making her way around.

The place of occupational interests in the total life space of young adults is at present associated with sex differences. There is still a marked tendency for men to concentrate on occupational identifications while women give these secondary place. Because of the interaction between identifications made in different areas of focal interest, if a young woman's commitments and interests are almost entirely centred on the institution of marriage, she is less likely to have deep commitments to occupational interests. Similarly a young woman who has deep occupational involvements is less likely to allow domestic and marital interests to swamp them. Many young women decide at this point whether they are going to adopt a 'conventional' woman's role—i.e. not work after marriage or the first child—and to develop their identifications almost entirely in the domestic sphere; their primary role is defined as future wife and mother; they are thus in a limbo from the time they leave school until they marry. Work outside the home is seen as short-term since (with few exceptions) they hope to marry and have children soon, and nearly all will then stop full-time (and probably even part-time) work though many will return later. As young adults, such girls are unlikely to pursue additional qualifications, to push for promotion, or to undertake extra work (except for money). Their work impinges little on the rest of their lives except in so far as it provides money for clothes for courting and so on. Socialisation for housewifery occupies much of the 'spare time' of such girls after they marry and before children are born.

Although major changes are now underway in the sex stereotypes associated with occupational affiliations, and more women are now concerned with maintaining some occupational interests, resistance is deeply rooted in society, and rears its head in unexpected institutions. Thus there may be ante-natal classes where the majority of expectant mothers are planning to resume occupational involvement shortly after their babies' births, but instead of getting the support and encouragement necessary for them to realise these plans, they receive talks based on the assumption that they will become full-time mothers and housewives, hitting them when they are most apprehensive about their abilities to 'mother' adequately. One informant relates that on first attending a mother-and-baby clinic with a new-born infant, she was first asked her husband's occupation, and then what her *previous* occupation was. She replied that she had been a 'student'. As far as she was concerned, her *current* occupation was 'town planner'. But when the health visitor asked no more questions, our informant realised that in the health visitor's terms, her current occupation was 'mother'. Pointing out this disparity only led to increased indignation when it became clear that there was little concern at the clinic with what her actual occupation had been—student, town planner or whatever—only for the fact that she was now a mother.

There is also increasing recognition that family factors generally may affect work patterns for men and women. Career decisions are influenced by mate selection in early adulthood (Rapoport and Rapoport, 1965); later job changes or training opportunities may be affected by family factors (Cogswell and Sussman, 1971; Pahl and Pahl, 1971). Studies of occupational socialisation, mainly American to date, show the importance of peer-group friendship in developing occupational competence. For many young adults—particularly men and particularly (though by no means exclusively) in the professions and skilled trades—job socialisation is an important element of their life interests and their preoccupation with social institutions. Furthermore a good deal of the informal work of incorporating ideas and ideals associated with an occupational group or institution is done while pursuing non-work activities—eating, drinking, chatting and gossiping, playing together or watching together.

We turn now to consider the next set of interests for channelling the focal preoccupation of identification with social institutions. These are connected with the interest in *developing more permanent heterosexual relationships*. These interests begin before the young adult phase, but now it is usual for people to form more enduring heterosexual relationships, whether or not they lead to courtship and marriage. A small minority of people do not want to marry at all; others wish to postpone marriage for a long while. The age of marriage, statistically, has been declining in recent years, but some new evidence from the USA indicates that the age of marriage is now rising. Still others want to marry as soon as possible and courtship and marriage interests become dominant for them in this stage of life.

There are variations in the way people pursue the attainment of a close and intimate relationship with someone of the opposite sex. For those wishing to postpone marriage there may develop a stable 'boyfriend–girlfriend' relationship with no marriage. While this does not necessarily conform to formal courtship styles of interaction, it may eventually lead to marriage. Students often enter into such relationships, as do men and women who wish to consolidate their occupational interests before embarking on marriage; others prefer such relationships to marrying at all. The usual tendency is to concentrate on an increasingly narrow range of acquaintances of the opposite sex—and to move from 'going steady' through a more or less formal engagement to marriage. One element in this 'mate selection' process is the testing out of compatibilities through the sharing of activities and interests. 'Leisure' facilities are important in this and a great deal of the courtship process among conventional couples—particularly in the early phases before a more home-centred 'saving' period is entered—is conducted in the context of leisure facilities. Paradoxically, once the mate is selected, the demands and exigencies of the relationship itself—especially in the early establishment phase which follows—leads to a squeezing out of the interests which helped to connect the couple in the first place. They may nevertheless remain dormant and be reactivated in later phases of the relationship. For less conventional young adults, other interests, for example occupational, may be important in establishing heterosexual bonds. These bonds may not result in marriage, though often involve living together.

Much of the writing on 'mate selection' from the USA has been concerned with showing how often like tends to marry like for a range of social background variables (such as religion, education, ethnicity), despite the recognition that personality attraction is often based on a complementarity of needs. The like-marries-like pattern is probably due not only to the fact that persons with similar backgrounds tend to be able to share interests and values more easily, but also that there are social pressures making 'similar' partners more acceptable to parents and others involved. Also, importantly from our point of view, like tends to meet like in 'leisure' situations as well as in schools which practise selective intake, in work settings which bring together people with similar backgrounds, and in residential neighbourhoods which are class-graded. However, young people are not just passive bundles of background variables, reacting to other 'bundles' according to the elements they share in common. They are active participants and manipulators of their courtship situations. Thus a couple may grow to be alike and may jointly change so that they take on characteristics which are different from one or both backgrounds.

Courtship studies indicate a conventional cultural process guiding the development of identification with marriage institutions. There tends to be a graded series of symbolic acts which indicate personal interest in getting further involved in the process. These acts are dating, 'pinning', taking the other home to see one's parents, announcing an engagement, giving a ring, starting a 'hope chest' and so on, until the actual legal rite of passage of the wedding (Rapoport, 1963). To the extent that the courtship has the character of a dominant life interest, the processes surrounding it make for a critical transition in life styles. Courtship, engagement and marriage bring about a reorganisation of one's relationships, interests and activities. The reorganisation begins in the courtship process. Once a couple have decided to get married, in the conventional pattern they not only tend to stop going out with others of the opposite sex, but they reduce 'going out' to places which require spending money because they become more concerned with saving. Courtship may then shift to a concentration on a complex of interests related to building a home, realigning one's friendships, one's relations with parents, in-laws, sibs and other kin and building up a mutually satisfactory array of activities, a social network and so on.

Young adults' involvement in forming more stable heterosexual relationships means not only severing of psychological cords binding infant to parents, but the negotiation of a new kind of relationship between adults. There is strong *interest in successful reintegration of relationships with family*. Those who have passed successfully through adolescent rebelliousness may be on easier terms with their parents emotionally; but there is still the need to negotiate new terms for co-existence in adult life. A boy may or may not follow his father's occupation; a girl may or may not be conventionally oriented in relation to her home-making and child-rearing roles; young adults may contribute to the parental domestic economy or, if they do not, there may be the need to agree terms for not doing so. The mate is also a potential 'in-law' to the individual's family, and these new relationships are often tested out in the context of 'leisure' and other activities—visits, shopping, shared outings, games and pastimes of one kind or another. Through these experiences, and the planning for the future, new relationships are worked out which become the platform on which a life style in the establishment phase to follow is erected. Those who form relationships that contravene the norms of their parents may have special difficulty in working out satisfactory new alignments with them. This was clearly so for Joanne.

Little is known of the part played by parents and other relatives in the development of meaningful interests at the young adult phase. Adolescents often express 'anti-' attitudes towards parents and attempts to influence young people often seem frustrating because of this. Indeed, many parents feel that during adolescence their children are withdrawn, counter-suggestible and likely to attach more importance to their peers' remarks than their parents'. This phenomenon is often illusory, but the atmosphere of tension is very real and seems to be an important element in the separation of the young person from his family ties during the quest for personal identity. To the extent that this quest has been adequately achieved in the preceding period, the young adult becomes a much more amenable person for his family and relatives to relate to. He may relate to his mother and father more as friends and to his siblings with less rivalry for parental attention and family resources. In so doing, while he is better able to pursue independent outside interests, he is also better able to share interests agreeably with his parents.

Findings from longitudinal studies in the USA suggest that critical attitudes towards parents and sibs, the rejection of their company, and the self-absorption of early adolescence, change from an attempt to usurp parental roles (challenging father's politics, outdoing him in a hobby, buying mother new curtains or other household goods to replace those the child considers unsatisfactory) to increased cohesiveness and harmony by the late teens and early twenties. The 'child' becomes less critical and more friendly, willing to help with younger sibs and their problems, contributing to the family budget, and planning a future for him/herself which may closely resemble the family career of the parents (see Butler, 1956; and a similar tripartite development outline in Miller, 1966). Also, once a decision to marry has been made, there tends to be a slowing up of external expenditure and time is spent in one or the other of the parent's homes to a much greater degree than previously, when the young people were 'out' and unreceptive to talking about it to their parents. The young man who cannot find employment —contrary to his own and his family's expectations and values— was seen to be severely handicapped in this adjustment process. His interest, confidence, and scope in courtship is likely to be impaired, he is unable to contribute to the family financially, and in all other respects his competence and initiative are likely to be viewed with considerable ambivalence.

The young woman may take a renewed interest in her mother and her mother's role as her thoughts begin to turn towards becoming a wife and mother herself; or this may await the parental stage. She may previously have resented the idea of learning anything related to domesticity but may begin to find these things interesting—particularly when the engagement phase has been reached. Many of course do not become interested in domestic skills but may find other ways of developing a new relationship with their mothers.

There are of course many other complexities in this pattern. Young adults may have left home or become involved in friendships with people who have little in common with their parents and who may be unacceptable to them. Joanne's world was so removed from her mother's that they could find little—even in the enjoyment and rigours of the grandchild's upbringing—to link them positively. In these circumstances the problem of 'giving up' the child may be particularly difficult for the parents, but in either case considerable involvement surrounds the various issues of what kind of job, what kind of friends and what kind of marriage the particular young adult is developing. For many young adults marriage may not be an important goal, and to the extent that their parents are conventional-minded this may be a source of tension between them; it may be specially difficult to work out satisfactory new alignments with parents and other kin in this case. Parents may feel that their influence is at its last point of direct exercise— whether or not it is effective. On the other hand, children influence parents as well as parents influencing children, and parents may also change their concerns and interests and move closer to their unconventional children.

Friendship interests though less well understood are of great importance during this period. A realignment of friendships goes on in the course of courtship; pairs tend to associate with other pairs and 'competing' relationships are gradually dropped, for example sports clubs, drama clubs, etc. Females tend more rapidly to give up potentially competing affiliations than do males. New relationships, less age-graded, may develop with friends from work and in community activities. But there are indications that the private interest groups for the pursuit of cultivated interests—clubs, associations, etc.—often resist the absorption of young adults, particularly those who do not have the 'right' manners or the right connections.

Many young people continue their patterns of peer-group affiliation into young adulthood without perceptible change—whether they are in sports clubs, interest groups, cliques or gangs like Hell's Angels. Delinquent gangs may harden into criminal sub-groups—just as interest groups may give way to a high level of professional cultivation. Even 'pairing off' on a heterosexual basis can be absorbed into many of these group activities without diversion—as when the Hell's Angel takes a girl who then dresses up to suit.

By and large, however, this is a period of change and transition. Movement away from home to take a job, going off to university, relating closely to a member of the opposite sex, the development of new interests associated with colleagues, may have the effect of loosening earlier associations. The old teenage groups and gangs may drift apart, and the young adult may at some point 'peel off' and see old associates, especially schoolfriends, less and less frequently. New friendships—in new locations around new interests—may be incompatible with the old ones and there may be little attempt to bring them together.

On the other hand, there are instances where the different cultural emphasis of young people continues into young adulthood and forms a basis for continuing affiliations. Instead of youth clubs or children's villages under the supervision of adults, young adults who reject the conventional life career of job and marriage, and differentiate little between life spheres, set up their own communities, with various counter-culture or new-culture emphases providing integrative foci. Conservation, revolution, communal living and health interests may combine with the more expedient motives of cheap housing and freedom from control by authority figures.

The importance of friends and the need to make friends in this period is great and often goes unrecognised. The function of friends is less for providing norms and standards through which the individual can form an identity in counterpoint to the norms and standards being offered by parents, teachers and others in authority, but is, rather, an important part of making relationships with social institutions—whether the established ones or variant and counter-cultural ones such as in some political groups, hippie communes and the like (Mills, 1973).

Once a young adult has left the protective setting of school and family and entered the institutions of the adult world—a job, and perhaps a new residential situation—he leaves the shelter sometimes provided by teachers, careers guidance officers, parents, club leaders and so on. Those who guard access to and regulate participation in other social institutions are less geared to the needs, doubts and uncertainties of neophytes. They may be intolerant of the disruptive effects of taking in new people and make access difficult. Isobel Emmett's work on 'social filters' has shown how one sort of filter operates for young people, as indicated in chapter 2 (Emmett, 1971b). There are age factors that cut across social-class perceptions of 'rough ways', and many adult institutions are simply not tolerant of younger members—because they question established ways and make demands which increase the burden of those operating the facilities. For those seeking to make their way in the world of adult institutions, the process of becoming accepted in such settings may be arduous. Here the function of friends is critical. Friends introduce one to activities, organisations and people whom they know. Friends coach one in the kind of knowledge, skills and behaviour that will be necessary to make one's way in an organisation—whether it is a matter of the rather subtle aspects of being liked and accepted, or the more mundane matters of how one makes reservations or other arrangements to be able to use facilities, or even to know that they exist.

The importance of having such friends or being able to make such friends cannot be overestimated in contemporary society. They take the place of family and community in simpler societies—particularly in the city setting. One of the emphases of 'alternative' culture is on the ready access to friendly behaviour and relationships. The language and the tone of a mass publication like *Time Out*, which is more geared to the young adult market than the publication *What's On*, is that of the friend. Friendly advice is given on everything from finding a spouse to squatting, where to eat, sleep, fornicate, spend money, and how to deal with police, taxmen, bureaucrats and others who ought to be one's friends but who misguidedly (through being victimised by a bad system or simply being imbedded in bureaucracy) are not.

To realise their friendship interests, people need some positive content with which to attract and sustain relationships. The more meaningful interests they can express, the better. Interest in 'relating' only, appears to be insufficient. This highlights the paradox of the young adult phase, a liminal period when the individual may feel considerably isolated. At a time when friendship links have much potential for facilitating more fluid transition to larger social institutions, the energies young adults focus on making those social identifications leave little residue to devote to sustaining other interests.

'Leisure' provision for young adults: helping to keep other interests alive

Neither the descriptions of the four sub-groups of young adults nor the illustrative case vignettes are the basis for a systematic analysis of how the preoccupations of people at the young adult phase play themselves out in patterns of interest and activities. They do however give a partial picture of some of the variation present in this phase within contemporary British society, and some of the issues for which 'leisure' provision may be relevant. There is a conspicuous lack of good research data on young adults in their various forms; this is striking when one considers the importance of this phase. Much more research needs to be done to delineate the variations in values and life styles present among young adults. Little is known about the processes whereby they express their preoccupations with how they relate to social institutions in terms of actual interests, and how the development of these interests is facilitated or inhibited by available provisions.

There is little provision that is exclusively geared to young adults. This is consistent with the difficulty of the sub-group in forming itself as a 'lobby', in contrast to younger consumers. The public sector makes no special provision for young adults once out of school and involved in interests that go beyond those of the Youth Service, except for those who continue higher education and become part of an institution of higher learning which has its own leisure facilities. Of course young adults may attend evening institute classes and the like, along with older adults. While we see no reason for young adults in particular to be special beneficiaries of leisure provision, we suggest in what follows why greater efforts in the public sector towards facilitation of young adults' interest expression could be of value.

There are some types of provision from the current facility array which young adults seem to favour. Most of them are now earning, and are able to utilise facilities like pubs, cinemas and similar entertainments offered in the commercial sector. Although they have not yet reached the peak of their earnings, at the beginning of the young adult phase at least, they are not yet committed to the effort and expense of home-making. The commercial sector has been swift in identifying them as a prime market for the kinds of provision that facilitate heterosexual contact and activity, especially for entertainments that can be pursued outside the home, along with the market they constitute for clothing, toilette, etc. While traditionally men have tended to bear the major burden of spending on entertainments, and young women on the accoutrements of attractive appearance, with the modern tendency for women to be active in the assortative mating game as well as men, the latter have also become high spenders on clothes and lotions to make them attractive.

The focal preoccupation of the young adult phase is identification with social institutions. For conventional-minded young adults in particular the most salient interests, other than those associated with work and career, centre on meeting and getting to know others of the opposite sex, as a starting-point in identifying with the family as a social institution. The highly traditional debutante's 'coming out' ball is a vestige of the earlier periods of relative seclusion of girls of 'good family' in settings where there was virtually no chance of having contact with members of the other sex. 'Coming out' into society was, for such individuals, a relatively overt rehearsal for the wedding ceremony. For most people the social mechanisms for mating are less stylised and constricting—but it is often in the context of 'leisure' facilities that this goes on, informally.

The sorts of activities that are relevant to the cultivation of interests in heterosexual relations and assortative mating take place in dance-halls, nightclubs, pubs, discotheques, sports centres and so on. The essential point is that heterosexual contact and social mixing is possible along with the main agenda. So a lecture, concert, discussion group, demonstration or exhibit can also serve as a meeting place. The bars and amenity areas associated with such public events are useful for this purpose. They are meeting places for young adults who seek others who show similar interests by virtue of being there at all. The art of the 'pick-up' and of exploratory conversations that establish suitability for continuing association are cultivated to the highest pitch at this point. It is legitimated in such institutions as the 'singles' bar' and for those who are either inhibited, inept or who lack access to opportunities, there are many computer-dating bureaux, match-making agencies and 'contact' publications.

The role of these venues also as meeting places points up the need for providers to shift towards more fluid entry and exit of activity groups. The 'social side' of sports clubs and evening classes is well established, but not only has the social activity usually been secondary to the activity which is the ostensible basis for the group, but attendance is usually required to be formalised and routine. At the other extreme, very casual 'meeting places' like exhibitions have little scope for people to get to know one another in a socially easy way. If the interest people have in meeting others is to be facilitated, scene-sampling (both for the *people* and *activities* involved), manifesting itself in high turnover of participants, must be facilitated as a legitimate activity. This require-ment seems important throughout the life cycle.

It should be emphasised that while heterosexual interest of a more serious kind is paramount at this stage (i.e. exploring what it is like to have a sustained relationship with a member of the opposite sex rather than just to have a date or a sexual adventure), it is not the only interest in which 'leisure' provision is important. The whole process of develop-ing a commitment to a line of work or career may also be affected by 'leisure' activities. Contacts made on holidays, pursuing activities and through friendly social relations may lead to changes in occupation and career. Visits with family and kin may also be important and this may be a period in which a new interest is taken in kin, to whom the young adult relates differently—as an individual with his or her own interests rather than as a child with certain kin attributes.

While we have suggested where leisure provision can facilitate fuller expression of the interests focal to the young adult phase, it has other potentials too. There is the tendency for young adults to squeeze all other interests out. This is especially so for conventional couples, whose inward-looking courtship often sets off what may be a prolonged period of *privatisation of interests* within the home of the resultant family. We believe there is a challenge to leisure providers to help young adults keep other interests alive. If energies are too scarce to devote to other interests, then it is important that young adults at least develop adequate bases on which to resume interests later, for that is the essence of resourcefulness. But sustaining an adequate base for activating dormant interests does require some familiarity with the skills and information surrounding those interests. There is a paradox here. While we have highlighted the social role of activity groups, the importance at this phase of exposure to the activities pursued by such groups cannot be overstated. This requirement is in contrast to that for young people, for whom concern with the techniques and information encompassed by formal academic and vocational teaching may well be de-emphasised in favour of expanded *informal* learning in social life.

If young adults do not maintain adequate bases for the resumption of meaningful interests, we believe they will sustain personal losses, often of a permanent or long-term nature. One drawback relates to the acceptance of the received social institutions of work and family in relatively uncritical ways, which for many gives this phase the character of build up to a climax of pleasurable expectation. Yet there are signs that increasingly, for the conventional woman in particular, the anticipation is greater than the realisation. Or, to put it another way, the honeymoon wears off rather more rapidly than the fairy-tale of 'happily ever after' allows—leaving a bored and disillusioned 'captive housewife' in the next phase.

A policy implication is that efforts should be made to keep alive and encourage other interests during courtship and early marriage. Current research shows a dropping off of all other activities, particularly by women, at marriage. There is a withdrawal into the home and domestic interests. This concentration, while perhaps functional for enjoyment in the new family, may create difficulties for emerging into a fuller life later on, particularly if there is not much resourcefulness to fall back upon.

For those who go on to higher education, the university or college setting provides a near-ideal environment in which to cultivate new interests and evolve new life styles—as well as to perfect and consolidate those already chosen. Yet while some experience the setting in this way, and feel their interests widely and intensely stimulated, often as never again, the studies show that many students feel highly constrained not to pursue anything but their course specialisms. Though universities and colleges impose constraints, they do foster a range of attitudes and responses to available social institutions from intensely conformative to intensely dissident. Satisfactory performance in the tasks presented by the institution, particularly in the more technical fields, requires disciplined concentration on an orderly accumulation of skills and knowledge. This may gratify those who are able to focus their potential occupational interests but may leave those with a broader conception of personal development with a feeling of frustration, anxiety or boredom. Universities recognise in varying degrees, that the problems posed are partly organisational, and there are experiments for providing opportunities within the framework of higher education institutions for developing interests along a broader spectrum than simply the vocational. This is being done by curriculum changes (introducing broader possibilities for study, with emphasis on humanities and social studies as well as technical fields), by work periods, travel periods, social contacts with non-university elements in the community, bringing in external people to university events and for the use of university facilities and so on. Increase in contact, reduction of seclusion and fostering of community interactions seems to be an important aspect of contemporary efforts to make university experience more relevant to the development of a whole pattern of meaningful life interests.

A policy implication, for both educational administrators and others concerned, is *to seek ways that the provision of educational institutions and those of the community may be interrelated*. Where there is a relatively narrow input within the college or university, as in some technical universities, this may have to be broadened; where there is too great a separation in a 'total community' of college life, as in some of the élite institutions, ways should be sought to provide community experiences, through work, holiday travel, regular interaction during the term, etc.

The unemployed highlight the importance of work beyond its obvious economic and social status elements. While there are exceptions, in general the lack of employment leads to an erosion of self-esteem, of social esteem and the capacity to develop constructive and meaningful life interests. What could be an opportunity with lasting benefits is all too often turned into a traumatic stunting of personal development, with enduring negative consequences for the individual.

A policy implication for the unemployed is the need to provide *activities which can serve to develop meaningful life interests*. These may, under some circumstances, be translated into vocationally relevant skills. But whether they are or not, the work required makes for morale and personal development that will facilitate an increase of resourcefulness which can be used for occupational or other adaptation later on.

Those who live according to 'alternative' cultures have evolved various alternative forms, ranging from a withdrawal from modal life patterns to active criticism and revision of them. While the resultant forms may not be generally acceptable, and some may not prove very viable, they do at least stimulate thought and change about dominant patterns.

In bending their lives entirely to the pursuit of meaningful interests, some individuals in these 'alternative' cultural groups have not only rejected the manner in which their elders have allowed their lives to be bent to the requirements of material culture and technology, but they have also attempted to find new ways of living that would be more satisfying. The fact that the results of such social experiments have been sometimes successful, sometimes indifferent and sometimes disastrous, does not gainsay their potential utility—both for themselves as a way of life that may be in varying degrees transitional and also for others who cannot or dare not experiment in this way, though they might like to.

Individuals and groups engaged in the pursuit of 'alternative' life styles want neither the disciplines of an orthodox acceptance of conventional patterns of job-family-community life, nor the specialised developmental courses of institutions of higher education. They wish to create lives that are meaningful in different ways. For various reasons— ranging from the view that they may be engaged in creating valuable artistic and social innovations, to the view that they may be psychologically disturbed and inaccessible to orthodox forms of treatment— greater toleration of these efforts is indicated. Suitable safeguards could be instituted, as they are, for example, in relation to pop festivals, against allowing these efforts to be seriously damaging to others, such as in matters of public health, noise pollution and drug abuse. Constructive links should be maintained with these groups; their members could be facilitated in moving in and out of the groups as their development warrants it. The provision of therapeutic communities along the lines of the Richmond Fellowship or the Philadelphia Society would help to make such linking institutions.

But above all, society as a whole may benefit if such experiments were used for a reconsideration of conventional assumptions about life. 'Alternative' societies are laboratories of social and personal experimentation. They are difficult to study and difficult to interpret but important for themselves and for those who are able to learn from experiences that many think of undertaking but do not actually have.

In addition to the function of 'alternative' ways of living as quasi-models for people—older and younger—the ethic of total pursuit of meaningful life interests is instructive. Although the proponents of 'play power' and others may overstate their case, they suggest the contemporary *challenge to leisure providers* to help keep the pursuit of meaningful interests vital in the lives of others (Neville, 1970). Specific suggestions enabling them to do so will be made in chapter 6.

4

The establishment phase
Life investments

Earlier phases of the life cycle have the character of rehearsals—explorations, preparations, tentative playing with ideas, relationships and activities. While this continues throughout life in some form, in the establishment phase people usually make more enduring commitments. The phase is long and variegated, occurring roughly between the ages of 25 and 55, depending on the stage of family and work cycles. The central preoccupation of people is with making commitments that constitute *satisfying life investments*. This does not mean that major commitments have not been made previously or will not be made later, but the process of investing in a meaningful life pattern is most salient at this phase. While patterns of living are diverse, the preoccupation with major life investments in work, family, friends, community activities, and with various abstract ideas, gives some unity to it. The investments consist not only of material commitments, but of personal interests and involvements; people invest bits of themselves as well as of their possessions in a pattern of life from which they expect satisfaction over the long run.

Over 90 per cent of the population marries, and by the end of the establishment phase most families will have had two or three children. Late in the period children leave their families for work, for further education or to start their own families. While there are families who have no children, we concentrate here on those with children.

The establishment phase has been popularly idealised in the 'getting married and living happily ever after' tradition. In this traditional model the husband is the provider, securely and permanently employed in a job that brings ever greater rewards until retirement; his wife is his helpmeet, a devoted housewife and mother whose external interests do not conflict with her basic job as home-maker, child-bearer and rearer. However, several changes are altering this picture.

Longevity and multiple careers have increased. Life expectancy is longer for both men and women. People look forward to a longer period of activity than previously. Men are likely to change their jobs, their employers, even their occupations, one or more times during their lives. Women (particularly as they marry earlier, bear fewer children more closely together and plan their family size) are likely to involve themselves outside the home for longer periods of their lives than previously.

So the stability of the idealised picture—one employer, one kind of work, one residence, one pattern of work and family relationships—is changing into a complex of different patterns with increased options. Career fatigue, technical obsolescence, voluntary changes and a host of forces in the industrial environment that make for dissatisfaction, reorganisation and rationalisations lead to more complex career patterns than previously and more flexible career planning—with implications for the organisation of life generally.

On the other hand, where flexibility and the multi-career is not possible or not practised, boredom may lead to explosive consequences. Where occupational or career fatigue is not recognised and dealt with, for example by cross-posting, job-enrichment, sabbatical leaves or other devices, there may be deleterious effects. In both England and the USA observers have attributed some unofficial strikes to this boredom and the need for excitement. Strikes create an element of exhilaration and high drama in routines which are otherwise deadening (Leeson, 1973).

Mobility has increased. This is partly related to the lengthening of productive life and the possibility of multi-careers, and partly to the rapid expansion of technology and its impact on large-scale industry. Increased mobility is required for those who wish to advance within large organisations; it is often necessary for those who experience technological obsolescence. Thus coal-miners, small-scale farmers and railwaymen have to redeploy themselves as their branches of the industry become mechanised and rationalised. Both at the high end of the occupational scale (where mobility is often associated with 'spiralling' upwards in the managerial-professional career structure) and at the low end (where mobility may be necessary to find jobs) there is a good deal of moving around in the establishment period. Even when this brings economic gain, it may be unrewarding psychologically for the worker or his family. Moves become less frequent in middle and late phases of the establishment period, and another pattern evolves, particularly for the more affluent. Second homes are acquired. Second home users are characteristically families with two children under 14 and the couple in their thirties (Downing and Dower, 1973).

New homes, new schools, new jobs, new cars and sometimes new wives and families are part of the investment 'portfolio' of the establishment period of life. The number of second marriages (like that of second homes, second cars, second television sets) rises in this phase. Between 1961 and 1970 the number of second marriages in which both parties had been married before increased in Britain from 21,000 to 32,000; second marriages in which only one partner had been married previously rose from 36,000 to 49,000 in the same period (*Social Trends*, 1972).

Affluence levels have changed. Multiple ownership and multiple experiences in ways of living are a product of affluence. Jules Henry (1963) has elaborated the effect of consumerism on American society, and shown how escalating productivity and wealth is kept permanently behind escalating wants, induced by a creative advertising and marketing industry. It has long been observed in somewhat less affluent countries like Britain, that the lower divorce rate and its concentration in the middle classes was partly a function of the economics (as well as the legal and moral problems) of divorce. So affluence and its pursuit have disrupted the traditional ideal dream of family life as well as bolstering it by creating a plethora of beautiful private milieux.

Publications such as *Social Trends* (1972) indicate that incomes rise in the establishment period, but little is known about trends in enjoyment. In the early establishment phase, there may be enjoyment in domesticity while there is still a 'honeymoon' effect, though financial commitments for home-making are heavy relative to incomings. To the extent that a family is mobile, this heavy commitment continues, with a press towards better quality and more detached housing, housing that is owned and that has amenities in and around it. As a sign of contemporary affluence, over half of the homes in Britain are now owner-occupied, but there are vexed problems about keeping the distribution of wealth reasonably equitable. While many meaningful interests and activities of the wealthy remain inexpensive ('the best things in life are free'), money does help—if only to get people to places where natural phenomena can be enjoyed without disturbance. On the other hand, there are many indications that the degree of striving required to achieve high financial rewards in modern society often extracts too high a price in terms of *joie de vivre*. Just as affluence does not automatically bring enjoyment of life, substandard conditions do not automatically entail misery. This is seen for example in people's attachment to housing in areas where there is an attempt to move residents to make way for modern housing or new highways (Gans, 1965; Fried, 1973).

At an individual level inequalities may be particularly apparent within the establishment phase of life. Those who have benefited by society's affluence are more clearly distinguishable from those who have not. There are sharp contrasts in life styles as well as some blurring of class inequalities. The relationship between private and public provision, local and national provision, town and country provision, differs by area. Efforts made at a societal level do not reflect the magnitude of changes that have occurred in the Gross National Product. One of the elements that will affect future development of interests and enjoyment is the amount society will put into 'leisure' as a social service.

Changes in sex roles have a fundamental effect on the ideal conception of the conventional family. The division of labour in the conventional nuclear family arose in the course of the Industrial Revolution, as an adaptation to the new conditions of urban-industrial life. Though based on traditional ideas of masculinity and femininity, the essential element in conventional families in modern times is the sharp segregation between the life of the workplace and that of the home; masculine qualities are assigned to the former and feminine to the latter.

In the workplace, where males dominate and control, the virtues are toughness, competitiveness, deferral of gratification and high aspiration. Parsons and Bales (1955) thought it was a pan-human tendency for men to take these 'instrumental' roles, while women concentrated on the 'expressive' roles within the family. The family, according to this conception, is a haven from the competitiveness of external life; it is ruled by principles of love, affection and support, with the wife helping her husband and not entering his world (except for emergency or diversion). However, under the impact of egalitarian ideas, universal education, revised conceptions of sex differences and changes in the nature of work, women are adopting work roles which are in substance and in concept increasingly equivalent to those of men.

The proportion of women who are economically active rose from 37·5 per cent in 1961 to 43·6 per cent in 1971. Men's participation in the economy dropped correspondingly from 86·3 per cent to 81·7 per cent. Women have entered more responsible and highly skilled jobs as they receive training equivalent to that of men and as prejudices in the workplace decline. Women, like men, increasingly see themselves as having a work and a domestic life. Women may work continuously or drop out of work for a limited period while their children are young and then re-enter the occupational world. New retraining schemes assist this pattern, as do company policies which provide extended maternity leave and benefits, together with opportunities to accelerate back into the career structure after re-entry (Fogarty *et al.*, 1971; Seear, 1971).

Women marry earlier than men and live longer, so their productive life (domestically and/or occupationally) is potentially greater than that of men. When women work, they receive retirement pensions earlier than men, though this practice may alter with anti-discrimination legislation. The tendency for women to work when they have no pressing financial need to do so, is a powerful social trend; they re-enter the work force while still relatively young with strong potential for training and advancement. Some studies show that this trend may be accomplished at the expense of leisure.

While some women work to use their talents and earlier occupational interests, others do so primarily to supplement their income. Some see working as a channel for enriching their lives—by developing their interests and increasing social contact; while for others work is, as for many men, an alienating experience. Many women feel nowadays that they must equip themselves with a 'second [work] skill' in order to face possible changes in their life situation. There is an increase in divorce, particularly among those who marry early; as divorced men seek second wives among 'the available pool of nubile spinsters', the divorcee is at a disadvantage (Chester, 1972).

Men's motivations in relation to work and family life are also changing. Increasingly men acknowledge a domestic role—ranging from being a helper to a full participant. Increasingly they are challenging notions of the nature and place of work in their lives. Manual workers put on pressure to 'enrich the quality of working life' in factories—and where this is impossible, to be paid compensation. Higher-skilled workers are questioning whether work should be so all important in their lives, making them into uni-dimensional men.

Changes in motivational patterns are manifest at times of job change. Firms recruit new members by 'leisure' inducements; other firms lose personnel because of the lack of such inducements. A South-coast English firm of solicitors advertises for an associate who 'likes to potter around with boats', western American universities attract top faculty by their proximity to ski resorts, 'head hunters' for multi-national corporations dangle the bait of non-economic inducements—early retirement schemes, travel to environments where work can be mixed with pleasure, etc.

As a consequence of these changes, life style options in the establishment phase are increasing. A man may work and not his wife; they may both work continuously or they may work in alternating patterns of each at half strength; they may work as a partnership or separately. The Norwegians have research under way on new patterns of 'work-sharing' in families, and many countries are experimenting with flexible work hours and shortening the work week (Fogarty *et al.*, 1971; Gronseth, 1972; Poor, 1972; Evans, 1973).

Three sub-phases of the establishment period

The establishment period can be divided into three sub-phases, demarcated by the children's development careers. The first sub-phase relates roughly to families with young children of pre-school age, the second to families with children still in school, and the third to families in which the children have left school. Such a classification has problems as well as advantages of phase-definition. A family in which the father is much older than the mother and retires or dies before the children leave school never, properly speaking, experiences the late establishment phase as an intact family. Similarly a family in which there is an early marriage and child-bearing while the couple is still in the educational system may experience their early establishment phase prior to either partner actually entering work. Similarly those who do not become parents, or defer becoming parents, may experience the preoccupations of these sub-phases differently. For them, the sub-phases may be less differentiated.

Within each sub-phase characteristic focal preoccupations effloresce and potential problems may develop. This does not mean that earlier preoccupations disappear, only that they are less salient for most, particularly for those who have handled them satisfactorily in the earlier phases. The three sub-phases can be described as shown in Table 2.

Table 2 *Sub-phases of the establishment period*

Sub-phase	Preoccupation	Potential problems
Early establishment (pre-school children)	Concern with *productivity:* choices and plans	Conflicts in the allocation of one's energies
Mid-establishment (children at school)	Concern with *performance:* effectiveness; competence at what is chosen	Conflicts of loyalties and obligations; dissatisfaction
Late establishment (children out of school)	Concern with *evaluation:* the meaningfulness of commitments (psychological 'pay-off')	Depression; boredom; feelings of entrapment, isolation: whether to change? What? How?

Psychologically the sub-phases may flow into one another and are differently experienced by different people. For some the transitions are smooth and nearly imperceptible, while for others there may be considerable turbulence around the transitional events, like having a child, or when the children leave home. For some there may be an early build-up of conflicts about the allocation of energies, doubts about investing oneself in a given course of action. Such a conflict may lead to early opting-out of a line of development—marriage, work career or a given interest. For others this kind of feeling may come later or not at all. The degree of turbulence experienced and concern with the issues arising out of the fundamental preoccupations depend on a complex of variables—personality, social class background, values and aspirations and the specific event in context.

Early establishment phase

The focal preoccupation of this sub-phase is with productivity; the characteristic problems surround the allocation of energies. 'Productivity' may be a concern in all life spheres. Apart from the economic productivity usually associated with occupational roles for those family members who have them, the family is likely to be concerned with other kinds of productivity too. Productive efforts may be invested in home-making; the Le Corbusier conception of the home as a machine for living is relevant however much families invest their homes with non-technological meanings. The same may be said of marital relationships and the tasks of child-rearing. However much they may be based on non-instrumental values—love and affection—most people have to 'work' with relationships to make them happy. One 'becomes productive' in the sense of producing marital satisfaction or rearing children satisfactorily. In their non-work lives outside the home people may be involved in other activities—cultural, community and social service, educational, and so on—which occupy their time and energy. The central theme is to become productive in *some* of this array of possibilities, how to group them, and what priority to give them. For some people it will be a wide and variegated spectrum, for others a narrow or specialised one. For all, the contemporary problems centre on choices, strategies and allocations of energies to different life commitments.

As we describe the patterns that are indicated in the available research literature, it is important to bear in mind that there is a *modal* tendency which characterises the greatest proportion of families in this phase, and that there are *variations* by region, social class, sex and personal orientation. But the picture is changing and there are influences that make the prevalent patterns of yesterday and today obsolescent tomorrow. It is therefore useful to look at the available information in terms of the principles to be derived, rather than in terms of the statistics which may shift rapidly.

In the early establishment sub-phase, if they stay together (the first year is at high risk of marital breakdown), most married couples have children. Most husbands concentrate their efforts on getting and holding a job and/or in developing a career. As the economic demands on the family are high at this point relative to the earnings curve, it is a period in which finances are 'tight' (Abrams, 1963). What is spent tends to go into the home, the centre of what is shared between men, women and children. For most the home is more than a mere shield against the elements. Though there are many in society who still are deprived of this elemental condition, it is a centre for the cultivation of interests, a place to store and display valued objects and possessions, a social centre for the enjoyment of friendship and conviviality in privacy and comfort. Available evidence indicates that with increasing affluence these 'middle-class' values in housing are diffusing more widely in the population.

By the early establishment phase, the family is likely to be living in their own home (Rosser and Harris, 1965). To the extent that they are able to afford it, they may move from rented to purchased accommodation, which may then evolve from an attached to a detached house, from a less desirable to a more desirable neighbourhood—often moving centrifugally from the urban centres in the search for privacy, quiet and comfort. In Britain there has been an increase in owner-occupied houses, in the standards prevailing in them and in the inventory of material possessions that they contain (Donnison, 1967; Hole and Attenburrow, 1966).

Madge (1968) points up implications of these trends:

In affluent countries, the rise of general space standards to the level previously reserved for middle class homes has coincided with, and may have helped to stimulate, the growth of individuation in the home. Whereas in the traditional working class home family life was lived collectively in the 'living kitchen,' today there is more stress on individual privacy and a greater tendency for members of the family to follow their own pursuits.

Pursuits within the home may differ by sex and generation. The male's preoccupation with productivity is likely to centre in the workplace, but for some men the home is parallel to or even more important as a channel of productivity than their work.

For most women the home constitutes the main channel for being productive at this phase. The conventional wife who enjoys home-making and has a compatible husband may find that domestic channels serve her needs to be productive and she may be happy in this period. A less 'maternal' woman, or one with a disagreeable set of living conditions or an unhappy marriage, may be dissatisfied with her domestic roles. If she is able to, she may cultivate other interests, as sources of satisfaction. This will usually be more difficult to effect in the occupational sphere than in the non-work area. For both wives and husbands this tends to be not only a home-centred sub-phase, but also a child-centred one. Play with children and the involvements of early parenthood are prominent interests.

While available research data on 'enjoyment patterns' is scarce, some material has been extracted from a study on highly qualified women (Fogarty *et al.*, 1971). From this study we have analysed data on 'enjoyment curves' from school through the early establishment phase for married men and women graduates, using a number of everyday activities which have a leisure character. The picture in Figures 5 and 6 emerges (Thiessen *et al.*, 1975).

Though limited to graduate couples, the data confirms in detail the general tendency to enjoy home-centred activities. Following marriage, most men shift their patterns of enjoyment from physical activities to

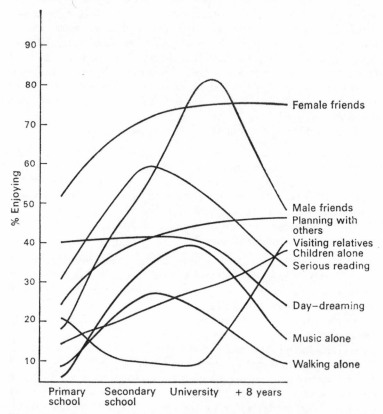

Figure 5   *Enjoyment careers: family-orientated married women graduates*

home-based ones. Survey data shows that do-it-yourself decorating, home improvement and pottering around with the car increase for men at this point (Morrell Publications, 1973). Women's main physical activity, dancing, drops off at marriage; they begin to cultivate 'crafts and hobbies', particularly knitting, sewing and other home-making arts (Sillitoe, 1969).

Married men and women in the graduate sample show a drop in their enjoyment of friends of the opposite sex, and both drop their enjoyment of day-dreaming and fantasies. They concentrate more on the here and now issues of home- and family-building. For women in this group the enjoyment of being with children peaks in the early establishment period. For men the enjoyment of children rises too but somewhat less so. This pattern may be different for other sub-groups; enjoyment of

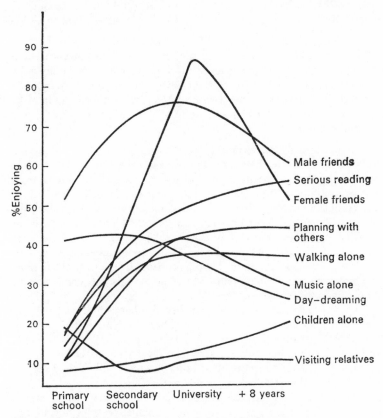

Figure 6 *Enjoyment careers: married men graduates*

children may come later. These data also show that women carry the main function of linking the family with other kin; this is similar to the pattern reported by researchers of working-class families. In the graduate sample men enjoy visiting relatives less than women and their involvements between home and work are more split.

The foregoing picture is an overall one. Variations in patterns of interest and enjoyment are related to different types of family structure. In the British graduate sample that we surveyed we found that the more symmetrical a couple is in their work and family roles, the more they enjoy everyday activities (Rapoport *et al.*, 1974).

In the *conventional* family (male as provider; female as home-maker) which has been dominant in all classes in the West since the Industrial Revolution, it was through middle-class affluence that women were at first freed from having to work. The model of middle-class suburban family structure is best described in Riesman's introduction to Crestwood Heights (Seeley *et al.*, 1963, vi):

> The husbands work all day in the city; they pride themselves on being practical no-nonsense men—a pride partly maintained by polarising themselves from their allegedly emotional starry-eyed wives. The wives have the leisure and education and energy to make a career out of suburbia, and to be anxious about themselves and their children.

In conventional families mothers have their children early and assume full responsibility for their care. This is *their* sphere of productivity. It is expected that they will enjoy and obtain personal fulfilment from domestic and child-oriented activities. Their psychological 'pay-off' in the gratifications of motherhood comes quickly (Rossi, 1968). A conventional husband, depending on his work, may be heavily involved in establishing himself in his job or career in this period. If he is lucky, he will have a job he enjoys. But he may have to defer some gratification until he reaches more seniority; doing the groundwork to establish himself may take a lot of extra effort at this point; this may compete with family and other interests.

The conventional family, being heavily home-centred, may be particularly strong in developing home-based interests. This is reinforced by the tendency for cash to be in short supply. What is available will be spent on home improvement and 'do-it-yourself' activities. For conventional wives the pursuit of other interests will depend on the availability of domestic help or child-care facilities.

A problem that can be seen at least in nascent form in this sub-phase centres on the man's concentrating his principal energies outside the family. This may have been accepted unquestioningly in the past but it is now a matter of reconciling more complex values and choices. To the extent that the wife is young and strong and is achieving satisfactions from home and babies, considerable sacrifices are likely to be acceptable to her in relation to her husband's outside commitments. But increasingly, he is expected to participate in the domestic and child-care activities.

A potential problem for the husband may be how much time and energy he can give directly to his wife and children when work demands on him are high and he is enjoying the challenges created by them. He may not only feel that he is failing to help his wife but that by being away from the family so much he is losing out on some of its enjoyable aspects—such as participating in the development of his children. At this stage too there may be an early perception of what might become a problem later, namely how to integrate his wife into his work life. He may recognise that if he does not do this, their interests could diverge. This could become a serious problem for the development and continuation of the marriage.

Another potential problem for the conventional wife is that of energy allocation: how much time to give to her children versus her husband, at what standard to maintain the home, and sometimes how much energy to devote to 'herself'. If husband and wife share home-improvement hobbies, one of the conflicts may be resolved. However, for women who have ambivalently adopted the conventional pattern—i.e. have no intention of returning to work but feel that they ought to or would like to—a feeling of entrapment may develop; this is the beginning of the 'captive housewife' syndrome. In later phases a family problem may arise unless new interest horizons can be provided for the wife.

The couple in the early establishment phase can easily be swamped by the demands of home and work and find themselves unable to allocate time and energy for maintaining their relationship *per se*; unless this is dealt with, husband and wife grow apart in a way that is difficult to reverse later. At this time too family problems may revolve around the children being deprived of their father during their waking hours and of having a mother who is irritable, overwhelmed and resentful.

The *new-conventional* pattern is defined in terms of the wife's intention to return to work after a period of withdrawal into domesticity following the birth of children. Behaviourally the new-conventional pattern resembles the conventional one in this early establishment phase. The man puts his productive energies into work channels and the women into home-making. As the distinctive feature of this type of family is the intention of the wife to return eventually to economically productive work, there is a range of attitudes and interests distinguishing the new-conventional from the purely conventional family. For one, the husband may take a greater part in domestic tasks, as a facilitating step towards his wife's return to work. The wife may use any available time to keep in touch with her occupational or other work-related interests by going to meetings, reading journals or seeing former colleagues. She may take a course that might aid her re-entry into work. These variations will depend on how long the 'out' phase of the 'in-out-in' sequence is expected to last, and partly on the type of occupation the woman has.

An early re-entry to work for the wife is defined as working again before her youngest child has entered school—placing the re-entry process in this early family phase. The likelihood of a wife wanting to re-enter varies partly with how conventional her own and her husband's norms are about women working. Other influential factors are availability of good child-care facilities and help, opportunities for flexible work arrangements in her environment and her husband's participation in family life. Some women experience a rapid decline in the enjoyment of having and caring for babies, and correspondingly a strong pull back towards work or other interests. For them there may be a foreshortening of the period of domestic withdrawal. For others the enjoyment may be more than expected and there may be a prolongation of the period of domesticity.

When the wife re-enters early, there are likely to be sufficient rewards for the couple to counterbalance the strains. The couple's dual earnings help with the home-making; each pursues an interest in work as well as at home so that the sacrifices of other diversions may not yet make themselves poignantly felt. On the other hand, tensions may reach an explosive point, threatening the relationship and the happiness of one or other member. These tensions will be affected by the degree of consensus that exists between husband and wife, the degree of overload she and the family experience in relation to her work commitments, the disapproval or support present in the family's social environment and so on.

The *dual-worker* family is one in which both wife and husband work continuously at their occupations as well as taking on domestic roles, even following childbirth. Couples vary in how committed each partner is to work as distinct from familial roles, how full-time and how egalitarian the situation is. Sometimes the wife works continuously but part-time; the work may be perceived as a hobby and of secondary priority in the family's overall affairs. The husband has his work and his home, the wife has 'two jobs'. More egalitarian dual-worker families are those in which both not only work continuously, but consider that each is to be given equal priority in the allocation of the family's energies and decisions. In the early family phase this may mean that a decision to move for an occupational opportunity may be equally important whether the job is for the man or the woman. The decision is made by both in terms of their overall interests. This is the kind of family described by Young and Willmott (1973) as one in which it is recognised that the couple has four jobs with each partner having an outside and an inside job; sustaining this pattern is difficult unless the male participates more than has been usual in domestic roles.

The strains of the dual-worker pattern are high for both partners and for the relationship (different though not necessarily greater than in other family patterns). The wife may sometimes be emotionally torn between home and work and feel that she does justice to neither. She may resent turning the baby over to a helper and at the same time she may feel that she cannot give as much time or energy to her job or career as she would like. The husband may feel that he is helping out quite a lot but that this is not considered enough; or, if he sees that his wife is under strain or failing in her wish to maintain both roles, that he is not pulling his weight at home.

During the early establishment period the couple experience their own and each other's personalities and capabilities in a new light. The wife may realise that work is more important to her than she has thought, confirming her wish to continue both interests, and that her husband is less helpful to her than he proclaimed his intention to be when discussing the situation in prospect. The husband may feel that while in theory he wants his wife to continue her job, he does not like it to interfere so much with his own work and other interests. He may resent her telling him that he does not really share the domestic responsibilities when he feels that he helps a great deal as compared with more conventional norms. As the strains and conflicts build up, other interests may get crowded out as one way of dealing with the role overloads. This may exacerbate the tensions. Alternatively the couple may diverge as each involves him/herself in separate interests.

Two vignettes illustrate these issues in particular families. In both, the husbands and wives were highly educated, but in both there were modifications of their marital structures as they faced the problem and tested their abstract ideas against the realities they were experiencing. The Peters expected that they would be a dual-career family, but Mrs Peters decided to make a change in the direction of the new-conventional pattern. In the Carlos family, the shift was in the opposite direction. Mrs Carlos assumed that she would drop out of work after childbirth, following something like the new-conventional pattern; but when she tried this she found that her work meant too much to her, so she and her husband (and her employers) worked out a situation in which the dual-career pattern was made more practicable for them. In both cases we try to highlight the implications for the pursuit of enjoyment and the development of meaningful life interests.*

THE PETERS are an example of a *new-conventional* family, in which Mrs Peters worked until the arrival of her first child and then left work for a period of full-time domesticity.

Mr and Mrs Peters are both civil servants and were in their mid-thirties at the time they were interviewed. They both came from

---

* In dual-worker as opposed to dual-career families, as case material not presented here confirms, the preoccupations and problems are similar, though their resolution differs due to differences in such factors as conditions of available occupations. In general there are greater opportunities for flexibility in the more highly skilled occupations.

families in which the fathers were in government service, though Mrs Peters's father had a slightly higher position than Mr Peters's and eventually went into a successful private practice in accountancy. So, while both grew up during the depression of the 1930s and had felt the stringency of financial shortages, neither had been really hard-hit by the poverty or insecurity that had afflicted many families.

Both Mr and Mrs Peters have younger sisters; his is two years younger and recently left the Civil Service after marrying a university teacher. Mrs Peters's sister is five years younger and married a solicitor. She is a 'lady of leisure', since leaving her job.

At the time of our interviews the Peters were living in a working-class suburb in North London; they were looking for a house in a more middle-class area. They had just had their first baby and Mrs Peters had decided to leave her job, intending to return to work eventually and to take on part-time work as she felt able to. At that stage, their life was very much taken up with domestic interests—the search for a new house, the new baby and associated new arrangements. They stated that like some of their friends (but in contrast with the general trend) they had married late and were involved with these issues at a later age than many people, but that they had accumulated considerable experience of life and seniority in their organisations so that they enjoyed certain advantages.

Mrs Peters was the more intellectual of the two sisters and was pushed to be a career woman by her mother, who had earlier been a promising scholar but had dropped out after a scholarship in a girls' boarding school. However, while she did not manage to make a career for herself, she made a decisive break from her working-class family background and acquired education, a vision of the possibilities that the world held, and a husband who was socially slightly above her own family. Mrs Peters's father was rather withdrawn, partly because he had a struggle to establish himself. While still in the Civil Service, he took an accountancy apprenticeship and established himself within a firm while the children were very young. This meant a lot of extra work; he was often tired and worked at night. Mrs Peters feels that she has a reasonably good, if not very close, relationship with both her parents but that they do not understand her present situation very well, i.e. her decision to opt for a period of domestic interests, which comes as something of a surprise to them.

Mr Peters's family was more working-class than his wife's; his father worked at a lower level of clerical work in the Civil Service. Also his parents were considerably older when he was growing up. His father was over 40 when he married. This meant a constraint on being expressive around home, particularly when he was in his teens, and it also meant that his mother was less orientated to domestic activities and child-rearing. He describes her as a 'very traditional, conformist sort of person', but one who did not like housework and was always frustrated because she had not had much education. His father is described as a very 'undomesticated man', who was thrown into a certain amount of self-help in the household to which he rose occasionally when necessary. Mr Peters feels that he is like his father in temperament—both being somewhat 'squirkish' and 'irreverent'—but father and son do not have a close relationship. He is closer to his mother with whom he shares interests into the present—like reading and going to the theatre. He feels that this may underlie his interest in intelligent women: 'I couldn't conceive of being married to somebody who wasn't intelligent. It would be so dull. I couldn't envisage being married to somebody who wasn't, in however loose a sense, rather intellectual.'

Both Mr and Mrs Peters entered the Civil Service as Administrative Class Officers (assistant principals) following their completion of university training. Mrs Peters had a degree in economics, while Mr Peters concentrated on history. Both worked in economics-related positions within the Civil Service. Mrs Peters had been in the Civil Service for nearly fifteen years when interviewed, and Mr Peters a year longer. They worked in the same department for some years before marrying.

Mr Peters has found his work continuously stimulating and has developed a high sense of identification with the Service and the work:

'There's no doubt about it, I went into the Civil Service because it was rather an achievement, coming from the background I did, to get into the Administrative Civil Service. Having been in the service for over fifteen years now, I find there are a number of things one enjoys. The relations with colleagues—the social side of the office—is pleasant, and one always learns from other people's lives, through what is admittedly something of a distorted mirror. As for the work, there are some posts that present tedious work that has to be slogged through but in the Civil Service there is always the prospect of moving on to something which may turn out more interesting. There is such a variety, that one can look forward to another post in which there will be more challenge—reacting to situations. Sometimes in the midst of a job when the pressure is on, it may seem tedious and frustrating but when one looks back you can see that it was quite interesting.'

Mrs Peters says that she has always enjoyed the work, but:

'I wouldn't say I was passionately work-centred. I enjoyed it and I think that if I was doing a job I'd want it to be interesting. I'm not passionately ambitious, I wouldn't like to get to the very top but I've also got the feeling that I shall be able to go back without losing too much position. They've now altered the regulations so that you can arrange to drop out and more or less pick up where you were. . . . I've got so much seniority clocked up as a principal, that I can go back without causing too many problems. It would have been difficult if I had been made Assistant Secretary, oddly enough, because I wouldn't have yet had time to do very much at that level.'

The Peters had known of each other's existence for some time, but had not taken a special interest in each other until he was posted abroad and she had made a couple of trips over on business. They went out together and found that they 'sort of fit'. They married when he returned from his overseas posting, and had been married for six years at the time of the interviews, which was just a few months after their baby had arrived. Mrs Peters says:

'When we got married, we hadn't any clear feelings about having a family. In fact, if anything, I was rather uninterested in the prospect. I think we agreed from the beginning that it was basically up to me because most of the consequences would tend to fall more heavily on me. . . . We took the decision not to start a family immediately and having done that, things just went on for some time.'

Their main life investments in the earliest stage of marriage went into being productive at work. Their strategy was to defer having children and concentrate on establishing themselves economically and professionally. Five years or so after marrying, when they were both in their mid-thirties, Mrs Peters broached the subject of starting a family:

'Partly age I think and partly one begins to feel a bit elderly . . . not elderly, but you know, time is passing, one is more aware of this when one gets to be about 35, I think. We were getting on almost too well. We're both fairly placid characters, rubbing along fairly well together—getting on well, we have a lot of interests in common and we'd settled down to a rather cosy existence.'

Aside from her wish to become productive in the family as well as at work, the problem of boredom seemed to loom on the horizon:

'I could see us getting very middle-aged and self-centred. And I felt that unless we took a decision pretty soon—this sounds pretty cold-blooded but various things were moving—and I began to feel that it would be nice to have a family.'

She also envisaged the potential problems of allocating her energies so much in the workplace that she would miss out on the domestic experience of infant care:

'Originally when we talked about it in the abstract, I rather envisioned going on working. But when it came a bit closer, I decided I
really didn't want to work full-time and the Civil Service doesn't
really allow for part-time work in our grade, so it was a straight
decision. Was I going to hand the baby over to someone else to look
after, or not? I decided not. I think I came to this conclusion before
we actually started the family.'

Mrs Peters thought all this through before raising the subject with her
husband, expecting that he might rather want her to continue with her
work. When she did tell him about it, he said that he was rather relieved.

Mr Peters felt that as they had waited before marrying, and then
waited while working, and had a modest kind of living accommodation,
they had achieved considerable financial viability by this time. This
meant that unlike some younger people who plunge into parenthood
early, they had the option of Mrs Peters stopping work. They were not
committed to heavy financial outlays which were based on the assumption of two incomes. He also noted that it is 'obviously more convenient
from the man's point of view, looking at it purely selfishly, if his wife is
at home'. However, he was rather surprised and thinks his wife might
change her mind and continue with her career—or re-enter earlier than
she thinks now. She expresses the classical view of conventional and
new-conventional mothers, emphasising the wish to get what pleasure
she can out of the actual life experience of having a baby and looking
after it while it is young:

'One romanticised it all a bit . . . but I feel that it would be an awful
pity to miss completely the young days. The Civil Service hours—
one's out of the house effectively from nine-thirty to seven at night;
it would just mean seeing the baby at the weekend.'

Mr Peters emphasises that another element in his feeling of relief had
to do with the fact that there would be so many logistical problems if she
continued to work. In the Civil Service generally, and with his wife in
particular, as she is so conscientious, there would be problems of how to
meet contingencies—emergencies that might arise at home, if the baby
were ill or the nurse walked out, etc. So that while neither of them is
particularly conventional-minded about the exclusive need for only the
mother to provide infant care, they recognise the difficulty in 'bucking'
the prevailing system. Also he notes that as they have got older, they
feel less inclined to take a dissident position: 'The general collective
advice in the environment—in this age of Spock and Bowlby—is very
much couched in terms of motherhood being a full-time occupation.'

So Mr and Mrs Peters have agreed, for an amalgam of reasons—her
gratification, his comfort, their joint management of logistical problems,

financial considerations—that the best solution for them was for her to drop work for the time being and then to return eventually, taking part-time and flexible work assignments from the Civil Service Commission in between.

Their shared *interests* in literature, theatre and sociability take form in reading, talking, seeing friends, going to the theatre. His parents are retired on the East coast, and hers in Surrey. They visit them inter-mittently. Their attitude, prior to the baby's arrival, was very casual about their house location and the standard of housing in general. These are changing and becoming more orientated to building up a comfortable home in a more socially suitable area. But for the time being, Mrs Peters's activities were centred on making their present home more comfortable for the baby. She did a great deal of sewing and used her time at home to brush up on her piano-playing. She had been a good pianist, but this had got rusty under the pressure of a full work commitment. Her musical interest is now being cultivated more vigorously during the time she has at home with the baby.

In summary this couple shows how the new-conventional pattern may emerge as a stress-relieving pattern, out of what started as a dual-career family structure. The stresses of the early establishment period were not actually experienced but anticipated and rehearsed mentally and in discussion. The shift was made to concentrate Mrs Peters's productive involvements in child-bearing and infant care. She did this after a period of establishing herself professionally, so that she could realistically expect to be able to return to work, when she was ready, under reasonable conditions. Mr Peters, who would have facilitated the dual-career pattern had his wife chosen it, is clear that he likes the added domestic inputs and the avoidance of extra strain, but is ready to return to the more difficult pattern when she is ready. An extra 'plus' in the situation is her greater leisure to revive an earlier cultivation of the piano.

MR AND MRS CARLOS are both architects who decided, after a brief ex-posure to the new-conventional pattern, to be a dual-career family. When they were interviewed, they were in their early thirties and had been married for four years. They had two small children; a nanny came in every morning. They were, at the time of the study, living in a flat in central London but planning to move to the country from where they would continue to work for their respective London firms, though with more 'take-home' work arrangements and a greater possibility for a comfortable home in the country near Mrs Carlos's mother, who would be able to help with child-care contingencies.

Mr Carlos was of continental origin. He had come to England to attend university and then remained on for architecture qualifications, finally marrying and settling here. Mrs Carlos is a middle-class English woman who from childhood had assumed that she would probably drop her career when she married; she always lived in a bright, cheerful, clean and conventional sort of home in the southern counties. Mr Carlos was somewhat cynical about her 'serious' approach to life but had a lively range of interests, a sharp wit and unquestionable professional flair.

Mrs Carlos, on completing her architectural training, entered a firm in which she rose to increased levels of responsibility, being recognised as a person who got things done and was reliable. Mr Carlos had been her assistant for a long time and was considered something of a Beau Brummell around the office, long on charm and short on career ambition. At first they were not particularly drawn to each other—on the contrary, they often 'fought like cat and dog'. She had other involvements and a young man of the 'right' sort from her home area wanted to marry her. He was quite the opposite type to Mr Carlos—quiet, taciturn, emotionally reserved. Mr Carlos took out many of the girls from the office and at first tended to regard her as an 'earnest nit, taking her work a bit too seriously'.

Their decision to marry looked, on the surface, to be one based on a complementary relationship between temperamental opposites. Each had something to contribute that the other felt he/she lacked. At another level, however, the marriage strengthened any latent wishes that she might have had to continue her career. He was not the sort of man to take over entirely and put her into a conventional role as a gentleman's wife. For him there were also additional functions that the marriage seems to have served. Marrying an obviously competent and established English professional woman dealt with any latent reservations he might have had about going back to his own country, in which he knew he would be something of a misfit after his training and experiences in England.

They both felt stimulated by one another, able to express their feelings and thoughts quite frankly, and capable of developing new interests and new patterns of living that they felt would enrich their lives:

> She: 'I married him because his kind of life appeals to me. . . . He was interested in so many things I had not even started being interested in; music and reading . . . and I would rather have somebody who is a bit extrovert and you have a good quarrel and it's all over.'
> He: 'I think basically it was because I enjoyed her company and I felt that she enjoyed mine, that we did an awful lot of different things together and enjoyed them . . . we could be completely candid with one another.'

While their marriage did consolidate their latent wishes—hers to continue her career (but in modified form), and his to stay on in England—their idea of a rich and varied life of cultivating new interests and forms of expression was not so readily realised.

In the first years of their marriage, the strains of operating two full careers and a conventional domestic pattern made themselves felt, crowding out many other pursuits. The sheer physical load of keeping a full-time job going and a home as well, particularly with the conventionality of Mrs Carlos's orientation to housework, was taking its toll:

'I was ill with a suspected duodenal and overwork . . . after we'd been married about two years. We had a very rough two years really . . . I used to have fits of hysteria because I couldn't cope . . . .Working full time . . . was much more tiring than I am doing now. I was so unhappy about the fact that we didn't really have a home. The house was dirty and I couldn't cope with the washing and ironing.'

Her husband's reaction was to take her out to a nice restaurant for a treat. This sort of solution has proved to work very well for some 'captive housewives' who feel cooped up at home. For a dual-career-worker like Mrs Carlos, it only made things worse as the housework did not get done magically. Her husband, his brother (who sometimes stayed with them), her father and people generally, expected her to carry on more or less as though she were a housewife—while they got on with 'important things', sipping sherry and talking politics. She became furious about this, but often said nothing, in order to preserve the relationship. It took her some time to recognise how conventional her expectations of herself were, for she had been brought up to expect that she would stop work when she had a family.

The strain built up—exacerbated by her success, for she was given a more senior job and found (as she knew from earlier experiences at school) that she really did not like being in a position of authority. By chance, the Carlos's had taken on a private job to do in the evenings during this period as well. Finally it became too much and she decided to give up her job with the firm.

She had two babies in rapid succession, working part time on commissions from the firm. During this period she realised how important the work, as well as the family, were to her. The firm also felt her loss and negotiations began about an arrangement that would allow her to develop professionally and take increased responsibility, but in a more freelance framework of flexible working hours:

'The job I'm doing has been a tremendous success and they like it so much that they want to increase the department and somehow arrange for me to do about three times as much work, not myself personally, but with some sort of small department . . . they want me to spend the whole of the hours I am willing to spend on the designs.'

This is difficult because if she concentrated only on designing without getting out and around, looking at the job, talking to the planners, etc., she would get out of touch. She would rather (and at the time of the interviews she began to explore the possibility of doing so) be given an annual fee and a great deal of flexibility to employ her own secretary, assistants, etc., on a sub-contracting basis, so as to get the jobs done in her own way. She could then take on 'X jobs a year' and get them done with an agreed budget in her own way. As an alternative, less attractive for her, she thought of increasing that small part of her work which was collaborative with her husband on small private contracts that had come their way. It seemed as though the arrangement with the firm would be agreed; the firm benefiting from the application of her experience to a wider range of new jobs and she benefiting by the flexibility to do the jobs in her own way.

Mr Carlos, after working at various architectural jobs ranging from house conversions to complete new office-block constructions, decided that his penchant was for interior design, and that he preferred working in a professional consultant–client relationship which allows for the provision of a professional service and the building up of a relationship between architect and client based on mutual respect. According to his wife he is very good at 'putting himself over' to clients. He has a design flair and a sense of history:

'To me architecture is simply the reflection of a particular period—sociologically and historically speaking—whether present, past or possibly future. If you understand the period you are discussing, and more than the period—the people—you start understanding their architecture—why they built and thought in that particular way.'

His own work was developed on a private basis and reflects his style and tastes. She has participated in it on a consultancy basis, trying out the experience of working together. He fits less well into a firm which requires diversification of effort. If he is asked to work on something that does not interest him, he finds it difficult to engage himself and so has sometimes been seen as lazy by colleagues.

The Carlos's have found, in their attempts to work together, that they have some complementary skills: his for administration and dealing with clients, hers for being methodical in planning through a project and tying up the details; his for getting a preliminary conception of a design solution, hers for its realisation. However, there are difficulties too and she in particular dislikes the insecurity of such a pair practice.

So the Carlos's had a very stressful early marriage phase, each work-ing flat out, tired in the evening and with less time and energy to cultivate their interests—including their sex lives—than they had envisaged. Added to this, the familistic customs of Mr Carlos's back-ground intruded, with his sister being sent to stay with them and being with them 'every minute', so adding to the strain. Mr Carlos, for all his goodwill and intermittent help in the household, has pursued a con-ventional male pattern in the domestic division of labour. He liked cooking and she enjoyed his cooking, so that was a help—but it was something that was an enjoyable part of the household work. He did much less by way of household cleaning or the more tedious aspects of infant care—leaving the burden essentially on her except for rather sporadic help when called upon to give it. Their life in a small flat was beginning to 'get them down', particularly when the older child became mobile. Mrs Carlos felt that the child needed the country, a garden and friends. She reduced her involvement in work to part time during the period of her pregnancy and the early months of each infant child; this relieved the strains somewhat but also made her aware of the im-portance of work in her life:

'I find being pregnant very satisfying and I find having a baby terribly satisfying. Really I would have one a year if I could afford it and could have a nanny. But afterwards you want to go back to your job again.'

Having the baby and having to care for it quickly became anti-climactic and the strains pulling her each way began to mount, in-creasing the sense of resentment and foul-temperedness, as she de-scribed it:

'I spend an awful lot of time feeling quite desperate and resentful . . . resentful that you can't spend more time on your work and resentful that you can't spend more time with your children, and resentful that you can't have both.'

She consolidated the dual-worker pattern as a result of learning about her own needs and values, rather than as a matter of preconceived ideas:

'It is since the second child was born that I have decided that I really shall go on permanently. I shan't give up work even if this job falls through. . . . I have always been involved, terribly involved [in my work] . . . the more I thought I would have to give it up, I didn't want to. But I thought I was going to have to, and it's only dawned on me that now it isn't really necessary. I can do both.'

Mr Carlos notes that she had reached a stage where she was an expert and could do interesting work, even if only on a part-time basis. Private work was too insecure. The fact that Mr Carlos too was having difficulties in his career, given the shortage of the kind of work he wanted and his unwillingness to do whatever came along, may also have firmed her own resolve to continue a regular career.

They have decided to concentrate on building a new home for themselves, and see it as solving many issues, though it is not free of problems. They acquired a piece of land in the country, near Mrs Carlos's family and near friends who have children and not far from where Mrs Carlos's sister is living. This promised to provide a network of helpers so that they would not feel the whole strain on themselves as in the city, where any illness of a child, or any difficulty about arrangements, had to fall entirely on their own, and usually her, shoulders. The fact that they are architects gives it an additional function, in that they could work on designing the house together, putting into work some of the excitement they had earlier experienced in collaborating, and putting their minds together collectively in a way directed towards solving some of the domestic problems. When the plans were finally made and building was in progress, they arranged to move close to the new home. She said:

> 'I just can't wait. I can't stand it here any longer. The flat is now much too small for the children. The youngest child is too big for the carry-cot and needs a proper cot but there is nowhere to put it. The children should have a garden.'

She wants a tricycle for the elder child and a pram that she can push, and others around for the children to play with.

It appears that the excitement of having children as an exclusive productive channel for her was only briefly satisfying; she needed both work and children, and worked out a way to do with flexible work arrangements and a home in the country near friends and family. For him, the productive channel of work was satisfying but insecure, and he was able to pursue his interests partly with her help, materially as well as morally. Producing their own home was exciting to them both, but he experienced a sense of mild foreboding about it all because of being more attached to city life. The home was not where he wanted it, but he helped to bring it into being, and it seems that he was willing to allocate his energies in a way that made it possible for her to function more comfortably. They are on the verge of a strongly focused pattern of 'do-it-yourself' home improvement, home and garden work and child-centred living.

Queries for their pattern of 'leisure' activity in the immediate future: how much will be outside the home? Very little, other than visiting relatives, we would expect. They seem to have participated in little social activity since their marriage. One would expect them to entertain their friends from town occasionally at their home, and to settle into a pattern in which the demands of home and career squeeze out most separate leisure, and consequently the attempt will be made to make these two strands of living as rich and enjoyable as possible.

Mid-establishment phase

This is the sub-phase in which some kind of a *plateau* is reached, though there are marked variations in just how steady the state is. Turbulence has its place here too. The early phase in the role-cycling process was one in which new challenges were confronted and the strains of adaptation were at their highest pitch. In the mid-sub-phase the pattern has become relatively established—at home, in work, and in relation to child-rearing. The man usually knows what his line of work is, what sort of husband and father he is and what pattern of domestic life he has adopted; the woman knows what sort of wife and mother she is and the way her domestic pattern is evolving. The central issue confronting people at this phase in their lives is that of *effectiveness in role performance*. They have usually settled into a home and a neighbourhood, and the children into schools. The long process of guiding children through their schooling and their own developmental phases is well under way. Depending on the specific conditions of housing, employment, schooling and community life, this may be a relatively stable and happy period, or it may be one of continuous strain with deleterious consequences for personal enjoyment, the marital relationship and participation in community life. Though this period may become routinised, it may also provide continuous new challenges.

The mid-establishment phase is potentially a period of great enjoyment. One's identity has usually been consolidated and there may be the economic potential to buy what one wants—excursions, food and drink, entertainments, travel and holidays. Because consumer wants accelerate in this period and are often acquired against future capacity to pay, high consumption may be accompanied paradoxically by the feeling of being 'strapped' for funds. The more vital issues of ageing and physical/psychological decline are not yet as apparent as they will be in the late sub-phase, and there is a push to enjoy life while one is still 'in one's prime'. Economic pressures and adversities can often be faced without severe depression in this period because of the feeling that there is the capacity to improve one's position.

It is in this period that there is a peak in *family-centred activities* both at home—such as television-viewing and gardening—and outside— such as in holidays, trips and excursions. Participation in activities that are pursued on an individual basis now drops off in favour of activities that can be carried out as a family. Thus male club-membership and sports activity, for example, recedes (as they did for women earlier) and activities like visits to swimming pools and galleries come to the fore (Sillitoe, 1969).

In the USA the concentration on home-centred activities is confirmed as the central productive effort that is shared between the spouses—with the husband's occupational work usually out of sight in the downtown business districts of the great cities. The life style in the middle-class suburbias studied by American and Canadian sociologists—the Crestwood Heights, the Park Forests and so on of the affluent, child-centred contemporary society—is based on consumption, in which rearing children is meant to be fun, and Spock and Gesell replace the Bible as a guide to moral conduct. The level of consumption is probably much higher still in the USA than in Britain. While the working-class suburbs as described by Gans and Berger, for example, differ from the middle-class suburbs in the degree of interest people show in cultural activities and the solidarity that can be produced through voluntary interest groups organised around educated housewives, the emphasis on child and home-centredness is a common element. Working-class residents are, as innumerable studies show (in England and the USA), more passive and less articulate in the pursuit of interests and activities. Middle-class suburban residents have not only more financial resources with which to pursue competitive consumer-based leisure activities, but also a higher level of education interests which can be expressed socially. *The potential social value of articulate interests is enormous, and only partly realised*—for example, in voluntary activities and community activities of various kinds. Yet suburban life has been characterised by conventionality and apathy about participating in interests groups beyond those of local or private concern. The distinction between 'local' and 'cosmopolitan', however, differentiates relevant sub-types, with the latter being much more interested in diversity, larger-scale interests and innovation (Lansbury, 1970; Gans, 1965; Berger, 1969; Seeley *et al.*, 1963).

Underlying the consumer model in leisure behaviour which seems so dominant in capitalist society at present, and strongly supported by those at the mid-establishment phase, are sub-preoccupations and interests that could perhaps find expression in less consumptive activities. The complex of gratifications surrounding the boost in second home ownership is illuminating.

For some this is a prelude to the later phases, offering a stepping-stone to a style of life that will be enjoyed following retirement, for others it is a status symbol. For most, however, the second home is perhaps best understood in the framework of *sensory gratifications* that are in focus during this period. The early establishment period was probably one where there was considerable sensory deprivation, apart from that obtained from the main tasks of that period. Husbands may have concentrated on establishing themselves in work with little time for gratifying other needs. Wives probably concentrated on domestic and child-bearing pursuits (or, as in the case of the dual-worker families, on making both streams of involvement work). Child-bearing has associated sensory gratifications for many women. But after several years of such concentration, there begins to accumulate a feeling that other gratifications are required to give life meaning. Anyway it is neither socially acceptable nor economically feasible to continually produce children for sensory 'kicks'. The gratifications that were characteristically neglected in the early period begin to clamour for expression in this middle period. For the urban dweller they include *natural* pursuits: contact with the countryside; contact with water by boating, swimming, etc.; gardening and growing things; camping out and walking. The rural inhabitant may have more need for the gratifications found in the city.

Movement seems to be another sensory need of this period—taking trips, driving, boating, etc., with apparently no purpose other than moving about, seeing things, experiencing different sights, sounds, smells and so on. Interest in *sexual gratification* may be renewed during this phase, perhaps through fear of loss of potency or the need to stimulate new experimentation, new reading and viewing interests, affairs, etc. Sometimes there is a renaissance within the marriage with a shared interest in the topic as it is purveyed outside, for example in films, nightclubs, magazines. Experimenting with new *taste sensations* such as those involved in trying out new dishes, new places to eat— 'eating Chinese', 'eating Pakistani', may be common now. *Competitive events* involving physical exertion tend to be vicariously enjoyed in this period. Sometimes, however, there is a renewal of interests in physical competitiveness, or doing something against one's own performance record—for example sailing around the world, climbing a mountain. Also there are many competitive pursuits, such as card-playing games, which can be enjoyed without a great deal of muscular exertion.

Watching television, films, plays and so on provide vicarious sensory gratifications, while *do-it-yourself* activities, ranging from home-decorating to the cultivation of hobbies, arts and crafts, woodworking, sculpture and pottery and so on, provide more direct gratifications.

Available research gives some support to an efflorescence of interests in this period (Allardt, 1958; Piepponen, 1960; Lansbury, 1970). Young and Willmott provide data which supports the idea of a tendency toward cumulative leisure activity. In their study this tendency was found to be associated with social class. The higher social class groups—managerial and professional families—were found to be more generally active in a wide range of leisure and recreational pursuits than the lower social class groups, the less skilled and manual workers' families (Young and Willmott, 1973). There is evidence from an American study by Kadushin (1966) that as part of the complex of cultural and recreational activities engaged in by more affluent urban Americans, one can find a thread of activity associated with 'psychiatric sophistication'—knowing about others' problems, having friends who have gone to a psychiatrist, going to see a psychiatrist oneself, etc. This may be the affluent intelligentsia's form of quasi-recreational dramatic activity that corresponds to the British working man's use of industrial action. Both have legitimate purposes in their own right, but they also may have these social and psychological functions which are recreational and integrative in character.

An important element in assessing a *pattern of enjoyment* for this phase is once again balance. Any of the pursuits mentioned above may be pursued excessively, thus creating problems rather than a solution to some of the issues of this sub-phase. The individual who becomes preoccupied with sex and pornography; the individual who spends too much time indiscriminately viewing television; the individual who becomes obsessed with food and overeats—may all be storing up trouble for themselves and their families, as well as dealing with the immediate pressures of the situation. The penalty for not providing some of these pursuits of enjoyment is boredom, psychological malaise or even psychosomatic symptoms of one kind or another.

Looking at the positive side, differences in family structure are likely, in this middle period, to be associated with markedly different patterns of enjoyment.

The *conventional* family faces a situation in which the *raison d'être* for the wife's total concentration on home and family begins to recede. Even for those wives who have not experienced the boredom and trapped feelings of the ambivalent conventional housewife, it is clear that they no longer need to concentrate their attention so exclusively on their children. The school system has taken over a good part of the children's time and the wife has fewer demands on her time than previously.

The conventional wife may use the extra time to raise the domestic standard of the household. She may renew furnishings and decoration run down by active youngsters. Alternatively she may decide to develop some other life interests—pottery, art, language study or whatever. Or she may become more active in community voluntary activities, giving time to the old, the poor, youth centres, the PTA and so on.

The housewife who finds herself for the first time in this mid-establishment phase with time on her hands, may feel like the redundant worker. She may, like the redundant worker, react by feeling depressed at the source of much of her gratification and meaning in life disappearing for most of the day. Or she may feel relieved and able to think about new pursuits.

But in many cases, children do not cease to present problems of care and parents do not find it easy to 'give up' their close involvement in the child's life. A mother may still want to pick the children up or to greet them after school, to hear of their exploits and to help them cope with their problems. She may press them to take ballet or music lessons, join the Scouts, or she may restrain them later on; from travelling too far, going too fast, being too independent, as she sees all of these involve thought, decision-making and often a struggle. Some women who managed well with their little infants may feel less effectual when the children reach this stage; whereas other mothers have the reverse pattern, beginning really to enjoy the children only after they become 'people' with views which can be discussed and with whom interests can be shared.

Depending on the particular persons and situations, the conventional wife may or may not feel that she has developed enough in this period. If not she may decide only at this point to change to the *new-conventional* pattern and think of returning to school or to work. However, this is a point at which it may be particularly difficult to translate attitudes into actions. Many conventional mothers lack the confidence to make this change after a period of absorption with child-rearing, and there is at present a shortage of facilitation for a wife's re-entry into some form of interest external to the home.

As for the conventional husband, he may have arrived at a plateau in his work, depending on the kind of occupation he has and his orientation towards it; he may 'freewheel' to some extent from this point onwards, giving more attention to his family, his home or his other interests. Alternatively he may have the kind of work situation which is depressing and enervating, in which he feels exploited and blocked. He may take on habits which are antithetical to those of home-building, and he may drink or gamble, or simply lie about too exhausted and depressed to do much with his family. For those men who are highly committed to their work and mobile into positions of increasing responsibility, there may be conflicts between home and work—with the demands of each being increasingly felt to be mutually exclusive. Fathers in this situation may feel in the later sub-phase that their children have grown up without their really getting to know them and that they have lost their respect— particularly if they continuously say that they are doing all this for the family, yet are never there. For the father the dilemma may be how to divide time between two areas in which he feels considerable involvement but which seem to be mutually exclusive. With the conventional husband, the feeling that his wife is looking after the home front ordinarily serves to bolster his choice of heavier career involvements, though he expresses concern with what is going on. This is perhaps best described in the studies of *managerial work and leisure patterns.*

Managers represent the situation which Parker describes as 'neutral', in that their recreational patterns are not necessarily connected with their work either by overspill or by compensatory contrast. One manager may be interested in theatre, while another cultivates golf and still another is keen on boating. However, recent studies of managers in various contexts begin to provide a picture of the processes at work in the establishment phase.

A range of studies of British managers show that they work shorter hours than their counterparts in the USA, Japan, Russia or Germany. They have, as a consequence, more time for other interests. Moreover, in their 'leisure time', they tend to do things which are more 'neutral' to career advancement—such as to cultivate their personal or familial interests, or simply to relax. Where they do otherwise, family strains arise (Stewart, 1967; Horne and Lupton, 1965; Child and Macmillan, 1972; Pahl and Pahl, 1971).

Child and Macmillan point out that while British managers work shorter hours and have more 'enjoyment-oriented' leisure pursuits than their counterparts in other countries (where even leisure pursuits tend to be instrumental to business interests or career advancement), they face a dilemma as companies become more international in organisation and more competitive (Elliott, 1960; Heckscher and De Grazia, 1959; Dubin, 1970). In the Child and Macmillan sample, younger managers are more likely than their elders to want to use their non-work time to escape from the job, while the elders—in the mid- and late establishment phases—are more likely to want to use leisure for social contact, keeping fit or relaxation. This may confirm Dubin's observation that younger British managers feel blocked in their career prospects; or it may reflect the new values in a social change situation where there is a positive wish to develop a more full-valued, less work-dominated life style.

The information from the Henley study gives a different picture—probably because it is managers who are not blocked who are sent by their organisations to Henley for the training experience that is transitional to positions of increased responsibility (Rapoport, 1970). Reanalysis of the Henley career data for this leisure study shows a *correlation between advancement up the managerial ladder and the sacrifice of personal and family leisure at this phase.* There is a cluster of highly interrelated variables which show statistical tendencies as follows: if the amount of time spent in work increases, then the amount of time spent at home with the family decreases, the amount of time spent individually on leisure decreases and the amount of time spent with

LFLC—H

the family on leisure activities decreases. In other words, there is a direct negative correlation between career advancement and family/ leisure participation among upwardly mobile managers. This is borne out by subsequent studies both in Britain (Beattie *et al.*, 1974) and in the USA (Gunter, 1974).

We have taken the managers only to illustrate the conventional pattern in this aspect, as most managers are conventional in their family lives and they are in an occupation in which this particular dilemma is often highlighted because of the mobility expectations.

In conventional families, conflicts may arise over how little the father is there, how much he has to travel, how late he comes home, how many meetings he must attend and so on. Another sort of problem that may develop in the relationship is that the husband has grown and developed through his work in his interaction with changing environments, different kinds of people and increasing challenges. The wife, in contrast, may feel or be felt not to have developed and the fit between the couple may thus have deteriorated. This problem may become acute when the children reach adolescence. There is a particularly strong psychological need for the parents to be together at this point; where there is little exposure to each other's thoughts and ideas and little chance to work through positions in relation to the management of the children, there are increased chances of family discord. The tasks facing families at this point are sometimes worked through over the issue of leisure activities and family holidays. There may be conflicts about what these should be, who should (or must) be included and so on. *The challenge that seems to face most families is how to evolve a pattern of activities and gratifications in their free and holiday time that will allow a mutually acceptable combination of shared and independent pursuit of enjoyment.*

In new-conventional families in the mid-establishment phase, a great deal of attention may be given to the question of how the wife should re-enter work, when it should be, what kind of work and what proportion of her time and psychological involvement it should take up. Many wives find it difficult to envision going back to work. They have run their own shows at home, had flexible arrangements set by their own considerations to a large extent, and they may feel at a disadvantage in the workplace. Perhaps they will have to take instructions from younger people who are felt to be at an advantage because they have had more recent training. If they followed the strategy of waiting to have children until they were more established, they will perhaps be in a better position occupationally, but their children may be younger than others of their age, and their pattern of obligations may be something that others in the age group have passed already.

So, while the man may have reached a plateau in terms of work demands, unless he is ambitious and still on the move upwards, the wife may have found herself facing a new challenge with the need to mobilise her energies—to take on new roles. Many women feel phobic about this and require extra help from someone—most probably the husband. Not all husbands approve of their wife's re-entry into work, and of those who do, not all are willing to do more than give lip-service to the idea. Really determined wives will find a way, even in the face of opposition from their spouses, as Audrey Hunt's report has shown (Hunt, 1968). However, those who are not determined enough to surmount the various obstacles may find it very difficult indeed.

Alice Rossi (undated ms.), in discussing factors that make for married women pursuing their delayed aspirations for higher education, describes some of the hazards of the process as follows:

> A woman who is as deeply committed to family and home involvement as she is to her current job or hopes for a higher degree may resolve the strain between this double commitment by simply postponing the graduate education to the future. A distant goal of securing an advanced degree by doing nothing for many years about starting work toward such a degree may be like the romantic expectation of many people that they will one day write a great novel, although they do no writing apart from occasional correspondence to acquire the skills needed to write such a book. . . . In the process, they may be accumulating a considerable burden of unmet expectations with which they will enter middle age and increase the difficulty of that life stage's task of working through an acceptance of the probable limits of achievement they will reach in their life time.

It seems then, that the new-conventional wife may have an orientation towards her work role that is rather close to that of a hobby—a meaningful life interest that is important to her but is her own affair and of a secondary order of priority—both in relation to the children and to her husband's work and comfort.

For the couple there is the problem of readjusting to the fact of the wife working, as well as the children being in school—which primarily affects the wife. Some men may feel guilty about their wives languishing at home while they are busy and away so much, or they may feel insecure economically and welcome the additional income. Other husbands, and this probably occurs in most families according to many reports including a recent one by Oakley, may be well-wishers and 'help a bit', but not provide basic structural changes in the domestic division of labour (Oakley, 1972). For the new-conventional wife this is usually not pressed. The tendency to accommodate to the situation and take a secondary role has become well established. She may not have the 'head of steam' of the conventional wife who is ambivalent about remaining a 'captive', nor does she have the high strains of over-load that characterises dual-workers.

The *dual-worker* families find the mid-establishment phase a bit easier—though perhaps not as easy as they might have assumed. Entry into school does not decrease the burden of child care as much as might have been anticipated; it is in this family structure even more than the others that the *gap in facilities for young children, say 5–13-year-olds, is most apparent.* It is often assumed that they are in school and that this will keep them busy. In fact they arrive home after school and need to be greeted and attended to; at holiday time too they have to have diver-sions. They may slip easily into a pattern of indiscriminate television-viewing, which is one way of showing that they need to be 'entertained' or have their energies and interests channelled. Or they may be left with 'minders' under conditions that Brian Jackson and his colleagues are now exposing as unsatisfactory (*The Times*, 23 July 1974).

By the mid-establishment phase, a pattern will have emerged whereby the strains of operating the dual-worker family are distributed in a certain way. The husband's work may become more exacting so that he may diminish his participation in family chores on the assumption that now that the children are in school there is less to be done. He may also tire of the effort put into the unorthodox domestic division of labour and feel the need for being cosseted. The pressure of the jobs of the marital pair may pull them in separate directions and lead to a feeling that they have grown apart. Studies by Harold Feldman and his colleagues in the USA have shown this to be a low point in the marital satisfaction trajectory (Rollins and Feldman, 1970). However, the earlier period will have provided for families of this type a greater joint investment in the family resources—material and non-material. If the strains of potential divergence are successfully dealt with in the middle period, these families are likely to have at their disposal an unusually large repertoire of interests, experiences and resources for the pursuit of their enjoyment and for the stimulation of their children.

Two vignettes illustrating some of these patterns and issues for the mid-establishment phase will be presented: one of a highly achievement-orientated manager and his family; the other of a dual-career family.

THE CHARRINGTONS are an example of a *conventional family in the mid-establishment phase.* Mr Charrington was the only son of an entre-preneur, who built up a successful company employing several hundred people in a manufacturing business in the West country. The company followed a familiar course for family firms of its type, with various relatives in key posts as the original founder moved upwards and the company became more bureaucratised, eventually 'going public' and finally being absorbed by a much larger international company. Mr

Charrington was the only son, was in a favoured position and from early days he showed initiative and drive; he was not the kind of 'crown prince' who expected to sail into the top jobs by virtue of his connections. On the contrary, he was an 'over-achiever', proving by performance beyond what might have been expected of anyone in his position that he held it on merit.

As a young person, Mr Charrington had been to the appropriate schools for a person of his wealth and upbringing, but never thought of going to university or training for a profession. He was always interested in the business and the family firm was part of his social environment from the earliest days. He recalls the life his father used to lead, arriving in the office at 9.30 a.m., perhaps having a long lunch time cricket match in the middle of the day and then knocking off at a reasonable hour to be with the family. There was much less travel and a regular pattern of family holidays.

When Mr Charrington completed his education at a public school, there was never any question of his doing anything other than going into the firm. He took a brief course in modern management methods and went to work in production. His work became part of the thrust that enabled the company to continue its successful development; when it became a public company he was in the line of seniors immediately available to take on directorships, regardless of family connections. He was so immersed in the company and its work that he had little social life outside. Though it was not quite the 'thing to do', he married his secretary, who fitted in perfectly with his pattern of absorption and dedication to the firm and its growth.

The Charringtons' early family life was in the conventional pattern described. The family had two children quite soon after marriage. Mrs Charrington withdrew permanently from work and created a home for them that was a base for her husband and gave the children a happy home life. Both children stayed at home until they were about 14, when they were sent to boarding school. The girl, who was academic-minded and ambitious, went because she was not happy in the particular local grammar school. The boy was sent because it was apparent that he was not academic-minded and the family decided that a broader type of character-building was wanted. They both seemed to have settled down in their respective boarding schools, taking school holidays at home.

When the children were smaller, the family followed a regular pattern of holidays. The wife and children went to the seaside in summer and Mr Charrington joined them at weekends. Mr and Mrs Charrington went off for weekends in other seasons to the Lake District, once a month or so, staying with friends who owned a small inn. As Mr Charrington became more prominent in his company and it became larger and more successful, his leisure began to be eroded. He left earlier in the morning and returned later at night. He took fewer holidays and travelled away from home more frequently. The pattern reached a climax when the company was absorbed into a large group and he was made a managing director of the group with headquarters in London. This meant that the week comprised three days at home and four in London with a shift of base, when the children went to boarding schools, to a new home closer to London. The new residence was chosen not only so that he could spend more of his nights at home, but also so that he could be closer to the airport, as his business had considerable investment and aspirations abroad.

Mrs Charrington has coped well with this, in the way expected of conventional housewives. While she has 'regretted that there hasn't been more time together', she has been busy looking after the children, and now that they have moved, building a new home. Her husband says that her main problem has been learning to be on her own so much.

At the time of the interviews Mr Charrington was so busy that everything had given way to work. He had not had a holiday with his family for two years and the pattern evolved of joining the family wherever they are holidaying when he can. His wife laughed when he received our letter requesting interviews on his leisure patterns, saying 'what leisure?' While he deplores his total absorption in work and the way it crowds out everything else, he is absolutely clear that he does it not only because he feels he has to (as he is so identified with the firm), but because he loves it:

'I like flying. I like meeting people. I like having a good meal and good talk. I enjoy overseas travel and seeing different places. I like to meet with our overseas managers and see how things are going.'

He also enjoys the VIP treatment he receives when visiting the local area manager in places where one of their companies operates. But his main 'kicks' are intrinsic to the work itself:

'I get my main kicks out of being successful; seeing a good profitable business going, and the contacts with people one meets in doing that and trying to clinch deals. It sounds a bit too dramatic but that is what gives me satisfaction.'

He notes that 75 per cent of his work is 'cooking work',—reading reports, dealing with day-to-day matters—but there is 25 per cent which is highly dramatic and exciting, and that is what the work is for. One of the reasons he works so hard is for that enjoyment; another is the need to prove to himself and to everyone around that he merits the position and is not just in it because he is his father's son: another reason is the special insecurity that comes with the isolation in top jobs:

'It is always difficult to foresee what is in the future, and I think that probably every business executive feels that life is a bit less secure than it was at one time . . . but I'm not a man who looks down advertisements. I have been in the company a long time and while I welcome responsibility and look for more of it, I think that it is ultimately because of the satisfaction of knowing that one is in control of a complete situation or a slice of a situation. While I can have that, I can be happy where I am.'

Recently Mr Charrington's group of companies have had management problems in a new venture on the Continent and he has had to spend even more time abroad trying to straighten things out. This has affected his family life not only because of being away more than ever, but 'because one goes home perhaps not in the sweetest of humours'. The mid-life crisis while not acute for him has not been entirely absent. In his quiet way he has to admit occasionally asking himself: 'Is it all worth it, or wouldn't it be nice to do a quiet but interesting job like running a country pub somewhere?' But these are passing thoughts, far from being the basis for action. He is concerned, however, with his wife's loneliness, and feels that he must do something now that the children are away so much and he himself is travelling increasingly. He has the idea of taking her along more frequently on business trips:

'She did accompany me for the first time on an overseas trip to the Far East last year. It was a trip at the speed I would normally do it, rather than a holiday trip, in other words, under two weeks for the lot—four countries. But she found that very interesting indeed. I think she could feel more involved from that point of view and it would provide a considerable interest. She enjoys meeting people. . . . The other area of outside interest for her is voluntary work and hospital visiting. She finds this interesting and satisfying.'

The pattern is evolving with enough gratification and increase in challenge to keep him involved, rather than acting on his escapist mid-life fantasies; and with enough of a possibility for her to join him in his work trips, together with an entry into community work, with enough gratification for her as well, in this phase where her children have 'half left the nest' and her husband is away.

The Charringtons' way of coping with the strains of the conventional family pattern in a changing world are instructive. Neither feels a misfit or ambivalent about the pattern but each is concerned to make it work well not only for the husband, whose benefits accumulate in the mid-establishment phase, but for the wife, whose main gratifications were in the earlier sub-phase. Their own resolution of the problems that have arisen—of conflicts between areas of involvement and in attempting to find a way that both husband and wife could continue to feel productive and perform well in their respective roles—provides the pattern for the later stage. Mr Charrington will probably continue to rise in his firm and to be effective in his work, achieving satisfaction at what he has accomplished; while Mrs Charrington will evolve a mixed pattern of life—partly the conventional suburban wife's social service and voluntary service pattern, and partly an increased sharing of her husband's experiences by travelling with him in connection with his work. This resolution has not been accomplished effortlessly but through sensitivity to one another's commitments and sources of gratification, and in an attempt to arrive at mutually acceptable solutions.

THE CARLSONS are a *dual-career family with two teenaged sons*—the younger is still at home, while the elder has just completed secondary school and is in the Merchant Navy. Mrs Carlson is a science manager and Mr Carlson a sales manager. They are in their mid-forties and have lived most of their married life in a detached suburban home with large garden and the comforts of a middle-class, professional-managerial life. They operate two cars and own a boat.

Mr and Mrs Carlson give the impression of being opposite and complementary in temperament. She is forthright and definite in her manner, attractive and humorous; she characterises herself as hard-driving and 'tough'. Mr Carlson is more easy-going and light-hearted with an amiable and friendly manner.

The way the Carlsons' family, work and leisure cycles have interplayed are clear from their accounts. The main themes of the interplay are family-centredness and complementarity of temperament and interests.

Mr and Mrs Carlson met shortly after the Second World War when she had qualified as a research scientist and he had returned from the Services and was considering a career in teaching. Both of them came from relatively poor backgrounds, though their parents had high aspirations for them. Mr Carlson came from Wales and his parents wanted him to escape the limitations of an area dominated by coal mining. He was close to his mother; they used to cycle together when he was young. Mr Carlson was attracted to the sciences from a young age. Though he was not outstandingly academic, he showed enough talent to be encouraged towards grammar school. He volunteered for the Royal Navy when he was 17 to avoid being drafted compulsorily into the coal mines. In the Navy he was trained as a radar technician and sent to the Far East. By the time he returned to Britain he was 21 and had set his mind on teacher training. His mother died a year after his return. His father retired to the country near his wife's family and lived long enough to see his son married with a first child.

Mrs Carlson came from the North of England; while her background was 'higher' than Mr Carlson's socially, it was characterised by a greater sense of hardship and psychological deprivation. Her father was a salaried civil servant in a place and at a time when salaried employees with steady jobs were considered lucky. This was during the depression of the 1930s. Her family was 'respectable' and she felt that she was cut out for something special. Yet she had and still retains a kind of fierce pride in her working-class origins and in her own drive and success in overcoming the handicaps this imposed in relation to having a professional career.

Mrs Carlson was close to her mother, though she sees that temperamentally she resembled her father in many ways, having his drive and his temper. Her mother was seen as a beautiful and entertaining person who longed for the warmth and gaiety of the family life she had earlier experienced but had not found with her husband. Feeling trapped and limited, the focus of her mother's interest centred on helping her daughter to escape to something better in life.

Mrs Carlson's father was fairly involved with his own activities; a greater part of the family budget than mother and daughter would have liked was spent on convivial activities with his masculine 'mates'. Mrs Carlson feels he did not really like females and treated her like a boy for much of her early life, showing her how to use tools and to play golf and cricket. In retrospect she thinks that the battles she had with her father—while very difficult to bear at the time—had the effect of toughening her: 'If I'd been a different sort of character, I'd have been wholly crushed, but he hardened me and I'm prepared to fight.' She believes that this toughness has helped her to fight the necessary battles to establish herself professionally.

Leisure activities brought the Carlsons together. He was an assistant warden in a youth hostel for one summer and she was hostelling with a girl friend. When they met they were both carefree and in high spirits. He had come out of the Navy, taken a temporary job he disliked and had just decided to enter a teacher training college. She had just finished her university training in chemistry. Though they decided immediately that they were right for each other, they put off their marriage for two years so that he could complete his teacher training. They married two years later, though he had decided meanwhile not to teach. She supported him—both psychologically and materially—in his wish to 'have a go' at a science course at university.

The division of labour they established involved each in doing domestic chores interchangeably. In the early days much was undertaken by Mr Carlson as he arrived home from his classes earlier than she did from her job. Mr Carlson says:

'We got into the routine that if there was something to be done, whoever was there would do it. She was working and I was studying and

I hadn't got much time for devoting periods to doing any particular job. If the floor needed sweeping or needed cleaning, we would do it without reference to each other.'

Mrs Carlson was developing her career successfully as an industrial research chemist when their first child was conceived unexpectedly. She says:

'In a way, looking back now I'm glad it happened because we would probably have kept putting off having a child and we would have found ourselves at this age and childless and I think that would have driven us both dotty.'

Retrospectively she is also grateful for the financial difficulties they experienced at the time, which dispelled any doubt there may have been about her continuing her career at that point:

'There was a very strong feeling against a mother working when I started, and I did not from choice, but because there was a tremendous financial compulsion. I think I could have easily fallen by the wayside if it hadn't been the choice of working or starving at that time . . . I could have fallen to social pressures.'

The birth was a difficult one for Mrs Carlson and it was several days before she could see the baby. Because of this the baby was bottle-fed which, like other tasks of infant care, Mr Carlson could manage as well as she. He performed all the essential baby-care activities interchangeably with his wife:

'When he [the baby] yelled for any reason and I happened to be there, I would pick him up and find out what the cause was and deal with it on the spot, rather than charging all round the house yelling for my wife. So, if it was a nappy change, I would just whip it off and do the change, do the necessary work and put him back again.'

They had their second child two years later (1956) and by then were able to move into a small house and to have a trained nurse, and later an *au pair*, to help. Mr Carlson had meanwhile resigned himself to not becoming a scientist but to taking another kind of job in a science-based industry. He became a sales manager for a chemicals company, and by 1959 they were able to move into a larger house in a 'good' London suburb nearer to Mrs Carlson's work. During this period of great strain on their relationship as well as their finances the Carlsons had little time to pursue other interests, involved as they were with the establishment of two careers and a home, and the rearing of their two boys.

The Carlsons' first child was 'easy', presenting few problems and having many of the accommodating and social traits of his father's

personality. The second son, two years younger, is more determined—
like his mother. He likes to be an authority and collects stones, natural
objects and all sorts of information. His parents see him as very strong-
willed, 'a handful' and 'obstinate', but as he grows older they see how
he develops his interests purposefully and with good effect. He plays the
clarinet and absorbs himself in this activity when he is 'feeling down'.
From the start, he was very bright in school; he learned quickly and
mastered reading and writing before his brother who was three years
older. The Carlsons handled the problem of the younger child out-
shining the elder academically by emphasising the importance of the
elder boy's ability in sports and his general talents in social situations:

> 'We took the line eventually that the older one is very good at sport
> and games and athletics and swimming, and he's good with other
> children. He became a patrol leader in Scouts—he could organise
> these sorts of things. The younger is clever but he is not so good in
> these things. It took a lot of doing to get it over to both of them that a
> person can't be good at everything. It's nice to be clever at school
> work but it's also very nice to have a nice nature and the older one
> has a nice nature. He's good with people and he's good at organising
> and he's good at athletics.'

The younger son is at grammar school and very involved in science. The
elder, having done well enough at O-levels but not at A-levels required
for pilot-training, has opted for a career in the Merchant Navy.

Mrs and Mr Carlson have contrasting types of career patterns,
though there are some substantive overlaps in their interest in science
and chemistry.

Mrs Carlson, from the age of 11, had been interested in medicine
or an allied field. Her naturalist interests had been stimulated very early
and she embarked on what was a long 'battle' for professional qualifications. Eventually she achieved higher qualifications in biochemistry,
moving from a hospital post to one in industry. This brought an increase
in immediate cash returns, and additionally the company was committed
to sex equality in careers. Mrs Carlson stayed on despite having two
babies, and achieved promotion. Retrospectively she describes her
career as follows: 'I never anticipated making so much of a success,
I'd not exactly planned a career, because the plans were very different
when I started.' At present she has settled into a senior post directing
a research laboratory and finds the job satisfying, stimulating and is
proud of her accomplishments. She separates her work personality from
her domestic personality, symbolising the switch by her white laboratory
coat:

> 'I'm very authoritarian at work. Well, I have to be. I think, looking
> at myself through their eyes, I'm probably at least 90 years old and

fierce. I'm not really, but when I say I want something done, I don't mean next week. I want it done now. I wear a white coat at work, and I do try to hang my working personality up with it when I leave the office.'

For many years she worked as a scientific officer, rising through the ranks until she reached her present management position. While she now enjoys many of the perquisites of higher status—large office, larger expense accounts and so on—she also experiences loneliness and loss of enjoyment of laboratory work. When asked what the most enjoyable part of her work has been, she answers:

'Thinking, "I wonder if I could get a certain effect if I did a certain thing", trying it and finding that I do. This is almost like a shot of heroin to a drug addict.'

Mr Carlson's work career contrasts sharply with his wife's. Rather than a purposeful development with diversions and difficulties over specific hurdles, he has had a number of false starts and disappointments, leading to radical reorientation. As a consequence, occupational establishment came relatively late for him. In his school days he was interested in metallurgy but this was discouraged by his parents. He showed a continuous interest in science but was not an academic performer; he preferred going along comfortably in a socially active and enjoyable way to doing the 'grind' work that leads to high marks in examinations. He joined the Services at a time when he would have had to make a definite commitment about his higher education; thereby avoiding dealing squarely with this issue for about four years. He left the Navy in 1947 at 21, taking a job he disliked, and began to think again about higher education. At this point he met his prospective wife and entered teacher training college, a compromise solution supported by his father. Mrs Carlson recalls:

'His father wanted him to have a good job, wanted him to teach. He was young and easily influenced at the time, I don't think he would be so easily influenced now. But his father was quite old by then and retired, so he couldn't help much.'.

Once in teacher training college, during which time they got married, Mr Carlson decided that he disliked that sort of work too. He transferred to a chemistry course at a university—something closer to what he had always wanted, but he experienced difficulties with the mathematics. By then it was 1953 and his wife was pregnant, so he took a job as an engineer, but left this after four months. At this point, with their finances strained to the limit, Mrs Carlson decided that she really must return to work after her maternity leave. Mr Carlson finally obtained a more suitable job in a chemical company, as marketing manager for the southern region. He operated from their home, using staff who also worked from their homes. His personality made it easy to establish contacts and his general knowledge of chemistry was useful. On this job he worked with the technical people in his company, to whom he turned to discuss problems presented by the clients. In order to do his job well, he had to be intermediary between the laboratory people and the clients, and he had to keep abreast of new ideas and processes. So he attended professional and trade conferences in the chemistry area, acquiring knowledge and contacts.

During this period, which extended into the late 1960s, Mr Carlson maintained an office at home, enabling him to cover domestic situations in a highly flexible way. He enjoyed his work very much, and describes his main satisfactions as follows:

> 'I had nobody leaning over my shoulder saying "you must do this and that." It was left to run itself, which fits very well with my mentality, because I don't like too much planning ahead.'

He also liked the idea of negotiating a sale in which he could find novel solutions for the use of materials. But for his ingenuity, a difficult technical problem might block a company's development. Sometimes he could achieve spectacular results, as when a company that no one would have heard of so benefited from his ingenuity with finding the right chemicals for the job that they solved a major problem and became well known in their field. His one disadvantage in that job was feeling out of touch with the organisation, and therefore at a disadvantage in career development. While he was not highly ambitious, and in fact he had refused an opportunity of promotion that would have necessitated the family's moving to the North (where his wife would not be able to get anything like the job she held), he wanted to move upwards to make up to some extent for lost time. So, after about seven years in the job, with little likelihood of promotion (because of the company's administrative bases in the North), he began to look around for a better career opportunity in the London area. Obtaining the job of sales manager for an American chemicals company in its London office, he now does similar work to that he did in his previous job, but because the British base for the American company is in London he is not remote from headquarters. Also, as he has become more involved in the American company's affairs, he has found that he actually prefers its general atmosphere. He says:

> 'My former company was quite nice, but terribly paternalistic. They liked to tell me what to do and they had lots of people around to tell you exactly what to do at all levels. I think they even had people to

tell the chairman what to do. All up and down the line it was a pile
of faceless men. . . . It's so big, like a government department. . . .
It's alright if one happened to be a cabbage, but I like something
where one is personally responsible. If one makes a success, fine, and
if one makes a mistake, one is close enough to the top to get the
ha'pence and the kicks.'

He likes being close to the top and the style of first names and spontaneous sociability. The open communications in the headquarters
office among the senior staff gives him a feeling of being in touch with
developments in a way that was never possible before. He feels that his
work is important to the company and that his chances for future
advancement are good.

The rise in pay that the chance entailed also helped to close the gap
between his income and his wife's. While they had agreed that they
prefer to share the economic load of the family rather than assume that
it should fall primarily on either of their shoulders—as when the opportunity for him to advance by moving North had come up—it still
rankled slightly that he had been unable to make up lost time in terms
of financial rewards. Neither of them are anxious to be 'top dogs' or
get a Rolls-Royce instead of their Fords, but feel that they want parity
in sharing the family's economic and domestic burdens.

The Carlsons' meaningful interests. The subjective definitions of
leisure used by each of the Carlsons reflects their individual outlooks
and styles. Mr Carlson defines leisure as 'useless occupation'. Mrs
Carlson says, in contrast: 'One of my great pleasures is to look around
the house and think, "Hmm, how can I improve that?" What could you
make, paint, change, wire or whatever?' While the origins of the Carlsons' 'do-it-yourself' activities in their spare time at home were in the
early establishment period of 'tight' finances, by the middle and late
establishment phases it is not mainly connected with financial considerations. Mrs Carlson says: 'If we get outside people to do it, they
never do it properly.' Mr Carlson goes along with this but more in
terms of the satisfactions he derives from having something done just
the way he wants:

> '[when I get someone to do it] it's very nerve-racking. I make sure the
> message gets home, but at the end there is a feeling of satisfaction
> that you've done something. If I hadn't done it, it wouldn't have
> been done. I don't even think a professional person could have done it
> the way I wanted it.'

In their home-based activities, as in their lives generally, the Carlsons
perceive their relationship as one based on complementarities. Mrs
Carlson says that she has a very good colour sense and visualises that

dimension of problems; also she is a good organiser. Mr Carlson adds: 'I'm the labourer.'

The same shift of emphasis occurred in her sewing activity. She had to make her clothing when she was an impoverished student. She now makes her clothing because she is not happy about how off-the-peg clothing fits her. She also does picture-embroidery.

In the early establishment days Mr Carlson worked with technical people to install household systems, partly to save costs. Their household is full of modern machinery facilitating the duel-worker pattern. This labour-saving equipment has helped increase their leisure time. Mr Carlson describes their cooker, for example, as follows:

'It's one of those automatic things . . . a cross between an IBM computer and a cooker . . . this is fairly standard in North America. It has various automatic things which help us to prepare the meal . . . gives you a chance to sit back and relax a bit rather than sweat over the hot stove.'

These machines provide the choice for them to do 'something else' or just 'sit back and do nothing'. Mr Carlson feels, however, that all these household activities are not 'leisure' in the strict sense, because they improve the material standard of the house and this is an important motivation in doing it:

'Leisure to me, is something completely useless, or relatively useless. Gardening is relatively useless for us, because we do not grow crops to eat. Growing flowers, bushes and trees is a relatively useless occupation in this sense. That's leisure. We sail our boat. We could go much more comfortably and efficiently on a commercial steamer, but on our boat we enjoy our discomforts. If I were interested in playing golf or other games, that would be a useless occupation.'

Mrs Carlson, however, considers herself to be more of a 'materialist' in general:

'I like to see some end. When I garden, I like doing it so that I can gaze at it. I like to make a floral display for the purpose of getting the satisfaction of looking at it. In gardening, I am aware of the fact that I can pick the flowers for this purpose, or perhaps I can pick some to give to friends. And sometimes I lie in the garden and there it is— it's nice, it's pretty, it's very nice to be there. This has a lot to do with it. And I like making things. I make all my own clothes. This started from sheer necessity and they looked like it too—but after doing it for quite a long time, I realised I was getting better at it and so I tried harder and got better still. Also, I had another problem. They don't seem to produce clothes in my proportions. Any garment I buy has to be altered and I always see the design I like in the wrong size, the wrong colour or whatever. So, I've taken to making practically everything, including topcoats. I decide on the colour, and the pattern and I do it at home.

Mrs Carlson's embroidery—which she calls 'sketch pictures'—is of a very high standard. She has been offered a fair sum for one displayed in their lounge but says that she would not embroider for sale or even sell one of her pieces unless she tired of it herself.

Thus, by the mid-establishment period, the past of each of the Carlsons has produced their current pattern—for example in the way in which things done for economies earlier are now done for satisfaction and to achieve specific desires or standards. Also there is an anticipatory element—particularly in Mrs Carlson's outlook, as she generally operates by objectives, in her development of interests, as in her work. The latest objective, in this phase, of a potential shift in future from hobby to occupation is just making itself felt. She says: 'I grow quite a lot of plants and I work two greenhouses. I think I could take to growing plants.' Mrs Carlson's interests are usually actively pursued—even in the sedentary activities like reading. She describes the time when she was in hospital and her husband used to bring her paperback books to read:

'We have a friend who used to travel a lot, and each time she travelled she picked up some paperback books and kept them all—shelves of them. When I was in hospital for three weeks I used to devour these books, so that when my husband went by their house for more books, he didn't say "can I have a couple of books?" He'd say "can I have a couple of feet?" '

Mr Carlson said he would 'borrow them more or less by the yard, put them in a cardboard box and take them to the hospital. She could read four a day with no trouble at all.'

Mrs Carlson's enjoyment career. Some of Mrs Carlson's present interests go back to her earliest days. Though she considers that her personality was toughened through conflict with her father and that she succeeded more or less in spite of the barriers he put up for her, she also acknowledges that both her work and her leisure interests have a grounding in some of his interests:

'he was very good at nature study in a self-taught sort of way. He knew a lot about birds and plants and he taught me a lot about that. I don't know how much he showed me, and how much I had "green fingers", but I could grow trees from cuttings.'

When Mrs Carlson was 6 or 7, her father gave her a patch of ground in the garden and some seeds:

'He gave me some nasturtium seeds and the seeds would come up. I still feel that thrill when you put in runner beans. There comes a hot day, and the ground cracks and you can almost see it growing. I find this enormously fascinating.'

When she was in her teens her father was ill and she had to look after the garden for him. This re-enforced her interest:

'We got on badly, and I had done bits of gardening before for him, partly under pressure. Now I learned a new kind of pleasure, not of growing individual plants or a row here or a row there, but of growing the whole outfit. I could put in rows wherever I wanted to, move things around, and I didn't care how much he grumbled. I looked after the whole thing and grew vegetables.'

Gardening and nature study (in which her mother also participated when they had no garden and the whole family would go on forest walks) were the earliest and most consistent interests in her life.

Reading was also an early interest that persisted. Her mother used to say that she would 'read the labels off the jam jars'. Her father used to take home books and other documents that had been left at his office, many of them very interesting and educational. She read voluminously, an interest encouraged by her mother. Despite the tensions in the family, there were some family leisure activities other than walks. They played cards quite a lot and this later served to integrate her husband into the family when they were married. Though she says that they were 'hopeless at cards', the Carlsons would play with her mother and father and have 'quite a lot of fun', partly at her father's expense. He was deaf and her mother could talk without moving her lips; she would enjoy passing signals that would end in the father's defeat.

There were some street games but these did not interest her much. She played cricket with the boys and the usual chalk, wood and ball games of the terraced-house streets of the day: 'all sorts of strange and complicated games. Sometimes hundreds of kids playing in the street— chalk marks all over the place, goals, cricket stumps, hop-scotch, hoops, yo-yos, etc. One doesn't see that so much now.'

The major turning-point in her activity pattern came with university entry. She was no longer living at home, so the garden was not in focus any more, nor the local friends or family. She had to work very hard at her course in chemistry at the university and had little time for other involvements:

'It was a cram course, it really was. I had to slog at it most evenings. I didn't go to dances much, although I would have liked to. I did go to an occasional one, but on weekends if the weather was fine it was usually out for a long walk or with a bicycle. There was a lot of nice country just outside Manchester, and no traffic because petrol was rationed. It was marvellous. You could ride your bike all over the road.'

Her pursuits became more focused on energy- or tension-releasing activities of a more compressed kind—swimming, tennis, cycling:

'We needed this kind of release because we spent so much time sitting down with books. In those days I did have a lot of physical energy. I'd feel almost electrically charged with it, and I needed to do something.'

The practical problems of making ends meet financially were dealt with in part by her learning to make her own clothes. Materials were rationed, but she went to a local market on Saturday afternoons and looked at bolts of cloth that had come from various sources, such as 'dropping off the end of a lorry'. They could be had cheaply and without coupons, so she would pick up a piece and then she and a friend would sit and talk over their sewing. The talk would be mainly political—not 'philosophical' or academic:

'I think that people of my background were more practical. One wanted to *do* something, to see some material change. We didn't sit around and talk about drugs and smoke pot and things like that. There seemed to be too much to do. . . . When the war broke out, one was aware that there were square miles of cities like Liverpool which had really the most dreadful housing. . . . That all seemed so wrong and when the war broke out and a lot of people went into the forces the lines of unemployed men disappeared from the streets. As labour became scarcer, opportunities opened for women and we were determined that all the mistakes that had been made after the First World War weren't going to be made after the Second. We all wanted to work for this and our talk had a very practical quality to it.'

She feels that many young people now seem much more concerned with their own personal experience and with 'aery-fairy' ideas. However, she sees a common element in the idealism at this stage of life:

'You feel that you can see things much more clearly at this stage. Such and such a situation is wrong. Things seem either right or wrong and there is no in between. There's not the "Yes, but . . ." that we feel now in our mid-forties. Sometimes one feels that one has so many qualifications now, knowing more, that one could weep for one's lost self.'

The interest in the countryside, nature study and appreciation was transformed during the period of greater independence from her family into youth hostelling in the holidays:

'We didn't have any money. I had always been interested in scenery, the hills and the sea. I had grown up by the sea and away from buildings and the people. The geology—the general structure of the countryside and the details, plants that grew there, etc., all of this appealed to me very much. The hillier the country, the better. So a lot of like-minded people at university would go out in groups and you could stay overnight in a youth hostel for about 3*d* . . . it was incredible. You had to provide your own sheets and the meals were very simple, but when you are 17 or 18 you don't worry about what the food's like. You only want something to eat. There's a great crowd of you and you have been out and got soaking wet.'

Mrs Carlson and one or two friends used to explore the Lake District on holidays. One particular friend, who was at college in the Lake District and was 'a bit older than I and was regarded by my parents as sensible', provided the companionship on the earliest trip, at 16. Thereafter groups from university were available as companions. They enjoyed what was for her an essential element—that of challenge and 'coping with nature', as well as the companionship and the escape from the city:

'There was a great big obstacle, nature. It provided bogs, tussocky grass, slippery paths, dolloping rains. But we were going to get there and we worked it out for ourselves how to get there. It wasn't exactly survival, because we weren't out in extreme conditions but they were conditions different from those met by most town-dwellers. . . . My son, for example, has never met with that sort of challenge before. But it seemed part of life. In the North of England we tended to be a bit more puritanical, and we felt a great virtue in suffering. So, if you went out on a trek through the hills, you got cold and wet and hungry. You felt it did you a lot of good.'

Mrs Carlson feels that her current pattern represents a *domestication of earlier interests*: horticultural gardening rather than wilder natural interests; embroidery along with sewing, etc. Facing the challenge of nature is still present in their boating, but even in this her form of participation is now more detached. Her husband and the husband of her friend and one or both of their boys may take the boat across the English Channel, but the wives will take the steamer and check into a hotel room, meeting them at their destination.

Mr Carlson's enjoyment career. Mr Carlson, like his wife, played in street games when he was young, but was never keen on them:

'I'm not keen on games. I played them—football, rugby, basketball, and at college I became interested in field hockey and basketball. But, I wouldn't say that I was enthusiastic about them. They were physical things to do. I got pleasure from charging about for an hour or two, and having a shower; and, when I got older, going off to the bar afterwards and having a few drinks and generally enjoyable evening after the game.'

Mr Carlson's father was keen on watching football and Mr Carlson went along with him but without great enthusiasm. He went to the international rugby matches 'not for the game, but for the general atmosphere of the thing. I wasn't terribly buoyed up if they won or depressed if they lost. Some of my friends got almost to the point of suicide!' In general his preference was not for competitive sports or organised games but for doing what interested him. He did not like playing games with too many rules. Like his wife, he progressed from walks with his father to riding a bicycle which took him farther afield, to making longer journeys which involved challenge and planning:

'We got to going further afield—up to the Brecon Beacons, pretty bleak! One had to learn how to plan such a journey. One must take note of the weather, the terrain and the timing of the trip in making decisions about when to go.'

Also like his wife, he started youth hostelling by accompanying slightly older friends but his initiation was earlier, at 14:

'It was a way of seeing the countryside for little cost, and during a time when it was impossible to go to any of the more holiday type of places. It wasn't possible to go to the seaside in those days except odd places near the city, all the other places were full of barbed wire and Army training grounds, and nobody went very far afield because of the danger of running into trouble.'

The family holidays were spent at seaside resorts, often on the north-west coast of Devon in boarding-houses. Alternatively, they went to his mother's relatives in Suffolk, where he enjoyed farm life:

'The farm life gave me a nice holiday because if we stayed on the farm there were things to do on the farm and we were never more than eight miles from the sea, so we had day trips to the sea rather than a fortnight at a boarding house. When I got a bit older, my parents took me away for the whole summer holidays down to the relatives, and I'd have a week here and a week there. I got passed around. They'd say "We've worked out an itinerary for you. It's all organised".'

The big break in Mr Carlson's pattern of activities and interests occurred when he entered the Services:

'When I went into the Royal Navy, I was in a crowd of people who were much of a muchness. We couldn't consider doing youth hostel-

ling during weekends when we were, for example, in Scotland doing
training things. It was too far from home to get home for a weekend,
so we would trot off to the mountains near Glasgow, not that they are
very exciting mountains, but they got us away from the city where
the training base was.'

After spending about a year 'scrubbing around' in various parts of
England, he was sent to the Far East where he had a lot of opportunity
for travel and new experiences: '. . . A very pleasant time of it, and
more leisure time than I've had in my life since.' During his earlier
days in Wales and in the Services at home, he had gone to dances, but
he does not think of them as leisure in the same sense that his outdoor
and boating activity was:

> 'I wasn't very keen on dancing, but it was a good way of meeting
> girls. In fact, in Cardiff and later in Glasgow, dancing was a very
> serious pursuit. It wasn't really what I would call leisure. People
> went to great pains to perfect their technique.'

Both Mr and Mrs Carlson are amused at the difference between dancing
when they were young and dancing as it is now experienced by their
children. Mr Carlson recalls:

> 'I remember the days when a fellow would come into the lab where
> I was working and announce that he had just learned a new step and
> this is how you do it. We'd all start doing it . . . all these very com-
> plicated movements which went with those foxtrots, and tangos and
> all that sort of thing. These complicated movements had to be done
> exactly right, with military precision. We were very serious about
> this. The main object was so that next time one went to the dance
> hall, you could be the boy that knew all the fancy steps and all the
> girls would fall at your feet . . . not that they ever did.'

Mrs Carlson contrasts this style, at which she had only achieved
moderate success under her mother's tutelage, with that of the present
generation:

> 'Nowadays our kids think dancing is to stand on one spot and wriggle.
> The music is purely incidental, and they've no sense of rhythm or
> tune. If you dance that way, you don't run any chance of treading
> on your partner's toes and you don't need any special skill.'

Both Mr and Mrs Carlson were gripped more by the outdoor exercise
and the associated pleasures than any of these indoor activities, even
the more active ones like dancing. It was in their shared pleasure of the
physical delights of the countryside that they met and joined their lives.
The family enjoyment career. The Carlsons' experiences contain both

common and contrasting elements. A common one is in the sheer enjoyment of the challenges of nature. As he put it:

> 'I suppose it is the sense of achievement—hell while you are doing it but lovely when it stopped—the head against the wall syndrome. We'd say, tomorrow we're going from A to B, and you have to master it, like climbing a mountain because it's there.'

She feels the same way about the challenge and the pleasure that follows—the '*après*-hike'.

> 'When you've been walking or climbing or scrambling hard in the open air, and when you've got wet, you've got enormously hungry and when you change into nice comfortable dry clothes, put plaster on the blisters, have a meal—it's so relaxing. You love everybody.'

He says:

> 'The sheer pleasure of putting on dry socks and dry pants, enjoying the really elemental things of life, I wouldn't change with a king or a president.'

They say that they have these enjoyments in common, 'otherwise we wouldn't have both been in the same place at the same time and met'. He emphasises more the sociability, following such an experience: 'In the evening, at these hostels, people come from all directions and we have a general talk-in, singing and making a damned fool of yourself . . . going out and drinking beer.' They kept up a certain amount of this kind of activity during their two-year courtship; when married a good deal of their energy went into home-making in London. Between the attempts to get Mr Carlson through his course, establishing a home and having children, the effects were in the direction of home-centredness for a good many years following marriage:

> 'When we had children, we tried to continue our interest in country walking, but we got very tired with lugging push-chairs in rough country. We discovered that you get further if you pull it than if you push it. Our first child was amiable, and he enjoyed bouncing up and down, but before long we found that our cross-country walking had to be cut down. Also, we were in the wrong part of the country. If we'd been in South Wales or the North of England where walking is so much more worth while, it might have been better, but around here you have afternoon-stroll country, not all-day hiking. It gives one no sense of achievement.'

The emphasis became very much on home and garden. When the Carlsons moved into their present home, the development was new and the garden had to be cultivated from scratch. She says:

'We dug this one with a pickaxe. I don't know if you'd call it leisure. There was an enormous sense of achievement. We had to clear the country like American pioneers in the West—mud and bonfires. We cut down 22 trees, dug out the roots and burned them. The kids enjoyed the bonfires and mudpies. They went into the mud. It was the kind of mud that you'd nearly disappear in and when you'd lift your foot out, you left a boot behind.'

The work of clearing the garden and cultivating were under control by the time their two sons were old enough to do more than play around while they worked.

For annual holidays in their family years, the Carlsons went abroad together—using first one pattern and then another in choosing a destination:

'Sometimes we'd go off on our own, leaving the children behind. We'd get into our car, take the Channel ferry across with some sort of vague destination in mind, like Germany, and just play it by ear— eenie, meenie, meinie, moe about which road to take. Or, later, we might take a package tour where you pay your money and they fly you to some God-forsaken hole.'

The package-tour idea was, Mrs Carlson says, brought on less through their preference than through the children's dislike of car travel:

'The object of the package tour is that we've got two children who really didn't enjoy riding around in a car like we do, who didn't enjoy looking at towns or museums or ancient buildings. Their idea was the sea and we thought, right, we'll fly to some place close that's reasonably easy on the eye, and the actual cost of the holiday wouldn't be much more than driving.'

Mrs Carlson thought, particularly when Mr Carlson was in a job that required a lot of driving, that when he got to the package-tour destination he would have wanted to collapse and rest. On the contrary, he would pop out immediately after their arrival and hire a car so that they could get around and see the environment:

'If you go on a package tour, you have to get away from the crowd where they land you by hiring a car. We've done that in Sardinia and other places, seeing far more of the country around than anyone else on the tour. One holiday in Tangiers, we found there were no cars to hire, but you could hire a taxi for the whole day for less than it would cost to hire a car normally. If we'd driven ourselves, we would have had to worry about bumping into camels and all that. So, we hired a taxi and as we can speak a bit of Spanish, we made friends with the driver and he took us to all sorts of non-tourist places. The oasis that everybody went to; well, we went to the next one.'

Some of these early-family-phase holidays were with the children, some without. They tended to take one holiday a year, for example skiing, with another couple, who were friends from Mrs Carlson's work. More recently they acquired a boat. This has been for the past three or four years a focus of family leisure activities, though it has now been stabilised as a primary pursuit of Mr Carlson. He describes the way the boat fits into their lives as follows:

'As with other bits of equipment we have, we've tried to get something that requires virtually no maintenance. It's a fibreglass construction, it doesn't need painting, all the moveable parts on it are made of stainless steel or bronze, which are non-corrodible. There is a company that takes our boat out of the water and keeps it out for us until we want it—near Southampton. Starting about May, we go down once or twice a month—depending on tides and weather—and sometimes I go with the family, and sometimes with male friends, making it a stag outing.'

Mrs Carlson explains why she doesn't always want to accompany her husband on his boating outings:

'I spend all my evenings in the week doing the washing and rushing around. I don't mind going down there occasionally, but I don't want always to be forced to be madly working for four or five days in order to go down and madly work again two more days on the boat. He's got a lot of friends who do want to go, so they do it more often.'

Mr Carlson says that there are a lot of people who want to go down with him and he often goes with a neighbour or friend from work. The way he describes the pleasure he gets from boating resembles very much the way he described the pleasure they had got earlier from cross-country hiking:

'Apart from getting places, and the pleasure of moving over water, there is also a mental exercise. You can't just let it go. You've got to work out winds, tides, what the weather is likely to be doing in the next 24 hours, planning ahead so that you never get yourself into a situation that you can't get yourself out of.'

Mrs Carlson organises entertainment for people at home, which tends to be at weekends rather than during the week, because of their both working. She enjoys quieter domestic pursuits now—embroidery, sewing and gardening.

The continuities of interest, both within their own life cycles and in relation to their parents' interests, is quite striking for the Carlson children.

The elder son, like his father, is very sociable and enjoys travel. He has followed in his father's enjoyment patterns and likes 'taking the mickey' out of them. He had been very active with his father in the boating interest. Now that he is in the Far East on a proper ship he writes home with mock sarcasm about their little 'craft'. He is described as being very gregarious, having a lot of friends and being very active with them. When they reached the adolescent stage of parties— over the last couple of years—he would tend to be the one who arranged such events at home, dealing with his parents in such a way as to get their support. Mrs Carlson's support was conditional on the parties not being destructive and on the young people clearing up the place after they were finished. She describes one such event, in which she returned and found the house full of long-haired youths and their girlfriends, with the gramophone turned up to maximum volume. They had just finished and were clearing up, as instructed:

'I came in and there was a young man with a vacuum cleaner, who said to me, "Hi." I said "Hi." He said "Do you live here?" I said "Yes, I live here." He said "Oh well, can you tell me where to put these?"—indicating a pile of just-washed plates. Then he put them in the proper place. That was just fine. Then they washed everything, there was no mess, just fine. I'd made it clear to Stephen that if there was any mess left over, there'd be no further parties, so he got the labour force absolutely organised. "You collect dirty glasses; you wash them; you dry them; you put away; you vacuum; you put the furniture back." Stephen was doing absolutely nothing. That's my boy!'

The younger son is more like his mother in his outlook. This takes several forms. He has always been a naturalist and taken to collecting things. He is not gregarious, tends to be something of a 'loner' with a few friends. Both boys were taught, from an early age, to cook, but the younger one shows a special talent for this and enjoys rather elaborate cooking and baking. He enjoys organising a menu and during school holidays caters for the family. While the elder boy's meals tended to be in the 'fish and chips line', the younger one makes special dishes. The younger boy's rock collection is displayed in the lounge. He not only collects things, but likes to be an expert on them:

'He'll name birds you never heard of; and now he's becoming interested in plants and he's tending to take up gardening. He acquires information. He's like a sponge. It builds up, and he likes to be an authority, so it comes out.'

Mrs Carlson says that he is like her in the way he uses his expertise. She portrays him talking about the garden layout:

'It would be nice if we had some so-and-so over there, and some such-and-such over there. Now, you go and buy them, and I'll show you where to put them. As to the actual putting in of the physical effort, there's not so much of that!'

So, just as Mrs Carlson lays out a work problem for her husband, her son does it for her, to their semi-amusement. His interest in the clarinet has a tension-releasing aspect. His father says: 'Whenever he gets frustrated he goes and plays with his clarinet.' He has also taken to target practice, in the garden with an air rifle used on a rusty tin hanging from a tree.

The family members share an interest in nature which has at least a three-generation span. Mr Carlson's maternal grandparents were farmers and he enjoyed contact with the land. He later enjoyed the challenge of cross-country hiking and travel in the Navy. Mrs Carlson's father was interested in gardening and nature study (an element of integration in an otherwise conflicted family situation). She was interested in nature and became a biologist; and she too cultivated her interests through physical contact with the countryside, in hiking, hostelling, etc. The boys, in their different ways, have shared this interest—the older boy now in the Navy himself, following his father's pattern; the younger being an amateur naturalist, following his mother's interest.

The part played in the family life by the boat is instructive. Like gardening, it is a multi-faceted pursuit. For Mr Carlson it is a continuation in a different medium of his earlier interests in natural challenge. Mrs Carlson has less interest in this but she goes along with the boating and finds new interests in it. She describes how the boat offers multiple interests as follows:

'A lot of our interests have a kind of integration to them. We're interested in geology; we're interested in meteorology; we're interested in the countryside—both in big chunks [mountains] and in the details of plants and animals—and we're interested in the way these things change with climate and latitude and all the rest of it. . . . Wherever we go there is something we're interested in, and it's all integrated. Then there's the boating. We like reading; well, you can read on the boat, and I can take my sewing on the boat and if we do have decent weather, I can actually bear to lie there for a couple of hours doing nothing, sunbathing. From the boat you can swim and if you're interested in fishing you can fish, and they fit together.'

They even manage to incorporate the boat into a holiday pattern where they have different wishes about mode of travel and accommodation. They went with another couple and their two children to Brittany. In each case, the wives preferred not to make the Channel crossing in the small boat. The two women and their friends' elder child (a daughter) went by commercial steamer and booked into a hotel in the port-town of destination. The two men and the two younger boys went by small boat. They describe the merits of this arrangement as follows:

> Mr Carlson: 'We had the best of both worlds really. We had land transport (because they took the car) and water transport (because we took the boat). We found that at the height of the French tourist season it was easier to get one large room in a hotel than to get two, and it was also more economic to use the boat as one of the hotel rooms. So the two females arrived at the town and booked into a hotel room, and the males stayed in the boat.'
>
> Mrs Carlson: 'You could get quite a big room with two double beds. So my friend and her daughter shared one bed, and I the other, and this worked out very well. . . . When the males arrived at the hotel [off their boat which was docked in the harbour], it was quite a sight. The sailors would walk in and the smartly dressed gentlemen would walk out. There was only one bathroom in the whole hotel and you had to pay 5 francs for the key. We managed to get four baths on that before she got suspicious and took the key back.'

They have worked out the optimal pattern for this stage of their family life cycle, with a brief spring holiday on a package tour (most recently to Corfu) and the boat reserved for various arrangements in the summer.

The Carlson family show how the pattern which crystallises in the establishment phase is determined by earlier influences and, at the same time, sets up a situation which is likely to affect subsequent developments.

Mrs Carlson, because of her particular constellation of earlier experiences and current circumstances, became economically productive earlier than her husband. Her productivity in the domestic sphere—having the children when she did—was almost fortuitous, though in retrospect she is glad about the way things evolved. Her husband, contrary to the modal pattern, had not crystallised the way in which he would become productive in work by the time of their early establishment phase, and this difference from conventional roles caused strains which they had to overcome. The 'problem' of allocation of energies was dealt with in an unorthodox way, and this provided its special mixture of strains and benefits as described. During this period—in which the early establishment phase had extensions from phenomena usually present in the early marital stage continued into the child-bearing period—there was not much possibility for developing outside interests, or even pursuing those which they had shared earlier. The involvements became intensely home- and work-centred with Mr Carlson's possibilities for developing satisfactory work interests rather severely limited.

Around the home, this family showed an interesting pattern in early establishment. The husband was at home working flexibly while the wife was out at work. Given the fact that this was a period in which building works were in progress, and the installation of machinery of various kinds was going on (as much to support the pattern they had as a sign of conspicuous achievement), the husband's participation in these activities gave the family more than they would have had if the wife had been at home. Mr Carlson worked with the workmen and thereby learned a lot about plumbing and machinery generally. This made it possible later on to share these activities with his sons, giving the 'do-it-yourself' activity more of an enjoyable family character than might otherwise have been possible. It is also in this early establishment phase that there is the steepest increase in requirements coupled with a relatively slower increase in financial wherewithal. Therefore the physical participation of the husband in the decorating, gardening establishment and so on, actually goes further to close the gap between incomings and outgoings than is usually possible. This meant the accumulation of lower debts, making it possible for the family to have other material objects, notably the boat, earlier.

The Carlsons are a family that work at *integration* as well as at the pursuit of the several *individual interests* of its members. This produces a situation in which there are *independent interests* (the elder boy in his parties with peers; the younger in his collections and his clarinet); *cross-generational paired interests* (father and younger son in cooking; father and elder son in boating; mother and younger son in naturalist collections; mother and elder son in reading); and also the *interests which can be shared* as a family—notably the boat which has the multi-interest character already described.

In the mid-establishment phase, the father as well as the mother began to feel productive and competent in their work as well as in their home roles, and the conflicts within the family and between the family and those with whom they were involved outside were worked through. This produced a situation at the time of the study—poised on the entry to late establishment—when it was possible for the life-audit that was going on to come out with definite plus balances on all scores. The boat was less an integrating vehicle than previously, but it had served its vital function in the middle phase and would continue to be used—perhaps differently in future. The garden was established and served its multiple functions, with new ones opening up in the future as the idea of a retirement hobby-cum-occupation begins to come into the picture. The feeling that prevails is that life has been meaningful and well lived. The Carlsons enter the later phases of life with a feeling of having met social as well as economic and physical obstacles and mastered them.

Late establishment phase (children out of school)

The late establishment phase is the period when children have left school. This may occur anywhere from the late thirties to early fifties, but with younger marriage and condensed child-bearing it tends to occur earlier. This phase overlaps considerably with the end of the mid-establishment phase and with the next phase of pre-retirement.

The main issue or preoccupation now seems to be *revision*. This involves the question of the meaningfulness of the commitments that were made, whether or not there is a psychological 'pay-off' in terms of feeling happy and satisfied, and whether one's life is adding up to a meaningful whole. Of course this has been going on already, but it comes sharply into focus now. The awareness of general decline in physical capacities is marked toward the end of this period, with difficulties arising in sight, hearing, memory, capacity to grasp and hold new information, stamina and so on. As Elliott Jacques has noted, this is the period in which death becomes more real in the psychological lives of people: this may lead to profound depression or act as a spur to new activity or creativity (Jacques, 1965).

The characteristic feelings that arise in those who experience turbulence in this period are restlessness, looking around to see if one might not do better with something else—another kind of life, another kind of wife, another kind of job. Quite often there is the feeling, particularly among affluent, middle-class professionals and managers, that they have everything they want and yet they are not happy. There is an unaccountable malaise. One is still vigorous enough and perhaps sufficiently well established to be able to do something about it if so inclined. By this sub-phase the children have probably become autonomous and may have left home, so that where their presence was a constraint in the marital relationship, it no longer operates so powerfully as such. There may be 'affairs', wives may feel abandoned and the proverbial 'empty nest' atmosphere may pervade the household. On the other hand, this period may be grasped by husband and wife to change their lives away from the home as central focus and to develop new interests outside.

Occupationally as well as in family life, this period is often experienced as an anti-climax. Men who are occupationally mobile will have reached their peaks and ordinarily they will have levelled off—not changing jobs as frequently, not getting as many rises, not being given as many new challenges. While this is the general picture, many men continue to rise and to confront stimulating new situations throughout their careers.

Information from many sources documents the decline aspect of the picture. Lidz (1968, 460) paints the picture from the medical-psychiatric point of view:

> Hair is growing grey or sparse, wrinkles appear, the abdomen gets in the way . . . the paper must be read at arm's length and then bifocals become a necessity . . . [there is an] increase in proneness to illness and dysfunction . . . the threat of sudden death from coronary occlusion [for the man] . . . [for women] malignancies take their toll . . . ill-health and death are potentialities that hover over him and those close to him.

Disturbances of personality, however, are less notable in this period because there is generally a tendency to discard unrealistic aspirations. The task is how to settle for what is possible, to resign oneself to all the things that might have been but which are now manifestly impossible. Depression—sometimes quite severe—may arise if there is a feeling that what one has to settle for is not good enough, or if one does not want to face the necessity at all. This may be as much a matter of inner conflicts arising from earlier experiences as of the current conditions of life. Very powerful aggressive feelings are sometimes displaced on to 'scapegoat' figures, or turned back against oneself if no one in the environment can be found to blame for one's dissatisfaction—only deepening the depression.

On the positive side, however, there are the potentials for great satisfaction in this period. If one is able to 'settle' for what one has or to make whatever adjustments are necessary to improve life's balance sheets, there is still the benefit of wide experience of life and a sense of perspective in knowing what is possible. For those who have done well in work, there are financial and social resources available, and the recognition that comes from achievement. A workman may become foreman or shop-floor steward; a manager may move into senior management or a position on the board; a professional person may be awarded an honour or elected to office in a learned society. If the on-coming younger men within the organisation, profession or workplace are not actually a threat to the older established man, he may enjoy helping younger people to develop, for it is now clear that he is not in any way directly competing with them. On the other hand, if the young pose a threat to the old, as is often the case in the newer industries with technical expertise having paramount importance, bureaucratic defences can be erected by individuals in their jobs to protect them against the real and imagined threats of the young (Hall, 1968).

Rothschild points out that there seems to be an ever-increasing gap between the time of one's peak powers and social recognition. Scientists do their creative work early and get Nobel prizes later on; generals achieve public acclaim and are made political leaders when they are old and feeble; leaders of enterprises who though adventurous early may in later years become set in their ways and unadventurous (Rothschild, 1973). Rothschild recommends early efforts at equipping the individual to come to grips with this stage. It is often too late to try when it is upon the individual. He notes that the traditional education system with its emphasis on rote memory places a premium on the accumulation of information which is bound to become obsolescent, and which can in any case be better stored and retrieved by the technological aids now available for people who wish to make use of them (1973, 29):

> With instant access to any information, the pupil would be freed to develop a far more wide ranging set of interests than is possible for him to pursue at present. This would doubtless both liberate the creativity that contemporary education so successfully suppresses, and, as a spin-off, provide a partial answer to the problem that increasing leisure has raised. With a wide range of interests developed from early youth, the distinction between work and leisure would be less sharp and obvious.

This is partly a matter of cognitive styles but it is also a matter of values. Soddy and his colleagues note that this is the period in which one might enjoy the fruits of a life of work, but that having been brought up in the puritanical tradition which says, in effect, that 'Satan finds mischief for idle hands', one is unable to relax and reap the fruits of it all. Thus, referring to 'do-it-yourself' activities, Soddy says 'the modern problem of leisure is that the individual spends less time being paid to do things in order to have more time to work hard for nothing' (Soddy and Kidson, 1967, 348). Soddy notes the spread of a second job —for which one may be paid or not. This is particularly marked for women, who may alter the saliency of their domestic role and their work role to suit the family phase. For the woman in the late establishment phase, the work role may become re-established, while for the man, it may be on the wane with a secondary interest taking greater precedence. Soddy notes that the tendency for men and women both to have two jobs (in addition to the man's domestic job) poses the 'problem [of] how to achieve leisure' (Soddy and Kidson, 1967, 349).

Another psychological problem that may be easier to deal with by early 'emotional inoculation'—i.e. preparation for the probable range of later outcomes—is that of success beyond what one might have expected. This is a problem for many men because of the psychological issue it poses of surpassing one's father—with the guilt and anxiety that this may entail for those who retain vestiges of earlier 'oedipal' problems.

Lidz mentions this as a common problem, elaborating on earlier observations made on this topic by Freud, in his classic paper on 'fear of success'. There are other problems, more sociological in nature, that attend success beyond what one may have anticipated. The change in life style may pose considerable problems as one moves from one group to another, with different norms and expectations, different backgrounds and preparation. Such is the phenomenon of the *parvenu*, successful and proud of himself but shunned and perhaps scorned by others of the same social status because of the way he (and/or his family) handle themselves in social situations.

For women the late establishment phase period may have more marked physical accompaniments with the menopause. The impact of the climacterium seems to be greater for women who have not developed outside interests, hobbies or occupations with which to provide psychological development and social integration after their children (and/or their husbands, for widows or divorcees) have left home. For such women, it is particularly crucial that new sources of self-esteem, psychological investments and incomes be found.

New interests—developed on a couple basis (if the couple is able to sustain the strains placed on the marriage at this stage)—may develop. Travel and programmes of educational interest may be taken up on a shared basis. The husband may enable his wife to take up a new interest or draw her into his—at the office or golf—and the wife may help the husband to deal with doubts or self-recriminations he may have about what he has *not* achieved in his life, emphasising the value of what he has. Grandchildren become a focus of active interests; the bond between grandparents and grandchildren is legendary and grandparents have an important part to play in the lives of their grandchildren.

The late establishment phase has some special problems in relation to leisure provision, because physical decline and a vulnerability to illness and disorder presents a problem for potential users of many facilities. Campaigns to get men, in particular, to take regular if moderate exercise in this period as a preventive medical measure against coronary illness have been only moderately successful. Sillitoe found a 'slight revival of interest in physical activities at this time', and noted that men are more likely to take up gardening at the expense of television-viewing (Sillitoe, 1969, 18). But though there is mounting evidence that judicious exercise can defer coronary illness, attempts to assure that it can be undertaken in the most beneficial way tends to encounter non-rational resistance. In this sense the exercise issue may be comparable to that of eliminating smoking or introducing fluoridation. A recent airline crash was attributed to the heart attack of its captain and there has been a call for gymnasia to be installed for flight crews' regular use at airports.

Swimming, jogging, bicycling, golf, tennis and other sports seem to be pursued on a regular basis only by a tiny minority in this age group, despite the rising use of sports facilities of all kinds. There is little tendency to initiate participation later in sports not experienced earlier; notable exceptions are bowls, which is popular among older people in warm climates and in the summer season, and golf, which is a sport that is rapidly expanding in popularity for people in this phase. Golf is a sport which women are likely to take up as well as men, and the age of the 'golf widow' may be on its way out for this phase of the family life cycle. 'Family golf' is practised in Scotland and may extend more widely. The frequent mention in Sillitoe's study of lack of facilities as a reason for not participating, particularly in this age group and among women, suggests that people in this phase of life are less likely to want to take any significant journey to get to a leisure provision. It must be nearby or will not be used—a finding which seems to hold for many sports facilities across the board, but *a fortiori* for people at this period of life. Sillitoe found, however, that the attitudes of most people in this late phase were relatively complacent. This is not an age in which people press for different conditions on the whole; rather there is a continuation of the earlier sub-phase's interest in getting into contact with nature, open spaces, trees and so on.

Current among clinicians and social scientists are a number of anecdotes which suggest some of the dilemmas of the leisure pattern (or lack of it) in this period. They relate it to the *failure of most people in our society to be prepared for the potentials of enjoyment at this period.* One of the anecdotes cited by Lidz had to do with a man who suffered from a coronary occlusion, following which he was told by his doctor not to go to business, smoke, play golf or have sexual intercourse, and to go to bed before eleven every night. He asked his doctor whether he would live longer if he followed this advice. The doctor is said to have replied, 'I can't say, but it will seem longer' (Lidz, 1968, 472).

It is too late to try to remedy a deficient activity pattern after a fatal illness has struck. The current research of J. N. Morris indicates the negative relationship between exercise and coronary heart disease (Morris *et al.*, 1973). Those who are aware of this, in their minds or in their hearts, may take pre-emptive action.

The late establishment phase is one in which the man may opt out, perhaps shifting from a more demanding career to a secondary one which may have been a hobby or a fantasied interest. Early retirement may be possible during which a less high-pressured interest may be developed. At the same time, the wife may want to re-enter work and adopt a pattern which makes her own life style more like her husband's. The problem arising in many marriages of the need to renew the relationship at this point may become acute. When the children are grown and more independent, and the audit of the meaningfulness of life occurs against the background that has been described, some couples arrive at a feeling of liberation, a 'new lease of life', relief that they have come through the struggles and accomplished so much against whatever odds and anxieties they may have envisoned. Many feel that they have come out better than they would ever have imagined, and they wish to put these achievements to use for the enjoyment of their lives. While what stretches ahead may be less than what stretches behind, it is now longer than ever it was before and the conditions for living it are more comfortable than ever. It is therefore possible to think of doing something entirely different, perhaps something one always wanted to do—and the late sub-phase may consist of a deliberate effort to bring into being fantasies that were kept at bay while the challenges of career, home-building and child-rearing were so all-absorbing.

This phase may then become a renaissance. Couples may make a new kind of relationship—almost like another courtship and honeymoon, in which they rediscover each other after having been preoccupied with other impelling demands for so long; they may find time to 'stand and stare' (Davies, 1971). They may cultivate an interest together in gardening, sailing, reading, theatre, walking in the country, crafts or whatever. They may talk more with each other than previously, and go on trips together, building up a new body of shared experiences on which the later years may rest as a foundation—creating new memories for the future, new excitements and exhilaration while they are physically still able to. In this, patterns of different family structures may merge. The dual-workers may work a little less, looking more like the new-conventionals. The old-fashioned conventionals may begin to think about doing something else—if not work, then voluntary activity or other interests which bring about the new phase of shared interests. Those who did not marry may find companionship—with a close friend of either sex and build up relationships as a couple.

There are many—and no one knows just how large this submerged, passive sub-group is—*who have no exciting, revitalising interest.* Their acceptance of ageing is too acquiescent. They feel 'finished', that they are old and that their chances for advancement in work or for a happy family life have passed them by, and they settle into a more vegetable form of the late establishment period—set in habits, routinised and passive, watching television, sitting at home, unstimulated and unstimulating. If depressed and unhappy, this can be seen as a wasteful pattern, a pattern which needs stirring up for, unlike adolescents (whom the late establishment people may surprisingly resemble in their new sense of 'freedom' and quest for excitement), the drive outward from the home is diminished, and it is too easy to sink into a passive and miserable lethargy.

Review of the case material: the dynamics and complexity of the establishment phase

The range of case studies we present in the preceding section, though not exhaustive of the types of family structure we identify, is sufficiently varied to illustrate that the phase is highly complex, and far from a stable state of happiness forever after. This complexity is pervasive at two levels: first of all in the definition of the life styles of individual people and families and, second, in the evolution of varying family structures in the early, middle and late periods within the establishment phase.

The case material highlights the basic themes of the phase for individuals and families: the extent to which some differentiate separate life spheres and others do not; the special salience for some individuals of a particular sphere—in work, family or other interests—or the equal salience for others found in all spheres; the ease or difficulty with which individuals can actualise their preoccupation with life investments by channelling it into meaningful interests in the various spheres; and the ease or difficulty with which they find satisfaction and enjoyment.

It is according to similarities and differences in the way life styles are woven that we distinguish three family structures in the establishment phase. The case studies illustrate some of the potentials and constraints for the development of meaningful life interests. The various forms of family structure that people evolve in this phase reflect their efforts to develop meaningful life investments. The structures—conventional, new-conventional and dual-worker—in turn affect the development of a pattern of investments and the enjoyment that can be derived from them. The case material also shows that the life style of any *person* within a particular family structure is more complex still.

The particular life style people adopt will hinge on their personalities and their resources; while we argue elsewhere that it is likely that those who adopt family structures which are most innovative and enjoy least environmental support may have to be particularly resourceful, re-sourceful people are to be found in all sorts of family structures, social classes and environmental settings. Ultimately individuals' resourceful-ness will play a critical role in how much satisfaction they derive from each sphere, all of which hold positive potential for realisation during this phase.

The establishment phase has conventionally been one marked by a *work commitment* as both essential to the economic survival of most families and as morally and socially valued. During this period, and with this orientation, a high degree of structure in life is erected by the job. Variations in work that have been stressed in most of the social science literature have concentrated on income and status of jobs, with their correlates for personal satisfactions. There is a thread of writing on the psychological meaning of work for people—in terms of validating their self-esteem, providing challenge, allowing them to develop and exercise their competence, providing social interaction with others and so on. There is less on how these factors may relate to the overall development of life interests at different stages, based on the underlying preoccupations at each stage.

In the establishment phase as in others, 'leisure' means various things to different people. When asked directly, people give a bewildering array of meanings. If we concentrate instead on how their preoccupation with life investments becomes translated into life interests and then activities, patterns are observable in the impact of work on individuals' life styles. To some extent, as Wilensky, Stanley Parker, Young and Willmott and others have tried to show, activity patterns relate to the type of job held: how remunerative, how flexible, how satisfying, how value-oriented and how organised in terms of relationships to other interests and other spheres of life.

For some people there is a clear block of their lives that is work which may be negatively or positively defined in terms of enjoyment, and there is a clear block that may be termed 'leisure' within which enjoyment may be pursued in various ways. We believe, and have the impression from the newer research including our own, that increasingly this model does not hold. Rather there are degrees of clarity in the definition between work and non-work interests; degrees of 'porosity' in the work situation—during which enjoyment may be obtained as part of the work situation; degrees of flexibility not only in the introduction of pleasurable elements to work, but in the dispersion of work into other situations. Once past the initial thrust of establishing oneself in the work situation during the early establishment period (and the salience that goes with the challenge), most males have gained sufficient ground by the middle period to enjoy the positive potentials of operating more flexibly in the world of work. Women who have worked continuously may experience a similar 'spacing out', especially as their children will now be in school, but for women who re-enter work only when their children are older, tensions may revolve around the need to establish boundaries to the work situation rather than enjoy the relaxing of boundaries that follows consolidation.

The establishment phase is a time when people's involvement in their family networks is potentially at its greatest. This aspect is largely excluded from the perspective of this book, which breaks into the life cycle at the adolescent break towards autonomy, and follows the individual through to his/her establishing a family, with life-cycle stage defined primarily in terms of the age and phase of its children. This focus limits the attention to adult people's relation with their own parents and other kin when they head families of their own (GAP, 1973).

We have not charted this adequately and neither does our case material reflect that in the establishment period people tend to occupy a pivotal place in a network of intergenerational relationships. They are also likely to be more widely involved then than at any other period in a family network on a horizontal plane—with siblings and their spouses, and cousins and their spouses.

Not everyone activates this network, but for many their involvement with at least some of these kin is likely to be very real. This may bring in its wake other responsibilities and obligations, pulling in a different direction from the ties establishment-age parents experience with their children. Thus parents may feel a need to spend Sunday lunch with an aged aunt; they may decline a promotion that involves moving to another town because that will mean leaving grandfather alone and he is believed to be too insecure about leaving familiar surroundings; or they may spend their holidays in one place visiting grandmother. Such pulls may have a marked influence on people's life styles, options and constraints. But they also involve an additional source of potential gratification.

Some people receive and passively adapt to the structures imposed on them, while others manipulate, change or create new ones. People also vary in the degree to which they differentiate or integrate different areas of their lives. Parker made this distinction in 1971, and it seems useful for describing the philosophies of living around which life invest-ments are made and later evaluated. If one holds the view that enjoy-ment can be obtained only if it is kept separate from obligations—work, family and the rest—one makes different kinds of investments (or reacts differently to the investments one finds oneself constrained to make) than if one feels that all life spheres are equally important, with enjoyment to be found in each. Busy people like the Carlsons and Carlos's may not operate with a leisure concept at all. They may have many interests and many involvements; some may be more enjoyable than others but none are leisure in the sense of a residual sphere of time. One has to structure one's time—'make time'— to pursue interests, whether in work, family life, friendship or com-munity living. For reasons which we indicated at the beginning of this chapter, there is the opportunity at this phase for an efflorescence of interests other than work and family ones.

There have been a number of approaches to studying interests that are highly relevant. These are figures on holidays, travel, use of open spaces, visits to places of interest, use of sports facilities, television-viewing, reading newspapers and magazines, attendance at cinemas and theatres, attendance at adult education classes and so on. Many of these are broken down by age and occasionally there is information about social groupings, such as whether or not families were involved together. There is much less from the individual's perspective, particularly in relation to how people organise conceptions of their use of time and patterns of activities. The simple recounting of activities in the framework of a time budget with the researcher providing the classification poses problems. One way that comes a little nearer to the issue of how people organise their interests in activities and make life investments relative to other spheres of life is in the use of the term *hobby*.

A survey in 1965 conducted by the Tavistock Institute examined hobbies in the context of a study of psychological stress and its alleviation. While recognising the shortcomings of the term 'hobby' as expressing meaningful life interests, it is perhaps closer than other terms currently in use. In the reanalysis of the Tavistock Stress Study data* it was found that accounting for the time spent on work, time allowed for eating and sleeping and other prescribed activities (washing, natural functions, transit from one location to another) leaves little or no time accounted for in the records of most respondents. It appears from this study that most people tend to transfer habits of behaviour acquired in other contexts into their 'free time' rather than acquiring new or creative patterns for this time. This underscores our view that 'free time' does not exist as a distinguishable entity for most people. Calling what they do while not at work 'hobbies' is often only a euphemism, making a virtue out of a necessity. Many genuinely enjoy what they do at work and choose quite freely to continue it in their free time. For others there is anxiety about work performance and the need to try to bolster this by extra effort outside the job situation; for still others there is a lack of resourcefulness about what to do with oneself. Table 3 shows the actual patterns of hobbies reported.

Table 3 reflects how widely the term 'hobby' is interpreted. Eighty per cent of the sample claim to have one, while prevalence of home-centred activities in this group accords with the findings of other surveys (Sillitoe, 1969; Morrell Publications, 1973). Women are less likely than men to have hobbies, and those they do have are more likely to be home-based. The Tavistock study showed the greater tendency of men to continue with some kind of active sports, both team sports and individual activities like walking and swimming. It also reflected that people of lower education and in the lowest socio-economic group had the greatest tendency to have 'no hobbies'; those who do tend to grumble more than people in other groups (Table 4).

The gambling refers to formal gambling activities such as **horse-race**

* This was done in collaboration with Linden Hilgendorf and Barrie Irving.

Table 3   *Hobbies reported in Tavistock national sample, 1965 (men and women, 21+)*

What are they:	N	%
Work continued in another form, e.g. studies	54	3·8
Home and family activities (useful activities distinguishing a good husband/wife/parent), e.g. saving, gardening, knitting, do-it-yourself, 'the children', etc.	913	64·0
Social activities (distinguishing a good citizen), e.g. Red Cross, charities, church, clubs, social evenings, entertaining, etc.	41	2·9
Skilled performance (non-competitive), e.g. model-making, collecting, crosswords, keep fit	37	2·6
Competitive activities (all sports and games)	130	9·1
Gambling, e.g. betting, bridge, bingo	26	1·8
Vicarious activity (all spectatorship activities or second-hand experience), e.g. reading, watching sport, touring	136	9·5
Submergent activities (non-productive activities where person is submerged, taken out of himself), e.g. playing music, walking, swimming, sailing, fishing, bird-watching	64	4·5
Exciting activities, e.g. skiing, motor-racing, dancing, rock-climbing	10	0·7

Total N = 1,411

Table 4   *Gambling and social class in Tavistock national sample, 1965*

Professional–managerial	Skilled non-manual	Skilled manual	Unskilled manual
0·6%	1·5%	1·4%	3·4%

betting and bingo. Members of the professional and managerial classes, though they do not indicate gambling as an activity, engage in other activities which have a gambling element—such as playing the stock market.

The Tavistock survey, like Young and Willmott's London study, showed that the higher socio-economic groups cultivate more skilled hobbies and spill over work into non-work time more, blurring the distinction between work and non-work interests (Young and Willmott,

1973). Education is relevant: those who left school under 15 tend to have 'no hobbies', or if they do, to have only home activities; those who completed secondary but not higher education tend more to play competitive games. For different sub-populations strategies for relating home and family activities to work and other interests vary. The bald reporting of the fact that most 'free time' is spent in home-centred activities (as is done in most surveys) can hide the problem of just how much this is, when it is, what it consists of and how differently family members work out their separate as well as their joint interests at home.

In the survey, type of dwelling (which partially relates to socio-economic status) had a bearing on hobbies in that those who live in detached and semi-detached houses have hobbies more frequently than those living in flats or terraces. The semi-detached, it seems, is the locale *par excellence* for the home-based hobbyists; those in detached housing show a greater proportion pursuing activities which take them out as well; and those in flats show a disproportionately high interest in 'vicarious' activities such as spectator events.*

Television-viewing is a phenomenon that deserves separate attention, and indeed volumes have been written on it and reams of tabulations compiled on use patterns (Blumler, 1972). Television, even more than the motorcar, has permeated the population. Colour television claimed a great portion of the 'leisure pound' across the board in the 1960s (Morrell Publications, 1973). Black-and-white sets are consequently available very cheaply second-hand, and found as second sets in homes with modest incomes.

For our purposes an important distinction is the frequency and selectivity of television-viewing. As with the use of alcohol, cannabis or other quasi-addicting experiences, there are differences between those who seek to broaden their experience and those who seek oblivion (Zinberg and Robertson, 1972). Many individuals may use experiences like television in a complex way—sometimes for escape, sometimes for broadening experiences. Within families there may be different combinations of uses and these may change over time. Being lulled into a fairyland of song, romance, titillation and violence may or may not be a more benign form of oblivion than that produced by hashish. It is certainly more accepted.

Television-viewing, the home-centred activity *par excellence*, reaches a high plateau during the establishment period. The life-cycle curve of nightly television-viewing, which is, of course, an imperfect indicator of non-selective viewing, is shown in Table 5.

* Aside from the fact that these are statistical tendencies and do not govern every individual family in these housing circumstances, there may also be quite different meanings attached to the term 'hobby' by members of different social classes. This may affect the correlations observed with housing.

Table 5 *Watch television every night (Tavistock sample, 1965), percentages by age (men and women)*

Age	%
21–24	33·1
25–34	47·5
35–44	49·3
45–49	42·6
50–64	51·2
65+	40·0

Total N = 1,798

This curve suggests the high plateau between the ages of 25 and 44, followed by a slight dip and then a sharply rising curve into the sixties. The peak represents the period in which there are children at home, the dip perhaps heralds the departure of the children. The subsequent rise suggests the different kind of interest in television in the later phases, going over into retirement.

The Tavistock study shows an interesting pattern of correlations. Women are more likely to be nightly viewers than men. Nightly viewing is negatively correlated with having a hobby. It is positively correlated, not only with 'no hobbies' but with stress symptoms. Even its anodyne function, therefore, is ineffectual in some ways for captive housewives. Steady probably unselective, television-viewing as a 'free time' activity seems, like gambling, to be more associated with the lower-educated, lower-occupational-skill groups. This is confirmed by other studies of the same phenomenon.

While the meanings of leisure in the establishment phase are both highly diverse and subject to change in response to social trends, they can be seen also to have a kind of unity. The unity is to be understood as a set of responses to the preoccupation with life investments—what to become involved in, how much, in what combinations, how to avoid conflicts of involvement and how to assure ultimate psychological pay-offs.

Leisure provision for middle years: identifying needs on a finer grid

We have described characteristics of people in the establishment phase of their lives, their preoccupations by sub-phase and how they develop interests expressing these preoccupations or conversely are blocked and frustrated in them and experience problems. Our approach reveals complex, varied and dynamic qualities; it points up the need for leisure providers to view families at this phase in a more highly differentiated way than is common. The starting-point for more responsive provisions is a more refined identification of sub-populations in this phase whose requirements we have shown to differ markedly. While our approach may help inform providers, so that what they provide is, in a sense, tailored to the specific population served, enlarging perspectives in this way may not be easy in the bureaucratic structures in which providers usually work.

The complexities of the sub-populations of consequent difficulties regarding provision are underscored when one considers a specimen case. We studied an area-based provider–user relationship, some of whose findings were reported in chapter 2. There we gave an account of the stereotyped ways in which leisure providers in the area viewed young people. There was also a stereotyped view of adult estate-dwellers. In this particular new housing development on the outskirts of town, the generality of people were perceived as displaced, transient, hard-working, hard-drinking, violent, unstable, materialistic, discordant in family settings, fathers uninterested in their families, a high proportion of working women—especially on night-shift, children left alone in the evenings without adequate care, mothers who do not work day hours, and especially those working night-shifts, unresponsive to structured activities during the day, difficult to organise.

Families with whom we discussed their own patterns in relation to leisure tended to describe themselves with reference to their perceived differences from, and conformities with, this image. However, the impressions gained of these families lends little reinforcement to any blanket conceptions of what estate-dwellers are actually like, though some elements of the image are grounded in realities.

Here we report discussions with two families both born in the town and now resident on the housing estate in which the study was centred. We present the most and the least resourceful of the couples interviewed. They illuminate actual people's experience in a concrete situation where the range of available provisions is known, revealing the ways they relate—and do not relate—to provisions for their use and with provisions elsewhere. They serve as 'actual trees among the providers' wood', and their experiences crystallise many of the points raised in the chapter.

MR AND MRS RAWLINSON have four children aged 8, 7, 5 and 3. Mrs Rawlinson works at night and Mr Rawlinson during the day. Most of the discussion was held with Mrs Rawlinson, her husband participating in a minor way on returning from work.

Mr Rawlinson is a painter. In summer there is plenty of work and he can change jobs easily and be quite independent. Mrs Rawlinson says her husband does not find his work especially enjoyable but the main problem is that the amount of work drops enormously in winter. That is why she started work three years ago, to supplement their income. Mrs Rawlinson had not been in paid employment since expecting their first child, and she resumed by 'taking in crackers', which was tedious work for only £3 per week: '. . . Then a friend said how much more you could get as a barmaid for the same hours.' She started at one pub, then changed to the pub where she now works as a function barmaid. Mrs Rawlinson derives considerable meaning from her work, in particular: 'Equality in marriage as a person. And extra importance. It's not only the money, but people seeing you as someone other than just a mum.' Nevertheless Mrs Rawlinson would like to give up her work. She says she only started it for the money: 'Now we're in a better position than we've ever been in before.' But she has become more involved than she had planned to. The previous winter she had worked only a couple of nights each week, but when she returned this season, the manager wanted someone for six to seven nights each week. She accepted this, but now feels the 40-odd hour week at nights, returning home at 1–2 a.m. each morning, is a burden. She feels she will not miss the non-financial satisfactions she derives from her work: 'If I weren't working, there's much more I could do—like get to learn more about archaeology, instead of just knowing I want to.' Also Mrs Rawlinson finds she misses sociability, for which she now has little opportunity in the evenings.

The level of activity in which Mrs Rawlinson engages in addition to her heavy work and demanding domestic commitments is high. She says she feels the need to be active because of, rather than despite, her domestic commitments.

She reviews her married years as a sequence of 'courting, stopping to see other people, getting a house and that—getting into a rut'. 'Getting into a rut' means that 'you lose interests, lose initiatives with other people, get fed up.' Mrs Rawlinson says they have managed to get out of the rut. This does not simply mean that they go out more. She says they had always gone out a lot—'to museums and castles, etc. with the kids'—but had never had any life of their own:

> 'You lose something of yourself by getting too involved in a house and children. The more you do, the more you want to do. My husband says I sound like I'm searching for something—well, there's so much to do, and you can waste it doing nothing.'

Mrs Rawlinson feels that they emerged from their rut before she went out to work, although she suggests that money is very helpful in keeping her out of the rut.

The Rawlinsons spend much of their leisure on family activities. Until a few years ago, Mr Rawlinson used to go fishing on his own at weekends when he felt he should spend more time with his family: '. . . Now we go mainly to parks—large ones, especially with outdoor swimming pools, or with boating lakes, and swings for the kids.' One of the parks they go to also offers water-skiing, and Mrs Rawlinson says: 'I'm dying to have a go, but it is very expensive—30s. for fifteen minutes last time we inquired.' On Saturdays Mr Rawlinson usually works; if he returns early, he takes Mrs Rawlinson to the town shopping. This leaves Sunday for their main day out. If Mr Rawlinson does not work on Saturday, they usually go to London:

> 'We go to London often, though not so much this year. We go to big houses and museums, or just wander round. We take dinner with us and come home late—around 10 p.m., but now that I work evenings we have to be home too soon, so it isn't worth it. The children themselves enjoy museums.'

Mrs Rawlinson finds out where to go from advertisements and books. She realises that they could not easily engage in the activities they do without a car.

Another family activity is camping, which they long wanted to take up, and eventually did when a holiday they had planned fell through. The Rawlinsons have never had a 'booked holiday', and have not been abroad. They go camping on weekends at water activity areas, or they go sightseeing, and they have also been able to take holidays. Last year they went to Cornwall. They were planning to go abroad this year, but will postpone that trip until next year, in order to introduce some friends who are novices to a camping experience. They plan to return to the Cornish site they visited last year. They are hoping to join the Camping Club of Great Britain: 'We looked into it, and I wanted to join, but we didn't, because we didn't have enough time to go to the weekly meetings; we thought we'd put it off until we could use it better.' Mrs Rawlinson observes how the length of their holiday has increased. Until last year, their holiday lasted only a few days; then last year they took a fortnight, this year they plan to have three weeks, and next year they hope to go abroad for four weeks. This is consistent with their financial position.

Mrs Rawlinson practises wine-making as a hobby and she sews all her children's clothes: 'I get the material from the Lancashire warehouse—it's cheaper that way.' She also does crochet, and enjoys both this and the sewing. Next she plans to make fishing baskets for her sons; she considers them too expensive to buy. Her special interest is in archaeology—'old castles, museums, etc.' She is not sure how this interest developed:

'We went to these Roman ruins when I was at school, but school isn't the time to learn. About three years ago I saw an advert in the paper for a series of six weekly film shows about archaeology in the central library. We went down; it was really marvellous. There were different speakers each week with illustrations of their digs.'

Mrs Rawlinson says she had been 'scared' to go, but to her surprise: 'It was not what I'd expected at all. It wasn't full of clever people.' She has tried to develop the interest:

'I wanted to look into archaeology in night-school, but found there was none in the town. So we both did photography instead, which was hopeless because the teacher dropped out at the last minute and was replaced by someone who didn't know much more than the people in the course.'

Mrs Rawlinson does not use the focus of provisions on the estate, the community centre, at all, although she used to:

'I went to the original organisers' meeting and was on the social and nursery committees, and was also helping with the playgroup—and starting the disco for the youngsters. We had loads of coffee mornings to raise money. I enjoyed it a lot, but then the conflict came: should I work there or for ourselves? I was doing both for a while but it just got too much, so I packed up the social committee. Then when I went back to work in October and the manager wanted someone for six or seven nights a week, I gave up the playgroup.'

But Mrs Rawlinson recalls some unpleasant aspects of her involvement with the playgroup:

'Originally we thought we were going to run it. We put in a lot of work getting things sifted out and going. Then when the council came to manage the playgroup, we were told it needed trained teachers. We felt disappointed and hurt. There was a feeling of friction caused by the council coming and pushing us out. They said we weren't all needed all the time, sort of "you can help when we tell you." We felt pushed out.'

Mrs Rawlinson says she used the library at the centre, to take out books on history and similar topics, but found them very technical. Though she enjoys reading a lot, she finds that working takes much out of her. In general, however, she says she does not know much about events at the centre. She used to when she was on the committee, but there is little publicity or information outside the centre. There is another element: 'If I found out there was a dance, I'd say let's go, but my husband would say no. He doesn't like going dancing with all the neighbours.' When they go to dances, they seem to go mostly in surrounding towns.

The difference in their attitudes that Mrs Rawlinson expresses here reflects their respective orientations to life on the estate. What does Mr Rawlinson feel about the estate? '. . . I don't think about it a lot—I don't do much in the area. It's just like a collection of houses. I'm waiting to get out—to our own place—a bought place.' Mrs Rawlinson feels she relates more to the area. While her husband volunteers, 'No one round here would miss me if we left', she feels she would be missed. They attribute this difference to 'personality', seeing him as 'more independent' (his view) or 'demanding, wanting everyone to match up to his standards perfectly' (her view). Mr Rawlinson feels he would not relate to the area more even if he were home during the day. He says he has no friends and the people are not the kind with whom he could make friends. In part also this difficulty in finding one's place socially in the locality (a difficulty shared by other men spoken to) is due to the relative absence of social overlay in a new environmental setting. Despite the closer manner in which Mrs Rawlinson relates to the estate, and her origins in the town, she does not identify strongly with the town. Her family moved North just before she married, and many of her friends have moved to other towns. She seldom goes to the town— 'nothing to go there for'. Not even her shopping creates a focus. She uses the estate shops perhaps once a week, otherwise her husband takes her each week to a supermarket in the town centre which gives gift stamps. She is saving stamps for camping equipment.

Mrs Rawlinson is both especially resourceful and perceptive. This shows in the response she volunteered when asked where she finds out about all the activities she engages in:

> 'I don't think it's information straight that counts. You may see an ad. but be scared to go—like I was with the archaeology lectures. It's the same with dances. If there's things you want to do enough, you will do them anyway—you won't sit back and wait to be fetched.'

Though Mrs Rawlinson feels her activities are likely to influence her own children positively, she cannot explain what has influenced her:

> 'If you bring children up to go out, to do things, and that, they're more likely to find things they like to do. I never went out at all as a child—I don't know how I got like I am. I had my first holiday at fourteen.
>
>   I never had transport or money and that. There was very little I could do before I met . . . [my husband]. I got married at 17. I used to do needlework and drama before I got married.

He was 19 when we were married. He used to have a motorbike when we were courting. The whole thing is based on getting married and having children, and then one finds it's not everything, just not enough. I had to develop from there.'

MR AND MRS SMITH, another couple, have lived on the estate for twelve years. They have five children—aged 14, 13, 11, 9 and 6. Much of the discussion centred on the teenage daughters and is recorded in chapter 2. In talking to Mr and Mrs Smith about themselves they showed little conception of a separate 'life of their own' at present. Their teenage daughters were having a marked impact on their parents' lives, both in respect of the increased financial pressures on the family resources and in terms of the extent to which the Smiths' concerns are concentrated on the daughters' developmental patterns.

The Smiths say that they 'try to engage in activities as a family', but that 'the big ones' no longer want to go out with them. Previously they could not go to a social club because their children were too small, now they are sure they could not get in anywhere and believe the waiting lists to be long. Their teenage daughters now desire autonomy: 'Before the kids were keen to go anywhere with us on Sundays—they were eager to go. Now they say: "Do we have to go?" '

Mr Smith is a fork-truck driver at a large factory in the area. Mrs Smith is not in paid employment. Mr Smith often works a night-shift and overtime on Saturdays; this influences his family's leisure possibilities. He says that his firm offers its employees a wide range of activities including horse-riding, judo, etc., which employees' families may utilise. He works at the branch in the neighbouring town and many of the facilities offered by the firm are in the branch of the town the Smiths live in. He feels that the journey is too long for them to make alone. Mr Smith also points out that participation 'requires quite large chunks of wages'. He feels the charge is reasonable, as 'the factory isn't the council', but considers it a burden none the less.

Still, the Smiths say that they are 'hardly ever in in the summer and always in in winter'. Where do they go? Mainly the family goes swimming at the pool in a nearby town, or to one of the nearby parks with swimming facilities, or to other parks in the surrounding area.

The Smiths have definite opinions about provisions on the estate. They feel the community centre is 'very fine', and Mr Smith says he uses the library there, and the coffee bar. The eldest daughters used to go to Red Cross there, and to the disco. The youngest used to attend the playgroup. Nevertheless the Smiths feel that the centre is too small, and that the charges for participation in activities there are too high: 'The centre was paid for by Harry Ratepayer, so why must we continue to pay each time we use it?' He has other grievances: 'The squash court has always been a sore point to everyone on the estate because of the snob barrier—£14 a year to begin with. It's not people on the estate who use it.'

So far the discussion has centred mainly on the Smiths' elder children's activities, on Mr and Mrs Smith's negative feelings about available provisions, and on some of the constraints they encounter in engaging in leisure activities. How do the Smiths positively express themselves? In fact their activity level seems relatively low.

Mrs Smith says she knits and makes most of the children's clothes. Otherwise the Smiths watch television and play records. Mr Smith says his hobby is wine- and beer-making. They say that their entertainment declined from the time they moved to the estate—twelve years previously. They feel this was due to an absence of provisions—indeed they had to wait some ten and a half years for the community centre. Nevertheless they see that other estate-dwellers have responded differently:

> 'There was nothing to do, so people congregated in the pubs. They leave their kids alone at night, without proper baby-sitters. Some people feel that if they don't go out, they go mad. The husbands go to the pub, so the women must go with them. A woman is quite entitled to relief from the same four walls.'

The Smiths explain how they differ from the norm they perceive. Nevertheless they appear sympathetic to it. Mrs Smith adds: 'Many women go to bingo at the Catholic school. They live all week just for the break that one night a week.' She relates that notice of the school sports day was given just that day, to which all the mums reacted with excitement, planning to go. They look forward to it with more excitement than she thinks would normally be warranted for a school sports day. So does she:

> 'My life does get boring, I'll admit. There isn't anywhere I could go in the afternoon. The centre caters only for old people in the afternoon. There is the playgroup in the morning. There is needlework, and that in the evening, but I want to be home in the evening.'

Has Mrs Smith ever considered helping to run activities? She feels that implies too great a commitment. She could not be flexible if the running of activities depended on her presence: 'I want to go to the centre when I want to go.' She points out that with five children, domestic crises are not infrequent. Her need for flexibility is therefore great. Mrs Smith suggests that several of her friends would like day-time activities. 'We get absolutely fed up. We watch the time till its three-ten—time to fetch the kids. If my friend doesn't come round to be fed up with me, and I'm alone, it's even worse.' Mr Smith has a sudden insight: 'It's the same though in the evening. After tea we sit and wait till ten, so we can get our drinks and go to bed. Each day the cycle is the same.' Has Mr Smith attempted to pursue any evening activities? '. . . . I would be interested in archery, for example, but know that if I went to join it'd be full.' Mrs Smith points out that he cannot know: 'You've never tried.' Would Mr Smith perhaps give it a go if he felt sure the reception at the other end would be welcoming? Mrs Smith lights up knowingly:

'Yes. Soon after we came to the estate, there was a coffee morning on at Friendship House. We had nothing to do, so my friend and I thought we'd give it a try. We went across and no one spoke a word to us all the time. We would never go again.'

Mr Smith smiles defensively and says that he has a second hobby—ghost-hunting—but is sure there would be no group for it in the town. He was unaware of a town guide that includes an inventory of activity groups. Then the Smiths recall that they both love old buildings, especially old churches—but they only look at them when on holiday. They feel that the children are not interested anyway.

The family spend their holidays at a coastal resort in the West country, where Mrs Smith's mother now lives. Previously, when her mother lived in the South, they used to holiday there: 'This way we can go for three weeks for the price of one week in an hotel. It's just the cost of the petrol really. And it's nice there, and the children can see their nanna.' Mrs Smith suggests that however difficult life on the estate is for her, it must be worse for a newcomer: 'Even I get fed up, and I can go up the road and meet someone I know for certain.' The Smiths paint a portrait of a young woman, who is a newcomer on the estate, and knows no one, while her husband is at least assured of contacts at work: 'She must be really lonely.' They feel that is a characteristic of new estates: 'All new estates are the same—just groups of houses, a generous sprinkling of pubs, and nothing else really. Especially in the winter, they're just places where there're houses. Thank heavens for TV in the winter.'

The *implications* of our analysis *for leisure providers* whose activities are orientated to facilitating enjoyment and positive experiences in living are several.

Block thinking about 'the family' at this stage is not effective. There are different kinds of families and their preoccupations and interests differ. More sensible formulations like 'working-class, urban families with children' give more of the picture, but it is also necessary to know what the family structure and norms are. Conventional families differ from dual-worker families and from families with irregular arrangements of one kind or another. The strengths and strains in these

different family situations—other than economics—will partly determine their 'leisure provision' needs. It is also necessary to know more
about families' environmental settings. Though we have not concentrated on this variable, even the provider–user study area is sufficient
to indicate that 'urban' environments, for one, differ enormously.
The housing estate is in an urban residential district, but lacks the
variety, choice and stimulus usually associated with urban living.

In order to refine the assessment of 'need', a two-pronged approach
is suggested: (a) to isolate categories of individuals 'at risk', who are
relatively unhappy, who suffer psychosomatic complaints, who feel
disadvantaged as to their chances for enjoyment of life; and (b) to
isolate categories of individuals 'at benefit', who are 'happy' and feel
that they enjoy life as a whole. Neither of these is directly correlated
with social class, though at the very low end of the economic scale,
where the 'cycle of deprivation' operates most powerfully, chances of
multiple 'risks' and problems pile up precipitously.

More is known about the dissatisfied, symptom-producing sub-
populations than about 'happy' and satisfied ones like the Carlsons, for
whom a feeling that life is good prevails. This is an area for further
research; it is neglected because 'happy' people are assumed not to need
further attention from society. We believe it is important to understand
them both as potential resource people, and to make provisions that
enable them to maintain their satisfactory levels. Knowing how they organise their lives, how they derive enjoyment and how they learn to
adapt to new situations, can benefit those less competent in these ways.
They may also, under favourable conditions and with skilful persuasion,
become leaders in activities which benefit from their skills and accomplishments, particularly in voluntary groups.

Several observations are relevant to a consideration of populations 'at
risk'. A person may have psychosomatic complaints (signifying stresses,
tensions, anxieties) and also be happy. Dissatisfaction may be associated
with stress symptoms but it may be inversely related to them; thus dis-
contents may be bottled up and precipitate symptoms. There is some
evidence of a 'cumulativeness of strains' that is analogous in a negative
way to the cumulativeness of leisure activities and associations mentioned before. A downward spiral of stress is sometimes established;
life goes from bad to worse. Hughes and his colleagues found a high
concentration of psychosomatic complaints present in communities
which also had a high concentration of physical illness and of socially
disorganised institutions and life styles (Hughes *et al.*, 1963).

One problem in establishing the presence of situations of cumulative
strain is in defining when behaviour represents a state of personal and
social disorganisation and when it is simply another sub-cultural trait.
Gambling and 'doing nothing' are examples. These may be escapist

activities which signify unhappiness and disorder, or they may be the norm for a group and have no such special significance, or they may have positive functions. We have already noted that gambling, an activity of many sub-groups, is more prevalent among lower-income than professional-managerial groups. It has a male version (the 'turf accountant's') and a female version (the bingo game). The prevalence in the lower social class groups of a high rate of gambling is paralleled by a high rate of television-viewing and a higher rate of psychological complaints. This, together with other research, suggests that low social status is itself a form of stress which has multiple and cumulative negative accompaniments. By the establishment phase, the resilience of youth is gone and the chances for finding one's way out diminish. There may be a gradual build-up of hopelessness and a sense of alienation if one is in a low-status job, and this need not only be economically low status. Our data show sex role to be a powerful factor.

We found from the data of the Tavistock Stress Study that the most vulnerable and least vulnerable groups for psychosomatic complaints and symptoms were as shown in Table 6. For the first group of

Table 6 *Sub-populations and stress symptoms (Tavistock survey)*

	Most vulnerable sub-group	Least vulnerable sub-group
Pains and ailments Not feeling vigorous enough	Married women not working, 35 + with children	Married men *under* 35
Shortness of breath ⎫ Palpitations ⎬ Sleep disturbance ⎪ Tension ⎭	Married women with children	Married men *under* 35

symptoms the presence of hobbies was a mitigating factor. Women who have no hobbies have an even higher symptom level. What hobbies women have tend to be home hobbies rather than other kinds, and this does not seem to be enough to mitigate the overall picture for the sub-group.

The implication of these findings for leisure provision is that *ways need to be found to encourage non-working mothers in the 35+ age group to become interested in activities outside the home.* This is not a simple mechanical undertaking. As resistances and anxieties have to be overcome, particularly in relation to taking on activities never tried before, active facilitation is needed. The despair of boredom and monotony, understimulation, 'getting in a rut', 'being fed up', is widespread. All the women in the provider–user study spoke of being 'scared', but so may men like Mr Smith. In a physical environment that is less highly committed than that housing estate, fewer thresholds to participation may suggest themselves. Socially, that case material underscores the likely benefits of sensitive mediation, which may invite even those women who seem least receptive over the threshold to involvement.

In the least vulnerable group, the young married men, there was the highest proportion of hobbies present for any sub-group in the population. For the second group of symptoms, hobbies seem not to have made much difference one way or the other.

It is interesting to note the contrast with the *least stressed* sub-group (taking these symptoms to be stress indicators). The younger group of married men, in their early marriage and early establishment phases, seem to have least stress. They are still full of hope and prospects for their work and careers; they are vigorous and perhaps retain many of the pleasures of their earlier associations and enjoyment of activities. Their wives are for the most part in the 'honeymoon' phase of the maternal and domestic role cycles and perhaps deriving maximum gratification from having and looking after small infants. This is, of course, a statistical formulation and does not illuminate patterns for variant groups for whom these tendencies do not hold.

The stress accumulates for women, coming to a peak in the mid-establishment phase, when the enchantment of domesticity may have worn thin and the divergence between their own and their husband's worlds has begun to rankle. Once again, the men's peaks of stress lag behind, coming more into focus in the mid- to late establishment phases. The contrast between 'his' marriage and 'her' marriage, made plainest in the establishment phase, is one that has been explored by Jessie Bernard, who produced evidence in the USA compatible with our findings from the Tavistock study, the Henley study, the PEP study and other available information (Bernard, 1972; Rapoport, 1970; Fogarty *et al.*, 1971).

Available information indicates the period between 40 and 50 as a particularly hazardous one for a coronary occlusion; heart attacks that occur later have a lower chance of being fatal. This is a predominantly masculine hazard. The work of Morris shows the importance of exercise in this period, and there have been interesting differences found in different occupations. The bus-driver, to use Morris's classical illustration, experiences greater stress than the bus-conductor (Morris *et al.*, 1973). But as important as actual occupational choice are the different approaches within occupations. Doctors experience greater stresses stemming from the demands of their occupation than members of other professions; but within the medical profession the approach or specialism chosen may have a critical effect. General practitioners generally experience greater stress than do specialists in relatively undemanding and 'successful' branches of medicine such as plastic surgery or dermatology; solo general practitioners who do not use any form of relief aid suffer more than do those in a team arrangement of some kind. The research doctor on the medical school faculty is more like research people in other professions in his life style than his hard-pressed medical colleagues in practice.

Those who are stressed in their work and careers are more likely in this phase to show not only the symptoms of psychosomatic illness, but marital discord and behavioural aberrations. We have illustrated this in the analysis of managerial careers as well as the examples just mentioned. Another interesting and dramatic illustration of stress reactions is *'dropping out'*. 'Dropping out' has been of interest from several points of view for many years. It is increasingly recognised to be a phenomenon not only of adolescence—where it often serves a developmental, exploratory function—but of middle age as well. 'Dropping out' may be a reaction to stress or it may be a positive move in the direction of developing new life interests.

Private detective agencies and matrimonial courts have for many years been concerned with the large number of men who simply disappear from home after leaving in the routine way one morning, never to be seen again. This used to be an exclusively masculine pattern, but since women have become more conscious of their exploitation as 'captive housewives', it has grown as a female as well as a male option. An article in the *New York Times*, 16 February 1973, notes this:

> Detective agencies that specialise in tracing missing persons report that the ratio of disappearing wives to husbands, particularly in large Eastern cities has risen from about 1 to 100 a decade ago to more than 1 out of 3 now . . . [the president of Tracers Company of America stated] 'Wives usually take off as a declaration of discontent and lack of personal fulfilment and with the encouragement of the emerging women's lib movement.'

The feeling of being exploited has grown among married women, particularly those with education and training who have had to give up opportunities to use their skills. By the mid-establishment phase their role seems to many to be, in Jessie Bernard's terms, a 'dead end job'. Absconding for many women may, as for men, simply reflect a poor marital relationship, an accumulated sense of despair at the drudgery and difficulties experienced, or an impulsive reaction to precipitating events, such as discovering their husband's involvement with other women. For middle-class, educated women, the reasons are probably similar to those of the middle-class, educated man who 'drops out'

in this way—namely the feeling that life is not adding up in a meaningful way and that new opportunities must be pursued. One of the people
cited in the *New York Times* article quoted above said:

> I'd see all the people around me, women my age, staying at home and
> escaping into pills, drinking and affairs. It was so wasteful, so tragic
> . . . . [now] I've discovered that I have a responsibility for my life
> and can take care of it damn well. That's a very heady thing.

The comments by a series of middle-age, middle-class male 'drop-outs'
interviewed in Britain by Eric Clark have a similar central point, though
in their case the 'dropping out' was occupational; for the small series
of cases he interviewed, the marriages remained intact. Directors,
brokers, professionals—all successful, all materially well off, all socially
accepted—nevertheless decided to leave their occupations and start
something entirely different during the establishment phase. This often
involved a build-up of discontent about the work situation because of
the gap between aspirations or wishes (not necessarily for *vertical*
mobility) and experience. Often it was precipitated, like the marital
'drop-out' by a relatively minor event which acted as the 'last straw'.
Characteristically it did not entail a search for less work or no work—
but for a different kind of work arrangement, doing something worth
while—that was personally meaningful; often this involved working
closer to home, more collaboratively with one's wife, and at something
that one could do with one's own hands—all trends which we have
noted above. Clark summed up the core of motivation for this kind of
'dropping out' in the words of one of the men: 'What we are trying to
do is build a business up around our lives—and not the other way
round' (Clark, 1973). By hypothesis, it is the man who went too far
earlier with the latter that feels the need to make a radical correction
now in favour of the former.

However, the life audit need not involve 'dropping out'—either
maritally or occupationally. It may involve slight adjustments of life
style or it may involve a confirmation that the psycho-social accounts
are relatively well balanced. In a marriage husband and wife have, after
all, shared a great deal and they may feel a sense of pride in what they
have jointly accomplished in their children's upbringing. Even if
adolescence has brought stormy weather, and even if there has been a
rejection by the children of the parents, they do have one another. They
may get on better with each other when the children are not present to
stimulate disagreements. Middle-aged spouses often come to terms
with each other as not perhaps the best in an ideal world; sometimes
sexual relations improve in this period, despite the subsidence of earlier
passions, because the couple know each other's needs and have found
ways of enjoying each other. Occupationally, there may be a similar

recognition that though one may not have conquered the heights that seemed possible in earlier years, some skill, experience, recognition and status has been accumulated and this may be satisfying. Rather than being excited by the competitive struggle, there may be greater satisfaction from the craftsmanship of doing a good job and from helping younger people to develop.

Heightened dissatisfactions arise when there are residues of envy, recriminations for failures, lack of support for the infirmities that become more apparent, despair if the sum feeling is that there has not been enough satisfaction or pleasure to balance the sacrifice and suffering. This may be due to an objective assessment of what has actually occurred in the establishment phase itself, or it may stem primarily from earlier unresolved feelings of envy, depression and resentment.

An impressive feature of life during the establishment phase is the degree to which families are home-centred. Interest in developing the home and garden, the growth of do-it-yourself home-improvement activities, the all-pervasiveness of the television set and the increasing prevalence of the family car all re-enforce this pattern. Our work indicates, however, that none of the block-hypotheses about family home-centredness are supportable. De Tocqueville's fear that home-centredness would obliterate creativity and social participation is only partly supported; many people cultivate both a rich family life and participation in a wide variety of external activities. The theories of the anti-family 'doomwatchers' like Laing and Cooper also are only partially supported in the sense that there are some populations at risk psychologically through their entrapment in families, but there are others that find fulfilment in family life. Similarly the economic determinists with their emphasis on the needs of the poor and the cycle of economic deprivation are only partly supported in relation to 'leisure'. While there are certainly people at the lowest end of the scale whose enjoyment activities could be called 'empty' or escapist—those who seek to obliterate life with all its pain and futility by drink, drugs, gambling, opting out of social responsibility, or succumbing to television addiction—the capacity to find interests and develop them for one's enjoyment is found at all levels of the social scale with the differences statistical rather than categorical.

We have begun the task of differentiating groups 'at risk' and those 'at benefit' from whom lessons could be learned and leadership enlisted; by doing this we have begun sorting out how improved balances of various kinds can be achieved in future and what contribution can be made by leisure providers.

5

Life styles for later years

Personal and social integration

In our society production (or reproduction) has traditionally been a dominant reference point in organising life patterns. During the establishment phase, when productive activities are at their peak, 'leisure time' is conventionally seen in relation to occupational activity—for recreation or reward. But as we stress throughout this book, life comprises not only work and non-work, but also family, personal interests, community relations and so on. Work is not the sphere of prime salience for everyone; the significance that people invest in each sphere varies, as do the ways they combine the spheres in their particular life styles. But individuals' involvements and life styles vary with life-cycle stage—as one set of preoccupations after another comes to ascendancy. This is nowhere better seen than in the later life phases, when a radical reorganisation is required in the lives of most people.

We deal in this chapter with a period starting roughly from the age of 55; these later or 'retirement' years overlap with the late establishment period. There is no universal dividing line, though for most people an important reference point is the statutory retirement age of 60/65 (in the UK), when State financial support is available for those who cease their regular work. The focal preoccupation of the phases we consider here is with achieving a sense of *social and personal integration*. This entails an effort to bring a sense of integration into one's whole life—a sense of personal meaning and harmony with the world around one. In more stable societies that revered the elderly and valued the contributions that they could make—accumulated knowledge, reflection, wisdom, experience, perspective—this preoccupation with integrity was more readily translatable into interests and patterns of activity than has been the case in our society. In contrast, we avoid 'knowing' what it is like to be old and what old people are experiencing. This is reflected in the way many people consciously neglect to make adequate pension arrangements where these arrangements are not made for them as part of a work contract. Ageing in a change-orientated society has tended to be equated with obsolescence and even death.

The studies that have been made of old people have been 'done on' them by people who have not experienced being old; this is also usually true of planning and provisions for the elderly. Accordingly this is a phase less well understood than the others. At the same time it is more important than ever to understand and come to grips with the issues people experience in the later years. Demographically this is an increasingly important section of the population; for this and humanistic reasons, the issues need to be understood so that suitable provision can be made both by professionals and people generally.

In the later years the 'recreative' element of 'leisure' has less relevance than in the establishment phase when, in many instances, it made sense to think of 'free time' activities in terms of their restoring the individual to productive efficiency. In the later phase the meaning of time un-committed to occupational demands is not likely to be different, but it changes as the proportions of the elderly grow and as society's under-standing of the issues changes. Before launching into our attempt to contribute to this understanding, it is useful to review some of the facts.

First, older people constitute an increasing proportion of the popu-lation of industrial countries. In the United Kingdom, for example, the proportion of the population aged 65+ rose from 5·4 per cent in 1911 to 13·2 per cent in 1971 (*Annual Abstract of Statistics*, 1974). This is partly because of medical advances making for greater longevity, and partly due to falling birth rates in succeeding generations. Prevention and cure of killing diseases of earlier life, improved diet, housing and public health conditions, safer and more satisfying work, have all con-tributed to the picture. While many chronic ill-health conditions con-tinue to plague the elderly (for example, arthritis, rheumatism, cardio-vascular or respiratory conditions), relatively few are completely dis-abled until they reach their late seventies. As Shanas *et al.* (1968, 18) have indicated in their transnational study: 'The person who is old is thought to be sick. . . . The fact is, however, that although widespread pathology exists among the elderly population, old age and illness are not synonymous. There is no such disease as "old age".' These re-searchers feel that the stereotyped picture of the elderly as infirm is exaggerated. They found that most elderly people remain active despite their ailments until their late seventies. The implication is that the elderly, like younger people with handicaps of one kind or another, need assistance in living with these conditions and perhaps help with finding ways to develop their interests in spite of them, rather than being 'put on the shelf' even with good care and attention.

The central event for most people in their later years in industrial societies has been that of occupational retirement. There are a number of trends and counter-trends in relation to the broader concept of 'work', but as far as formal employment is concerned, the main trend is towards increased proportions of people retiring at the statutory age. It is unclear whether the figures reflect primarily the increase in optional post-retirement activities, or an increase in employers exercising their option to retire older people as industry undergoes rationalisation (Table 7).

Table 7   *Age-specific activity rates for males in older age groups (per cent)* (Social Trends, *1972*)

| | Actual | | Projected |
	(1961)	(1971)	(1981)
45–64	97	96	95
65+	26	19	16

While in the establishment phase workers have remained employed at a fairly constant rate, the economically active among the older pensionable population has decreased. The activity rates for age groups below the statutory retirement age are also falling, through earlier retirement, increased unemployment and those classified as 'long-term sick' (Townsend and Bond, 1971). Long-term illness may reflect a face-saving option for those who find it difficult to obtain new employment following a redundancy. It is easier to register as sick than to face the stigma of unemployment. These trends are present not only in England but in other nations as well, notably the USA (Sheppard, 1970) and in Scandinavia (Shanas *et al.*, 1968). The conception that older people wish to continue working needs revision except in a minority of cases. They wish to be 'occupied' and to have the companionship as well as the extra income a job provides. But the more general wish is to be able to enjoy a satisfying personal life—a wish that is more difficult for them to realise than many may have envisioned.

Research findings indicate a sharp distinction between the people who had favourable attitudes to retirement and those who had unfavourable attitudes (Crawford, 1971; Jacobsohn, 1970). Not only are there sex differences with more men than women being willing to retire at the statutory age, but favourable and unfavourable attitudes are not as contrary to one another as they appear on the surface. Jacobsohn found that 62 per cent of men in three industrial plants were willing to retire as compared with 41 per cent of women. The difference was attributed to women having less arduous jobs, and to their participation in the workforce being more voluntary. We add the observation that for many women who work at this phase of their lives, it is a second or third 'career' into which they have relatively recently entered following a child-rearing phase. This means that they are less likely than men to have experienced the build up of career fatigue. The contrast between married and single women's statistics supports this argument (Table 8).

Table 8 *Age-specific activity rates for females, married and unmarried, in older age groups (per cent)* (Social Trends, *1972*)

	Actual (1961)		(1971)		Projected (1981)	
	M	U	M	U	M	U
45–59	40	67	53	64	64	64
60+	11	10	16	8	19	7

M = married; U = unmarried.

Thus, for women, the proportions working in the older age groups are increasing and the difference between the patterns prevailing for married women and for unmarried women are being obliterated in the 45–59 age group. This is largely because of the erosion of the conventional pattern of married women as life-long housewives.

Jacobsohn's study also shows that neither the favourable nor the unfavourable attitudes towards retirement are based on an awareness of the sort of life available following this event. Those favourably inclined are often so disposed because of their wish to escape the boredom and rigours of the job; those unfavourably inclined are often so disposed because they fear the uncertainties and probable economic hardships of life on a pension. For men the economic loss seems to weigh more heavily in anticipation than for women, for whom the loss of social affiliation is more often indicated. In an American study of ageing and personality, Reichard and his colleagues found that the point of greatest anxiety about oneself, one's health, one's capacity to cope economically, etc., comes just prior to retirement rather than after it. According to how these anxieties are dealt with, the subsequent adjustments may be relatively 'mature' and satisfying, or relatively embittered and hostile or self-deprecating (Reichard *et al.*, 1962). This underlines the need for anticipatory preparation made by organisations like the Pre-Retirement Association.

Another body of data centres on what people actually *do* in later life. For some, activities seem to be a continuation of earlier patterns. Fishing (particularly for men), gardening and sexual activity (which, contrary to another cultural myth, may remain a source of pleasure for older people) are examples. In other respects the patterns are age-specific.

Old people are much more likely than younger ones to engage in less physically active pursuits—TV-viewing, reading, sitting, thinking, walking. The more affluent drive for pleasure and to sightsee. Idleness as a significant way of passing time—looking out the window, napping, just sitting—becomes more characteristic of the very old.

Research on the determinants of activity in later years seems to indicate a significant trilogy: education, income and health. Where all three are high, the activity rates are high. If any one drops significantly, the pattern rapidly becomes relatively passive. This should not be taken to mean, as Riesman and others have pointed out, that activity is in and of itself a 'good thing' in this or in any other age group. But taken in its most general form, most people want to be active in some way; where they are unable to be so, they feel their lives are empty, that they are unfulfilled and depressed. Taking activity in its broadest sense —to include meditation, reminiscence, conversation, as well as the more physical activities—there are not only variations in patterns, but these variations are associated with different degrees of satisfaction and they are determined by an interplay of earlier experiences and supports in the transition itself. While this general formulation is true for all of the phases we have described, the weightings and configurations are different for each phase. Older people have a heavier load of early experience (or lack of it, as with education) to overcome; at the same time they become more dependent on current provision than at earlier phases in working out their personal and social patterns of integration.

One of the key issues is how much or how well older people can learn. As Drucker pointed out in the late 1960s, we are living in an 'age of discontinuity', in which the capacity to learn is critical at every period (Drucker, 1969). Lowell Eklund, reviewing educational research, observed that the capacity to learn is affected significantly by previous educational experiences (Eklund, 1969). Castells and Guillemard, in their recent French study, confirm this, and conclude that people tend to continue in retirement the same sorts of interests they had previously, but with a 'deteriorated reproduction' of their earlier pattern—which means, for the lower educated, fewer interests and more passive, vicarious forms of involvement (Castells and Guillemard, 1971).

Our educational system—initial, higher and continuing—is somewhat fragmented and is not primarily orientated to inculcating the capacity for continuous learning. Therefore the challenge confronted by older people, 'learning to learn', is perhaps greater today than it will be in future. The difficulties currently encountered are not entirely indicative of what may lie ahead. As Dumazedier and Ripert have observed for this phase, the statistics show what people do and do not do; they do not show what satisfactions they derive or what they are *capable* of doing. While this observation applies to all phases, it is particularly true for older people (Dumazedier and Ripert, 1963).

It is impossible to say how much the rising generations of younger people, with their new interests and activities, will follow the patterns of today's older people and how much they will forge new patterns. The diffusion of 'culture' to wider ranges of the population through mass education and mass media is bound to have an effect, as will new programmes of recurrent education, improved health pensions, housing and other facilities.

Another issue is that of economic resources. At the national level, the concern is with balancing production and consumption in the economy, an effort in which retirement age and pension provision is one relevant factor among many. As modern State pensions do not usually keep pace with rising costs of living and as there are 'earnings rules' which make it difficult for people effectively to supplement their pensions, the financial plight of older people is often acute. However public sympathy for the situation of the elderly has helped to make their cause a popular one politically. In the report by the Rowntree Committee in 1947, the point was made that while continual attention had to be given to the pension issue (recently become particularly acute again), to the extent that this is dealt with, the issues become increasingly those of personal and social needs of elderly people. In this context continuing work is one way of dealing with some of the personal and social needs (Rowntree, 1947). Those with private wealth or private annuities may be better equipped financially to retire, but they also tend to be in occupations which allow them to continue indefinitely—unlike lower-skilled workers who may be forcibly retired by their employers. They may continue to practise a profession, write, sit on a board or consult until they are infirm or die. The occupational picture for older people is a mixture of historically derived patterns, with different conditions for members of different occupations or professions. There are some occupations which allow for late-life careers—magistrates, members of management committees, commissionaires, wardens, custodians, chauffeurs and some public service workers. Conditions vary by locality and by industry, and with the state of the economy. There are many paradoxical elements, such as the fact that work is becoming more agreeable and less degrading, while at the same time, the emphasis on work as a principal life interest is lessening. Different individuals, in different situations, will want different life resolutions in their later years and their employers, social service agents and families will support different patterns. It therefore seems eminently sensible to conclude as the recent OECD report did (Hackett, 1970, 89), that

there would seem everything to be gained by making retirement schemes more flexible. Flexibility is in fact an absolute 'prerequisite' for giving practical effect to such a fundamental tenet as man's right to work notwithstanding any extrinsic consideration, including that of age.

But the implementation of a flexible pattern is highly complex. Britain, with its non-compulsory pension scheme available, is in theory 'flexible'. However, there are many constraints on the individual as to whether and how he will exercise this flexibility. Apart from different occupations providing different possibilities for continuation in the late life phase, 'flexibility' is affected by the state of the economy, the state of a particular industry, the transferability of pensions or other conditions of employment. Also there is the prejudice against employing older people in the workplace, particularly in new situations where they have not built up familiar patterns and relationships. And previous educational attainment affects people's capacity to visualise what they will do when the structure of their everyday life that is provided by occupation is removed.

It is now increasingly recognised, both through social-psychological research and through impassioned pleas such as those of McErlean, that there are many positive contributions of older people to the national economy, such as reliability, judgment and loyalty. However, the prevalent negative stereotypes emphasise other features such as loss of motor capacities, memory and agility. There are moves towards legislation against age discrimination, but as yet no safeguards are universally available (Slater, 1973; McErlean, 1973).

Another set of constraints governing people's development of life styles for this phase is a complex of factors involving family and kin relations, housing and residential situations. Recent research by Shanas and her colleagues, by Rosenmayr in Vienna and by a number of British investigators including Tunstall and Crawford show that while there may be an increase in home-centredness and constriction of travel and activity, old people (at least under 75) are nowhere as isolated as has been stereotypically presumed (Shanas *et al.*, 1968; Rosenmayr, 1966; Tunstall, 1966; Crawford, 1971).

The emphasis in the past has been on the forces making for isolation of the elderly from their families. Mobility figures show the tendency for young people to move away; household composition studies show the relatively small proportions of households incorporating an elderly relative in the house (something for which our society is neither physically nor psychologically geared); mortality figures show a tendency for women to outlive their spouses and to have a lower chance of remarrying than men—making for a special sub-group of aged widows or divorcees living in relative isolation. On the other hand, it is now known that there are more relationships—and more mutually helpful relationships —being sustained across generational levels than has been presumed. Even among the two-thirds to three-quarters of households which are *not* multi-generational, the tendency is to live nearby, to visit frequently and to provide mutual assistance of various kinds (Riley *et al.*, 1968; Townsend, 1957; Rosenmayr and Köckeis, 1962). In the USA 80 per cent of older people live within an hour's drive of at least one of their children. In Great Britain and Denmark the proportion is nearly 90 per cent. The tendency to maintain proximity is stronger for individuals living in relatively intact working-class communities like Bethnal Green and in agricultural communities, than for individuals from white-collar and professional backgrounds, among whom there tends to be a greater mobility.

In general older people seem to wish to sustain as long as possible a separate household. Technological improvements and higher levels of affluence have made it possible for many to do this without losing contact with their families, even with greater geographical mobility on the children's part. If they are not part of the ageing population which lives below the poverty line and who are 'deprived and frustrated' (30 per cent in the USA), the telephone and high-speed transportation facilities enable them to keep in frequent contact, and to sustain a closeness (Andrus Gerontology Center, 1974). While these findings serve to correct older stereotypes, they also make it plain that the issues are complex. There are variations in the degree and type of family contacts sustained, and a residual group, small but important, where family supports are entirely lacking—both of one's own generation (spouse, siblings) and inter-generationally (children/grandchildren). The type and degree of family interaction in this phase is different from previous phases, and it is essential to understand the differences as well as to document the presence of such interaction if informal policies as to leisure provision are to be developed. This understanding is still very rudimentary, though some research has been directed precisely in this direction (Shanas and Streib, 1965).

What used to be referred to in terms of 'role reversals' in these relationships (the younger members become the breadwinners, the older members the dependants, the younger become the decision-makers, the older the followers, etc.) is now seen in more complex terms. New relationships are being worked out and they vary with circumstances. Sometimes a widowed grandmother will help to 'cover' the domestic scene for a young wife/mother who wishes to continue her work career, sometimes not (the grandmother herself may be still at work); sometimes a grandparent will help with domestic coverage while parents take a vacation away from home; sometimes visits by children are accompanied by practical help with housework, sometimes not; sometimes youngsters are interested in the wisdom and advice of the elderly relatives when in a personal crisis, sometimes not. The potentials of the grandparent role have often been mentioned, but they are still relatively little explored in relation to the pitfalls—for example the 'in-law problem'. Rosenmayr suggests the concept of 'revocable detachment' to describe this relationship—encompassing *some distance* (rather than isolation), but *some involvement* as well. The revocable quality cushions the relationship against potential intergenerational conflicts, but to be operated successfully requires considerable sensitivity and maturity on both sides, filial and paternal (Rosenmayr, 1966; Reichard *et al.*, 1962).

Positive potentials for the older individual include the possibility of developing a life style which is 'genuine', not status-seeking, legitimately geared to impulse gratification rather than deferring gratifications. Older people may be less constrained by 'the clock' and the 'rat race' of competitive struggle; they may as a consequence be freed to develop a sense of self-actualisation, cultivating many interests and ideas long cherished but recurrently put off because of the pressures of work performances and other responsibilities earlier in life. A number of social theorists have pointed out that in a society as affluent as ours, enjoyment of late life ought to be regarded as a 'right', something to be pursued unashamedly; retirement should be seen as having been earned rather than as a burden on the economically productive portion of the population. Older people should be seen as potential resources, using this period of their lives to pursue interests that may have social as well as personal value. Older people are potential role models for the rest, having something special to contribute with their resources of wisdom and experience, and their concern with perennial issues such as the meaning of life. Primitive societies, particularly those close to a survival level, often abandoned their oldest members to face death alone; but they also revered the elderly, and they rarely segregated them. While the most productive societies provide the greatest welfare benefits for the aged, they do not necessarily value older people most highly.

The social security system of advanced societies allows but does not facilitate this possibility for personal fulfilment and social appreciation of the elderly. Lack of facilitations is not merely neutral, it may lead to disastrous consequences, as seen in some of the negative indicators. These included isolation, apathy, depression and general deterioration of capacities as individuals move into relatively undefined, undervalued, powerless and dependent social roles. Looking at the overall picture, it would seem that we may think of the problem of developing meaningful life styles for the later years in terms of four propositions: (a) The task of reconstructing one's life style is likely to be salient in later years, whether the individual formally retires or not; (b) Some people are well equipped to approach this set of tasks, while others are less so, denying it as long as possible or even dreading it; (c) The core challenge is to evolve a life style for the later phase of life that is satisfying and enjoyable, rather than becoming dissatisfied, bitter and unhappy; (d) The development of meaningful life interests is crucial in this process. In analysing the tasks and the influences governing response to them, we consider the period of later life in three sub-phases: pre-retirement, retirement and old age.

Three phases of later life

Here we attempt to describe the phase-specific issues and preoccupations of later life. Social trends are leading to retirement being directly applicable to many women as well as men. In conventional families—where women remain housewives exclusively—the impact of the man's retirement is also great. Some people arrange not to 'retire' but to work until death or total incapacity. Others retire and find it intolerable and so re-enter work, sometimes several times until they are no longer able to do so. Not enough is known of how this is affected by people's preoccupations at this time of life. We are only beginning to go beyond studies of the impact of retirement on specific patterns of life such as consumption or housing and to ask whether there is any relevance for the way people think and feel about retirement or what interests they have cultivated earlier, to the way in which they reorganise their lives and the kinds of satisfactions they are able to derive.

Occupational retirement is an event of great magnitude in people's lives. After retirement, however, there tends to be a significant period before people are really 'old' and physically disabled. For this reason, it is sensible to divide this phase of life into at least three periods. As with preceding divisions of this kind, there are no precise ages for the transition points; both biomedical and social-administrative changes affect the boundaries. The sub-phases we distinguish in later life are imprecise, but each can usefully be thought of as having an associated preoccupation related to the larger preoccupation with integration, and each has a characteristic set of potential problems and rewards (Table 9).

Pre-retirement

Underlying the pre-retirement period is the preoccupation of *anticipation*. Occupational retirement is in the air. It may or may not be in the mind of the person entering this phase. This is a phase in which the difference in outlook between providers and the people provided for may be most marked (Rosow, 1962). Providers want people to think

Table 9 *Sub-phases of later life*

Sub-phase	Preoccupation	Potential problems	Potential rewards
Pre-retirement (55–60/65)	Anticipation of occupational retirement	If denied, inadequate provision for future	Development of new interests
Retirement (60/65–75)	Realignment of commitments	Failure to readapt, depression, withdrawal	Consummation
Old age (75 +)	Life before death	Physical incapacity and despair	Satisfaction

about preparing for retirement and their old age as early as possible. Employers, unless they are enlightened or seeking to precipitate early retirement, also tend to avoid issues about retirement (other than routine administrative provisions through pensions plans); they feel that if people think too early about their retirement, they will be less involved in their work.

The preoccupation with *anticipation* that goes on the pre-retirement phase may thus take different forms—including denial, inconsistent behaviour and the wish to hasten the process by retiring early. During the late establishment and pre-retirement periods, people may become dimly aware that they will enter the sub-population of 'older people'— after having been 'middle-aged' for some time. Moving forwards, being 'retired' has personal and social implications. Personally one is moving towards an undervalued group of people, people who may be seen as burdens on younger members of the population, and about whom there are many negative stereotypes. Many people do not want to be 'old'. Yet recognising that one is 'getting on' may be essential to planning. While there may be an anticipatory interest in older people during this period, there is sometimes an attempt to dissociate oneself from membership with that group. This accounts for a great deal of the ambivalent behaviour observed. People may feel 'there, soon, go I', and not want to know about it.

The sex imbalance which commonly begins in the late establishment phase (when the conventional wife loses her 'cardinal role' while the husband is still at the peak of his) may alter now, particularly if the wife re-enters work. Alternatively she may rebuild her life within the 'empty nest' where she concentrates on the control of day-to-day management in household affairs. A sense of estrangement between husbands and wives may develop in this period; the world of the woman intensifying more than ever on the home while that of the man consolidates around masculine associations outside. The issues of child-rearing may have reached a tension peak when the children were adolescent and the corrosive effects not yet repaired. Husband and wife may have grown apart and feel they had little in common. This is the phenomenon referred to in some American studies as the 'hollow' or 'devitalised marriage', where the couple feel it is too late to make another start (Cuber and Haroff, 1965; Rollins and Feldman, 1970; Blood and Wolfe, 1960).

A number of people have noted the reawakening of a sense of closeness to kin later in life, as well as the reawakening of religious interests. People may go far afield in search of opportunity, then return for a reunion with their parents later in life. Parents whose lives centred round their children reach a stage where they expect something back from them. In industrial societies these tendencies may be affected by the presence of support alternatives, e.g. in housing and pension schemes (Young and Geertz, 1961).

Earlier marriages and fertility have made people grandparents earlier. In the USA many become grandparents before the age of 50—in the late establishment phase. For conventional women who do not re-enter work following their children's departure from home, this provides interest as a grandparent. The potentials of the grandparent role as an aid to young families who may wish to have a more dual-worker pattern has been noted (Fogarty, 1975). Gorer has also suggested there is a mutuality in this. He notes that the 'alternating generation' relationship between grandparents and grandchildren has positive potential for both, and he suggests that schools ought to be established to cultivate it in our own society where there are so many special problems of social change (Gorer, 1961, 7-19):

It would be necessary for both men and women to attend such schools, and they would both have to bring to them a certain amount of humility. Men who have been successful in their careers would have to admit that there were areas in life about which they were ignorant; women who have raised their own children to successful adulthood would have to admit that in many cases the techniques and practices which they employed were no longer completely acceptable today—the refusal to admit this is one of the most fruitful sources of disagreement between mothers and their married daughters in this country. In such schools it might be possible for grandparents and grandchildren, or their equivalents, to attend together. Both could learn through teaching. The young can give their elders a new view of the world. The people who are now nearing retirement age

have experienced more change in their lifetime than any other
generation in the known history of the world. If they can recall and
explain this experience of change, they can greatly enrich the youngest
generation's ability to face a world in which change is likely to be
continuous.

However, recent research has indicated that the grandparents' ideal is
no panacea. First, many women will not be available for heavy investment in this role because they themselves want to go out to work
following their period of child-bearing. They may not wish to enter
their children's families in a quasi-work role, sharing the division of
labour in the household. Grandparents may wish to visit, play with
their grandchildren, go on outings and give them treats, but not to
take responsibility for them. In other instances, the reverse situation
may apply; the interest in this alternating generation relationship may
be asymmetrical with the older people being more interested in it than
the younger (Streib, 1958; Townsend, 1957; Neugarten and Weinstein,
1964). Social mobility and social change have also produced intergenerational differences in value orientations which may complicate
situations which bring them together over shared tasks. The 'in-law'
relationship has always been a problematic one, and does not disappear
with affluence and a higher general level of education. Hill and his
colleagues have found that the maintenance of a relationship between
the alternate generations often depends on active efforts at 'kin-
keeping' by the middle generation, particularly the women (Hill *et al.*,
1970).

For men, anticipatory preoccupations relate to the issues of the
world of work. The historical tendency in our society has been towards
the supervaluation of the place of work, particularly in men's lives, and
on the necessity of the male to be the breadwinner. Work also organises
most of people's waking lives, sets their patterns of relationships, and
occupies their thoughts. For men it is conventionally considered an
essential element in being 'real' men, good providers and in effect a
'good' person. The idea of living without working rouses images of a
meaningless, frightening, undefined void. For this reason, there is a
tendency (described in the research cited above) for anxiety levels to rise
to a high pitch prior to retirement. There may be a tendency to deny
the importance of the event of occupational retirement, let alone some
of the other disabilities associated with growing old. Anticipation of
some of the tasks to be performed requires an effort: to make explicit
what one's likely course will be, to face the issues and to do what is
necessary to deal with them. Modern enlightened industrialists recognise that the gold watch at retirement is not an adequate way of dealing
with the human problems of retirement; they realise 'the value of

helping their employees to plan ahead as an integral part of their personnel policy' (Adamson, 1972). Trade unions have traditionally regarded retirement reforms as a major part of their programme of social action; they have sought to bring about government action in relation to retirement and pension allowance. A variety of co-operative ventures between employers and trade unions exist. Alternatively workers desire an economic underpinning which will provide options for reorganising life styles in later life.

The ascendance of the idea of multi-careers is important in preparing for the opportunities and challenges that come when regular work ends. With the idea of recurrent education, machinery may be developed to make this idea a possibility, supplanting the now archaic notion that retirement is or ought to be a time of 'pure' leisure.

However, there are many problems both of provision and of effective delivery of such services. From the findings of basic research projects such as that at Bristol under Crawford-Hillbourne, and action pro-grammes such as those of Age Concern and the Pre-Retirement Association, it can be seen that there are a set of microsocial factors that affect the anticipatory work of reconstructing a new life style following retirement. These will be facilitated by institutional changes but will not disappear. They include: financial—the tasks of making preparation for pensions, investments, insurance, etc., well enough in advance, and understanding what is going to happen and when; legal—the tasks of preparation for making wills, transferring property, pre-paring for other legal aspects of inheritance, maintenance of control of assets, etc.; housing—the tasks of preparing to meet changes in housing needs and capacities, which have financial and legal as well as personal, familial and social aspects; health—knowing about the hazards of old age, benefits of judicious exercise, etc.; employment—assessing possibilities, types of jobs and problems; voluntary work—discovering openings, assessing feasibility, creating new possibilities; new interests —training, education, development of hobbies, enterprises; personal adjustment—dealing with feelings about loss of roles, doing preparatory work for new roles, developing self-concept for later life; familial relations—dealing with new patterns of family relations, between the generality and between husbands and wives.

These topics—which form the framework for many pre-retirement courses—reflect the experience both of research and of professional practice, that the readjustments at this phase involve the whole gamut of life sectors. Individuals reorganising their lives vary in resourceful-ness, and consequently in the degree to which they need personal assistance. It is for older people, however, that the paradox of demand is most apparent. That is, the healthier, more highly educated and economically self-sufficient are the more active and show the highest demand for services of all kinds; and it is they who do the most effective preparatory work towards reorganisation of their lives as they move into this stage. Consequently, providers of services and facilities—for example in the pre-retirement association—are confronted with the challenge of how to reach the less active, less resourceful, less expressive individuals. It is these people who are at risk for negative outcomes as the existential challenges of this life phase overtake them.

A key issue, especially for leisure provision, is how to counteract the stereotype that older people are disadvantaged, disabled, incapable of cultivating new interests and building new life styles for later life. This is commonly believed both by the public at large and by the individual person traversing this life-cycle transition. The perpetuation of negative stereotypes of elderly people's learning capacities, even within educational institutions, is a barrier to the further development of appropriate programmes. Breakthrough into the development of new programmes will require the capacity to grapple with entrenched pessimism within the field as well as with the intrinsic social and educational challenge. But there are some grounds for optimism.

First, there is the morale issue. To the extent that the capacity to learn, to develop new interests, or express interests in activities, is a function of educational level, there is room for optimism. The minimum age of school-leaving has risen since the present retiring population went to school in the early decades of the century and there is a tendency for pupils to stay on longer than the statutory minimum age. In 1961 about half the pupils left school at the minimum age, whereas in 1971 only a third did. Also more people take adult education courses of one kind or another and the orientation to learning has become more active.

Belbin, in a report testing out in various settings his earlier work on the Discovery Method of training as applied to older people, demonstrated the utility of the method. While his work is on people in the late establishment phase, it is relevant for older people as well. He states (1969, 22):

> The results of the four projects taken together seem to justify the conclusion that with appropriate training at an age higher than usual for training (covering an age span 41–55) constitutes no serious disadvantages. The gain from using these methods adequately compensates the older learner from the loss of learning ability attributable to age and often produces a situation of near parity between younger and older learners.

The issue of *preparing older people for developing other interests has been relatively less explored*. Nevertheless, the emphasis on permanent or recurrent education is gaining ground internationally. The importance of morale in self-directed learning has been taken into account by a number of experiments from William Morris's times through contemporary experiments in non-vocational adult education. People with cultivated interests have been found to have a greater repertoire with which to face retirement than those who have lower educational attainments and a lower level of cultivated interests prior to retirement (Havighurst, 1954). However, there is no direct continuity, and many studies show that interests and activities which may have been functional previously lose their appeal or their feasibility in retirement. Many earlier interests develop as a counterpoint to work. Where work is stimulating, interests making for solitude and rest may have been cultivated and this may be counter-productive for post-retirement interests. Similarly family pursuits may be neither as attractive nor as feasible in the later life stages when children have left home to set up their own families. Costly pursuits may become inaccessible on reduced income. There are new problems of synchronisation of retired people's interests in the context of a community life organised around the rhythms of the workaday world.

For all these reasons, the issues surrounding the development of interests which are satisfying in later life are not confined to the less educated. Those with more highly cultivated interests and the habit of learning—whether developed in the formal educational system through recurrent training, or on a hobby basis—are more responsive but they too may need to be facilitated in realigning their interests and activities to meet the new situations they confront.

The issues surrounding the *marital relationship* are also complex. The post-parental phase in people's lives has lengthened. Most couples can think of fifteen years or more of active life following their children's departure from the home. During this period, wives may begin a new occupational career and the husbands may retire. Husbands and wives tend to confront one another on more equal terms than in the late establishment phase, when both are at work or a little later, when both are at home. The data suggests that this is a period of challenge. There may either be a *rapprochement* and the basis for a new couple relationship, or there may be estrangement (Goldberg, 1970). A case study illustrates the processes described in the pre-retirement sub-phase.

THE ALLPORTS. Dr Allport is a physicist working for a government research laboratory. When he and his wife were interviewed, they were at the threshold of the pre-retirement period—he was 55 and she 55. They live in a semi-detached house on an estate associated with the scientific research unit where he works. They have lived there for many years and are well established in the community which is based largely on work associations.

Family background. Dr Allport's father was an engineering draughts-man in the North-east who died when Dr Allport was 14—the year he took his O-level examinations. The family was in relatively tight financial straits thereafter. His mother took in lodgers and when his grandmother died both houses were sold and another bought for the joint household.

Early on in his life it was recognised that he had good academic ability and his teachers groomed him for a Cambridge scholarship in mathematics. One of the school-masters who was also a Scout-master showed an interest in his non-vocational education and, for example, introduced him to foreign travel by way of a trip to Belgium. This was his first contact with another culture. He went on to Cambridge where he got first-class honours in mathematics and physics.

Mrs Allport's father was a wine and spirits merchant in Scotland until his business 'dried up' when the district went 'dry'. He then moved to North-east England. Having been badly hit psychologically by the collapse of his business, he was seeking a new job. He had always been 'handy with a spanner', was a keen cyclist and got a job as a maintenance man in a steel works on the North-east coast. The family grew up in this area, sharing an interest in music and other community activities. There was a close family feeling which persists, and the brothers and sisters and their families usually gather at Christmas to the present day, though both parents have long since died.

The Allports met at school and married during the war.

Work history. Dr Allport always did well in science and mathematics. He studied mathematics at Cambridge, and then changed to physics because he had always enjoyed the subject at school. He entered the Services in the Second World War with no clear career objective. He worked briefly as a physicist in Canada following the end of the war, but returned to England after marriage, taking a job with a government laboratory. He has remained committed to this laboratory with few regrets ever since. There were several other options in the course of his career that he might have taken up. Occasionally he wonders if they might have been better for him—one in medical research, one in another research lab, and two in universities—but he is now in a senior adminis-trative post and does not think of further developments within his profession—in or out of his employing organisation.

Mrs Allport was trained and worked as a secretary until the birth of her first child. She has not had serious occupational aspirations. While she does not like some aspects of housework, she knew from the begin-ning that it would be that way, and has determined to do the whole job as well as she can, taking the boring with the gratifying and making a package of it.

She considers that one of the most important aspects of her job as wife and mother has been to be available for the children while they were still living at home. The three children went to nearby schools and often one or another of them would come home for lunch. When this happened she was able to really sit and talk with them one at a time; she feels that parents who do not do this really miss one of life's most valuable experiences.

Like Dr Allport, Mrs Allport also harbours occasional thoughts about alternatives, for example, wishing that she had obtained a teaching qualification so that she could return to teaching now that her children are grown. One interest that she has cultivated is pottery, which she took up in the early years of her marriage and continued to do. Though she has had some tentative ideas of turning this into more than a diversionary interest, she has so far not done so.

Family history. The Allports are now alone in their house following the launching of their three children. The eldest daughter, nearly 30, is in Canada. A second daughter, who is married in London, has a degree in mathematics and a job in the civil service. Their son is studying at a polytechnic.

The family was always organised along conventional lines, Mrs Allport doing the child-care, cooking, cleaning, sewing and routine domestic work (with help 1–2 mornings per week) and Dr Allport doing the repairs and gardening in which she joins.

While the children were young, they both rose early and he was off to work and the children to school. He worked long hours when he was a laboratory scientist; though sometimes difficult for her, she reckons that it is wrong for a wife to resent her husband's absence at work. The strains were perhaps greatest when the children were going through their O- and A-level examinations and needed a good deal of attention. The family also experienced 'normal' adolescent rebelliousness which they considered 'healthy' and below average, but which caused some anxiety and tension in the family. The elder daughter was an adolescent when the Allports were in the USA for a year, and when she took on some of the precocious habits of American high-schoolers her parents were dismayed.

Now that the children are away Mrs Allport rises later, so Dr Allport usually makes his own breakfast, gives her a cup of tea in bed and departs. Their evenings are now more free because he no longer has his time dominated by laboratory experiments lasting until all hours, though he travels more.

Life interests. Dr Allport does not distinguish his 'leisure' interests from other things he likes doing at work and at home. He enjoys his work, though he would have preferred to keep in touch with the scientific side of things and often finds the administrative problems of getting the bureaucracy to move frustrating. In earlier years, he was highly absorbed in his work but kept a number of other interests going—choir, chess club, tennis, bird-watching, reading, listening to music, theatre and gardening.

The Allports helped to keep some boundaries in the family by making individual bed-times for the children, and by defining territories for activities—for example, homework in the children's own rooms, the main room for the parents, or for family group activities such as card-games before the children's bed-time.

Mrs Allport finds certain aspects of her domestic work enjoyable, such as the cooking. Gardening they define as 'work' when they have to do it whether they feel like it or not, and as 'leisure' when they do it because they feel like it. Dr Allport's approach to his non-work interests is like his approach to his work. He makes a list of things that need doing and goes around doing them (or getting them done) and ticking them off the list.

Dr Allport was active in sports and in scouting in his youth; Mrs Allport ran a Brownie pack. Both have had a consistent interest in music. A recent development in Dr Allport's interests is associated with his moving into an administrative job and missing the scientific side. He has developed an interest in the application of science to the study of archaeological remains, and thinks that he may pursue this interest in retirement.

Mrs Allport has been developing her pottery interest, spending most of one day a week at the local technical college. She also enjoys the company that goes with a class. Both have been active in the local community, entertaining and eating out with friends. They have tended to go out on average about once a week—for example to theatre, dinner or visit.

Dr Allport now feels that he would like to retire on the early side of the 60–65 range, and perhaps develop his archaeological interest. They are likely to want to stay in their home, enjoying frequent visits from their children, and now grandchildren. Mrs Allport would like to continue to develop artistic activities—perhaps getting her own pottery wheel.

Retirement

The experience of the retirement period has its own cycle, at first involving something like a holiday with a sense of relief or euphoria, a 'honeymoon' quality. Then there may be a time of depression, apathy and withdrawal after frustrating experiences; the duration of this varies and may be followed by effective realignments, personal and social.

This is the pivotal period in later life phases, with *realignment* as its focal preoccupation. There is much awareness that retirement is a life crisis for which many people are unprepared; that it takes them into a life-cycle stage in which society does not provide adequate social roles; that it has specific health, economic, familial and social problems associated with it, that can make it traumatic (like becoming redundant or becoming chronically ill and disabled) rather than developmental, as with transitions that have more obvious regenerative potentials (such as marriage, childbirth).

Problems of money, social relationships, health and housing dominate the concerns of people in this phase. The issues of social relationships and meaningful life interests continue throughout the phase, making for potential threads of continuity.

Earnings affect not only consumption patterns, but some continue to work and to earn at levels not appreciably diminished by their age. But for every Picasso, Rubinstein, De Gaulle, or Oliver Wendell Holmes, there are many more individuals who are manifestly slower, manifestly less alert, manifestly less self-confident as they enter these later years. If they work at all, they gravitate towards less demanding jobs—and correspondingly lower-paying and lower-status ones. This is less a problem for individuals who do not depend on their jobs for their self-esteem; it may not be difficult for a street-cleaner to consider redeploying himself as a caretaker, or a maintenance man to consider redeploying as a groundsman; but for a manager to take on such tasks may require psychological adjustments of a fairly radical kind. On the other hand, professional and managerial workers have greater financial, occupational and other resources for redeployment of their activities which may ameliorate the problem of readjustment following retirement.

Anxieties about illness, and being separated from one's loved ones when one may need help, tend to increase with age. There is often a period of high anxiety about what one can do physically to feel safe and yet not to be a burden, particularly if one is alone in this period. Because of the high mortality rate of males in the immediate post-retirement period, many widows confront the dilemma of what combination of work, family relations and new housing will be viable.

Each new generation of retiring people has a different history and set of experiences, so some of their problems change in character; but it is important to seek to understand the experience for the relatively constant and enduring elements. One of the more influential of studies is the work by Cumming and Henry (1961), which posits the 'disengagement hypothesis' that seeks to do this. The theory of disengagement was put forward as a counter-proposition to an earlier sociological theory—that of 'engagement' which was developed by Cavan and others. The earlier theory proposed that the most satisfying life integrations would be found where there was continuity between middle and old age. This theory implied that a high level of activity and involvement should continue throughout life, though suitable substitutes would obviously have to be found when people are forced physically to relinquish earlier activity patterns because of ageing (Cavan *et al.*, 1949). Cumming and Henry's work on retirement concentrated rather on the finding that old people tend to seek social withdrawal following retirement. They found that retired people not only gave up their occupational life, but also many other relationships, showing a general decline in commitment to social norms and values. Cumming and Henry's interpretation of their findings was that the increasing withdrawal into self-gratifying interests and activities, is a developmental process and that the multiple role disengagement facilitates this rather than produces it. Withdrawal, according to their view, is functional for the individual as well as for society in that it prepares the ageing person for his approaching terminal withdrawal and minimises the effect of death on himself and the social system (Cumming and Henry, 1961).

The prevailing view by Rose, Talmon and others is that both theories have some relevance (Rose, 1964; Talmon, 1968). Continuous engagement means continuous meaning in life and social relationships, and gives structure to activities. On the other hand, it may perpetuate a life of strain, it validates the whole complex of work/effort and activity as the most worthwhile pursuits and does not allow for the cultivation of enjoyment values. The kind of disengagement that Cumming and Henry describe does occur and may have some of the functions they attribute to it, but it is not intrinsically biological (as Talmon and others who have done cross-cultural work have demonstrated) and it is not even universal within our society. In Britain the disengagement hypothesis has been found to have only limited applicability (Bracey, 1966; Crawford, 1971). In Crawford's study both men and women divide about evenly as they approach retirement as to whether they have predominantly positive or predominantly negative orientations to the impending transition. For both, but particularly for the favourably orientated, the findings are that the anticipations may often be short-lived. This is consistent with the findings of Jacobsohn reported above. Crawford goes more into the implications for the marital relationship. She found in her study of English couples in Bristol that the retirement event has different significance for wives and husbands—as might be expected given the differences of the place of work in the lives of conventional men and women in our society. Husbands tend to be less keen in anticipation about having more time with their wives after retirement than are wives. This is particularly true for husbands whose previous enjoyment has centred on masculine company in the workplace. Thirty-five per cent of wives (the highest proportion of responses) indicated that seeing more of their spouses was one of the pleasant elements anticipated about retirement; only 15 per cent of the husbands chose this aspect (Crawford, 1971). The lack of planning for what people will do as a family after retirement has been one of the main findings of a number of studies in the 1960s (see, for example, Kerckhoff, 1966; Prasad, 1964).

This contrast by sex and men's lack of awareness of the implications both for themselves and for their wives of the retirement transition is extremely important. In conventional families where there is a sharp segregation of male and female roles, neither the men nor the women are prepared for what is to happen. Many men tend not to understand that their wives have a personal life organised around the central fact that men are not there during the work days; and many women accordingly find it difficult to incorporate a masculine presence around the house for more than the accustomed times. One wife is reported as saying, 'I married him for better or worse, but not for lunch'.

These contrasts are related to social class as well as family structure. Manual workers are less negatively oriented to retirement than nonmanual workers, presumably because their relative drop in income is less and the intrinsic satisfactions in their jobs which have to be given up at retirement are also less. However, manual workers find it more difficult to adjust to a home- and family-centred pattern following retirement, and are less resourceful in developing new interests. Middle-class workers are more equipped to deal with the realignment tasks from a relearning point of view, and may be relatively familistic in their values, but they may experience the status-loss more severely. In this Crawford's British findings agree with those of Rosow in the USA, where the pattern of middle-class workers is to deny the ageing process and dissociate themselves as long as possible from identifying with their age-mates (Rosow, 1967).

More is known about the retirement sub-population as a population at risk (from apathy, depression, suicide, loneliness and so on) than about their happiness potentials. We know from studies of the family cycle that though the tendency is for happiness and satisfaction to decline from a pinnacle at early marriage, there tends to be, under some conditions, an up-turn in late life, when couples make a new relationship with children in the background and work optional. Data from studies like those of Blood and Wolfe, and Rollins and Feldman, show a 'U'-shaped enjoyment career, taking marital satisfaction as the main variable—with a high point just after marriage and the lowest point when the children are adolescents still at home. Strains are high and the romantic elements in the marital relationship itself may have worn thin by this time. This may be followed by a renewal or enriched quality of attachment following the departure of the children, in the late establishment phase. Then the curve may either continue to rise or decline slightly again following retirement. The more negative possibilities, with the emphasis on estrangement in this period, are reported in the East London studies and in Kansas City (Blood and Wolfe, 1960; Young and Willmott, 1957; Rollins and Feldman, 1970; Cumming and Henry, 1961). Factors making for more positive outcome for happiness in old age (despite the constraints of lower income, ageing and the social problems of withdrawal of family and of social esteem) are less well documented.

Three ways are suggested as leading to an increase in the positive outcomes in this period, and minimising the negative outcomes. The first is implied in the work of Emery and Trist, and of the people like Schutz who specialise in recovering people's capacity for joy (Emery and Trist, 1973; Shutz, 1967). They relate this to the achievement of a better understanding of one's inner life motivations, inhibitions, conflicts and so on. Emery and Trist note, basing their observations on psychoanalytic work, that the depressive tendency is one that has lifelong relevance. It is given structure in infancy in the handling of the negative feelings towards the mother, who is the source of most of life's earliest pleasures and enjoyments. The complexities of handling feelings of love and hate, of anger and envy, of optimism and despair early in life become critical as foundations for the achievement of happiness in later life.

A second approach is more at the level of how people organise their lives. Beric Wright's approach reflects this preventive medical stance (1972, 9):

> the man who dies of a broken heart soon after retirement is a classic case of too little challenge or stresslessness. He has his house, his pension and his family, but he has lost his identity, his purpose and his status. He has nothing to do and nowhere to go—so he fizzles gently out from emotional deprivation. Success in retirement depends on a lot of things . . . but one of the most important factors is happily to shed the anxieties, or boredom, pressure and routine of going to work every day and replacing them with purposeful enjoyable activity which keeps you gently on the hop until bed-time.

Third, there is a more social approach that is associated with the construction of new communities with the express purpose of creating life styles that foster enjoyment and happiness in older people. Two recent articles give accounts of life in those purpose-built retirement communities. 'The Affluent Ghetto' describes the idea of an 'age-group ghetto' as a new development in American styles of living. Older Americans with sufficient funds have clubbed together in Sun Cities, which have become sufficiently profitable to mushroom in many states in the USA. These are 'fun-oriented towns' where no resident under 50 is allowed and where many of the citizens are, as they say, '80 years young'. Some of the Sun Cities, sometimes called 'Leisure Worlds' or 'Youngtowns', are part of the new emphasis in the USA on creating purpose-built environments to suit specific life styles. In these cities cultural patterns are preserved, 'like flies in amber', according to the tastes of the age groups that inhabit them; and they are able to live happily together without fear of riots, hippies, smog, campus unrest or inter-racial tensions. 'The world outside [can go] clean mad', but it need not affect them (Leslie, 1971).

Such age-graded communities have many advantages. No one disparages the people in them for being old; they need not feel disadvantaged in terms of keeping up with anything and obsolescence is slowed down by slowing down change in the environment. These communities are not swept with new fads and fashions, but with reminiscences—in the music, films and events that were shared in the past. Ceramic classes, 'slim-and-trim' clubs, tricycles for old ladies are available to all, erstwhile wallflower spinsters become once again mainstream members of the community way of life.

In 'Radical Retirement Chic', a preventive interventionist view is taken and retirement is defined as potentially an age for the realisation of one's most meaningful life goals (Harris, 1973). Summarising the Canadian research and experience, Harris notes that what differentiates those who experience this phase as a negative one (withdrawing, feeling embittered and a failure) and those who experience it positively (keeping active, sociable, or at least enjoying their choice of passivity and relaxation) is whether or not they have planned for it. At the heart of this is the process of self-examination, definition of personal goals, assessment of means and resources and planning to make the two come as close as possible from as early a date as possible. If this is successful, it is possible to enter the retirement phase and arrange what one wills as a life style—travel, change of residence to a warmer climate, a later-career enterprise of some kind, further education, sport or voluntary community work. In Canada, as in the USA, there are retirement villages which create environments which cater for the tastes of old people (less noise, less rowdy behaviour, attention to landscaping and other amenities) and above all provide friendly communities. Canadian planners (as in the USA) are discussing the possibility of communal living groups for the elderly, an idea which is a reality in Sweden.

Thinking positively about how to make the post-retirement phase of life an enjoyable one is *not* to be confused with Utopian thinking. The Canadian counterpart of the English idealised notion of a seaside cottage is a farm away from noise, dirt, pollution and close to nature. This may be a Utopian ideal or not, depending on how aware the individuals are of the realistic issues, and how prepared they are to cope with them. Harris notes that people are better equipped to cope if they know of the higher mortality rates in rural areas, and therefore take precautions to assure good contact with medical services. In parts of Canada there are hazards that become known to year-round dwellers (such as five feet of snow for weeks on end) that casual vacation visitors do not see. This is comparable to the experience among British retirees, who find that year-round living on the Costa del Sol or Mallorca may be less fulfilling than they had thought from holiday visits. Canadians and Americans like travelling but the reality-testing approach requires that elderly people recognise that they are no longer teenagers, and may require different modes of travel and accommodation than when they were youth hostelling. The keynote of this community approach to building a new life style in retirement is enjoyment. The power of the community's sanctions must, in many instances, be strong to undo the effects of earlier conditioning. People now retiring have been taught to devalue non-work activities, to feel guilty about doing things for sheer enjoyment, to defer gratification and to worry about the future. The 'new lease on life' that emerges in such communities seems to be in dealing with immediate problems of organising time enjoyably. It also seems to be able to override psychological problems of facing eventual disablement and death. Bringing the process out into the open seems to be useful for people who are experiencing it. There are no terrors as great as those generated in the unconscious mind about such very fundamental and primitive concerns as who is going to look after one, bury one and perhaps shed a tear at one's grave. The answers to these questions are provided in these age-graded specialised life-style communities, so that the business of cultivating meaningful life interests for the life before death can be got on with.

There are no age-graded specialised communities of this type in Britain, though some local areas are heavily populated with older people, and there are some purpose-built housing developments for the elderly. Many British retired people try to cope in the ways described in the two cases which follow, of ordinary working-class people, lacking either in the wherewithal for bungalows by the sea of the environment for bespoke life-style communities.

MR WILKINS is a retired Jack-of-all-trades. He attended a pre-retirement course the year before retiring but he continues to work at the same job from which he has officially retired. He characterises himself as a working man, born of working-class parents. His family background was somewhat complex, and the history of events in his family contributed to his present orientation that life is pretty well stacked against him, no matter how hard he tries.

Family background and early interests. Mr Wilkins's father was a sheet-metal worker. His father's father was a shop-keeper in Soho, who ran off with a French girl and subsequently made a lot of money in France. He died rich but left all his money to his French family. His mother, who was a cripple, came from a wealthy family who had lost everything in a bank crash. On her side of the family were King's Counsellors, Grand Masters in the Freemasons and other luminaries, and a lot of money which never saw the light of day as far as Mr Wilkins was concerned. He had two brothers, one of whom was killed in the First World War.

So Mr Wilkins began life 'at the bottom'. He left school at the age of 15, when his father was out of work and his mother already crippled. He 'stopped' at a firm for about eight years with the idea of becoming an apprentice in an interior decorator's firm. He found that he was too old to be apprenticed, so simply worked to learn the trade informally.

When he was young, and continuing to some extent through his life, Mr Wilkins was very athletic. He belonged to an athletic club in central London and he used to run, jump, box, wrestle and do weight-lifting with the club. During the war, when he worked as a fire warden, he rowed for the Fire Service. He felt that he might have been an outstanding athlete:

'I threw my chances away. I don't think there was anyone to touch me at the time but I wouldn't take it serious. Racing, the first race that I ever had was a novice's race. I done twenty-five miles in 1·11. That was on steel and I was still learning; I had a new bike—only got it on Saturday and rode it in the race on Sunday. The fastest was only 1·6.'

He feels that what he lacked was someone to facilitate his development:

'If I had had somebody to give me the right instructions. . . . I can train people now but there are very few people around who do it. You can pick a fellow out, a very good chap, a boxer say, light, fast, precise, he knows what he's going to do. He doesn't get any encouragement. There's no one in this country will pull him out, push him, organise him into a team to work together. We haven't got that. Or, a chap that runs. See the way he places his feet, the way his toes come down, you watch these things. You say, he'll make a good runner—a good ten-miler there.'

While Mr Wilkins recognises that there are some people who are trying to do this—for example, coaches encouraged by Sports Council support—he feels that there are too many people who are out to do others down:

'There was a chap in our club that was boxing along with me, and he was one of the finest boxers that ever could be on the market. He was smart. He was clean. So what happened? He was too good for his grade, so they put him up against a good chap, gave him a good hiding and he wasn't interested any more. What did they say? "That'll take him down a peg or two." Chap loses interest that way. He says that's enough. Same thing happened to me. I was wrestling and there was nobody on the team good enough. So, I wrestled with the instructor. I beat him three falls to one—bang, bang, bang. But up went his hand. They gave him the medal. Why? Because they said he was more scientific. I said, if that's wrestling, that's it.'

This thread, beginning with his family background, going through his interests and job history, completes over and over the cycle of quick interest, disappointment, and a feeling of having been done in by unfair forces. He feels that his mother's father instilled in him certain qualities which, while virtuous, have often led to his own defeat. His father, whom he refers to as a 'proper Victorian', taught him always to be truthful and honest, never to be a cheat:

'I'll be truthful and tell the truth. I'm no good at telling lies because if you tell one, you've got to tell another to cover it and you can't remember the first one. If I don't like something, I'll tell you straight what I think.'

This policy of being straight and expecting others to be the same way has got him into many experiences which have disillusioned him and left him bitter. The story continues with his father's wartime experiences and after:

'When my brother was killed in the war, the insurance people caught my mother for half of what she ought to have had on the policy because he was killed in the Battle of Jutland, on a ship that was sunk. As the policy paid £20 to cover expenses and he didn't need a burial, they only paid her £10.'

Mr Wilkins has a very pronounced 'they'-orientation towards governments and large organisations:

'I could turn your hair at what goes on, if I had the right time and the right place, what they do and what they don't do. These big organisations, they've got a line and they will not draw over that line that says fullstop or comma . . . that's where you end, and you can't go over that. That's that. Now their policy stated in the event of death you get so much and so much—I don't know if it said anything about war risks or anything else like that, I was too young to know. But she went down to the insurance office and all they would give her is half money. . . .

I'll give you another case. In the newspapers they used to have insurance. If you took the *Daily Chronicle* or whatever it was for so many weeks, you were insured. Now the old lady joined that insurance. She had the papers regular. She fell off a chair putting the curtains up and she didn't break her ankle, but she had two large lumps from milk fever and walked like a cripple. She went to the doctor and he said get back home to bed and I'll come and see you . . . you must stop in bed if you mean to get compensation, which she did. She wrote to the paper, and they sent a man down. He said, "What happened?" She said, "I was on that chair, I fell off the chair and hurt my leg." "Right, then what happened?" "I went to the doctor." "I see," he says. We got a letter a few days later. "You were not totally incapacitated. You went to the doctor." That was the catch, in the small print, you had to be totally incapacitated. There's only one way to be totally incapacitated. That's if you're dead. They've got you every time.'

Mr Wilkins's work history has a similar collection of experiences, culminating with his dilemma about retirement. After having left his first job to take up what he thought was going to be an apprenticeship in decorating but which turned out to be a decorator's mate's job, he had a series of job experiences many of which had the same character. When he was in his twenties, the economy was in trouble and he had to go without work periodically. Added to this, his mother died and his father was left living with him and his brother. One of Mr Wilkins's jobs was with a sheet-metal company. He met one of his workmate's sisters. She was a 'local girl, worked at the same factory at the same time'. Her father had been a foreman at the company but had been 'discarded' and as a widower was living with his children. The decision to marry was linked closely with Mr Wilkins's next change of job. Mr Wilkins's girlfriend suffered from pleurisy. Her doctor was a member of an exiled group of European élites who had a club. The club needed a husband–wife couple to live in and work as steward/stewardess:

'[The doctor said to her] "You're not in a fit condition to live in a house all on your own, with sisters and brothers you're looking after, as you're the oldest, and looking after your father. That's why you're ill. You're run down . . . now, if you were married, I know of this job at the club, where you get so much a year, so much for dinners, so much for teas, so much for shoes and odds and ends, and rent-free, a very good job." He said "If you were married! Your young man, has he mentioned getting married?" She said "I've only been going with him six months." Well, anyway, knowing the conditions I was living under at home—it was like a prison—when she spoke to me about this, I said "How long does it take to get married?" She said "I don't know." I said "Find out." And she found out that you could get a special licence and be married in three days for £2.10s.'

Given the bad housing conditions on both sides, he said that she should tell the doctor that they'd take the job, and they did. But it did not turn out as painted. The place was 'full of ex-nobility who treated you like dirt'. He told them after a while, that if this was the way they treated people where they came from, he could understand their having been pushed out:

> 'I was up at four o'clock in the morning getting the boilers ready for the hot water for bathing; cleaning the shoes, then out to the tennis courts to pull the roller round—that was hell to pull around. I was pretty tough in those days but it was getting me down. I'd be up 'til three o'clock with one of their parties, then up again at half past four. I got no sleep. My feet were wrecked. In the end I had such a row that I said I'm not having this any more. They told me to get out. Instant dismissal.'

He went back to decorating work but it was sporadic and uncertain. What he was able to save in the good seasons, he used up in the bad. He worked with the Fire Service for a few months during the war as a dispatch rider:

> 'The house got blown up, I got injured. I got phlebitis, thrombosis, cerenitis, and something else as well. I'd been in the Fire Service three months, three weeks and four days but because I hadn't been there four months they stopped my pay. So I had no money coming and I was left with a game leg. . . . I went back and they offered me some charity but I slung it back at them. I gave it back as soon as I was on my feet.'

It was at this point, after the further misfortune of having had his wallet stolen with all his savings in it, that Mrs Wilkins decided to go out to work. She got a job 'collecting' (rents) and eventually went on to the office staff at the Council. By this time their first child was in school. Mr Wilkins tried going into the decorating business for himself but his hard luck pursued him relentlessly:

> 'I was working for twelve solid months on my own—doing well. Suddenly it broke, kicked the ladder from under my feet again. It rained and it poured for six solid weeks. I couldn't get inside work and the few pounds I'd saved went. So I lost that. Every time I get so far and then something like that happens.'

Mr Wilkins's estrangement from his brother came about through similar circumstances. Once when Mr Wilkins was out of work, a friend who was working for a company that pressed gramophone records told him that good money could be had on piecework there. He applied for the job and was told that it was a skilled job. He asked if he could work without pay while he learned and he was allowed to do this. He continued doing this job in winter, between decorating jobs. Once when his brother was out of work, he came looking for a job. But Mr Wilkins wasn't able to get him in. This so upset him that he became spiteful:

'He had a very jealous nature and when I couldn't get him a job, he thought I'd done it deliberately. Now when the summertime was coming on, and the record orders were only coming in small batches, you know it was time to pack up and get back to building work before all the jobs were taken up. Then later on, I was out of work for twelve weeks, walked over half of London and couldn't find a job. I'd asked my brother and he told me there was nothing at his place. Then someone told me that they was crying out for people down there for the past three months—just took on two yesterday. When I told them that my brother worked there, they said "didn't he tell you?" I said "No, he said it was full up." They said "If I had a brother like that I'd know what to do with him." So when I saw my brother I told him what I thought of him and we never spoke after that.'

Later the brother died without Mr Wilkins knowing though his wife was a second cousin. The relationship had degenerated completely.

At one point of unemployment, Mr Wilkins was walking around and noticed some men working on the canals. He asked the chap in charge if they had any work for a maintenance man and he said that he would be willing to start right away. He was given the job and has been with the waterways ever since, over twenty years.

Even this experience, however, has been tainted by the workings of a cold bureaucracy. Though his job was regular and he has been able to save, he found out only at the end of his career that he was not eligible for a new improved pension scheme which came in after he was too old to join. As a consequence, he has continued working on a reduced basis with the waterways. He says that because he is such a good and willing worker, they not only keep him on but send him on awkward jobs. So, once again, as a consequence of his honesty and competence, he gets the worst of things. If there is an awkward repair job on a lock that involves shifting heavy timbers, for example, he will suggest that they send someone younger who's lounging about. The reply is: 'No use sending him. He'll only make a botch of it.' As a consequence he gets landed with the hardest jobs.

After they left their job at the club and Mr Wilkins went back to decorating work, Mrs Wilkins became a full-time housewife. They had their first child after eleven years of marriage—a boy—and she remained at home until he was in school. After Mr Wilkins lost his savings while unemployed, she went out to work and took a job as a council rent-collector. When one of the collectors was coshed, they considered that the job was too dangerous and she went to work in the accounts office of a local firm:

> 'She's pretty good at figure work you see. I'm no mug myself when it comes to figures, so we worked it between us. Anything she got stuck in, we worked out together. The mistake she made was not paying the full stamp, she could have packed up work at 60 and drawn the full pension. But like everything else, unless someone sits down and tells you, puts you wise, you lose it.'

The trouble is, he adds, that sometimes people sit down with you and tell you not to worry and as a consequence you are still landed in trouble: 'In those days people didn't realise that if they'd go into an insurance scheme, it would guarantee them an income.' Mrs Wilkins worked on that job until her next child arrived and then dropped out for three years; after that she returned to work for the Council where she is still in their accounts office.

Family history. The Wilkins's married when he was 22 and his wife two years younger. She was working in the same firm as he and they then took a job together in a club as steward and stewardess. She stopped work when her husband went back to decorating and until her first child was in school. There was a twelve-year gap about which we have little information.

After working for a period of about twelve years (there is a gap of sixteen years between the age of the two sons) the second child arrived. Mr Wilkins said that he does not know about his wife but he had in mind having another child as a way of holding together the marriage, because with all his troubles and her working, 'things were coming apart a bit'. Having the second child caused only a three-year interruption in her career, and when she resumed again they proceeded on a more even keel.

The two boys are now grown; one still lives at home and the other is married. The married son works for a banking and investment company as a bond salesman and is doing very well. He seems to be firmly entrenched in a middle-class life style, and his parents see him and his family once a week: 'He's got a nice house on the green; he has two children and good luck to him.' His son has given him advice about investment bonds and insurance, but 'it's too late now. I've missed the bus'. Also, though he works for a big and wealthy company with investments all over the world, he himself has everything put into his house—paying off the mortgage: 'Interest rates are so great now that it takes what he earns to pay his way.' Mr Wilkins regards this as something they, as a family, have let the boy do, rather than expecting him to repay them.

The younger son, though still single, also has his own house, which he is paying off with the earnings from a good job. He was always good at art and would have liked to become an artist. However, the teacher at school discouraged art as a career. Mr Wilkins says:

'Here again you get led up the garden path. The chap at the school said to me about this boy: "He's a beautiful artist, drawing—wonderful." So I went to see a chap who is an art master, and he said: "Don't put him into art, whatever you do. There's no money in art." So I said: "Right, go to the tech., son, and learn a trade. Engraving." '

He went to tech. and learned engraving, but when he got his first job as a photogravure worker, things came to grief over a conflict between work and leisure interest:

'He went into the job, taking the training. He also belonged to the Scouts. And they wanted one of the boys to go to France. After he'd been there for a year, he was entitled to one week's holiday. Now, the stay in France was two weeks. He asked the governor if he could have two weeks holiday, one extra week, and he said "No." I said: "Well look son, I've kept you for sixteen years and I can keep you for another one. You go to France. It might be your only opportunity. You take your week, then take another week. If he says anything, well it's up to him. If you're a good chap, they'll keep you." '

This attempt to stretch the system might have worked out except that when the boy returned from France he was suffering from dysentery and could not return to work for three weeks. He lost the job. Following that he worked for a while in an estate agent's office, then entered the Services and trained as a cipher. After returning from service in the Far East, he took a job with a large insurance company and is now a district manager.

Retirement transition: problems of integration. Because Mrs Wilkins has not paid her national insurance stamps, she could not begin drawing her pension at 60. Because Mr Wilkins was not eligible for the company pension scheme in his own employment, he had to depend on a lower level of pension than he might have had. This has meant that both of them have continued working past the age at which they would have liked to retire so as to accumulate enough money to do what they would really like to do:

'I'd like to go down to the country, buy a nice little house and have a boat. I had a little place lined up that I thought would be nice. My wife's got a sister on the South coast. Her husband is 79, an electrician and a very nice fellow. He says to me, "I wish you was down here with me. When you're on your own, it's pretty tough going." I said, "Yes, if I could come down there, we'd have a boat, do a bit of fishing, we'd cultivate the garden, grow our own veg. and we'd go out and enjoy ourselves, buy a car, drive around." "I wish you could get down here," he said. "So do I," I said. We kept that in mind. "If I hear of anything I'll let you know," he said. Then I applied first of all to the local council, then to the place down the coast. I told them that there were places down there, but they said "You're not eligible." It seems I just can't get away from them. You see, if I could just get a little place down in the country near the seashore. I don't want much, just a little place in the country. And I can't get it because they turn to you if you're 65 and say it's not for you.'

Mr Wilkins saved a few hundred pounds but found that prices had gone up. So he waited and saved more, but prices went up faster. He is now trying to get an exchange of council houses with someone down at the coast. He would take a smaller house for his larger one. Mr Wilkins is bitter about not having planned for this earlier. He has met people on the South coast who do little jobs—taking money for amusement parks, for deck chairs, etc., and they are quite happy with it, particularly if they made the move earlier when it was possible to buy a little house for a few hundred pounds.

Meanwhile his present life is one that could be enriched, he feels, if provisions within the urban setting were available. Once again 'they' had not done things to make life come right for the likes of him:

'Look, when you get to our age, you've been working all day, you come home, you're tired. You sit down, you have your tea, you begin to read the paper. What's on telly? There's a good play or there's not a good play. I do the crossword. Right. I try to make the brain work, when it won't, it takes me all night. I fall asleep. What's the time? I wanted to see so and so. I fell asleep. . . .

What you want is to get something to take you out of the house. It should be something that the wife is in agreement with you on and she'll come with you. In an estate like ours, there's an institute but you can't go there. First and last time we went there, there was a young kid who was threatened by some chap with knives. The whole trouble today on our estate with us people is that there's no supervision. Your streets are dirty. If you want to go out, you're afraid. Afraid to go out and come home late in case you get knocked about. What would interest me would be something like a village hall. You know Mrs Brown and you know Mrs Jones. You say, tonight there's a dance on. There's a discussion. If you go on your own, it's not far. Now here, where can I go? I have to take a bus ride everywhere. It's

4p. Whichever way I go, it's a fixed fare, 4p before I get anywhere. It was all country when I first came here. The LCC didn't provide any parks. Then they just built, built, built. All around—private estates, private houses. The old river where we used to walk is all polluted now. They've even fenced it off so you couldn't walk there if you wanted to. They could have put seats there. People could have sat there. But you can't go down. Sunday afternoon, lovely sunny day. Where can you go? The park? It takes half an hour to walk there. Sometimes more by bus because you have to wait twenty minutes for a bus. If you want to go to another park, you've got a great bloomin' hill to go up—half a mile up and half a mile down the other side. You've had enough, especially if you've been pushing a bike to work all week.'

Mr Wilkins is bitter at the chances he lost—the way they have 'done him in' or he has 'missed the bus'. He is also bitter about the way in which provision for leisure has either been ignored or has been provided in such a way as to make it difficult for older people. Mr Gills, whose case follows, seems to be more resourceful in getting a satisfying sense of integration in later life despite the upheaval of marital separation.

MR AND MRS GILLS lived together at the time of the interview, but they were not communicating with one another and had not had an ordinary marital relationship for years. He retired a year before and she was due to retire shortly. They plan to disband the household at that point and each will then have another living arrangement.

Prior to retirement Mr Gills was a street-cleaner for the Borough Council. His wife worked as a cook at the local police station. Following retirement, his life became increasingly centred on the local church where, in addition to his participation in the religious and social activities, he worked as a voluntary custodian handyman.

Early family background. Mr Gills was born in a London working-class district and lived there all his life. He was born in a house that has since been pulled down to make way for council housing, and went to the local school opposite:

'My father was an expert china and glass packer, which was a job in itself. He got paid a little bit extra than the other movers because he done all the china and glass packing. Him and two friends of his, they saw the rise of the man they worked for. He started with a pony and trap, and when he retired I think the old man got left about a thousand quid, and so did the others.'

Work history. Mr Gills left school at 15 and took a job at the local 'tea-grocer's', a hundred yards down the road:

'Hours were long, pay was low. Of course, you lived cheaper in those days. Half-past seven at night, Monday to Wednesday, half-past one on Thursday, eight o'clock Friday, nine o'clock Saturday, were the closing times. And when it came to Christmas, you never knew what time you were going to get home. It could be eleven o'clock.'

His work as a general helper and delivery boy took him all through the neighbourhood and into households of all kinds. He was known to be honest, reliable and willing. He liked the life—talking to people, out in the fresh air a lot, and looking into things generally.

At some points he helped his father in his work as a furniture mover. He did other jobs, for example for a furniture repair shop, upholstering and delivering. Then because he really missed being outdoors, he went into his 'real love', gardening:

'I got a job for a firm that did greengrocery, fruits and gardening. . . . I worked there for a number of years . . . and I seen this district alter. . . . All these people around that way had maids in those days. Not one but two or perhaps three or four. There was a house that had a lady, a gentleman, son and two daughters, and he had five maids and a butler, and a valet and a chauffeur. That's a long time ago . . . but I know because I used to go and collect the order every day.'

He recalls having had his twenty-first birthday party while on that job. He was given a birthday party by his sunday school superintendent at the local church. This job went on until he entered the Services in the Second World War. He had just married and had two children when he left for war service. Following demobilisation, he had a hernia operation and then took a job with the Borough as a street-sweeper, a position which he held for twenty-three years until retirement.

Mr Gills characterises himself as a person who likes and knows how to get on with people. He observes that the superintendent would always stop him when he saw him on his sweeping job and have a little chat with him

'because, he said, there was only two of the road-sweepers who knew how to speak. We gave him his correct due—called him "sir"— rightly so too. We knew how to speak to him and how to ask for anything.'

This politeness towards his social or organisational superiors was something that he had learned to cultivate earlier in his job as the greengrocer's delivery man. He recalls that many of the people in the mansions around used particularly to ask for him:

'See if you can get that young man to check our order. He does check all the stuff and he's allowed in the kitchen and he checks it off and puts it in the vegetable rack and says "Sorry madam, they forgot to put in so and so. Are you in a hurry for it?" And if they said "Well, I would like it for lunch," I used to get it for lunch.'

In his road-sweeping job, he was very obliging to the supervisors, and until his doctor called a halt, he would customarily return to the office for an overtime clean-up after doing his regular sweeping duties.

Family life. Mr Gills married prior to the Second World War, when he went into the Services and was away for several years. He and his wife have two children, both married now and with children of their own. When the second of their children, the boy, left home, the Gills made no more pretence of harmony in their relationship, and he moved into the boy's room.

Mrs Gills never shared his interest in religion, or in the people he met through the church. Since his retirement, with more and more of his time and interest being taken up with church activities, the tension has mounted; by the time of the interviews there was no communication between them at all. The actual break occurred over a trivial set of disagreements about taste in television-viewing which, obviously, symbolised deeper disagreements:

'One night I came into the front room where we have the television set. Now I'm not a lot struck on television. I prefer my transistor set and I get a kick out of it. I take it with me every night when I go down to the church . . . I go down there to keep a watching brief that there's no vandalism goes on, and I take my transistor along . . . well what I like on television is a bit of sport. I don't like all sport, I'm not all that gone on football. I think we have too much football rammed down our throats, far too much, nine or ten months of the season. My favourite game is cricket. Anyhow she came in and I had so and so on. "Oh no, I don't want that. There's a much better programme on the other side." You've never seen such a load fo rubbish in your life. This went on for two or three months. I never got anything I wanted, so I used to jack off to my room, see.'

This became so loaded between them, that it has persisted as a sign of the breach in their relationship. He says that he still continues to give her her 'wage', though he is on a pension. However, they both know that the relationship is finished.

Their daughter maintains a close relationship with Mrs Gills, who plans, when she retires from her job in the coming year, to take a council flat near this daughter who lives in another town. Mr Gills only found that out accidentally. Once when he was visiting his daughter, he went into the local Council office and asked about the availability of housing, with the idea that he and his wife might move closer to their daughter following retirement. He was told then that Mrs Gills had already registered for housing there, but only for one: 'It was then that I smelt a rat.'

This had come as a bit of a shock to him as he had already not only looked into the housing, but had visited the local Borough Engineer's office and given a demonstration of how well he could work the 'path hoover', a machine for vacuum-cleaning public pathways. He had, by his account, impressed them very much and they offered him a job. Now that he heard about the housing situation and his wife's intention to move down there on her own, he has given up this line of thinking.

He has a less close relationship with his son, who has moved to another district and is rarely seen by either of them. He has, however, developed a very rich array of activities around the church, which includes the possibility of another 'domestic career' as well.

Post-retirement interests. Since his retirement, Mr Gills has built on his love of visiting and 'chatting people up'. He has looked up a number of old friends and filled his book with appointments and commitments to an extent that would resemble a busy professional man's book. One of the friends that he went to see—someone he had known from childhood days—turned out to be also lonely and wanting companionship. This was Evelyn:

> 'Why I particularly went to see her was that we were boy and girl sweethearts. But I wouldn't have married her. No. Her station in life was very different from mine. She was born with a silver spoon in her mouth but she didn't want that to interfere with our friendship. We had all the same things in common—our love of church work, our love of sunday school teaching, our love of people, and above all our love of missionary work. That is a great thing.'

Evelyn's husband was killed in the war. She has a daughter who is in divinity school, training to become a woman minister in the church. Mr Gills has become so close to the family, with this daughter not having known her own father, that he is now called 'dad' by the girl. The reopening of the relationship with his childhood sweetheart has brought new light into Mr Gills's life:

> 'She and I used to go out to missionary meetings and do little shows together when we were children. And they knew it [that we liked each other] and my mother and father knew it. They loved her. She often came home to us to have a cup of tea instead of having one sitting with a napkin on her knees. She was a great girl. But today's today. . . . We've become very close again and when my wife leaves, we'll become closer still.'

Aside from renewing this old relationship, the church occupies his thoughts and activities day by day. His diary book is full of things to do —many of them regular commitments as voluntary caretaker, and other events associated with the church round. He is so busy with church work that he finds he can't get over to visit his son and daughter as often as he might otherwise like to, which, it seems, is probably for the best:

> 'The church asked me if I got a bit of free time. And as soon as I took up that job [caretaker], one or two others came up. The second one that came up was junior church registrar, keeping all the records of the children who come to church on Sunday mornings. Keep all the registers, and the birth dates and death dates and that's how we go on. One thing leads to another.'

He also does a bit of Sunday School teaching, something he has done since he was 14:

> 'I enjoy it. It's a hobby of mine actually. Although I'm a practising Christian, it's something I really enjoy. I thoroughly enjoy it. Next weekend we've got a gift day. Once a year we have an envelope and put extra in it. We have a show on Saturday. Every organisation in the church does a fifteen or twenty minute show, a turn of some description. We've got a dancing troupe, women's hour, sunday school, Boy's Brigade, Girl's Brigade—they all do a turn. Then we end up with all the ladies and gentlemen of the staff singing three hymns, led by myself.'

He keeps up with missionary news and goes on trips with church groups. For example, later during the week of the interview he was going on a trip to another church with the welfare leader of the church, where there was to be a presentation for another welfare worker who was retiring. There is an annual church outing to the country and various other events which keep him constantly 'on the hop'. When his wife retires and moves out, Evelyn will move in with Mr Gills. Then they will start a new life together, and will share the church interests.

The Wilkins and Gills show how preoccupation with realignment gets expressed in the retirement transition, as well as how it is affected by earlier experiences and anticipations. For the Wilkins the search for integrity will involve coming to terms with an idealised longing to settle in a home by the sea. For Mr Gills the church provides a focus of interests and activities, and for the realignment of his domestic life. For Mrs Gills, her children and grandchildren provide this focus, and she has arranged separate housing near them.

Old Age

Previously, agencies concerned with old people considered their field to be people of 60+. With increasing longevity, better health and a different attitude to life, people are active longer and it is on the 75+ group that concern is now focused.

Within our framework this is a phase in which the focal preoccupation of the people concerned is with *life before death*. People tend, in this phase, to be more alone. They are likely to have lost their spouses, many of their friends and own-generation kin. Younger kin are likely to have moved away, and the patterns of the preceding phase of playful encounters, giving treats and taking children on outings is likely to become more difficult, physically and financially.

This is an age of special vulnerability to physical disorders, and to psychological distress associated with ageing. Disorders like arteriosclerosis, uremia, diabetes and strokes are more likely to occur. There is greater likelihood of people suffering from malnutrition, from hypothermia (particularly in conditions of poverty in winter) and from accidents and injuries from falls.

There are also emotional problems that come with the disorders and incapacities of old age, together with increasing loneliness, isolation, feelings of insecurity and not being wanted, feeling that one is forgotten, 'put on the shelf', 'discarded', and a 'spare wheel' in social groups. Images of the lonely meal, the long staircase to the cold flat, malnutrition and the wasting of the body, all belong to this period. The increase in behavioural problems—untidiness, forgetfulness, repetitiousness, occasional childishness—makes it more difficult to break through the inhibitions and a vicious cycle gets under way which may lead to depression and even suicide.

There are a number of groups in Britain which combine research in the area of the aged with an attempt to influence policy or action programmes. We shall mention only three, the National Corporation for the Care of Old People, Age Concern and Political and Economic Planning (PEP), because of their research components.

The National Corporation plays a role that is complementary both to the specialist public sector social services and that of other bodies which have a more specific interest in problems of the elderly. It seeks to monitor changing conditions bearing on the age group with which they are concerned, and to stimulate and support both research and innovative action experiments which reflect contemporary felt needs in the field. In this way, they move flexibly from one area of involvement to another as the need becomes recognised and taken up as part of an ongoing programme. Day-care centres and local welfare services, for example, have moved from a phase of struggling to become established as an idea through broad acceptance as government policy. Earlier work of 'pump priming' served its purpose and the Corporation has shifted its sights to new horizons. An information service is provided with the aid of a register of research, and the Corporation commissions position papers on policy implications of special issues emerging from contemporary research, for example, on housing, geriatric nursing, and special issues of health care and accident prevention.

Age Concern is a national action group, which conducts its own action-oriented research and seeks to apply the results promptly and directly to influencing policy. Examples are in economic, nutritional, and transportation problems of the elderly, and the stimulation and support of voluntary groups, often of very diverse backgrounds and orientations—such as Task Force, Samaritans, etc.

Political and Economic Planning (PEP) has been interested in services for the elderly as one of a large range of topics on which they conduct policy-oriented studies. The PEP study by Barbara Shenfield and Isobel Allen (1972) outlines some of the needs and problems in the organisation of voluntary services for the elderly. They found that visiting home-bound old people is required in cases of social isolation or inadequate care by either families or other responsible sources. It is of two types: an intermittent calling in to 'keep in touch' with people at risk of being in need of care services, and a closer kind of relationship for regular support and personal services. The first can be more easily accomplished on a broad base of voluntary effort, and even made part of the role of other local service workers such as street-wardens, depending on the local situation. The second requires a more highly organised effort and training. Both have important morale functions and can contribute significantly to old people's preoccupation with sustaining positive experiences in the terminal period of life.

There are other specialist groups concerned with the aged; the most relevant are probably the medical professions (particularly in the field of geriatrics), architects (particularly in relation to special housing) and clergymen (see Riley *et al.*, 1969). Medical studies have concerned themselves with the disorders of older people and issues of their care. Hospital versus community care, the role of families, voluntary workers, nursing and other forms of surveillance, are some of the topics that have been under discussion and research.

In the housing field the controversy has been between those who favour special housing for old people and those who uphold the view that the best solution is to maintain age-heterogeneous communities— so that intergenerational contacts can be fostered for mutual benefit and kin relationships can be sustained. This view is partly based on positive advantages of age mixtures, and partly on a revulsion against negative concomitants of segregation. Lewis Mumford (1966) has emphasised the positive and, Peter Townsend (1957) the negative considerations. Townsend found, in a study of old-age institutions that the majority of residents deplored having been sent there, and that their morale was adversely affected. Furthermore, more than half were considered able to cope for themselves with little or no assistance. The call, thereupon, was for the abolition of old-age institutions, and the transfer of care of the elderly to the community—along similar lines to the reformist movement against the old-fashioned custodial mental hospitals in the 1950s.

The position now generally favoured is one of multiple options. Given the improvements of housing that have occurred since the days that produced the kinds of old people's homes studied by Townsend, the idea of institutional care is less foreboding. A semi-segregated residential pattern seems desirable to many now, one in which an elderly peer group culture can survive, where there can be conveniently located and appropriately stocked and managed club rooms, hobby rooms, shopping facilities and so on. Games and activities popular with older people and in which they can succeed are fostered; shuffleboard, billiards, croquet, ceramics, flower arrangements, etc. (Rosow, 1961; Madge, 1969; Andrus Gerontology Center, 1974).

In Britain there have been positive results from their *grouped flatlets for old people* scheme. This scheme, which reflects the international trend in dealing with problems of old people's housing, has been favourably received in terms of family contacts, visiting neighbours, sociability and the availability of communal facilities, of alarm systems, nutrition, safety and psychological issues arising from the risk of isolation and loneliness (Ministry of Housing and Local Government, 1968).

This pattern seems to work best, however, in a situation where special residential facilities are located in or near neighbourhoods in which the residents also have external relationships with friends, relatives and others. As long as this network of informal relationships is relatively intact, the resident can enjoy the safety, protection, health and welfare services available in the segregated grouped-residential accommodation, while at the same time having the benefits of interaction as feasible with others in that age group. Talmon sums this resolution up as follows: 'A partly segregated age-homogeneous setting maximises opportunities for contacts with peers and protects the aged from invidious evaluation, yet at the same time does not cut them off from outside contacts' (Talmon, 1968, 195). A number of studies of such semi-segregated settings in the USA have shown that there can be extensive social participation and intensive use of the facilities provided by the housing management if these are sufficiently geared to the needs of old people. This allows for a community life within the housing estate, which may be sufficient for many and for others an increasing option (Kleemeier, 1954; Hoyt, 1954).

The idea of a bungalow by the sea, or a cottage or farm in the country, is one that grips the imagination of older people, as we have already indicated. Studies like that of loneliness by the Women's Group of Public Welfare for the National Council of Social Service (1972) and the sociological *Retiring to the Seaside* by Valerie Karn show that the problems associated with this dream make the idea of having a cottage in the country less realistic for people in this age group than their predecessors in the early post-retirement period (Karn, 1974). It may bring unanticipated problems—such as the burdens of a home, lack of employment opportunities, overloading of medical and welfare facilities in popular retirement areas, with the difficulty of carrying on when one of the partners (usually the male) dies. As there are few areas of geographical attraction compared with the many areas from which old people come, the choice tends to be between retiring to a beautiful place remote from kin and friends versus staying in an area where kin and friends are available whether or not it is geographically desirable. In the USA, in resorts like Southern California, Arizona and Florida, and in England in the South-eastern resorts and the Devon–Cornwall area, there are small proportions who have both. But more of the population of such places have opted for the environmental amenities though it means remoteness from kin. The alternative, which is seen in the better examples of clustered flatlets for the old, provides communal features of care in communities where the older person has roots and ties.

Old people are prone to suffer from adverse comparisons with themselves at earlier stages of their lives. This leads to a state referred to by Kleemeier and colleagues as 'desolation' of mind. In resorts, or in age-segregated housing estates, the residents are less prone to the deleterious effects of such individual comparisons, because they can compare themselves with others of similar age. Because they are, as a group, disengaged from the constraints of the workaday world that govern urban and suburban life, they can make their own schedules and timetables to suit their capacities. They are 'all in the same boat' in terms of lessened kin contact and the special problems and anxieties facing the elderly, so they can form mutually supporting friendly relationships.

Helping old people in this phase not only to keep alive interests they had cultivated earlier, but to continue to develop new interests, is considered important by many observers (NCSS, 1972).

While older people in the age group under discussion are less able to be physically very active (though there are exceptions), they may retain lively mental interests. Failing eyesight and hearing can be supplemented by electronic devices and other aids to continuing, or even developing, interests in visual, auditory or tactile experiences. Modern

LFLC—L

technological devices increase physical mobility of the handicapped, so that visits to libraries, for example, may be possible. Maintaining an interest in toilette—hairdressing, chiropody, etc.—is a way of helping older people to maintain morale and self-esteem. The telephone allows contact for the house-bound. Intercommunication devices make it possible to keep in touch with an old person who may fear sudden illness. Pets are particularly useful in helping older people to feel needed—even if only to feed the budgerigar—and to have company. Prayer and meditation for the religious, and perhaps an interest in religion as history, as art or ceremony or philosophy for those who are not, is another area that may be cultivated late in life. It is also the channel, traditionally, for helping to attain the equanimity for facing the ultimate transition to death (Goldberg, 1970; Tournier, 1972; NCSS, 1972).

In recent times there have been efforts to provide secular counter-parts of the functions served by religion in assisting elderly people to achieve tranquillity in their final experiences of life before death. In psychiatry, for example, there is the growth of interest in the pheno-menon of dying, helping dying people and those close to them to face death. In this last period of life before death, old people cling to things they know, their treasured objects, environment, people and memories. Losses, which exhaust more parts of what the real world has to offer, are suffered as psychic wounds, and the work of bereavement for the elderly person is particularly painful. In the earlier retirement period it is dysfunctional to keep 'alive' in oneself lost relationships. Thus the widow who always feels her lost husband is with her, hears his voice, feels his touch and so on, closes over the possibility of making other relationships. In the terminal period, on the other hand, such internalisation of thoughts, feelings and imagery—through reminiscences and other forms of internalisation—brings about a sensed wholeness and integrity in life. This makes the disengagement process more tenable as an idea (Parkes, 1972; Cumming and Henry, 1961).

General issues in the light of the case material: integration and new meaning in life

Many of the issues raised in the literature are illuminated in the case studies. The importance of viewing people in the later phase of life in a less stereotyped and more differentiated way is particularly apparent. The meaning of leisure in later life is complex and variable. Not only are there the various circumstances of family, work and community life against which leisure definitions are couched for all of the sub-groups, but in the case of the elderly there is the withdrawal of many of these structures and the consequent possibility of new, optional patterns—all of which in a sense are 'leisure'. This is why the popular conception of old age is that it is an age of leisure. It is in fact far more problematic than that conception implies.

The people we have described, and those reported in the literature, find that the unstructuring of their lives that occurs with occupational retirement is a mixed blessing. For many the liberation of the individual and his family from oppressive routines is—both in anticipation and in realisation—rewarding. For others it is traumatic and resembles bereavement; it may be experienced as part of a massive loss of physical faculties, of social relationships, perhaps of a home and neighbourhood as well as of a job. The tasks of mourning and bereavement that this entails may be great and, as with all such losses, accomplished with varying degrees of effectiveness. The range of responses—from the 'angry' one of Mr Wilkins to the new and happier realignment of involvements of Mr Gills—illustrate the variability. While there is an element of truth in the observation made by Susser and Watson that retirement resembles the sick role in its exemption from specific positive prescriptions—you do not have to get up in the morning at a certain time, you do not have to go out to work, you do not have to provide for the family economically—this simile has its limitations. To repeat Shanas's observation: 'there is no such disease as old age.' What there is, is a challenge—a critical status transition—which may be traversed and responded to positively or negatively (Susser and Watson, 1962).

For scientist Dr Allport, retirement offers an opportunity to revert to his first love, the laboratory bench—from which success had removed him as he moved into higher administrative echelons. He began before retirement to think about and plan how to apply his scientific knowledge to his interest in archaeology; he found an opportunity to reorganise his life in a satisfying way. Already living in agreeable country surroundings, it was not part of his fantasy to find a little cottage in the country. Both he and his wife found within the same environment the possibilities for a satisfying new life pattern for their later years. Not so for Mr Wilkins and his wife. His earlier interests did not lend themselves easily to reapplication; nor did the Wilkins have the money to resettle in a satisfactory situation which would allow a new form of outdoor activity. Mr Wilkins had a life-long, class-antagonistic attitude towards bureaucratic functionaries and professionals. He found that he had to cope with these agencies increasingly—for housing, insurance, employment and so on. He was unable to move out of a somewhat embittered stance and his outlook was coloured by anger on a whole range of issues.

In the task of reconstructing a new life style appropriate for the individual's circumstances in the later years, the economic factor is important, though not always in a crude way. Though handyman Wilkins's aspirations were impaired by his lack of cash, his anger and bitterness had deeper roots than that. Conversely, in the case of a surveyor whom we interviewed (whose case is not reported here), there was no 'objective' need to earn professional fees to sustain a satisfactory standard of living following his retirement, but he felt angry at the constraints placed on him by the earnings rules. He felt that his capacity fully to exercise his professional skills was impaired; he was too scrupulous to evade taxation, and too unresourceful to evolve other ways of using his talents for the mutual benefit of himself and the community outside the traditional fee-for-service framework. Though many more individuals are occupied in jobs that provide informal sources of return—whether in cash or in other benefits such as food, shelter, clothing—than the official statistics reflect, the issue of money and its link to personal and social esteem remains problematic (Le Gros Clark, 1960). The whole network of associated issues—earnings rules, pensions arrangements, training and access to jobs, the abolition of discriminatory practices, and the formation of a co-ordinated pro-gramme of voluntary group activities with and for older people—provides a formidable set of challenges, for the rest of the community as much as for the elderly (Snellgrove, 1965).

The two-sidedness of the challenge—that facing the older person, and that facing society—is more than a simple doubling of problems. There are dynamic issues involved that can only begin to be understood at present. People fear to confront older people not only because they provide economic burdens on the more productive members, and because they impose expectations that cannot be reciprocated because the others are elsewhere occupied—but because they rouse feelings difficult to cope with. They rouse feelings of guilt, and anxiety about the process of ageing which everyone will have to confront, but many avoid as long as possible. The depressive elements in the ageing process are seldom seen as a set of conditions that are real and part of life and can be coped with. They tend to be pushed out of awareness or trans-iently responded to by making a contribution to 'helping the elderly'. And yet depressive trends and manifestations are important elements to be confronted in this phase.

Expressions of loneliness and despair and statistics of morbidity and suicide may pertain only to a small proportion of the elderly, but there is a reason beyond that of rousing public concern for giving them attention. They are tips of a very broadly based 'iceberg' of social-psychological issues which may be disregarded if it is thought that the issues are primarily specialised ones of health care for a smallish group (Sainsbury, 1955; Tunstall, 1966; Townsend, 1962).

The call for better conditions of housing, health care, diet and so on, is essential, but it may not be enough. Only a small proportion commit suicide, but many are engaged in a suicidal life style in which they neglect themselves, sink into almost imperceptibly deepening levels of despair and end their lives with a feeling of uselessness. To deal with the issues of giving meaning, dignity and a sense of fulfilment to life in this last stage, providers should understand the underlying social-psychological issues of the sub-population as a whole, not merely those who complain of illness or inequity. Our data re-enforce the observation of Joan Eyden in her view of available literature on social policy towards the elderly (1973, 204):

> We still know too little about what it means to be old in modern society; we have too little detailed information about the external situation of the elderly and about their hopes and fears, the stress and strain due to ageing, the compensations and satisfactions which may also be theirs.

Our data do suggest, in common with other analyses, that kin relationships are important in old age, but not in a way that can easily be encompassed by generalisations like: older people become increasingly home- and family-centred; older people experience a reversal of role relations with their children; older people take up and expand their grandparental roles. These statements may be true, but there is considerable variation and complexity in their relevance and applicability to specific situations. The art of ageing gracefully in relation to one's kin seems to involve the formulation of a new balance of involvement and distance in these close relationships. In the case of the Gills, the resolution was different for Mrs Gills (who drew closer to her daughter and family) and for Mr Gills (who developed a new quasi-marital relationship and drew away). In the case of the Wilkins, where there was upward social mobility by the two sons, a modification in the quality of the relationship is seen. The children are doing well and Mr Wilkins says 'good luck to them'. He neither expects that they can help him very much (given the strains of establishing themselves) nor that he can help them very much (though he did take the opportunity in the interview situation to explore the possibility that the interviewer might be interested in purchasing an annuity from his insurance salesman son). We found little to support the idea that family relations fill the gap left by retirement from work. We did not extend our exploration into the later phases, where physical illness and disability dominate the life patterns evolving. However, everyone in the mid-stages whom we interviewed made it clear that they would welcome an expansion of neighbourhood and community facilities that would reduce their burdens of travel, make a familiar and secure setting for cultivating new interests, and allow for a final period of life integration in a setting of calm and dignity. There are a range of services now envisioned and operated by community-minded social agencies like Age Concern, Task Force and the various statutory and non-statutory helping groups. There is a mushroom growth of neighbourhood and voluntary groups, 'over-sixties' clubs and so on, which manifests society's concern with the issues presented by the very old. The need for co-ordination remains, more markedly than ever as the complexity of activities increases. It is in the borderlines between medical and social care, family and community relationships, work and hobby, that the greatest attention is required. This is because older people have often been disregarded because they have not been classified as belonging in one or another of the welfare categories. If they are to be facilitated in making life resolutions that achieve integrity (rather than the less constructive resolutions that may be observed), their special interests must be recognised.

At a societal level, and in the long-term perspective, our interest in older people is a part of the moral order in which we live. The treatment of old people—like that of women, children, minorities and people generally—reflects the kind of society we have built. Irving Rosow has said passionately in his essay on 'Old Age: One Moral Dilemma of an Affluent Society' (1962, 191):

> The crucial people in the ageing problem are not the old, but the younger age groups, for it is the rest of us who determine the status and position of the old person in the social order. What is at stake for the future is not only the alienation of the young from each other and of men from men. There is no real way out of this dilemma, for young or old, without a basic reordering of society's aspirations and values, of which the ageing problem is but a token.

More immediately, the family remains a major potential resource in attempting to work out resolutions which fit particular cases. The exploration of alternatives for elderly people can, of course, be undertaken impersonally through an ever-more effective and co-ordinated social service system, but the kind of resolution that allows elderly people to manage things in their own way—to feel that they can cope, that they can do something for themselves and are good spouses, parents and grandparents—depends on working through with these close figures the kinds of resolutions that suit the individuals concerned. Many old people are not involved with family relationships, and others will prefer to work out resolutions apart from their families. This does not counteract the more general tendency for these late-stage resolutions to be made most effectively in collaboration with family members. But this is not an easy process. Many observers have noted that as older people drop the façades of impression-management that they may have adopted in making their way in life earlier, they may be more difficult to get along with. But there may also be a more 'genuine' sense—a sense of 'integrity'—that will require that stereotypes of various kinds be discarded both by older people and by others: old people are not all 'sweet dears', or 'old grumps'; nor are they all lonely and miserable or angry or resentful. They vary, as do their circumstances and their resources. On the other hand, as with other life-cycle stages, they confront common isssues as a sub-group in the population—at the core of which is the need to reconstruct a life style appropriate for the circumstances of their later years. This is an active process, requiring revisions not only of activity routines and consumption patterns, but of interests and relationships; these will be heavily influenced by those which they had prior to reaching this stage, but which will be capable of being reworked productively. Leisure providers may facilitate this process.

Leisure provision for later years: continuing life

There are a number of points on which considerable consensus has evolved in considering provision for people in this phase of life. They are reference points from which to inform policies, though, as we have indicated, they are still incompletely understood.

First, retirement from the occupational world need not be taken as the end of productive enjoyable living. Because of the complex of demographic and technological factors described, a meaningful life stage remains available for those who can grasp it and realise its potentials. With increased affluence (overall, though not for some), older people not only live longer but also look younger and are more fit physically. Second, a successful transition to retirement depends largely on preparation: society could facilitate this. While some people are more prepared than others in terms of their storehouse of knowledge, experience and resourcefulness in learning to develop new interests, few are free of the need to make major life-style realignments. Third, the task of achieving integrity at this phase of life is neither exclusively individual nor exclusively social; it involves interaction between individual, family and social agencies in the context of an enlightened public opinion.

Pre-retirement programmes could be developed on a far wider scale than exists at present. Ideally pre-retirement education should be a life-long process, in which it is not hidden from young people that they will one day have to reorganise their lives as old people. The young and middle-aged need to know what it feels like to be old, what older people's aspirations and views of life are, and what the trials and tribulations as well as the joys of later life entail. The orientation to life as a continuous developmental process, with recurrent educational experiences, is likely to grow. In the meantime adult education, 'recreational', industrial, and other sources of support should be used to facilitate the retirement transition of men and women now approaching it, in 'crash' courses rather than not at all. Research is needed to evaluate various programmes: to determine what kinds of people are responsive to them, to help those who are not responsive (to their own detriment), and to study intervening factors between intention and realisation in the process of adaptation to retirement.

It is important to distinguish what happens following statutory retirement age—and for anything up to fifteen or twenty years afterwards—from what happens if and when there is marked physical and psychological disablement. In the first phase there tends to be a period of psychological depression and social withdrawal, as with other losses and the 'mourning' that goes with them. If the work of mourning is accomplished and there is recovery and a new lease of life, there is still the opportunity for another 'late career' which emphasises enjoyment rather than external achievement. This late enjoyment career can be facilitated by working through the losses entailed in retirement.

Provision could be oriented to inventing and upgrading more social roles for later life. This would connect with the development of more flexible retirement options. Whether an individual retires at a fixed age or retires gradually, he or she may need facilitation in redeploying interests and energies. A certain degree of upset is expectable (though not necessarily there) in the process. Given the lack of structure in later life, considerable scope for social invention is needed—both by older people themselves and by 'providers'. Local service roles could be developed and adapted so that older people could contribute to as well as benefit from their existence. Anti-age-discrimination measures in the workplace should be broadened to encompass other areas of life, including the social services. Some of the new roles can come from within the field of 'leisure provision'; this means not only helping those who need help but, perhaps even more important, employing as helpers those who can give it, or develop so as to be able to give it. Coaching, caretaking, and a range of service and support activities could be developed so that older people give something to others, and in so doing help themselves. Work positions in which older people now function, for example, wardens, groundsmen, caretakers, could be restructured and upgraded, giving their occupants more of a sense of participation in the whole enterprise of provision. This is not so much a matter of better pay and material conditions of work, as of better communication, improved patterns of participation and organising the job so that there is feedback of appreciation from users of facilities to service personnel who are often taken as part of the scenery, dehumanised or even resented.

New experiments which integrate housing, health care and leisure provision are of increasing interest. Different solutions will be required for different kinds of family and neighbourhood situations and different degrees of affluence. To the extent that older people wish to disengage from the neighbourhoods in which they have lived and worked, they may want to live in other types of communities which have special properties supportive of them as a subpopulation. Natural experiments of towns which have become retirement villages show that some environments are friendly, helpful and supportive to older people and in these environments there is higher morale. It is difficult to change 'natural' communities and by no means certain that one can construct 'bespoke' old people's estates, neighbourhoods, or villages that will have these properties. Nevertheless this seems to be a direction in which there are promising potential developments.

Understanding the culture of old people's colonies is interesting not only in the framework of organisational management for social, medical and other services, but in and of itself as a type of community in the contemporary social scene; like ethnic and other communities, it provides interesting social phenomena. These are communities in which people deliberately attempt to slow the pace and impact of change, deliberately lower performance standards and expectations and deliberately cultivate enjoyment. As with other human experiments with culture-building, studies of these societies may help not only their own adaptation, but they may provide lessons for others.

Programmes of public education about old people are needed not only for themselves, but for other age groups. There is a large area of cultural inadequacy in general techniques for relating to old people. This arises partly because there has been a great increase in the proportion of old people in Western societies, and because older people were previously somewhat discarded and shunted aside into back rooms, rural retreats, and other institutions apart from the rest of society. Now there is a challenge to develop appropriate attitudes and behaviour patterns for relating more constructively. It is widely felt to be morally wrong and humanly wasteful to deny the existence of older people and put them away; it is equally wrong to act as though they had no special difficulties or problems in living with their families or in society generally. Public education programmes would aim at correcting erroneous images of older people and countering the fear that many people have of facing and relating to old people. This is a responsibility that cannot be discharged by economic provision alone, essential as these may be. It is one that requires the humanisation of social attitudes towards the elderly. To do this the roles of community workers who come into contact with home-bound old people need to be enlarged so as to increase and enrich their contacts. Voluntary workers, traffic wardens and, at a more highly trained and involved level, social and personal service workers are important in this. They can learn to do things with old people, to spend time interacting with them, to listen to them and to learn from them. Both sides might gain from such encounters by an increased appreciation of how to enjoy life and by improved methods of working together towards shared goals. Older people are prime social resources, with time, skill and potential interest in contributing to playgroups and so on.

For all these purposes, *research on the social and personal phenomenology* of ageing and old people is necessary. We need systematic life histories of different kinds of old people in which we explore their experience of becoming old, how they perceive the process and the people who relate to them. We need to know about different sub-populations—before retirement their expectations about life after retirement, how this actually works out after they have retired, what they hope from the rest of their lives. Equally we need to know from first-hand knowledge of the people associated with those who retire and become elderly, what they feel and do in the process. This way we may be able to understand the possibilities of *rapprochement* between them. Such research needs to be based on qualitative, systematic case studies. Knowledge gained this way will supplement the picture of demographic and quantitative indicators of the ageing process. What we need now are studies of old *people* rather than studies on old *age* and its problems.

6

Leisure provision

Specialist providers cannot do it all

We start this chapter with a critique of some ways in which leisure provision in Britain is being institutionalised. Our presentation is not comprehensive, nor does it do more than point to what in our opinion are considerations for future development. As our basic terms of reference for the study on which this book is based were defined from the users' vantage point, the processes at work in the world of providers were necessarily marginal to our considerations.

Nevertheless, if our approach to the leisure topic is to have value beyond conceptual clarification, and to be useful for the implementation of leisure policy, we must at least begin to put ourselves into the position of providers and attempt to understand what some of their problems are, and what issues lie ahead for making their work articulate more closely with the preoccupations of the people for whom they are providing.

An attempt to beam into the world of providers immediately points up the issues surrounding institutionalisation in the contemporary leisure scene. On the one hand, nearly everything in the environment is a potential leisure *resource*; on the other, there is a call for the provision of specialist 'leisure' or 'recreation' facilities. While we do not wish to undermine the efforts of the specialist leisure providers at this point—indeed we believe their role is more crucial than ever—we note that the institutionalisation process is demarcating leisure as a specialist and distinct sphere of activity, a process which may be critical from the users' perspective. It is important to clarify what we mean by 'leisure facilities' in contrast to 'leisure resources'. Christopher Alexander, in his incisive urban planning essay, 'A City is not a Tree', pinpoints the difference unequivocally (1971, 416P17):

Another favourite concept of the CIAM theorists and others is the separation of recreation from everything else. This has crystallised in our real cities in the form of playgrounds. The playground, isolated and fenced in, is nothing but a pictorial acknowledgement of the fact that 'play' exists as an isolated concept in our minds. It has nothing to do with the life of play itself. Few self-respecting children will ever play in a playground.

Play itself, the play that children practise, goes on somewhere different every day. One day it may be indoors, another day in a friendly gas station, another day down by the river, another day in a derelict building, another day on a construction site which has been abandoned for the weekend. Each of the play activities and the objects it requires forms a system. It is not true that these systems exist in isolation, cut off from the other systems in the city. The different systems overlap one another and they overlap many other systems besides. The units, the physical places recognised as play places, must do the same. In a natural city this is what happens. Play takes place in a thousand places. It fills the interstices of adult life. As they play, children become full of their surroundings. How can a child become filled with his surroundings in a fenced enclosure? He cannot.

Our view that leisure can best be seen as part of life interests is very similar to that of Alexander, though perhaps less categorical. The paradox is that the specialist leisure provisions are also necessary. Alexander himself does not exclude the importance of 'leisure facilities' but urges rather that they exist in relation to, not divorced from, the rest of life.

'Leisure and recreational resources' institutionally provided are mainly controlled—with different patterns in different places—by private, commercial and public providers. Sometimes the same kind of facilities may be provided by all three. Private facilities include those which are owned and administered by private clubs and organisations, and others which are operated by industrial or business concerns for the benefit of their members. Commercial facilities are provided by individuals and organisations with the express purpose of making profit. They range from solo or small family-scale facilities to those operated by large-scale organisations.

This area of the commercial sector's involvement has been referred to as the 'leisure industries', although there is no single set of these. The term refers rather to a loose collection of different types of enterprise with different histories, different financial and organisational properties, and different problems, embracing areas like: entertainment, in which we would include the whole range of dining and catering industries; gambling; tourism, holidays and travel; provision for trippers, including stately homes, estates and gardens, leisure parks and so forth; leisure equipment, including equipment for organised sport ranging from traditional team games to the sophisticated and highly technical equipment of water sports, skiing and mountaineering; hobbies, including do-it-yourself; home and garden products and the mass media, including books, visual aids, records, colour slides and tape cassettes.

Individual units in the 'leisure industries' involve themselves in many combinations of these areas and mammoth entertainment organisations, like Rank and Mecca, tend to diversify within a group of industries. The commercial sector is also involved in the provision of leisure facilities such as swimming pools and tennis courts in private housing estates. It seems that leisure opportunities enter little into the detailed design of houses. However, flexibility in the use of component parts of houses and flats has made it possible to cater for changing leisure needs in the family life cycle and these considerations may enter more effectively into design considerations in future.

Many of these 'leisure industries' have attempted through market research to understand more clearly the consumers' interest, if only in the narrow band of attracting support and investment for their particular product. In other instances no market research has been undertaken and the success or otherwise is purely coincidental; in still further instances the demand is created by advertising supply-cum-marketing techniques. These marketing and research techniques may have value in the public provision field as well, where there is the wish to understand motivations and aspirations of players and potential users of leisure facilities.

The voluntary sector, local and national, is also basically private, though it has a somewhat public sector ethos. This is in part due to public support for voluntary bodies—through financial support, access to public facilities and back-up administrative services. Voluntary output may, under appropriate circumstances, be mobilised for small public cash input. The manning of public facilities by volunteers has been little tried. There is considerable potential in play leadership schemes, at advice bureaux and on library counters, in domiciliary library services and in the administration of allotments (or better, 'leisure gardens') for this kind of effort. Using composite bodies such as local arts councils and sports councils to act as mediators between voluntary organisations and the local authority can be the key to many exciting possibilities. Simple 'pump-priming' for individual projects such as new or improved facilities for clubs and other voluntary organisations may reap a reward much larger than the sums involved.

Voluntary organisations include sports bodies and arts bodies on a widespread basis. Many quite small towns have local advisory sports councils and the number of local arts trusts and councils has grown steadily. There are also hobbies groups of all sorts, some more exclusive than others. Some are purely local, others are local branches of bodies like the British Bridge League and the Royal Horticultural Society. Youth movements were formerly a key grouping in the voluntary sector, and since the war national uniformed youth groups like the Boys Brigade and the whole scouting movement have been trying to change their image to attract a wider participation. Meanwhile service-linked youth groups have proliferated, and young people are now also included together with adults in a wide variety of public service organisations like Task Force and conservation corps. There is a range of these voluntary movements, more modern in ethos and participatory in nature, that have become a conspicuous part of the contemporary scene. Play movements are one example. Play leadership of children and young people and the movement of pre-school playgroups appear to offer considerable opportunities to enrol adults, especially parents of the children involved. Neighbourhood movements are mushrooming; many die with particular problems, but sometimes they persist and enlist ordinary people in agencies like tenants' associations, community associations, neighbourhood councils, age-group clubs. Similarly there has been a growth of pressure groups and amenity societies, though many of these, like the Council for the Preservations of Rural England and local branches of the Civic Trust and Inland Waterways Association, have a more persistent and formal character.

There are a number of other heterogeneous bodies with involvement in the leisure field that have even more of a public ethos, though in fact they are usually private or voluntary and occasionally even have some commercial interest. Most have charitable status and commonly enjoy some government funding and connections; they are often seen as quasi-governmental bodies. Some examples are the British Film Institute and National Film Theatre, the National Trust and the Central Council of Physical Recreation. While not directly accountable to government, these bodies are often cautious, as though they were, and tend to choose councils which perpetuate this position. They are beginning to co-ordinate their efforts and there is a flow of people among them and related bodies.

The links these bodies have with government on one side and professional associations and institutions on the other, give them potential for a high-calibre attack on specific problems. The kinds of interested professional associations include: the Institute of Landscape Architects, the Royal Institute of British Architects, the Association of Recreation Managers, the Institute of Recreation Management, the Institute of Baths Management, the Library Association, the Institute of Parks and Recreation Administration, the Town and Country Planning Association and the Royal Town Planning Institute. It is noteworthy that many of these institutions, particularly those containing the word 'recreation' in their designation, are of comparatively recent development.

We shall consider public agencies in more detail in the portrait of institutionalisation which follows. Essentially public facilities are mainly of two kinds: those provided by a public authority specifically for leisure use and those provided out of public funds where leisure use is either secondary or restricted to some sector of population. Examples of the first category are urban parks, swimming pools, libraries, museums and country parks. Examples of the second category include facilities in educational establishments, those administered by the Armed Services, forest areas and certain types of water facilities such as domestic supply reservoirs or canals.

We have referred a lot to an 'institutionalisation' of specialist leisure provision that is going on. Our basis for postulating the existence of the process is the increase in such phenomena as the allocation of funds specifically for leisure provision; the creation of committees and roles specifically responsible for leisure issues, and the building of new kinds of facilities justified by concepts of the public's leisure needs. The *Institute of Recreation Management Yearbook*, for example, comprises a directory of the many agencies now involved in this specialist field (Spon and Spon, 1973). Once having said this however, it is necessary to recognise that at this stage in the institutionalisation process, there is enormous heterogeneity in the provisions available in any given place, in the priorities placed on them and in the ways in which they are administered. There are also problems of communication, co-ordination and conflict resolution among the various interested parties. Self-conscious attempts at rationalisation have been made in recent years, but the issues remain salient and in some instances become exacerbated as demand becomes more articulate.

Providers differ in the extent to which they see themselves as part of a common effort. Whether or not a unitary philosophy is either necessary or desirable is itself a key issue. At a high level of abstraction (e.g. the pursuit of the greatest good for the greatest number, happiness for all, improving the quality of life), providers agree that their aims are in the same direction. But at the level of implementation, conflicts of goals and of methods become salient. What weight should be given to housing versus recreational needs in the reclamation of an urban water basin? In the past these issues might have been decided automatically or opportunistically. Today the decision process is more complex and therefore more difficult, though 'better' where it is 'people-oriented'.

Our approach to a better understanding of the provider–user nexus is best undertaken from the local community level, extending from this to the 'regional' and national contexts. The past decade's development trends in leisure provision in the public sector, especially in the local government domain, display in greater magnification than others the critical contemporary issues in the field. In addition, focusing on the local authority serves as a reminder that we are primarily concerned with *individuals and communities*.

The legislative base that underlies public sector provision does not reflect a coherent national policy on leisure. There is no overall set of statutes: legislative powers that exist are mixed and characteristically arise through the passage of an Act based on a report or a White Paper. Many Acts have relevance; for example Public Health Acts, Housing Acts, Allotment Acts, the Physical Training and Recreation Act. These mainly provide enabling powers. In some cases the Acts set out constraints within which provisions may be made. Obligatory provisions are few. Moreover the statutes themselves reflect philosophies and objectives current in political thinking at the time they were passed, and many become increasingly less relevant to the contemporary situation. The general picture in the public sector therefore is one in which there are many optional powers but little that actually *must* be done. What is done depends on the initiative of local authorities and on the government's programme, which is in turn responsive to the wide range of historical, financial and political influences which operate at any given time.

However, the scope for initiative in the public sector is considerable. In addition to its legislative powers, local government is also a pivotal point for private or commercial development, for it holds crucial planning powers and is often the major land-owner in the community. Thus it may also be well placed to take a lead with mixed public and commercial enterprises.

In addition to the rather universal provision of parks, baths and libraries, local authorities may provide facilities like theatres, sports centres, country parks, museums, local history centres, community centres, adventure playgrounds, golf courses and indoor bowls rinks, activities like renewal of derelict land or waterways, pre-school playgroups, play leadership schemes, horse shows, pageants and entertainment events of all kinds. Local education authorities may interpret adult education widely and thereby cater for clubs, groups and classes in a wide variety of activities, or confine their activities to a narrow band of formal classes. Local government may also promote all sorts of activities without any particular legislative base. Examples are: town-twinning between towns in the United Kingdom and abroad; tourism promotion; support for local arts and sports councils; local committees or groups concerned with quality of life; and pump-priming or various activities such as traditional crafts.

It is within this permissive statutory framework that the wide diversity in how local authorities in fact interpret and develop their roles is observable. Many have generated considerable action, creativity and leadership. Yet there remain local areas where inactivity prevails and there is an impression, particularly at rates-fixing time, that aside from using leisure as a little 'icing on the cake' it can easily be dispensed with when budgets are finally fixed. And, in times of even tighter financial pinch, 'leisure' is particularly vulnerable. Slogans like 'beds before boats' are difficult to rebut when an urban water space is up for reclamation or rehabilitation; but once lost, the waterway's chances for reappearing on the urban scene are very slim indeed.

The differences in activity or inactivity around the development of resources do not coincide with the differences in potential. There are many reasons for this, among which are the complexities of jurisdiction. Confusion as to the role and function of different kinds of local authority even among professionals in local government administration, with all their overlapping functions and layers of powers, has been further compounded by recent local government reorganisation.

The distinguishing features over the last decade as regards leisure provision in the public sector have been the efflorescence of activity in this field and heightened consciousness about the scale of involvement appropriate to public authorities. Indeed, over this period, the scale of local authority leisure provision has escalated enormously and almost unnoticed. Public servants whose training and outlook have been geared to much more modest budgets, organisational methods and quite small-scale projects, now find themselves faced with enterprises that are highly complex, involving large staff and requiring skills for which they have not been prepared. The management skills that are now required involve officers with financial accounting (from the point of setting charges to the accounting system), involvement in multi-disciplinary teams, the use of study groups, the development of career-planning strategies, information and computer services, public relations on a large scale, industrial relations and so on. There are signs that these requirements are beginning to be met in new courses of professional training. Professional courses for administrators and managers have been initiated and are being undertaken at universities and polytechnics.

Yet what is perhaps most remarkable about the development of leisure provision is how swiftly attitudes to the role of leisure in society and its place in public responsibility have altered. To paraphrase, at the beginning of the last decade the view that leisure provision was mainly 'icing on the cake' was common. The stance taken in the House of Lords Select Committee Report on Sport and Leisure (1973), that 'the public is entitled to a good time', reflects a marked change of emphasis. Not only was leisure increasingly viewed over this period as a legitimate sphere, but also increasingly as a coherent enterprise. Consequently people in the then emerging leisure field were advocating the creation of an integrated machinery in government to facilitate an improved approach to leisure provision, all the more important because of the new light in which it was seen. Molyneux wrote (1968, 154), for example, that:

> to give effect to this philosophy [of the importance of recreation in its own right] urban recreation has had to operate through a pro-liferation of departments, and through statutes which carry such tell-tale names as 'evening institutes' and 'further education'.

It was those in the vanguard of the new approach to leisure provision who mostly held these views, and it was therefore in the quarters where the most positive efforts were being made that the call for integrated leisure departments came strongest.

Parks, baths, libraries, etc., were all seen to add up to an encompassing sphere, leisure or recreation, provision for which, to be effective, should not be diffused among a string of departments. In parallel with the view that leisure is a coherent sphere, the notion that it is also a distinct—or at least distinguishable—sphere implicitly gained ground.

The first integrated leisure department in Britain was formed in 1968, in the County Borough of Teesside, and others have followed since. The formation of these departments has doubtless been influenced by (some argue have directly resulted from) the larger forces for innovation in management approaches in recent years. These include the Maud Report on the Management of Local Government (1967), the Mallaby Report, which followed shortly after, and most recently the Bains Report (1972).

The departments for leisure services which have been established cover arts, sport and general leisure and amenity. The experiences of these authorities which have developed such directorates have only begun to be assessed, and monitoring and further study is generally acknowledged to be desirable.

One local government officer described the trend to us as follows: 'Some local authorities have nevertheless attempted to grasp the nettle and to view recreation provision and opportunities in a global sense for the communities they serve.' The advantages of this approach appear to them to outweigh the bureaucratic difficulties and obstacles involved. A review of the case for the integration of leisure services highlights the issues pressing for institutionalisation in the world of providers.

The case for the composite department is based on several premises. Advocates claim, firstly, that a much better use of existing resources and more effective development, siting and administration of new facilities can be achieved by this realignment of the departmental and service committee structure. In addition they argue it is then possible to work more effectively with planning, education and social services departments of the authority. This then facilitates drawing up a comprehensive plan for community leisure opportunities, by bringing together into one major leisure service what were formerly a series of 'Cinderella departments'. Leisure provision can thereby be promoted more effectively as a major factor in the physical and financial plan for the authority. It is thought that such a department is able also to provide more effectively the focus for increasing leisure opportunities, by interpreting closely the roles of departments which were created originally with other objectives, but where leisure has assumed a major role. Monitoring changing interests and trends would facilitate the feedback into the social and physical plan. It is widely accepted that there is a need to generate more positive policies to take into account the varying needs and aspirations of the community, making known existing opportunities for participation and creating new ones. Protagonists of leisure coalitions believe that such departments are better placed to take initiatives and work closely with voluntary organisations in this.

The range of responsibility of such a department can be wide and fairly comprehensive. The inventory of amenities and facilities may vary between authorities. A typical plan constituting a point of departure for a new composite leisure department could comprise the following, viewing the categories from the urban sector outwards:

(a) Urban open space—including local amenity areas, children's play areas, sports grounds, allotments, local parks and larger parks around sizeable areas of developed or undeveloped space, including water space. Within certain areas of open space it is important to consider also a number of specialist facilities of more than local significance such as golf courses, linking networks of footpaths or bridleways, rural museums, artificial ski slopes, riding areas and motor sports centres.

(b) Open country facilities—including areas of open space and water, more remote from the urban environment. Here one considers amenities such as picnic areas, country parks, water recreation areas, walking and riding routes.

(c) The third category might be termed indoor facilities generally— including meeting rooms, small exhibition areas, small halls, craft shops, branch libraries, district swimming pools, sports halls, museums, squash courts and so forth.

(d) Finally, there is the category of specific indoor facilities which may be of more than local neighbourhood significance but which are required in larger communities to serve more than immediate local needs. Here one could include central libraries with specific reference services, major local collections or regional and internal library loan services, specialist museum collections, gala swimming pools and high-diving facilities, concert halls, indoor bowls centres, theatres and art galleries.

Such an analysis of requirements may at first sight be awesome and overwhelming, and for those with responsibility for getting provisions on the ground, it doubtless is, but there is a sense in which we see it as rather limited and only illustrative of some potential initiatives in a local area. Shops, pubs, hairdressers, streets, side-walks, transport termini and so on are excluded from conventional categories of amenities and facilities; yet they are an essential part of the fabric of life which people may enjoy.

More specific ways in which some believe the composite department to be more effective in exploiting existing resources and planning new facilities at local level are envisaged as follows. For example, meeting rooms and small halls may already be in existence from private sources, particularly lay churches, and available for further use over and above their existing use to the mutual benefit of new users and existing owners. Other provision can be developed through private and commercial resources if there is a department actively exploiting possibilities. Within the public sector local authorities can utilise possibilities for dual-use of education and other public facilities and jointly plan new schemes with other departments, for example, the Education Department and the Department of Social Services. Cultural, sporting, entertainment and a local area's general needs for meeting rooms and small halls with related social, refreshment and car-parking provision, are all capable of development; they provide a focal point within the local authority and a physical and financial plan for their establishment is fostered. Others may question whether departmental restructuring is required to bring about collaboration at a very local level. Indeed some suggest that if realignments are to occur at all, they should begin on the ground and then proceed upwards to the authority itself. Predictably many of the arguments have two sides. While protagonists may suggest that the existence of a department with central responsibility for leisure interests can react swiftly to changing trends in demand, and vary the uses to which flexibly built facilities are put, others point to the need for safeguards against bureaucratic tendencies of rigidifying and conservatism.

However, for those authorities which have established comprehensive leisure departments, the overriding problem is that of developing a coherent philosophy which will rationalise either the maintenance of separate areas of influence and responsibility in what they now see as a unitary problem area, or allow them to be merged.

There is as yet no coherent rationale for the unification of leisure providers' efforts other than those associated with fiscal or political considerations. This is reflected in research in the leisure field. Most studies undertaken so far have been facilities-oriented, rather than looking at alternative patterns of provision in relation to users' needs and wishes. No way has yet been developed to integrate the two approaches.

A similar disjunction seems to be emerging at *a regional level*. From the providers' point of view, there are several forces in favour of regional collaboration. One is the need for a mutually beneficial framework between urban and countryside provision; this can only be reached through collaboration between authorities and with various regional agencies. Others include the fact that many facilities draw on regional or larger catchment areas, for example, golf courses, concert halls, seaside resorts, water recreation areas, as do some activities, such as pop festivals, and that many minority provisions can benefit by regional pooling, for example, air sports and motor sports centres, museum services, linear and national parks. The motorcar, aptly described by Rodgers as the major 'recreational tool' of our culture, brings a larger than local use and a regional catchment for many activity areas (Rodgers, 1969). From the users' perspective, however, 'regional' is a difficult scale to relate to easily and for the sizeable percentage of the population who will continue to be without personal transport, the term will continue to be of more marginal significance (Hillman *et al.*, 1973).

Nevertheless, there are specific regional agencies which have emerged in the last decade with a responsibility to develop and co-ordinate regional planning in various areas of leisure provision. Arts associations and regional sports councils are typical examples. Other regional agencies include tourist boards, national parks planning boards, river boards and water authorities. Nearly all have some grant-aiding function, but there is a lack of overall philosophy guiding the separate developments, a lack of uniformity in the boundaries within which they work and resultant difficulties in communication within regions which cross local authority boundaries. At a regional scale at least, there is as yet little expectation that composite leisure agencies, as opposed to specific ones, have any relevance. Meanwhile, the apparent advantages in regional provision could be explored in greater depth and the successes and problems experienced by regional projects like national parks and the Lea Valley Regional Recreation Park could be analysed. The regional agencies will require a dialogue among themselves, to build on common factors and functions and thereby to understand more clearly the problems of strengthening their own service, particularly to local authorities.

Extending the perspective to *central government*, the issues are revealed once more in sharper focus. Characteristically they surround the cases for and against a Ministry of Leisure.

At present responsibility for leisure is spread through many departments somewhat fortuitously. The pattern represents a heterogeneous and somewhat conflicting series of prohibitions, regulating, enabling, taxing, planning, directly providing, researching, grant-aiding and co-ordinating functions. In nearly all cases leisure or recreation is a minor role in the government departments involved. Specific government spokesmen have been established for the arts, sport and countryside recreation during the 1960s. In some cases the government agency responsible is contained within the government department, though frequently staffed by Civil Service administrators and professionals operating within the Civil Service. The role of central government agencies reflects not only their specific histories, but a lack of coherence in central government generally about what is wanted in the leisure field. At this level as well there is no coherent or unified leisure philosophy, though the Lords' Select Committee Reports are influential in this direction (1973). There are many different ideas, partly implemented in specific local situations, without consensus about what the desirable directions for such developments are.

Yet arguably, there are advantages in this situation. Government agencies offer examples around the country of creative developments in various leisure areas. Creative provision for people at local level may occur irrespective of coherent models and a unified policy. Diversity and lack of coherence may stimulate imaginative developments. Conversely losses may stem from 'top-heaviness'; for example, stereotyped sports halls, swimming pools and golf courses may not deal as universally or as enjoyably with people's needs. The Sports Council and the Arts Council of Great Britain are concerned with developing a variety of regional and national projects, to encourage local authorities to evolve creative ideas and attempt innovations, often with financial support for their experiments. The Department of Health and Social Security is concerned with pre-school play. The Home Office urban aid section offers assistance for new ideas and projects through its urban aid programme. The Countryside Commission has sponsored important management and research projects such as the Goyt Valley Traffic Experiment, where a joint project with the Peak Planning Board developed a specific scheme to handle the invasion of the motorcar into this vulnerable and unique area of countryside (Miles, 1972). Within just this type of mosaic framework, a good deal of pump-priming, stimulating and catalytic initiatives may generate action at local level, especially if the agencies from which they emanate are in a position to offer financial support and other back-up services.

What then should be the role of central government itself? Should there be a Ministry of Leisure? If it is claimed that there is a lack of clarity in government about what is wanted in the leisure field, and when it is known that, for example, one agency finds it needs to operate in fifteen or more government departments in order to effect its policies, there would appear to be a *prima facie* case for drawing in all the minor leisure roles of these departments to one ministry. Such a ministry could conceivably provide a focus for leisure-planning, rationalise the anomalies in grant-aid assistance from government departments and agencies in the field, hammer out a common philosophy for provision at both local and regional levels, and develop research programmes around technical problems of facilities, management policy and socio-logical/psychological areas of motivation and aspiration.

But aside from all the real political obstacles to such a development and the question of the relative weight it could carry if it were able to take off at all, the overriding objection from our point of view is that any *unitary* philosophy of leisure in its own right will be at variance with the meaning of leisure in the reality of many people's lives. While it is probably necessary to integrate leisure provision at local level to make it feasible to create facilities and stand up to the competing claims of more time-honoured programmes, the case for national integration is less clear, especially in view of the dangers of rigidity and uniformity that may accompany an official or formal philosophy. A Ministry of Leisure? Probably not. A Ministry of the Quality of Life, Paris-style? Perhaps. At least Giscard D'Estaing's new creation also warrants careful and dispassionate monitoring.

In summing up this critique, we wish to emphasise three points we consider to be of paramount importance in leisure provision. While there is a justifiable concern with the accomplishment of tangible goals and products—parks, pools, sports centres and the like—there is a continuing need to consider the less tangible aspects of how these facilities function. By this we mean attention to their location, lay-out, presentation and management from the point of human relationships with users. One of the hazards of the institutionalisation process is that these aspects may be assumed to follow automatically. This assumption is proven over and over again to be inaccurate. Similarly, if it is con-sidered desirable to monitor facilities, provision for this must be built into budgets and kept in. Otherwise, being intangible, it may become a casualty in the chronic scramble for scarce funds. Rosow, writing about provision for the elderly, formulates it in *generally* valid terms (1967, 2):

> we are generally much more sensitive to material than social needs, and think more readily in concrete than abstract terms. It is easier to visualise a particular building or formal program than social in-stitutions. Objects and organisations provide tangible reassurances of effectiveness and success. On the other hand, concepts and relationships are intangible. They implicitly confront us with dis-quieting issues of *meaning* which the material approach often clumsily but readily ignores.

The institutionalisation process is subject to vicissitudes. After an initial period of flux in which modes of operation, roles and procedures, budgets and powers are worked out, a *modus operandi* is evolved. When this crystallises, it is difficult to alter unless a crisis occurs, in which there is an 'unfreezing' and new institutionalisation processes come into play. The institutionalisation process in relation to mass 'leisure services' in Britain still has some fluidity. Roles are being established, departments formed, fields staked out, lines of authority and influence established. Insights achieved at this stage may be more influential than later when things are humming smoothly according to agreed principles. We hope that it is neither too early nor too late (and therefore doomed to await a future crisis of reorganisation) to point out that, while 'leisure services' need to be provided and institutionalised at this point in time, in the long run leisure departments should be orientated towards their own eventual elimination. In keeping with the view that we express continually in this book, while it may be politically strategic at this moment in history for local authorities to have leisure departments or their equivalent to obtain the financial and other backing for providing necessary services, in the last resort, leisure interests are most appropriately seen as part of general life interests which shift through the life cycle and which may occur in various spheres. *Providing for them separately assumes the segregation of life into different spheres which is only one pattern among many.* The leisure field is institutionalising at great speed, but the process has been going on for a relatively short time. It may thus still be possible to build in an orientation to the whole life which will enable leisure providers to minimise the development of vested interests in segregated and specialised leisure services.

This is, perhaps, asking too much of enthusiasts at a time when institution-building is so sorely needed. However, the trend at the people's level is towards cultivating interests and enjoyments as part of life rather than something separate and set aside. The implications of this for providers are enormous. They involve various attempts to enrich the quality of working life, to enrich the quality of family life, to enrich the quality of community life, in addition to increasing the stock of available resources.

The world of concern of providers operates semi-independently of the interests of people. While the two worlds of providers and people function according to their own internal preoccupations, it is the provider–user interface which is crucial in assessing the value of facilities. But what criteria are to be used for evaluating the use made of provisions by people? An economic model of supply and demand is a first step in most planners' thinking when coming to grips with these problems. But knowledge of what lies behind or outside observed demand is also important in planning and providing facilities. We have approached the problem of developing this 'deeper' knowledge and perspectives by the critical analysis from first principles of understanding substance, variation and change in people's motivations. It is beyond our scope to attempt a thoroughgoing analysis of the organisational constraints on providers' agencies; but whatever these may be they should not override an awareness of the preoccupations and interests of the human beings for whom the provisions are being planned and managed. For this reason it is necessary to repeat that institutionalisation (in the form of large-scale, bureaucratic organisations) has hazards in relation to the cultivation of personal interests, however rational it may be for the provision of facilities. These hazards should be made explicit, kept in awareness and guarded against. They include impersonal handling, block-thinking, inflexibility and access-barriers.

Nevertheless, leisure provision (pursued with the appropriate reservations) has positive functions. The provisions are not just to take up surplus time or to attract surplus disposable income; they should enrich the quality of life. A simple 'philosophy of leisure' will not do this. What is needed is a 'philosophy of life', and for this it is necessary that providers sustain a 'person orientation' as well as a 'facilities orientation'. People's capacities for developing personal interests are critical in this. The interest capacity is essential not only to enrich life, but to safeguard against hazards of social isolation, occupational redundancy and alienation in an 'age of discontinuity'. Interests serve as threads of continuity around which lives may be organised. They relate individuals to their own pasts and futures as well as to others in their social and natural environments. We think these considerations should be given serious attention, obvious though they may seem, and they should be recurrently reviewed, unnecessary as this may seem. In support of this we cite comments on the Department of the Environment's report on *Children at Play*. A newspaper editorial leader indicated that the very detailed research drew conclusions which seemed obvious to the informed reader, namely that children are more likely to use play facilities if their families live in flats nearer the ground, that children want to bicycle but find the streets unsafe and the parks off limits, and that taking bicycles on buses and tubes and trains is difficult (*Evening Standard*, 19 March 1973, our emphasis):

> Goodness knows what this extremely thorough survey cost to mount. It might seem a trifle daft to some that it needed to be mounted at all, when the conclusions that it comes to could generally be provided by the most feather-brained housewife after two seconds' thought.
>
> After all, the finding that most outside play takes place 'near dwellings' and that therefore play areas should where practicable be sited close to them is scarcely world shaking.

Nor should it come as news to anyone that the nearer children live to the ground, the more they play outdoors; and that if they live anywhere above the first floor this propensity is sharply reduced.

Yet it is precisely because this will evidently be news to so many housing estate managers and architects that the survey is not daft at all. On the contrary it is extremely necessary.

It is stupid, when thousands of children get killed and injured each year, that recreational grounds are not more often provided close to where the children live.

We have become dim about people and families while becoming brilliant about machines and large-scale organisations. It is not necessary to smash or throw out the machines and organisations (indeed they are needed more than ever), but it is necessary to design them and apply them *with people in mind.*

No provider or consortium of providers can meet all the complex and changing preoccupations and interests that we have outlined (and we have only sketched major patterns with no claim to comprehensiveness). Yet it is this *orientation to people* and the varying and changing needs that should be the central consideration—complementary to, not pushed aside by the orientation to facilities and their preservation. The propositions we set out below specify some attitudes that would facilitate people's pursuit of their interests, complementarily to the creation and functioning of the facilities themselves. We see these formulations as essential underpinnings for practical suggestions.

The present report has a number of limitations. Some pertain to the current stage of the work, others to our particular research experiences. To the extent that we are aware of them, we indicate them as areas for further research. We have a better knowledge of middle-class than working-class activities and interests; a better knowledge of urban (particularly the older metropolitan) situations than the rural, suburban and new development situations, and a better appreciation of the public sector than the private or commercial sector providers. These limitations do not imply our evaluation of the relative worth or importance of the different sub-groups; indeed we explicitly recommend that supplementary work be undertaken to correct the deficiencies.

It is not our intention that the propositions which follow be construed as a blueprint for leisure providers, but rather as a set of guidelines which may be useful for them and those delivering other community services, for researchers in the field and for the people with whom they are concerned. Our main recommendation is that *a people-orientation* be adopted. This orientation can improve the work of leisure providers not only in their own attempts to meet aspects of the 'leisure explosion' with concrete provisions of various kinds, but in their potential efforts, along with other kinds of providers, to *humanise* our society.

The first six propositions which are at the core of our thinking relate to 'people', the remaining six to 'providers'.

PROPOSITION 1: *The public is entitled to a good time.* The idea of the pursuit of happiness as a human right is enshrined in the preamble of the American Constitution, is being written into British policy-influencing government documents (Lords' Select Committee, 1973) and is a clarion call by visionary leisure providers (Hudson, 1973).

PROPOSITION 2: *The public is not a block.* They come not only in different sizes, shapes, sexes, but have different focal preoccupations, different interests and behave variously under different conditions. People vary as well within any age group. In this book we have presented four types of young adult, for example. There are many more at least as important, particularly among young metropolitan dwellers. Block thinking about 'the family' is also not effective. There are different kinds of families and their preoccupations and interests differ, Age, sex and social class are not sufficiently comprehensive as variables guiding policy. Formulations like 'working-class, urban families with children' give part of the picture, but it is also necessary to know what the family structure and norms are. Conventional families differ from dual-worker families and from families with irregular arrangements of one kind or another. The strengths and strains in these different family situations—other than economic—will partly determine their 'leisure needs'.

PROPOSITION 3: *Nor is the public a collection of isolated individuals.* Each is influenced from birth by a succession of different forces, operating through phases of the life cycle. These influences are personal (i.e. involve internal motivations as influenced by earlier experiences), interpersonal (i.e. stem from close relationships with other significant people, for example family members, friends, teachers, neighbours), institutional (such as the school ethos and curriculum) and sociocultural (that is the larger set of norms and values diffusely present in the culture). These influences bind individuals together in a variety of social groupings and networks.

PROPOSITION 4: *There is no agreed definition of leisure that is common to people in our society.* There is enormous variation, overlap and blurring about what people consider to be 'leisure'. This blurring seems to be increasing rather than decreasing.

PROPOSITION 5: *People have preoccupations which change at different stages in their lives.* These preoccupations may be translated into interests and the interests may be channelled into activities. Characteristic preoccupations seem to persist through generations. This is why we couch our formulation in terms of underlying preoccupations rather than the more surface manifestations of their expressed interests and activities. It is important to try to distinguish between types of research on

fundamental problems and research that is of a more immediate and practical kind. A fundamental problem is how to give young people the chance for physical stimulation and 'action' in the urban setting. A more immediate and practical issue is how to get bicycle tracks built into roadway or park systems. Here there are innumerable problems of design, architecture and structure, as well as of public opinion, before bylaws can be changed, budgets allocated and programmes undertaken.
PROPOSITION 6: *Activities are not direct expressions of interest.* A specific activity can be used to express many kinds of interest; and a given interest can find expression in various activities. No given activity can therefore be considered to be uniquely required for specific interests. Gardening can illustrate the vitality of interests that may surround such an activity which appears as a simple check list item in many activity surveys. The *Sunday Times Magazine*'s special series on gardening quotes their gardening consultant's basic attitude to gardening as 'fun', an extension of people's tastes and pleasure into the open air—eating, drinking, playing, even sleeping: 'We encourage people to think twice about anything they are enjoying and to wonder if they wouldn't enjoy it more in the garden' (*Sunday Times Magazine*, 11 March 1973). Some of the uses to which gardens are put by contemporary families include: a new and creative hobby—creating a beautiful scene; helping things to grow; providing safe play areas for the children—swings, climbing frames, sports areas; entertaining, patio drinks, cook-outs; outdoor room to relax in, sunbathing, reading, resting; sanctuary for animals, birds, fish, wild areas, miniature countryside wilderness; growing food, harvesting own fruit and vegetables for the table; practice at garden sports (tennis trainer, golf putting areas, etc.); exercise (digging, cutting, mowing, raking, climbing for pruning, trellis and easy carpentry work); growing area for presents, such as flowers for presents in a hothouse.
PROPOSITION 7: *An institutionalisation process is going on in the leisure field.* While recent, it is occurring rapidly.
PROPOSITION 8: *Institutionalisation entails the agreement on a standard definition of leisure, of formal roles and responsibilities, formal allocations and visible distinctive products,* distinguished from other elements of life.
PROPOSITION 9: *Institutionalisation tends to give rise to a gap between the goals and procedures of the providers and the needs and desires of those provided for.* This is an unintended and undesired consequence of institutionalisation. Institutionalisation is required to meet the demands of the leisure explosion. But in becoming institutionalised, leisure providers create a gap between their own ways of thinking and operating and those of the public, many of whom are organising their lives in such a way that there is no clear differentiation between different sectors.

PROPOSITION 10: *A conception of provision based on interest-fulfilment would include a much wider range than only those institutionalised as leisure/recreation providers.* Schools, adult education centres, housing associations, work organisations, can all therefore be seen as institutions with potentials for satisfying people's interests.

PROPOSITION 11: *This conception opens the way for policy formation based on a principle of multiple use of existing facilities* on a broad basis and the development of new specialised facilities.

PROPOSITION 12. *Developing new solutions will involve the necessity to work with complexity, ambiguity and uncertainty.* This is likely to require the capacity to deal with defences and resistances. These capacities are likely increasingly to become part of the role requirements of providers.

These propositions constitute a set of guidelines, an orientation, which we suggest ought to be kept in mind when policy-makers in leisure or leisure-related fields develop their positions. We see that their position is a difficult one to straddle for all this implies that providers must be alert to a *dual-role*: one that is *facilities-orientated* (creating and managing the physical resources), and another that is *people-orientated* (being sensitive to channelling and cultivating the resourcefulness of the facilities' users). Neither is enough on its own.

How are these two agenda to be reconciled? We neither can nor do we wish to provide a blueprint for action. We suggest, illustratively, the kinds of practical implications these propositions might entail. At first glance they may seem to be too ambitious, given the difficulties in launching even a relatively straightforward programme of building sports centres, leisure centres, parks and auditoria. In a way they are. On the other hand, many of the suggestions emanating from this orientation are—like the proverbial 'best things in life' (nearly) free. The following examples are derived from our study. They are not exhaustive nor are they systematically presented. They have come to our attention in the course of our exploratory work, our thinking and experience.

Providing for variety involves a network approach to facilities. Providing more than one of a facility, like a coffee bar, may be better than one, even if it goes against principles of economic rationality. Having at least one 'alternative' coffee bar provides for people's interest in variety; it gives options for sampling differences in a changing scene of interactions. If there are difficulties from an organisational point of view in providing two, one might be self-programmed, manned by voluntary workers. This might provide possibilities for experimentation and innovation with design, contents of the service and so on. It might also provide an element of constructive competition with the establishment. This principle suggested itself strongly in the user–provider case study.

At present there is only one refreshment centre apart from the pubs, on the estate. This is located in the community centre. A second coffee bar would undoubtedly make a positive contribution not only because the centre bar is often closed and small in relation to demand, but because a second—if, say, it were commercially run in the shopping square— might assume a different atmosphere, attract a new clientele and provide a choice of venues for casual meetings.

There is another sense in which variety and a network approach to facilities is important. Where an environment is deficient in this respect, people feel that their actions are more exposed. Some estate-dwellers felt very self-conscious entering the community centre for example. In a physical environment that is more varied, fewer thresholds may present themselves, at least to the use of *some* facilities.

A people-orientated approach must be geared to the complexities of people. Head-counts of use of a facility are not enough to gauge the correctness of a policy of provision. Potential demand must be assessed; satisfaction must be assessed; inhibitions of populations who are reluctant to express their interest must be overcome; the development of interests must be facilitated. For young people this will often mean guiding their interests into areas that are exciting without being too dangerous, spontaneous without being too chaotic and disorganising, limit-testing without being irresponsible, and which allow for trying out new interests without fearing failure or negative sanctions. Young people's interest in experience often requires a tolerance of disorder. Not everyone can achieve this. Local level involvement of people who are in personal contact with those who come to use a facility is important, so that a balance can be maintained between permissiveness and constraint. This is particularly important in relation to young people's quest for new experiences, which may bring them into areas where they test the limits of social tolerance, of their own physical or psychological tolerance, and which may arouse anxiety or court danger for themselves or others. Too much regimentation and constraint shuts off the possibility for experience; too much permissiveness courts danger and shuts off other experiences. Tolerance of ambiguity, of complexity, of apparent chaos and disorder, walking the tightrope of facilitating development and controlling danger—all require very special kinds of leadership.

The indications for constraint are most prominent in leisure provision for young people. On the other side are problems of 'passivity'. While this problem holds particularly for older groups, it is true also for some young people. This may be a matter of fear and inhibition, it may be lack of knowledge or encouragement. This is not to say that young people are either vigorously active or subdued; any one individual is potentially both. It is therefore not enough for us simply to provide facilities. Young people, particularly those who are less comfortable, more restless and searching, want to know the reason why; they want to try for themselves; to see how things work, and what's over there. At the same time, they are easily put off, skittish, often disappointed avoidably through not having the appropriate 'awakening' experiences provided. This requires positive efforts to influence or 'animate' those who are shy, inhibited or defensive.

There are sub-groups in the later life-cycle phases which require positive encouragement to develop interests even more urgently. For example, young adults, particularly conventional-minded ones, tend to become preoccupied with courtship and marriage to the exclusion of other interests. It is also known that while satisfactions are high during this period, the constriction of interests to the domestic sphere may lead to difficulties later on. Much less is known, however, about the mechanics of this constriction and how it can be countered. Research is needed to compare, for example, the responsiveness of young couples to new interests on a joint versus a sex-segregated basis; on a local versus a centrally located basis and so on.

Involuntarily unemployed young adults are another of the sub-groups we have presented that needs special leadership. It is well known from studies of the unemployed that a demoralising, depressing tendency is set in motion when the possibility for employment is involuntarily withdrawn. This is devastating enough for heads of households, but for young adults it may crystallise negative self-images and attitudes towards work and society that will have life-long effects. Research is needed on the effects of various attempts to activate and channel the interests of young people under these conditions—for example through community industry, public service, adult educational programmes.

Some 'populations at risk' through under-involvement with personally meaningful interests stand out more clearly than others. We suggested earlier (see p. 265) that the implication of the Tavistock Stress Study findings for leisure provision is that ways need to be found to encourage non-working mothers in the 35+ age group to become interested in a range of activities, particularly outside the home. This is not a simple undertaking that works mechanically. As resistance and anxieties have to be overcome, particularly in relation to taking on activities never tried before, active facilitation is needed. The adults' case material from the user–provider study indicates the delicate balance between potentials and problems in interest development. Most of those talked to spoke of despair or boredom, monotony, understimulation, 'getting in a rut', 'being fed up'. They too resist formality and insistence on commitment. All the women speak of being 'scared' but so may men like Mr S. Socially the case material underscores the likely benefits of sensitive mediation, which may invite even those women who seem least receptive over the threshold to involvement.

In all these cases—and differently for the different sub-groups involved—what seems to be required is a kind of *animation*, as the French call it. This involves *people who are facilitators, activators, mediators, who bring together people and resources to facilitate the development of interests*. This is a pastoral role that involves initiatives in the community —not just setting up facilities and contenting oneself that if people come the facility is successful. This does not imply that people must be constantly active; nor that they should be active if they do not want to be. The activators are important to help those who are inhibited, unresourceful and socially isolated to take the necessary plunges to bring them into contact with sources of development for their potential life interests. Spencer Hudson envisages these potentials in the context of non-specialised, local-level leisure centres that Dixey (1974) advocates. In his complimentary review of Dixey's book Hudson suggests (1974, 1499):

> The maison de la culture analogy is perhaps less apt, as these French sport centres tend to have a standardized physical design, which should be anathema to the general proposition [of flexibility and non-specialisation]; their important facet which is not mentioned is the role of the animateur—the term translates badly suggesting a manipulator of puppets, whereas it really relates to a man or woman who can breathe life into the whole enterprise. It is on such leaders, and the management arrangements behind them, that local recreation centres will succeed or fail. The persistence and depth of public consultation will be crucial, and this requires flexible and relaxed staff.

Facilitating the cultivation of interest requires new skills. New policies of recruitment and training are likely to be required. Orthodox recruitment and training practices may not lead to the selection of suitable people. The 'right' kind of person may not be the one who is conventionally drawn into either management or the public service fields such as education, local government or social work. Investigation is necessary into what kind of person and training would be best to cultivate this people-facilitating orientation.

As regards the need to constrain over-activity, destructiveness, exuberance, etc., we believe that a requirement of channelling rather than restriction is implied. This may involve either facilities or activities. In both cases the curbing of activity should be part of a programme which provides alternative channels rather than simply blocking the offending ones. Curbing the motorcar in the Goyt Valley succeeded because alternatives were provided, via minibuses and footpaths. Curbing vandalism may succeed if energies can be channelled into more acceptable forms of aggressive activity—from football and boxing gloves to contests, building works and similar outlets. But for the 'honeypot' strategy to be successful, the underlying attractions of whatever is seen to indicate alternative provisions need to be adequately understood.

Providing for stimulation and for quiet; sociability and solitude requires a design and management approach which allows for zoning and phasing of experience, and the linking of different kinds of facilities. This kind of problem becomes particularly acute in settings where there is not a great deal of overlay and complexity of provision; where the population may be too sparse for commercial investment in provision, and where the social environment is relatively homogeneous. In these settings the quiet-and-solitude part of the cycle is over-provided, while the stimulation-and-sociability part (particularly where there is the desire for novelty and new experience) is under-provided. New and imaginative combinations of facilities, local and regional, public and private, should be thought about in relation to this problem. This might involve public providers acting in ways not ordinarily thought of as legitimately part of their realms, for example pump-priming a commercial coffee bar or cinema.

We repeat our earlier suggestion, namely that it would be helpful also if providers shifted their emphasis in favour of more fluid and varying participation in activities. At present there is widespread insistence of 'joining', 'registering', 'enrolling', 'signing up', all of which carry an expectation of subsequent regular attendance. This not only means too much commitment for some, but it eliminates the scope for scene-sampling. The need to facilitate personal experimentation appears all the more necessary if the venues where activities may be pursued are recognised also as contexts for meeting different types of people.

The 'good family base' ultimately is one that facilitates meaningful interest development for all members of the family. This enables provision both for shared—at least integrating—interests within the home, and for linkages between the home and the outside world. External linkages are of two sorts. We have discussed at length the involvement with outside interests of family members as individuals. We know relatively little about the pursuit of integrative outside interests by family members as a family.

The scope of leisure interests for the quality of family life requires more research. Because of the negative impetus of adolescents who are making breaks with their childhood ties as part of their identity formation, there has been an emphasis on disorganising elements in relation to family life at this time. Young people are often awkward, rebellious, withdrawn; they do not communicate with their parents, they do not want to share activities, they are critical and dissatisfied. So great has been the emphasis on family problems at this period, that little is known about what families actually do together. And yet there is consensus that family influence is not yet at an end for young people at this point. It is likely that leisure can serve an important integrative function, and enrich family life at a point where this quality is under strain.

While young people are inordinately sensitive to being preached to, taught, controlled or otherwise made to feel like children, they may value doing things that are purely enjoyable with other family members or at least with other family members around. Much more needs to be known about what these pursuits are, under what conditions they can be made to serve family integrative functions while at the same time not constricting young people's development. Some family leisure may be used to maintain links between members even while separation processes are at work; it is therefore particularly important in relation to the adolescent child's development.

Within the home at present television has a near monopoly on family interests, and it seems to lack power as a family integrating device. Shared areas of interest that agencies may help to cultivate centre round do-it-yourself activities, gardening and sport, which transcend generations and sex divisions. Physical resources, in the vicinity of the home, for stimulating and expressing such interests are often deficient. Local authorities may make a positive contribution here. The range of facilities and activities permitted in public housing estates is frequently restricted; the 'no ball games allowed' sign, for example, is ubiquitous. Lessons may be learned from monitoring the array of facilities that have developed spontaneously in neighbourhood-minded areas like London's Mecklenburgh Square.

The scope for local leisure facilities, shared by a small cluster of homes, cannot be over-stressed. The most important focus of interest for young families in particular is around the home, although they often experience loneliness because of this. The provision of leisure facilities in close association with housing is not adequately developed at present. Even the wealthy with their gardens, high-fidelity sound reproduction equipment, play space and so on, have potential problems. There is the danger of isolation, particularly of the mother and child within the household. Leisure facilities in association with housing could include: children's playgroups, social groups for mothers, child, father—in various combinations—meeting rooms, sports facilities, open spaces and communal gardens, barbecues and play equipment.

It is not only the young 'house-bound mother and baby' who would benefit from such provision. It is a great advantage also to dual-worker families to have leisure facilities near at hand. For such families, having any *shared* enjoyment pursuits is often very difficult. To keep two careers going and at the same time run a household requires an enormous amount of work from the wife (particularly if her husband does not really share with the domestic side of things). Even if they contribute fairly equally to the domestic work, there are strains partly because of reduced time available. For such couples there is a problem of liberating enough time for leisure interests and the route to this may be by way of more mechanised goods to ease household work and child care; more convenience foods, goods, clothing, sheets, etc.; more 'leisure' activities that can be integrated in a small home or flat and associated with home-building tasks.

Arrangements for flexible work hours may make it possible to work more evenings and have afternoons free. This would allow for time together between mother and father, father and children. Emphasis first on mother's having flexible work time will not, in the longer run, be adequate. The emphasis will have to be on flexible work time for both so that the move towards sharing the tasks and the enjoyment pursuits can be maximised.

There are some current examples of family-integrative leisure provisions outside the home. In the commercial sector there are family holidays and camps at all price ranges. In the public sector there are university programmes where the academic plant is turned over in summer for course work, with accommodation provided for whole families. Another university holds a 'Family Sports Week', emphasising physical activities. In a public school located in a part of the country of outstanding beauty, there are summer music programmes which allow for whole families. The tricky element seems to be the combination of sharing and separateness. Sometimes family members want to do different things in a shared context, as when they all go off to the country together in the family car, but disperse when there. Sometimes they want to pursue activities together. There are very frequently obstacles to this. A father and son may wish to do woodwork together, for example, but the father may well find himself constrained to an adults-only class, and the son be confined to the purview of the Youth Service. At least two London adult education institutes have opened their facilities to families on Saturday mornings. A much less regimented and ongoing multi-use of leisure facilities than is common has considerable potential for supporting family relationships. Complexes of provision as in the more imaginative urban parks is another way that this problem may be approached (Pinfold, 1973).

Relations between young people and adults in general need to be fostered. There are generational problems in relation to both family and non-family leisure provision. Young people are keen to sample experiences on their own or with friends, to experiment with new interests, to try their hands at different tasks. Yet they often feel excluded or devalued

in the adult world, and may react by a reciprocal exclusion and devalua-
tion of adult society and culture. Even if there are no formal rules
assigning which age groups go where, 'social filters' act to exclude many
young people from adult interest groups and vice versa (Emmett,
1971b). Thought and action experimentation should be given to how
these gaps can be bridged.

Provision of self-programming, voluntary activities serves the interests of
several sub-populations, often reciprocally. Young people want to be
active, to be autonomous, and to do something that will have an impact
—whether moral or physical—on their environments (Stevenson, 1972).
Older people want to do something that allows their experience to be
put to useful application. Very old, disabled people want selective
sociability. Community service activities could allow more consciously
for the mixing of different age groups complementarily (as with Task
Force) as well as separate efforts for specific problems (as with young
people's conservation corps activities, or the more occupationally conceived effort in community industries).

On the young people's side, there is the question of how to engage
their energies in such a way as to derive enjoyment and a sense of growth
and identity. If a schism develops between 'us' (young people) and
'them' (the politicians, planners, providers), the potential benefits of
shaping and using facilities that can be provided only through the
larger community resources may be lost. While there are movements in
the direction of increased participation of all sorts of people in planning
and policy-making, including young people, this is a field that is far
from well thought through or understood. Young people are not
usually part of organised lobbies, and when they do organise to demonstrate for a particular interest, they often do so in ways that antagonise
their elders in the establishment positions that count in such matters.
What is needed is more work on the issue of how young people can make
their needs and wants felt other than by demonstrations which have an
anti-social, counter-cultural focus. Nor is the 'token' young person on
the decision-making councils of planners and policy-makers the answer.
Bridging the gap between young people and those who plan and manage
their facilities is a field for imaginative action research.

People need personal mobility. For young people this is a matter of
adventurousness, speed, excitement, movement, slight danger, showing
off. For all age groups it is a matter of getting around and about—for
business, shopping, pleasure, sociability, Hillman has shown that personal mobility levels are not as high as often imagined (Hillman *et al.*,
1973). While some solutions are well recognised though not implemented—for example free bus transport—others seem to be surprisingly
overlooked. With urban traffic problems and the dangers of motorcycles
and cars on the road, particularly in the hands of the young, why are

there not more cycle tracks, cycle networks, cycle throughways? The answer seems to be in relation to the absence of effective cycle lobbies rather than in economic or other terms. It is very difficult to cycle in urban areas; and yet this may be one of the pre-industrial cultural elements that needs to be reinstituted in a post-industrial society that is more aware of the body and the need for exercises, and more concerned with pollution and its noxious effects. Why not build it into roadways; why not convert old roadways for cycling? Why are networks of cycling tracks not put around towns and tracks built through parks instead of having cycles prohibited?

The role of schools in leisure provision is critical. *Provision for living* is important at all ages—from the identity crystallisation phase through the last spurt in old age. Learning to live cannot be 'switched on' at prescribed hours, or late in life without preparation. Training in resourcefulness (cultivation of the RQ) and appreciation of both the yields of interest recultivation and the habit of learning are intrinsically satisfying. Contemporary conceptions of schools are both age-graded and specialised. This is beginning to break down in the idea of 'community schools', 'open schools and universities', multiple use of school facilities, colleges and universities. Much more work in de-schooling is necessary, and new and imaginative ways of bringing not only the facilities, but the people in the different bands of experience into interaction with one another. This is not only from the perspective of those 'outside' who could benefit from freer access to the facilities of education establishments, but from those 'inside' whose perspectives are often very restricted.

A study of the relevance of education for the enjoyment of leisure provisions could be productive in a number of areas. There is evidence that individuals who left school very early are deficient not only in the substance of their formal education, but in the habit of learning. This reduces their capacity to develop new interests in situations later confronting them, and this has been observed to impair adaptation to such life events as unemployment and retirement. Less attention has been given to how the type of education obtained affects the enjoyment and quality of living. Emphasis on intellectual learning and academic performance may be relevant for occupational success but its relevance for life enjoyment is less clear. Increasingly it is likely that educationists will turn their attention to the construction of curricula which aim to *educate people for living*. Studies are needed to assess how different kinds of educational experiences relate to the capacity for performance and enjoyment; the capacity to stick with and master tasks *and* flexibility to readapt.

The overall problem of *enrichment of life* in existing life sectors— work, family life, school and community life—is one that needs major attention. Providing separate facilities—such as leisure centres and sports centres—can only be part of the answer, and often reaches only those least needing the benefits of public leisure provision. Major experimentation with these enrichment programmes is now called for— in the workplace, in the family, in the community. Interactive initiatives from groups like Interaction with its 'fun art bus' and 'Almost Free Theatre' are a growing part of the contemporary scene. Because of their flexible operation over a whole range of contexts, they have the potential to diffuse enrichment widely. John Hoyland (1974) reports in the *Guardian* on the Bath Arts Workshop:

> In fact, the theatre group (just one of the BAW's activity contexts) is possibly the most perfect expression of what the BAW is about, which might be described as the *application of imagination to ordinary life*. What's more, the theatre group's flair and humour infects everything the BAW is involved in. A coach outing for old people is liable to be held up by highwaymen on horseback half-way to its destination.

To approach the issue of non-economic aspects of need, we suggest a two-pronged approach: (a) to isolate sub-categories of individuals 'at risk', those who are relatively unhappy, who suffer psychosomatic complaints, who feel disadvantaged as to their chances for enjoyment of life; and (b) to isolate sub-categories of individuals 'at benefit', those who are 'happy' and feel that they enjoy life as a whole.

Information about the dissatisfied, symptom-producing sub-categories is more available from our exploratory studies than on the more 'happy' and satisfied sub-categories. This is an area that requires considerable further research; it is a neglected topic because of the assumption that such people do not need further attention from society. It is our contention that they are important to understand as potential resource people and in order that provisions that enable them to maintain their satisfactory levels may be made. Knowledge about how they organise their lives, how they obtain their enjoyment and how they learn to adapt to new conditions in their lives can benefit those less competent in these pursuits. They may also, under favourable conditions and with persuasion, become leaders in activities which benefit from their skills and accomplishments, particularly in voluntary groups.

We have begun the task of differentiating groups 'at risk' and those 'at benefit' from whom lessons could be learned and leadership enlisted. This is a start to sorting out how improved balances of various kinds can be achieved in future and what contribution can be made by leisure providers.

Providers need to know more about their users. For this, improved methods of communication must be developed. Two-way exchanges of information in particular are required. Providers need to know more about their users. Market research is one approach; use of lobbies is another; use of techniques for public communication and participation (from video-tape to neighbourhood councils) is another. It is necessary to undertake community research to discover minority groups and social isolates who do not respond to existing approaches in order to know whether they exclude themselves by choice or through deficiency of the providers' methods; for example, old and disabled people living on their own. Here social workers, milkmen, pub managers, corner shop-keepers, traffic wardens, health visitors and other peripatetic care-givers in the community may be useful collaborators with leisure providers—as are teachers and school/college administrators in relation to other areas.

We also need to know far more about what life is like at certain stages of the life cycle. We know relatively little about young adulthood, a critical period in individuals' development of meaningful interests, and we know almost nothing about later life. The sort of knowledge required for a more responsive people orientation suggests that studies need to be 'made of and with' rather than 'done on' people at these stages.

Others about whom we know too little are those pursuing alternative life styles. Many young people want neither the discipline of an ortho-dox acceptance of conventional patterns of job/family and community life, nor the specialised developmental courses of institutions of higher education. They wish to create lives that are meaningful in different ways. For a variety of reasons—ranging from the view that they may be engaged in creating valuable artistic and social innovations, to the view that they may be psychologically disturbed and inaccessible to orthodox forms of treatment—these efforts ought to be tolerated. Suit-able safeguards should be instituted, as they are, for example, in rela-tion to pop festivals, against allowing these efforts to be seriously damaging to others, for example in matters of public health, noise pollution and drug abuse. Constructive links should be maintained with these groups; their members could be facilitated to move in and out of the groups as their development seems to them to warrant it. The provision of therapeutic communities on the Richmond Fellowship or Philadelphia Community models are examples of such linking institu-tions. Research is needed on the subsequent fate of alternative society 'drop-outs'. The phenomenon is so new that it is not known what proportion and what type of young adult makes a permanent career of marginal living and what proportion use it as a 'trip' from which they make their way back into a more established pattern of life, and with what consequences for them. Only after such research is done can further sensible policies be recommended. 'Dropping out' is increasingly recognised as a phenomenon of middle age as well; in this phase it may be a reaction to stress or it may be a positive move in the direction of developing new life interests. We believe that *individuals and groups engaged in the pursuit of alternative life styles should be tolerated within limits of social constraint, but with readiness to help if help is wanted: such experiments should be used for a reconsideration of conventional assumptions about life.*

A people-orientated approach requires that certain dilemmas be resolved about majority versus minority interests. This will involve issues surrounding both privileged and disadvantaged minority groups. Assumptions made by architects and planners about giving the masses what they really want (even assuming that the problems of assessing this were solved) are problematic in relation to minority provision. Many minority groups dislike mass tastes; catering for this kind of variety is intrinsic in the democratic process, particularly in a changing society where minority tastes of today may become majority tastes of tomorrow. Problems of cost and distribution of benefits must be worked out, especially when the minority tastes are expensive (for example squash). Yet this issue must be kept in mind with planning not only for *variation*, but for the *future* as well. Planners need to take initiatives, stimulate initiatives in the population and respond to initiatives where those are shown. Getting people to think about what they have or might have, and working with them to plan for the future, is immensely complex, but necessary. Users also need to know more about what is provided and how to use it.

The communication of information about provision and potential provision—directions, listings, guides to use, routes, hours of opening, charges, etc.—needs to be much more highly developed, at both local and national levels. Information needs to be more widely diffused. Apparently obvious channels are sometimes overlooked, for example checkout points at supermarkets; the usual local authority networks for the distribution of pamphlets, such as libraries and health centres, are insufficient. Many elements of provision can be variously described and classified, and people may give up in despair or fail to discover the information they want through not knowing what agency to contact. Centralisation of information or intelligence services on leisure has begun on a private consultancy basis for the rich: it should now be diffused for more general use. *Time Out* magazine suggests the comprehensive range of information which could be readily available by dialling one central number.

Yet even with a sophisticated information system and even if they were aware it had something positive to offer them, some people would never contact an agency. A withdrawn and isolated young mother, for example, experiencing a bad transition to her post-natal role, is unlikely to ring an agency to find out where mother-and-baby water recreation is available. She may well not have heard of this pursuit, nor realise its potential for a positive experience for herself and her child. She may even be unable to swim. If it is left up to her, she will probably never make contact with the opportunity. It seems clear to us that if the challenge is to be taken up at this level, institutional leisure providers cannot go it alone. The responsibility must surely be spread wider, engaging the collaboration of health visitors, social workers, educationists and people generally—as good friends and good neighbours.

7

Leisure

The individual, the family and society

In chapter 1 we discussed some threads of social change. These are relevant both to providers and to their publics, though in different ways. The view of contemporary social change on which we based our analysis suggests the possibility of a 'new culture' emerging. This 'new culture' —if it came about—would combine elements of industrial society with a new interpretation of elements of pre-industrial society. It is this new synthesis, which might develop into the so-called post-industrial society, that is focal to our point of view.

In human history generally there has been an interplay between two trends of concern: one, geared to the more instrumental tool-building and -using, economic survival considerations, has been termed the 'technical order' by Redfield and others (Redfield, 1953). The other, which is more concerned with the quality and meaning of life, human relations and the cultivation of satisfactory social experiences was termed the 'moral order' because it traditionally centred in society's system of sacred logics, its religious and ceremonial life. To broaden the latter conception for use in modern life, this second order of human concern is perhaps better termed the 'human order'.

The dynamics of human social evolution, as observers from Marx and Hegel onwards have held, involves a tension between aspects of a culture. When one seems to go too far in its grip on human institutions and people's motivations, a counter-culture arises which asserts the primacy of the other. In the counter-culture there is a 'transvaluation of values' in which what was considered good under the established system is seen as bad. The negative consequences of the established order are felt acutely; and its benefits less so. There are many examples from history. The Renaissance efflorescence in architecture and science can be seen, in part, as a reaction against the stultifying domination of religious constraints in pre-Renaissance times; the Industrial Revolution and the growth of capitalism has been seen as another such reaction. Antiphilistine reactions, anti-hedonistic reactions, anti-militaristic reactions and so on, punctuate the history of mankind.

There is a strong trend in contemporary social thought that suggests that we may be in an era of such reaction, against the negative consequences of a society dominated by technology and its associated characteristics, such as the tendency to large-scale and larger institutions. While it seems that it is *size* that is dehumanising, we are prepared to tolerate much of it in pursuit of raising the average standard of life. Nevertheless, *along with* this toleration, there are indications of protest and a desire for finding ways of humanising society as well as making it more equitable.

The counter-trends imply more than the youthful protests of hippie counter-cultures. It is more than radical protests of political parties seeking to overthrow the established economic system of the ownership of production (in some instances to replace it with an equally technologically-dominated one). It is a more pervasive, if unco-ordinated, set of reactions in different spheres *against* both the consequences of a technologically-dominated social system, and the value assumptions according to which this social system has functioned. The reaction against pollution, noise, war, expedient morality, individualism and egocentricism, materialism and public corruption all add up to a revulsion against an order which promotes technology too single-mindedly: Slater (1971, 9–10) gives an account of the extremity to which technological domination of people's lives and values has gone in the USA.

> Technological change, mobility and the individualistic ethos combine to rupture the bonds that tie each individual to a family, a community, a kinship network, a geographical location—bonds that give him a comfortable sense of himself. . . .
>
> We seek a private house, a private means of transportation, a private garden, a private laundry, self-service stores, and do-it-yourself skills of every kind. An enormous technology seems to have set itself the task of making it unnecessary for one human being ever to ask anything of another in the course of going about his daily business. . . .
>
> We less and less often meet our fellow man to share and exchange, and more and more often encounter him as an impediment or a nuisance: making the highway crowded when we are rushing somewhere, cluttering and littering the beach or park or wood, pushing in front of us at the supermarket, taking the last parking place, polluting our air, and water, building a highway through our house, blocking our view, and so on.

The reaction against the contamination of nature has been spearheaded by the eloquent and impassioned appeals of Rachel Carson and Barrie Commoner. Hannah Arendt, René Dubos and John Maddox have adopted views expressing the need for a new synthesis with varying degrees of emphasis on how technology could be used to deal with the problems its earlier masters created (Arendt, 1968; Ward and Dubos, 1972; Maddox, 1972).

A similar process is evident in the world of business and industry. The radical critique of business, documented by Perrow, has served to mobilise a wider-based programme of reforms, now expressed in international moves to 'improve the quality of working life' and to increase the sense of social responsibility of large business organisations (Perrow, 1972; Davis and Cherns, 1974).

There is a radical critique of the state of morality in contemporary society, ranging from religious revivalist groups (Jesus people, Divine Light people, moral rearmament people) to more secular reactions (humanist societies). Some of these movements are themselves anti-bureaucratic with reference to their present institutions; others are present-day versions of the kind of moral protests that have been periodically seen since early industrialisation (such as nineteenth-century sects).

There are groups that criticise the whole fabric of personality and motivation attached to the technological society with responses ranging from total rejection by some underground, hippie, squatter and communal groups to more piecemeal efforts to 'dis-inhibit' individuals by encounter groups and sensitivity-training groups. An example of the critique of the total national character came initially from the psycho-analysts' consulting rooms. Franz Alexander, for example, wrote (1951, 259):

> The analyst sees his patients—physicians, lawyers, engineers, bankers, advertising men, teachers and laboratory research men of universities, and clerks—engaged in a marathon race, their eager faces distorted by strain, their eyes focused not upon their goal, but upon each other with a mixture of hate, envy and admiration. Panting and perspiring, they run and never arrive. They would all like to stop but dare not as long as the others are running. What makes them run so frantically, as though they were driven by the threatening swish of an invisible whip wielded by an invisible slave driver? The driver and the whip they carry in their own minds. If one of them finally stops and begins leisurely to whistle a tune or watch a passing cloud or picks up a stone and with childish curiosity turns it around in his hand, they all look upon him at first with astonishment and then with contempt and disgust. They call him names, a dreamer or a parasite, a theoretician or a schizophrenic, and above all, an effeminate. They not only do not understand him—they not only despise him, but they hate him as their own sin. All of them would like to stop—ask each other questions, sit down and chat about futilities—they all

would like to belong to each other because they all feel desperately alone, chasing on in a never ending chase. They do not dare to stop until the rest stop, lest they lose their self-respect, because they know only one value—that of running—running for its own sake.

Characteristically, early radical critiques are overstatements. So-called 'doomwatchers' serve the function not so much of documenting reality, as of mobilising a broader-based liberal response. The latter then has more effect on mobilising political and industrial forces that are necessary to make policy changes towards a new synthesis.

In educational institutions early experiments of 'progressive schools' attempted to humanise the educational process but they had the characteristics of other 'anti-institutions': they overstated the protest against the constrictions of achievement-orientated, goal-orientated, authoritarian conventional schools. In the contemporary educational scene—as in other spheres—there are 'old-school' and 'new-school' approaches; the latter are less unstructured and more varied in their emphasis than the original experiments which were geared more to an 'anti-'orientation. As progressive schools seek to reconcile themselves with the need to get young people into the existing system of higher educational institutions and the 'real world' of work and community, they become more like (though still different from) the institutions against which they originally protested (Bernstein, 1967; Strelitz, 1972).

There is also a radical critique of sex roles in society, and in an over-lapping framework, of the family as it has evolved in the context of industrial society. The sex role protest is not confined to the family, though the family is a key institution in defining and giving structure to sex role conceptions. (Greer, 1972; Friedan, 1963; Rossi, 1965; Mitchell, 1966; Epstein, 1970; Rapoport and Rapoport, 1975). The anti-family critique, independently of the sex role issue, is directed towards the intense concentration of involvements within this small and socially rather isolated unit, to the detriment of the personality structure of those reared within it (Laing, 1971; Cooper, 1970). For the 'new culture' to evolve, diverse patterns have to be tolerated with some people persisting to opt for traditional arrangements while others radically depart from them. It is important in thinking about new patterns of sex roles and family life—and of life styles generally—to include *variation*: namely ranges of behaviour, various solutions to the same problems and alternative patterns for achieving satisfactions (Fogarty *et al.*, 1971; Rapoport and Rapoport, 1971; Bernard, 1972; Rapoport and Rapoport, 1975).

In considering the larger framework within which our observations about family and leisure make sense, we refer to a number of observers of social change who are particularly able at diagnosis and prognosis.

Bell, de Jouvenal, Emery and Trist, Kahn and Wiener, Michael Young, Slater and others have written persuasively about their observations (Bell, 1974; de Jouvenal, 1957; Emery and Trist, 1973; Kahn and Wiener, 1967; Young, 1968; Slater, 1971). To some extent, they express the view that though one may not be able to tell exactly when a change will occur, it is sometimes possible to tell what the outlines of the change will be. This is of course controversial and not universally applicable. Hoyle is said to have observed that if the best minds in medicine had been brought together at the end of the last century to predict developments in medical diagnosis, they would have gone far wrong because no one would have foreseen the invention of the X-ray. Taking the more general case, and allowing for the possibility of new inventions—social as well as technological—sensitive social observers alert us to processes and trends which are important to heed.

The thread that integrates many current thinkers is that there has been an overemphasis on material considerations, technology, economic indicators, massiveness of scale, impersonality of modes of functioning and other characteristics associated with the development of industrial society. Slater refers to this technologically dominated culture as the 'old culture' and suggests that there are signs of a 'new culture' emerging which stresses co-operation (instead of competition) sharing (instead of individualistic accumulation) and the cultivation of human happiness (rather than achievement). The replacement of the old by the new culture does not occur automatically. It requires effort and conflict at many levels—from individual motivation to institutional management—to bring about these changes. The changes themselves are by no means universally desired; and even to the extent that they are, there are internal constraints—motivational and institutional—which militate against them.

For the 'new culture' to develop, it is necessary for change to occur both at *an institutional level, involving the restructuring and redirecting of social institutions, and at the level of individual character and motivation* on a widespread basis. The latter is a more long-term strategic process. For this to occur, people will need both the will and ingenuity to change. The former involves them in struggles against their own socialisation experiences within the 'old culture'; the latter involves them in struggles with external persons and institutions with 'old-culture hang-ups', such as ad-men 'pushing' old-culture technological values. An example of this is Slater's description of the ad-men's pitch on a flying saucer for every home (1971, 149):

How would you like to have your very own flying saucer? One that you could park in the garage, take off and land in your own driveway, or office parking lot? . . .

Within the next few years you may own and fly just such an unusual aircraft and consider it as common as driving the family automobile.

In the 'new culture' people would surely not want an

> invention that will blot out the sky, increase the noise level which is already intense to unbearable levels, pollute the air further, facilitate crime immeasurably, and cause hundreds of thousands of horrible accidents (translating our highway death toll to the saucer domain requires the addition of bystanders, walking about the city, sitting in their yards, sleeping in their beds, or strolling in the park) each year?

Is the American public really so insane or obtuse as to relish the prospect of the sky being as filled with motorised vehicles as the ground is now?

In bringing about the more pervasive changes in character and motivational structure, families play a crucial part. Families constitute near-total environments for individuals in impressionable years; they are deeply significant—for better or worse—in moulding individuals' basic wants, aspirations, values, interests and behaviour patterns. In the life-cycle pattern of attachment and separation, many of the issues which are present as conflicts and contradictions in the larger social order are played out. Cohort after cohort of young people break away from the patterns received from their parents, and then as they enter the similar structural conditions of prevailing social institutions (family, work and community) they are pressed to repeat the old patterns. Yet changes occur and it may be that we are at a point of conspicuous change now.

There are differences in the degree to which analysts of current change processes perceive the extent, pace and dynamism of change. Michael Young does not believe that we are involved in anything near as revolutionary as do Emery and Trist; Kahn and Wiener assume that we are involved in major changes but concentrate on economic indicators. Our own view is close to that of Emery and Trist, whose framework is one of the most useful available and is presented in summary form in Table 10.

This model of the 'new culture' by Emery and Trist reflects an array of trends also noted by other observers. To the extent that these trends are increasingly evident, we would expect 'the people' (i.e. consumers or users) increasingly to aspire to them. The case material presented in the four chapters on 'the users' lends support to this. It is especially true of the younger age ranges and raises the point that the *innovative perceptions of today may well reflect the modal patterns of tomorrow*.

In the USA some of the trends have gone further than elsewhere. It is possible to learn from them and to try to dampen some of the 'negative' aspects of the change process with its conflicts and defensive reactions. An example in the environmental field is seen in exercises like those of the Field Studies Council, who run courses to demonstrate to industrial managers the deleterious effects of a *laissez-faire* policy on the environment: 'We want to avoid the situation in America where industry and conservation no longer talk to each other and industry is permanently in the dock or sheltering from brickbats' (*The Times*, 7 June 1973).

Table 10 *Changes in emphasis of social patterns in the transition to post-industrialism (Emery and Trist, 1973, 154)**

Type	From	Towards
Cultural values	achievement	self-actualisation
	self-control	self-expression
	independence	inter-dependence
	endurance of distress	capacity for joy
Organisational philosophies	mechanistic forms	organic forms
	competitive relations	collaborative relations
	separate objectives	linked objectives
	own resources regarded as owned absolutely	owned resources regarded also as society's resources
Ecological strategies	responsive to crisis	anticipative of crisis
	specific measures	comprehensive measures
	requiring consent	requiring participation
	damping conflict	confronting conflict
	short planning horizon	long planning horizon
	detailed central control	generalised central control
	small local government units	enlarged local government units
	standardised administration	innovative administration
	separate services	co-ordinated services

* The terms used are intended to be self-explanatory, but reference may be made to McClelland (1961) on achievement; Maslow (1954; 1967) on self-actualisation; Tomkins (1964) on the regulation of negative affects (such as distress) and positive affects (such as joy). The need to regard corporate resource as belonging to society as well as the corporation became a major theme in *A Statement of Company Objectives and Management Philosophy* (Shell Refining Co., London, 1966), elaborated by Paul Hill in *Towards a Management Philosophy* (Nigel Farrow, London, 1971).

We suggest that we are in a period of considerable turbulence and social change. The social environment in which we live is both complex and fluid. There are trends and counter-trends: inequalities and reactions against inequality of benefits derived from modern technology; and there is anxiety and uncertainty about how to cope with the complexity. A central issue is how to sustain communication and integration among the parts of an increasingly complex society.

Examples of the complexities of the change process can be seen in the institutionalisation of leisure provision. When a new programme is instituted, some people participate in it because of their revulsion against technological values and some participate as a positive affirmation of a specific interest. Countryside conservation groups, for example, include people who act out of protest against the spoliation of the countryside by industry and heedless trippers, and some who cultivate countryside amenities for the positive value of such cultivation. Still others want things left as they are—the preservationists. Communication and integration must be sustained both between the constituent sub-groups and between the group as a whole and the larger society.

Leisure institutions and social change

There is some evidence that leisure providers are seeking consensus about their goals, strategies, tactics and organisational means for achieving them. There is widespread feeling that there should be a broadly based effort to meet the challenges of the 'leisure explosion'. In chapter 6 we indicated the range of leisure providers in society. The character of the services provided varies as does the orientation to the place of leisure provision in society's institutions and the part that leisure provision should play in social change. Notwithstanding the variation, there does seem to be concern with providing *humanising* efforts. The danger is that the rampant institutionalisation of leisure facilities will succeed according to 'old-culture' rather than 'new-culture' standards.

The 'humanising' efforts of providers sometimes take the form of an attempt to spread middle-class values and behaviour patterns to working-class people; it may be assumed, erroneously, that 'embourgeoisment' is equivalent to humanisation. Helping people to express their 'humanness' in the face of a society dominated by machines, competitive super-organisations and so on, requires a diversified approach. To 'stay human' in the kind of society we live in, individuals need ways of cultivating their personal interests, sharing interests with others and feeling they are getting a fair share of what society has to offer. Leisure providers could play an important part in this 'humanising' process. But this is more simply said than done.

The goal of 'humanising' society can only be achieved if efforts are made in many of society's institutions, and providers of all sorts of services will need to make efforts in this direction. If leisure providers decide to invest special efforts in this cause, they need to conceive of their role more broadly than is the present tendency; they need to be interested in the enjoyment component of many different institutions. If the cultivation of meaningful interests is left only to specialists, the need for change may be lost. To make an analogy with physiotherapy, it is useful to massage tired muscles and provide exercise for someone who sits all day in a poorly designed seat, but it would be more effective to improve the seating design that would make such remedial measures less necessary. So with leisure provision. It is clear that there are—and may always be—some sub-populations (like middle-aged captive house-wives with few cultivated interests and older people with lower educational experiences) who will need specialist remedial attention of one kind or another, in which leisure provision may play a major part. On the other hand, structural alterations in family roles, the preparation of people for retirement and the alteration of retirement practices as well as restructuring life styles for the later years are likely to be more effective.

Within each of the life sectors in which there are elements anti-thetical to the enjoyment of living, 'anti-human' elements, the problems are different. Thus if leisure providers adopt a simple uniform policy, it will not be applicable to all of life. The enrichment of working life is a concern of industrialists with or without the help of recreationists. It requires special talents and methods of approach that are different from those of community work or family work.

Some providers reinforce the tendency for leisure institutions to become separate, and for their facilities to be set apart from the specific sub-populations who might need them most. This is a frequently encountered concomitant of the institutionalisation process in schools, hospitals and religious and political institutions where organisational concerns may take over the centre of the stage at the expense of their constituents' concerns, even though the very existence of the in-stitutions depends, ultimately, on the constituents. Where institutions grow apart from the preoccupations and interests of their constituents, we refer to the provider–user gap. This gap is a central problem in today's complex society.

Bridging the *leisure gap* is usually attempted within the framework of the institutionalisation process. There is a need for leisure facilities, so recreational officers are appointed by local authorities, leisure industries spring up to meet demand, various leisure projects and programmes evolve. These are necessary if the 'leisure explosion' is to be saved from becoming simply another manifestation of the devastating conse-quences of *laissez-faire* social expansion: clogged highways, littered countryside, bored sub-populations and uncontrolled building pro-grammes—all with their secondary and tertiary consequences, in a chain of deleterious effect.

The speed with which leisure is being institutionalised provides other opportunities as well as hazards. The prevailing range of approaches is not yet crystallised. There is room to experiment, to assess, to evaluate different approaches, and to evolve a mixture of approaches which facilitate changes toward the humanisation of technological society generally. *Leisure providers are in a unique position historically to use their actions as levers of social change.* They may be able to play a more significant role in social change processes than most realise. There are many overlaps in the institutional structure, and individuals can satisfy their interests in different social settings and through different activities. If providers are there to help people to satisfy and develop their interests, their work can go on through mediation and liaison—in schools, workplaces, communities and families.

This may seem to be more ambitious than what is presently under way. It would be understandable if the harried leisure provider with difficulties in getting his local council to allocate funds for a sports centre would consider it to be an intolerable overload. There is, however, a counter-argument.

The quest for more and bigger and better facilities may provide one answer, but it is an answer that on its own is consistent with the technological emphasis. It is facilities-oriented if left to the 'bare bones' of provision, and in the worst eventuality could contribute to the effect it could be countering. It may contribute more institutions of an impersonal, bureaucratic kind to a society already overburdened with such juggernauts. Where these facilities are required, concern should be focused on the human factor: human mediation between providers and users, human elements of making the facilities enjoyable and so on. This is, in most instances, an additional burden. But, in other instances —schools, workplaces, families—the extension of humanisation measures via leisure provision, carefully considered in this light, can constitute a boon. The facilities already exist: there are schools, factories and families. Individuals not only are able to, but often do, satisfy many of their interests within these settings; often they do this inefficiently and many get left out who need not have been. In many institutional settings those responsible for the institutions would themselves welcome infusions of humanistic enrichment programmes.

There are many examples of this in industrial organisations throughout the Western world. In families—which are great bastions of privacy—there are similar possibilities. Under the norms of traditional and industrial society, the father role has been evaluated according to such 'non-human' criteria as to how many children he sired or, more recently, how much success he has achieved materially. A more important consideration, under 'new-culture' norms, is how 'good' a husband and father he is. This implies a form of relatedness to members of his family which is rewarding in human terms. With increased leisure in the sense of more time away from the workplace, this has not automatically occurred, as our studies and others of the establishment phase have shown. There is often a retreat to isolated pursuits such as television-viewing; to withdrawal into segregated interests which inhibit inter-action, and failure to develop shared, interactive interests. This is particularly important for those lacking a background of cultivated interests, which relates in part to social class. Yet cultivated interests are recognised as crucial not only for community integration, but personal happiness and mental health. For example, in a recent study of fathering, the following connection was made with the leisure explosion (Biller, 1971, 127):

> With increased leisure time, there is a growing potential for fathers to become involved with their children. In families which enjoy relative economic security, the father can spend much time with his children. However, many fathers seem to be much more concerned with their long-term occupational status than with their family's psychological well-being. In many families, priorities can be altered without undue economic hardship.

Involvement alone will not heal the scars of malfunctioning families, but involvement which is informed by ways of making human relation-ships more satisfying, positive ways rather than merely therapeutic interventions after the damage has been done, is what is needed. This could become the business of the leisure specialists.

There is enough to be disturbed about in modern life, enough to mobilise our defences *against*—and leisure providers should not eschew this world of peril and woe. However, there is a part of each of us that seeks fulfilment—a promised land, a heaven on earth, a new culture that allows the best in human potential to flourish and be enjoyed. In Samuel Taylor Coleridge's time, the dream took form in times past:

> In Xanadu did Kubla Khan
> A stately pleasure dome decree:
> Where Alph, the sacred river, ran
> Through caverns measureless to man
>   down to a sunless sea.
> So twice five miles of fertile ground
> With walls and towers were girdled round:
> And there were gardens bright with sinuous rills,
> Where blossomed many an incense-bearing tree;
> And here were forests ancient as the hills,
> Enfolding sunny spots of greenery.

In days of aristocratic leisure, such cases were in fact decreed—but for the enjoyment of the few. Today, and tomorrow, leisure providers, joining with these provided for, can share the dream of Xanadu and build a semblance on a wider base (Hudson, 1973). This is, after all, the dream of many. This vision does not imply a new kind of opiate for the masses, but a basis for humanising the technical order. The cultivation of interests will not guarantee whole-life satisfaction—any more than have the modern varieties of pleasure dome—Disneyland, Bunny Club, Club Méditerranée or Olympic-size sports complex. Neither will interests provide existential answers for everyone's lives but they will go some way towards creating meaning. This is illustrated by Saint-Exupéry's parable of the Little Prince and the Merchant:

'Good morning,' said the Little Prince. 'Good morning,' said the Merchant. This was the merchant who sold pills that had been invented to quench thirst. You need swallow only one pill a week, and you would feel no need of anything to drink. 'Why are you selling those?' asked the Little Prince. 'Because they save a tremendous amount of time,' said the Merchant. 'Computations have been made by experts. With these pills, you save fifty-three minutes in every week.' 'And what do I do with those fifty-three minutes?' 'Anything you like. . . .' 'As for me,' said the Little Prince to himself, 'if I had fifty-three minutes to spend as I liked, I should walk at my leisure toward a spring of fresh water.'

People's interests are not necessarily complicated, nor expensive to fulfil. Pursuing them may take many forms. Not everyone uses their time in the same way to derive meaning. What is important is that people do find meaning in the present of their lives.

Bibliography

Principal references

Abrams, M. A. (1963), 'How and Why We Spend Our Money', *Twentieth Century*, 134–8.

Abrams, M. A. (1974), 'This Britain: 1. A Contented Nation', *New Society*, 21 February.

Adamson, C. (1972), 'Turning Point', letter to *Retirement Choice*, vol. 1, No. 1, 4.

Albemarle Report (1960), *The Youth Service in England and Wales*. Report of the Committee appointed by the Minister of Education in November 1958. Command 929, HMSO, London.

Alexander, C. (1971), 'A City is not a Tree', in G. Bell and J. Tyrwitt (eds), *Human Identity in the Urban Environment*, Penguin, Harmondsworth.

Alexander, F. (1951), *Our Age of Unreason*, Lippincott, Philadelphia.

Allardt, E. (1958), 'Community Activity: Leisure Use and Social Structure', *Acta Sociologica*, vol. 3, 165–72.

Andrus Gerontology Center (1974), *Housing Needs and Satisfactions of the Elderly*, University of Southern California.

Annual Abstract of Statistics (1974), Table 7, Office of Population and Census Statistics; General Registrar's Office (Scotland); and General Registrar's Office (N. Ireland).

Arendt, H. (1968), *The Human Condition*, Chicago University Press.

Bailyn, L. (1970), 'Career and Family Orientation of Husbands and Wives in Relation to Mental Happiness', *Human Relations*, vol. 23, no. 2.

Bains Report (1972), Department of the Environment, Study Group on Local Authority Management Structure, *The New Local Authorities: Management and Structure*, HMSO, London.

Barker, D. (1972), 'Young People and their Homes: Spoiling and "Keeping Close" in a South Wales Town', *Sociological Review*, vol. 20, no. 4.

Beattie, R. T. *et al.* (1974), *The Management Threshold*, British Institute of Management, London.

Belbin, M. (1969), *The Discovery of Method*, OECD, Paris.

Bell, D. (1974), *The Coming of Post Industrial Society*, Heinemann, London.
Bell, Q. (1972), *Virginia Woolf*, vol. II, Hogarth Press, London.
Bengston, V. L. (1970), 'The Generation Gap; a review and typology of social-psychological perspectives', *Youth and Society*, vol. 2, 7–32.
Berger, P. L. (1969), *The Human Shape of Work*, Macmillan, New York.
Berger, P. L. and Kellner, H. (1964), 'Marriage and the Construction of Reality', *Diogenes*, vol. 46.
Bernard, J. (1972), *The Future of Marriage*, World Publishing, New York.
Bernstein, B. (1967), *Class, Codes and Control*, Routledge & Kegan Paul, London.
Biller, H. B. (1971), *Father, Child and Sex Role*, Heath Books, Lexington, Mass.
Blood, R.O. and Wolfe, D. M. (1960), *Husbands and Wives: The Dynamics of Married Living*, Free Press, Chicago.
Blumler, J. (1972), 'Television as a Focus of Audience Gratifications', unpublished manuscript.
Bone, M. (1972), *The Youth Service and Similar Provision for Young People*, HMSO, London.
Bracey, H. E. (1966), *In Retirement*, Routledge & Kegan Paul, London.
Bradburn, N. M. (1969), *The Structure of Psychological Well-being*, Aldine Press, Chicago.
Briggs, A. (1965), *Victorian People*, Penguin, Harmondsworth.
Briggs, A. (1969), '1980: The Organization of Leisure', *The Times*, 11 October.
British Tourist Authority (1973), 'The British on Holiday', mimeographed.
Brothers, J. and Hatch, S. (1971), *Residence and Student Life*, Tavistock Publications, London.
Brown, E. H. P. and Browne, M. H. (1969), *A Century of Pay*, St Martin's Press, New York.
Butcher, H. J. and Rudd, E. (1972), *Contemporary Problems in Higher Education: An Account of Research*, McGraw-Hill, New York.
Butler, R. (1956), 'Mothers' Attitudes Towards the Social Development of their Adolescents', *Social Casework*, May/June.
Cambridgeshire and Isle of Ely Education Committee (1970), *The Village Colleges*, April.
Carter, M. (1966), *Into Work*, Penguin, Harmondsworth.
Castells, M. and Guillemard, A. M. (1971), 'La Détermination des practiques sociales en situation de retraite', *Sociologie du Travail*, vol. 13, 282–307.
Cavan, R. S. *et al.* (1949), *Personal Adjustment in Old Age*, Science Research Association, Chicago.
Chester, R. (1972), 'Current Incidence and Trends in Marital Breakdown', *Postgraduate Medical Journal*, vol. 48, 529–41.
Child, J. and Macmillan, B. (1972), 'Managerial Leisure in British and American Contexts', *Journal of Managerial Studies*, May.
Clark, E. (1973), 'Life at the Middle', *New Society*, vol. 23, no. 536, 56–7.
Clawson, M. and Knetsch, H. J. (1966), *Economics of Outdoor Recreation*, Johns Hopkins Press, Baltimore.

Cogswell, B. and Sussman, M. (1971), 'Family Influences on Job Movement', *Human Relations*, vol. 24, no. 6, December.

Cooper, D. G. (1970), *The Death of the Family*, Vintage, New York.

Cooper, M. (1974), 'People Who do not Want a Career', *The Times*, 5 June.

Crawford, M. P. (1971), 'Retirement and Disengagement', *Human Relations*, vol. 24, no. 3, 255–78.

Crichton, A. *et al.* (1962), 'Youth and Leisure in Cardiff', *Sociological Review*, vol. 10, no. 2, 203–20.

Crowther, G. (1959), *Fifteen to Eighteen*, vol. 1, Central London Advisory Council for Education, HMSO, London.

Crozier, M. (1972), 'The Relationship Between Micro- and Macrosociology', *Human Relations*, vol. 25, no. 3.

Cuber, J. F. and Harroff, P. B. (1965), *Sex and the Significant Americans*, Penguin, Baltimore.

Cumming, E. M. and Henry, W. (1961), *Growing Old*, Basic Books, New York

Davies, B. (1971) 'Planning Resources for Personal Social Services', Seth Memorial Lecture, Edinburgh.

Davis, F. (1973), 'On Youth Subcultures: The Hippie ⎺ .riant', McCalib-Seiler Module Series in Sociology, McCalib-Seiler, California.

Davis, L. E. and Cherns A. (eds) (1974), 'Quality of Working Life', *Problems, Prospects and State of the Arts*, vol. 1, Free Press, New York.

De Jouvenal, B. (1957), *Sovereignty: An Inquiry into the Political Good*, Chicago University Press.

De Tocqueville, A. (1945), *Democracy in America*, Vintage Books, New York.

Deutsch, H. (1968), *Selected Problems of Adolescence*, Hogarth Press, London.

Devereaux, E. C. (1970), 'The Role of Peer-Group Experience in Moral Development', in J. P. Hill (ed.), *Minnesota Symposium on Child Psychology*, 94–100, Minneapolis University Press.

Dixey, M. G. D. (1974), *Local Recreation Centres*, National Playing Fields Association, London.

Donnison, D. (1967), *The Government of Housing*, Penguin, Harmondsworth.

Douvan, E. A. and Adelson, J. (1966), *The Adolescent Experience*, Wiley, New York.

Dower, M. (1965), *The Challenge of Leisure*, Civic Trust, London.

Dower, M. and Downing, P. (1973), 'Attitudes to Man and the Land', paper to Salford Symposium on Work and Leisure.

Downing, P. and Dower, M. (1973), 'Second Homes in England and Wales', prepared for the Countryside Commission, London.

Drucker, P. F. (1969), *The Age of Discontinuity*, Heinemann, London.

Dubin, R. (1956), 'Industrial Workers' Worlds', *Social Problems*, January.

Dubin, R. (1970), 'Management in Britain; Impressions of a Visiting Professor', *Journal of Management Studies*, May, 183–98.

Dumazedier, J. (1967), *Toward a Society of Leisure*, Collier-Macmillan, London.

Dumazedier, J. and Ripert, A. (1963), 'Retirement and Leisure', *International Social Science Journal*, vol. 15, 438–47.

Eisenstadt, S. N. (1956), *From Generation to Generation: Age Groups and Social Structure*, Free Press, Chicago.

Eklund, L. (1969), 'Ageing and the Field of Education', in M. W. Riley *et al.* (eds), *Ageing and the Professions*, Russell Sage, New York.

Elder, G. (1971), *Adolescent Socialization and Personality Development*, Rand McNally, Chicago.

Elliott, O. (1960), *Men at the Top*, Weidenfeld & Nicolson, London.

Emery, F. and Trist, E. (1973), *Towards a Social Ecology*, Plenum, London.

Emmett, I. (1971a), *Youth and Leisure in Urban Sprawl*, Manchester University Press.

Emmett, I (1971b), 'The Social Filter in the Leisure Field', in *Recreation News*, Supplement no. 4, July, Countryside Commission, London.

Eppel, E. M. and Eppel, H. (1966), *Adolescents and Morality*, Routledge & Kegan Paul, London.

Epstein, C. F. (1970), *Woman's Place*, Univ. of Calif. Press, Berkeley.

Erickson, E. (1950), 'Growth and Crises of the Healthy Personality', in *Symposium on the Healthy Personality*, Supplement II, Josiah Macy Jr Foundation, New York.

Erickson, E. (1953), 'On the Sense of Inner Identity', *Health and Human Relations*, Blakiston, New York.

Erikson, E. (1958), *Young Man Luther: A Study of Psychoanalysis and History*, Norton, New York.

Erikson, E. (1959), 'Identity and the Life Cycle', *Psychological Issues*, vol. 1, no. 1.

Etzioni, A. (1961), *A Comparative Analysis of Complex Organisations*, Free Press, New York.

Evans, A. A. (1973), *Flexibility in Working Life*, OECD, Paris.

Evening Standard, 'Play Space', editorial, 19 March 1973.

Eyden, J. L. M. (1973), 'Elderly People', in M. H. Cooper, (ed.) *Social Policy*, Blackwell, Oxford.

Ferguson, T. and Cunnison, J. (1956), *In their Early Years: A study of Glasgow Youth*, Oxford University Press, London.

Fogarty, M. (1975), *Forty to Sixty—A New Generation*, Bedford Square Press, London.

Fogarty, M., Rapoport, R. and Rapoport, R. N. (1971), *Sex, Career, and Family*, Allen & Unwin, London.

Fried, M. (1973), *The World of the Urban Working Class*, Harvard University Press, Cambridge, Mass.

Friedan, B. (1963), *The Feminine Mystique*, Dell, New York.

Freud, A. (1958), 'Adolescence', *Psychoanalytical Study of the Child*, vol. 13, 255–78.

Freud, S. (1957), 'Those Wrecked by Success', in J. Strachey (ed.), *The Complete Psychological Works of Sigmund Freud*, vol. 14, 316–40, Hogarth Press, London.

Gabor, D. (1972), *The Mature Society*, Secker & Warburg, London.

Gans, H. (1965), *The Urban Villagers*, Free Press, New York.

Gavron, H. (1966), *The Captive Wife*, Routledge & Kegan Paul, London.

Goffman, E. (1961), 'On the Characteristics of Total Institutions', in *Asylums*, Anchor Books, Doubleday, New York.

Goldberg, E. M. (1970), *Helping the Aged*, Routledge & Kegan Paul, London.

Gorer, G. (1961), 'An Anthropologist Considers Retirement', in Institute of Directors, *Problems of Retirement*, 7–19.

Greer, G. (1972), 'Middle-class Husbands, Working-class Wives', *Sunday Times*, 13 August.

Gronseth, E. (1972), 'Work-Sharing Families', paper presented at 12th International Family Research Seminar, Moscow.

Group for the Advancement of Psychiatry (1973), *The Joys and Sorrows of Parenthood*, Scribner, New York.

Gunter, B. G. (1974), 'Family Consumption of Leisure', paper to 8th World Congress of Sociology, Toronto, 20 August.

Hackett, A. M. (1970), *Flexibility of Retirement Age in the U.K.*, OECD, Paris.

Hale Committee (1963), *Interim Report of the Committee on University Teaching Methods: The Use of Vacations by Students*, University Grants Committee, HMSO, London.

Hall, G. S. (1968), *Senescence, the Last Half of Life*, Appleton, New York.

Harris, M. (1973), 'Radical Retirement Chic', *Chatelaine*, Toronto, June, 28, 90–3.

Harrop, K. J. (1973), 'Planning Publics', letter in *New Society*, 5 April, 36.

Hatch, S. and Moylan, S. (1972), 'The Role of the Community School', in *New Society*, 21 September, 550–2.

Havighurst, R. J. (1954), 'Flexibility and the Social Roles of the Retired', *American Journal of Sociology*, vol. 59, no. 4.

Heckscher, A. and De Grazia, S. (1959), 'Executive Leisure', *Harvard Business Review*, July.

Henry, J. (1963), *Culture Against Man*, Random House, New York.

Hill, R., Foote, N., Aldous, J., Carlson, R. and MacDonald, R. (1970), *Family Development in Three Generations*, Schenkman, Cambridge, Mass.

Hillman, J. (1974), 'One in Three Without Car', *Guardian*, 10 April. (Figures quoted are from *1971 Censuses of England and Wales: Availability of Cars*, HMSO, London.)

Hillman, M. *et al.* (1973), 'Personal Mobility and Transport Policy', *PEP Broadsheet*, no. 542, vol. 39, June.

Hole, W. V. and Attenburrow, J. J. (1966), *Houses and People*, HMSO, London.

Hollander, P. (1966), 'The Uses of Leisure in the USSR', *Survey*, July, 40–50.

Horne, J. H. and Lupton, T. (1965), 'The Work Activities of Middle Managers', *Journal of Management Studies*, 14–33.

Hoyland, J. (1974), Report in 'Arts Guardian', *Guardian*, 4 September.

Hoyt, G. C. (1954), 'The Life of the Retired in a Trailer Park', *American Journal of Sociology*, vol. 59, No. 4.

Hudson, S. (1973), 'The Ideal Directorate of Recreational Services and the Need for Positive Discrimination', Sports Council, London.

Hudson, S. (1973), *The Ideal Directorate of Recreational Services and the Need for Positive Discrimination*, Sports Council, London.

Hudson, S. (1974), 'Review of Local Recreation Centres', in M. G. D. Dixey, *Municipal Engineering*, vol. 151, 16 August, 1949.

Hughes, C. *et al.* (1963), *People of Cove and Woodlot*, Basic Books, New York.

Hunt, A. (1968), *A Survey of Women's Employment*, HMSO, London.

Illich, I. D. (1971), *De-Schooling Society*, Calder & Boyars, London.

Jacobsohn, D. (1970), 'Attitudes Towards Work and Retirement Among Older Industrial Workers in Three Firms', Ph.D. dissertation, London School of Economics.

Jackson, B. (1974), '£10 a Week: Child Minders in Experiment', *The Times*, 23 July.

Jacques, E. (1965), 'Death and the Midlife Crisis', *International Journal of Psychoanalysis*, vol. 46, no. 4.

Jahoda, M. (1963), *The Education of Technologists*, Tavistock Publications, London.

Jephcott, P. (1967), *Time of One's Own: Leisure and Young People*, Oliver & Boyd, Edinburgh.

Joint Unit for Planning Research (1974), *The University in an Urban Setting*, Heinemann, London.

Kadushin, C. (1966), 'The Friends and Supporters of Psychotherapy on Social Circles in Urban Life', *American Sociological Review*, vol. 31, no. 6.

Kahn, H. (1972), *Synoptic Context No 1: On Prospects for Mankind*, Hudson Institute, New York.

Kahn, H. and Wiener, A. (1967), *The Year 2000*, Macmillan, New York.

Kaplan, M. (1960), *Leisure in America: A Social Inquiry*, John Wiley, New York.

Karn, V. (1974), *Retiring to the Seaside*, Age Concern, Surrey.

Keniston, K. (1971), *Youth and Dissent*, Harcourt, Brace, Jovanovich, New York.

Kerckhoff, A. C. (1966), 'Family Patterns and Morale in Retirement', in G. Simpson, I. Harper and J. C. McKinney (eds), *Social Aspects of Ageing*, Duke University Press, Durham, N.C.

Kleemeier, R. W. (1954), 'Moosehaven: Congregational Living in a Community of the Retired', *American Journal of Sociology*, vol. 59.

Kovar, L. C. (1968), *Faces of the Adolescent Girl*, Prentice-Hall, Englewood Cliffs, New Jersey.

Laing, R. D. (1971), *The Politics of the Family*, Random House, New York.

Lansbury, R. D. (1970), 'The Suburban Community', *Australian and New Zealand Journal of Sociology*, vol. 6, no. 2. October.

Larrabee, E. and Meyersohn, R. (eds) (1958), *Mass Leisure*, Free Press, Chicago. (Criticised in *British Journal of Sociology*, vol. 10, 1959, 268–269.)

Laslett, B. (1974), 'The Family as a Public and Private Institution', in A. Skolnick and J. Skolnick (eds), *Intimacy, Family and Society*, Little Brown, Boston.

Lee, T. R. (1970), 'Urban Neighbourhood as a Socio-spatial Schema', in H. M. Proshansky *et al.* (eds), *Environmental Psychology: Man and his Physical Setting*, Holt, Rinehart & Winston, London and New York, pp. 349–70.

Leeson, R. A. (1973), *Strike—A Live History, 1887–1971*, Allen & Unwin, London.

Le Gros Clark, F. (1960), *Growing Old in a Mechanised World*, Michael Joseph, London.

Leigh, J. (1971), *Young People and Leisure*, Routledge & Kegan Paul, London.

Leslie, A. (1971), 'The Affluent Ghetto', *Sunday Times Magazine*, 3 January.

Lidz, T. (1968), *The Person: His Development Throughout the Life Cycle*, Basic Books, New York.

Lords' Select Committee (1973), *First Report from the Select Committee on Sport and Leisure*, HMSO, London, March.

McClelland, D. C. (1961), *The Achieving Society*, Van Nostrand, Princeton, N.J.

McErlean, J. P. (1973), *Pre-retirement and Retirement*, Dickens Press, London.

Maddox, J. R. (1972), *The Doomsday Syndrome*, McGraw-Hill, New York.

Madge, J. (1968), 'Housing', in *Encyclopedia of the Social Sciences*, Macmillan/Free Press, New York.

Madge, J. (1969), 'Ageing and the Fields of Architecture and Planning', in Riley *et al.* (eds), *Aging and Society*, Russell Sage, New York.

Maizels, J. (1970), *Adolescent Needs and the Transition from School to Work*, Athlone Press, London.

Mallaby Report (1967), *Staffing of Local Government. A Report of the Committee*, HMSO, London.

Marris, P. (1964), *The Experience of Higher Education*, Routledge & Kegan Paul, London.

Marsden, D. (1975), *Workless*, Penguin, Harmondsworth.

Maslow, A. H. (1954), *Motivation and Personality*, Harper, New York.

Matza, D. (1964), 'Position and Behaviour Patterns of Youth', in R. E. L. Faris (ed.), *Handbook of Modern Sociology*, Chicago University Press.

Maud Committee on the Management of Local Government (1967), *Management of Local Government*, HMSO, London.

Maw, R. and Cosgrove, D. (1972), 'Assessment of Demand for Recreation: A Modelling Approach', Built Environment Research Group, Polytechnic of Central London, Discussion Paper, April.

Miles, J. C. (1972), *The Goyt Valley Traffic Experiment, 1970–71*, Countryside Commission, London.

Miller, D. (1966), 'Leisure and the Adolescent', *New Society*, vol. 7, no. 193.

Mills, R. (1973), *Young Outsiders in London*, Routledge & Kegan Paul, London.

Ministry of Housing and Local Government (1968), *Report of the Footpaths Committee*, HMSO, London.

Mitchell, J. (1966), 'Women, the Longest Revolution', *New Left Review*, 40.

Molyneux, D. D. (1968), 'Working for Recreation', *Journal of the Town Planning Institute*, vol. 54, no. 4, April, 149–56.

Morrell Publications (1973), *Report on the Leisure Industries*, London.

Morris, J. N. *et al.* (1973), 'Vigorous Exercises in Leisure Time and the Incidence of Coronary Heart Disease', *Lancet*, 17 February, 33–9.

Morse, M. (1965), *The Unattached*, Penguin, Harmondsworth.

Morton-Williams, R. *et al.* (1968), *Young School-Leavers*, HMSO, London.

Mumford, L. (1966), *The City in History: its Origins, its Transformations and its Prospects*, Penguin, Harmondsworth.

National Council of Social Service (1972), *Loneliness*, Bedford Square Press, London.

Neugarten, B. and Weinstein, K. (1964), 'The Changing American Grandparent', *Marriage and Family Living*, vol. 26, 199–204.

Neville, R. (1970), *Play Power*, Jonathan Cape, London.

Oakley, A. (1972), *Sex, Gender and Society*, Temple Smith, London.

O'Brien, T. (1972), 'Young Nick', *New Society*, 17 February.

Odaka, K. (1966), 'Work and Leisure', as viewed by *Japanese Industrial Workers Paper* at the 6th World Congress of Sociology, Evian.

Pahl, J. M. and Pahl, R. E. (1971), *Managers and their Wives*, Allen Lane/Penguin Press, London.

Parker, S. (1971), *The Future of Work and Leisure*, Praeger Publishers, New York.

Parkes, C. M. (1972), 'Health After Bereavement', *Psychosomatic Medicine*, vol. 34, no. 5, 449–60.

Parsons, T. and Bales, R. F. (1955), *Family: Socialization and Inter-action Process*, Free Press, Chicago.

Patmore, J. A. (1970, 1972), *Land and Leisure*, David & Charles, Newton Abbot/Penguin, Harmondsworth.

Perrow, C. (1972), *The Radical Attack on Business*, Harcourt, Brace, Jovanovich, New York.

Piepponen, P. (1960), *Harrastusta Valinta (The Choice of Leisure Activities)*, Wsoy, Helsinki.

Pinfold, E. (1973), 'Urban Parks for Youngsters', *Journal of the RIBA*, March, 146–53.

Poor, R. (ed.) (1972), *Four Days, Forty Hours: Reporting a Revolution in Work and Leisure*, Pan, London.

Pym, D. (1972), 'The Myth of Employment', unpublished paper at London Business School.

Rapoport, R. (1963), 'Normal Crises, Family Structure and Mental Health', *Family Process*, vol. 2, no. 1.

Rapoport, R. N. (1970), *Mid-Career Development*, Tavistock Publications, London.

Rapoport, R. and Rapoport, R. N. (1965), 'Work and Family in Contemporary Society', *American Sociological Review*, vol. 30. no. 3, June.

Rapoport, R. and Rapoport, R. N. (1971), *Dual-Career Families*, Penguin, Harmondsworth.

Rapoport, R. and Rapoport, R. N. (1975), 'Men, Women and Equity', in H. Feldman (ed.), *Proceedings of the 1971 Groves Conference*, forthcoming. Also in *The Family Coordinator*.

Rapoport, R., Rapoport, R. N. and Thiessen, V. (1974), 'Couple Symmetry and Enjoyment', *Journal of Marriage and the Family*, August.

Redfield, R. (1953), *The Primitive World and its Transformation*, Cornell University Press, Ithaca, New York.

Reich, C. (1970), *The Greening of America*, Random House, New York.

Reichard, S., Livson, F. and Peterson, P. G. (1962), *Ageing and Personality*, Wiley, New York.

Riesman, D. (1954), *Individualism Reconsidered*, Free Press, Chicago.

Riley, M. W. and Foner, A. (1968), *Ageing and Society*, vol. 1, *An Inventory of Research Findings*, Russell Sage, New York.

Riley, M. W., Riley, J. W., Johnson, M. *et al.* (1969), *Ageing and Society*, vol. 2, *Ageing and the Professions*, Russell Sage, New York.

Rizzo, R. (1972), 'Vagueness in Haight-Ashbury: A Study of Socialization', unpublished ms., Graduate Program in Sociology, California State College, Hayward.

Robbins Report (1963), *Higher Education*, HMSO, London.

Roberts, R. E. (1971), *The New Communes*, Prentice-Hall, Englewood Cliffs, New Jersey.

Rodgers, B. (1969), 'Leisure and Recreation', *Urban Studies*, November.

Rollins, B. C. and Feldman H. (1970), 'Marital Satisfaction over the Family Life Cycle', *Journal of Marriage and the Family*, vol. 32, no. 1, February.

Rose, A M. (1963) (ed.), *Ageing in Minnesota*, Minnesota University Press, Minneapolis.

Rose, A. M. and Peterson, W. A. (eds) (1965), *Older People and their Social World*, Blackwell, Oxford.

Rosenmayr, L. (1966), 'Family Relations of the Elderly', 7th International Congress of Gerontology, Vienna.

Rosenmayr, L. (1972), 'Towards an Overview of Youth Sociology', *International Social Science Journal*, vol. 20, no. 2.

Rosenmayr, L. and Köckeis, E. (1962), 'Family Relations and Social Contacts of the Aged in Vienna', in C. Tibbits *et al.* (eds), *Aging Around the World*, vol. 1, Columbia University Press, New York.

Rosow, I. (1961), 'Retirement, Housing and Social Integration', *Gerontologist*, vol. 1, 85–91.

Rosow, I. (1962), 'Old Age; One Moral Dilemma of an Affluent Society', *Gerontologist*, vol. 2, 182–90.

Rosow, I. (1967), *Social Integration of the Aged*, Free Press, New York; Collier-Macmillan, London.

Rosser, C. and Harris, C. C. (1965), *The Family and Social Change*, Routledge & Kegan Paul, London.

Rossi, A. (1965), 'Equality Between the Sexes: An Immodest Proposal', *Daedalus*, 1964, reprinted in J. Lipton (ed.), *Women in America*, Russell Sage Foundation, New York.

Rossi, A. (1968), 'Transition to Parenthood', *Journal of Marriage and the Family*, vol. 30, no. 1.

Rothschild, Lord (1973), 'The Melchett Lecture, 1972: Too Old?', *Journal of the Institute of Fuel*, January.

Rowntree Report (1947), *Old People: Report of a Survey Committee on problems of ageing and the care of old people*, Oxford University Press for the Nuffield Foundation.

Sainsbury, P. (1955), *Suicide in London: An Ecological Study*. Chapman & Hall, London.

Sandford, N. (ed.) (1962), *The American College: A Psychological and Social Interpretation of the Higher Learning*, Wiley, New York.

Sandles, A. (1973), 'The Battle for the Leisure £', *Financial Times*, 30 April.

Schofield, M. (1961), *The Sexual Behaviour of Young People*, Longmans, London.

Schofield, M. (1973), *The Sexual Behaviour of Young Adults*, Allen Lane, London.

Schumacher, E. F. (1973), *Small is Beautiful: A Study of Economics As If People Mattered*, Harper & Row, New York.

Seear, B. N. (1971), *Re-entry of Woman to the Labour Market after an Interruption in Employment*, OECD, Paris.

Seeley, J. R. *et al.* (1963), *Crestwood Heights*, Wiley, New York.

Shanas, E. and Streib, G. F. (1965), *Social Structure and the Family: Generational Relations*, Prentice-Hall, New York.

Shanas, E. *et al.* (1968), *Old People in Three Industrial Societies*, Routledge & Kegan Paul, London.

Shenfield, B. and Allen, I. (1972), 'The Organisation of Voluntary Service: A Study of Domiciliary Visiting of the Elderly by Volunteers', *PEP Broadsheet*, no. 533, London.

Sheppard, H. L. (ed.) (1970), *Toward an Industrial Gerontology*, Schenkman, Cambridge, Mass.

Shutz, W. (1967), *Joy: Expanding Human Awareness*, Grove Press, New York.

Sillitoe, A. F. (1971), *Britain in Figures*, Penguin, Harmondsworth.

Sillitoe, K. K. (1969), *Planning for Leisure*, HMSO, London.

Slater, P. (1970), *The Pursuit of Loneliness*, Allen Lane, London.

Slater, R. (1973), 'The End of the Road at 40', *Journal of Personnel Management*, vol. 5, no. 5, 31.

Smith, C. (1966), *Young People at Leisure: A Report on Bury*, Manchester University Press.

Smith, C. (1968), *Adolescence: An Introduction to the Problems of Order and the Opportunities Presented by Adolescence in Britain*, Longmans, London.

Snellgrove, D. (1965), *Elderly Employed*, White Crescent Press, London.

Social Trends, no. 1, 1970; no. 2, 1971; no. 3, 1972; no. 4, 1973; Centr Statistical Office, HMSO, London.

Soddy, K. and Kidson, M. (1967), *Men in Middle Life*, Tavistock Publications, London.

Spon, E. and Spon, F. N. (1973), *Institute of Recreation Management Year Book*, Institute of Recreation Management, London.

Sports Council (1971), *Research Priorities for Sports Provision*, 2nd Report of the Sociological Surveys Study Group, London.

Sports Council (1972), *Indoor Sports Centres*, HMSO, London.

Stevenson, D. (1972), *Fifty Million Volunteers*, HMSO, London.

Stewart, R. (1967), *Managers and their Jobs*, Macmillan, London.

Streib, G. (1958), 'Family Patterns in Retirement', *Journal of Social Issues*, vol. 14, no. 2, 46–60.

Strelitz, Z. (1972), 'Joint Use of Urban Facilities', unpublished M.Phil. thesis, University of London.

Strong, E. K. (1955), *Vocational Interests Eighteen Years After College*, Minnesota University Press, Minneapolis.

Sugarman, B. N. (1966), 'Social Class and Values as Related to Achievement and Conduct in School', *Sociological Review*, vol. 14, no. 3.

Sugarman, B. N. (1968), 'Involvement in Youth Culture, Academic Achievement and Conformity in School', *British Journal of Sociology*, vol. 18, 151–64.

Susser, M. and Watson, P. (1962), *Sociology in Medicine*, Oxford University Press.

Talmon, Y. (1968), 'Ageing: Social Aspects', *International Encyclopedia of the Social Sciences*, Crowell-Collier-Macmillan, New York.

Thiessen, V., Rapoport, R. and Rapoport, R. N. (1975), 'Enjoyment Careers and Structures', in J. Cuisenier (ed.), *Family Life Cycle in European Societies*, Mouton, Paris.

Thompson, E. P. (1970), 'The Business University', *New Society*, no. 386, 19 February, 301–4.

Tomkins, S. S. (1964), *Imagery, Affect and Consciousness*, Springer, New York.

Tournier, P. (1972), *Learning to Grow Old*, SCM Press, London.

Townsend, P. (1957), *The Family Life of Old People*, Routledge & Kegan Paul, London.

Townsend, P. (1962), *The Last Refuge*, Routledge & Kegan Paul, London.

Townsend, P. and Bond, J. (1971), 'The Older Worker in the United Kingdom', paper read to the International Centre for Social Gerontology, Paris.

Tunstall, J. (1966), *Old and Alone*, Routledge & Kegan Paul, London.

Veal, A. J. (1973), 'Notes on Attraction, Preference and Choice in Recreation', Working Paper no. 5, Birmingham Centre for Urban and Regional Studies.

Veblen, T. (1957), *The Theory of the Leisure Class*, Allen & Unwin, London.

Ward, B. and Dubos, R. (1972), *Only One Earth: The Care and Maintenance of a Small Planet*, Penguin, Harmondsworth.
White, D. (1972), 'Spending on Sport', *New Society*, 28 December.
White, R. W. (1952), *Lives in Progress*, Dryden Press, New York.
Wilensky, H. L. (1960), 'Work, Careers and Social Integration', *International Social Science Journal*, vol. 12, 543–60
Willmott, P. (1963), *Adolescent Boys of East London*, Routledge & Kegan Paul, London.
Wolfenden Report (1960), *Report of the Wolfenden Committee on Sport*, Central Council of Physical Education, London, September.
Wright, H. B. (1968), *Solving the Problems of Retirement*, Institute of Directors, London.
Wright, H. B. (1971), 'How to Live Long Enough to Enjoy your Pension', Institute of Directors and *Financial Times* Conference, 2 June.
Wright, H. B. (1972), 'Stress and Retirement', *Retirement Choice*, October.
Wynn, M. (1970), *Family Policy*, Michael Joseph, London.
Young, M. (ed.) (1968), *Forecasting and the Social Sciences*, Heinemann, London.
Young, M. and Geertz, H. (1961), 'Old Age in London and San Francisco', *British Journal of Sociology*, vol. 12, 124–41.
Young, M. and Willmott, P. (1957), *Family and Kinship in East London*, Routledge & Kegan Paul, London.
Young, M. and Willmott, P. (1973), *The Symmetrical Family*, Routledge & Kegan Paul, London.
Zinberg, D. (1972), 'Student and Faculty Attitudes towards Science: An Analysis of Variance', unpublished report.
Zinberg, N. and Robertson, J. A. (1972), *Drugs and the Public*, Simon & Schuster, New York.

Additional references

Anderson, B. E. (1969), *Studies in Adolescent Behaviour*, Almquist & Wiksell, Stockholm.
Anderson, N. (1961), *Work and Leisure*, Free Press, New York.
Brightbill, C. K. (1963), *The Challenge of Leisure*, Prentice-Hall, New York.
British Travel Association and University of Keele (1967), *Pilot National Recreation Survey*.
Burton, T. L. (ed.) (1970), *Recreation, Research and Planning*, Allen & Unwin, London.
Burton, T. L., with Veal, A. J. (1971), *Experiments in Recreation Research*, Allen & Unwin, London.
Caillois, R. (1962), *Man, Play and Games*, Thames Publications, London.
Cullingworth, J. B. (1964), 'Planning for Leisure', *Urban Studies* vol. 1, no. 1, 1–25.
De Grazia, S. (1962), *Of Time, Work and Leisure*, Twentieth Century Fund, New York.
Donahue, W. *et al.* (eds) (1958), *Free Time: Challenge to Later Maturity*, Michigan University Press, Ann Arbor.

Donald, M. N. and Havighurst, R. J. (1959), 'The Meaning of Leisure', *Social Forces*, vol. 37, 355–60.

Dunning, E. (ed.) (1971), *The Sociology of Sport*, Frank Cass, London.

Foote, N. (1954), 'Sex as Play', *Social Problems*, vol. 1, 159–63.

Glasser, R. (1970), *Leisure, Penalty or Prize?*, Macmillan, London.

Goetschius, G. W. and Tash, J. M. (1966), *Working with Unattached Youth*, Routledge & Kegan Paul, London.

Greater London Council Planning Department (1968), *Surveys of the Use of Open Spaces*, GLC, London.

Havighurst, R. J. and Feigenbaum, K. (1959), 'Leisure and Life-style', *American Journal of Sociology*, vol. 64, 396–404.

Havighurst, R. J., Munnichs, J., Neugarten, B. and Thomae, H. (1969), *Adjustment to Retirement*, Humanities Press, New York.

Hill, R. and Rodgers, R. (1964), 'The Developmental Approach', in H. Christensen (ed.), *Handbook of Marriage and the Family*, Rand McNally, Chicago.

Himmelweit, H. *et al.* (1958), *Television and the Child*, Oxford University Press, London.

Hoar, J. (1961), 'A Study of Free Time Activities of 200 Aged Persons', *Sociology and Social Research*, vol. 45, no. 2, 157–63.

Huizinga, J. (1949), *Homo Ludens*, Routledge & Kegan Paul, London.

Hutchinson, E. (1970), *Learning and Leisure in Middle and Later Life*, Pre-Retirement Association, London.

Kaplan, M. and Bosserman, P. (eds) (1971), *Technology, Human Values and Leisure*, Abingdon, New York.

Kleemeier, R. W. (ed.) (1961), *Ageing and Leisure: A Research Perspective into the Meaningful Use of Time*, Oxford University Press, London.

Law, S. (1967), 'Planning for Outdoor Recreation in the Countryside', *Journal of the Royal Town Planning Institute*, vol. 53, no. 9.

Liebow, E. (1967), *Tally's Corner*, Routledge & Kegan Paul, London.

Linder, S. (1970), *The Harried Leisure Class*, Columbia University Press, New York.

McIntosh, P. C. (1963), *Sport in Society*, Watts, London.

Mead, M. (1960), 'Work, Leisure and Creativity', *Daedalus*, vol. 89, no. 1, 13–23.

Meyersohn, R. (1972), 'Leisure', in A. Campbell and P. Converse (eds), *The Human Meaning of Social Change*, Russell Sage, New York.

Outdoor Recreation Resource Review Commission (1962), *U.S.A. National Recreation Survey*, Washington.

Phillips, A. A. C. (1970), 'Research into Planning for Recreation', Countryside Commission, London. See also *Journal of Market Research Society*, January 1971.

Riesman, D. (1958), 'Leisure and Work in Post-Industrial Society', in E. Larrabee and R. Meyersohm (eds), *Mass Leisure*, Free Press, Chicago, 363–85.

Riesman, D. (1964), *Abundance for What?*, Chatto & Windus, London.

Roberts, K. (1970), *Leisure*, Longmans, London.

Rowntree, B. S. and Lavers, G. R. (1951), *English Life and Leisure: A Social Study*, Longmans, London.

Salaman, G. (1974), *Community and Occupation*, Cambridge University Press, London.

Scheuch, E. K. (1960), 'Family Cohesion in Leisure Time', *Sociological Review*, vol. 8, July, 37–61.

Smigel, E. O. (ed.) (1963), *Work and Leisure: A Contemporary Social Problem*, College and University Press, New Haven.

Smith, M., Parker, S. and Smith, C. (eds) (1973), *Leisure and Society in Britain*, Allen Lane, London.

Sussman, M. B. (1972), 'Family, Kinship and Bureaucracy', in A. Campbell and P. Converse (eds), *The Human Meaning of Social Change*, Russell Sage, New York.

Szalai, A. (1972), *The Use of Time*, Mouton, The Hague.

Townsend, P. and Wedderburn, D. (1965), *The Aged in the Welfare State*, G. Bell, London.

Wolfenstein, M. (1958), 'The Emergence of Fun Morality', in E. Larrabee and R. Meyersohn, (eds), *Mass Leisure*, Free Press, Chicago.

Index